Anthropologies of Guayana

Native Peoples of the Americas

Laurie Weinstein, Series Editor

Anthropologies of Guayana

Cultural Spaces in Northeastern Amazonia

EDITED BY
Neil L. Whitehead and
Stephanie W. Alemán

The University of Arizona Press
Tucson

The University of Arizona Press
www.uapress.arizona.edu

© 2009 The Arizona Board of Regents
All rights reserved. Published 2009
First paperback edition 2016

Printed in the United States of America
21 20 19 18 17 16   7 6 5 4 3 2

ISBN-13: 978-0-8165-2607-9 (cloth)
ISBN-13: 978-0-8165-3361-9 (paper)

Cover photograph: A Palikur woman painting a vessel on the lower Oyapock River in French Guiana. Photograph courtesy of Stéphen Rostain.

Publication of this book is made possible in part by the proceeds of a permanent endowment created with the assistance of a Challenge Grant from the National Endowment for the Humanities, a federal agency.

Library of Congress Cataloging-in-Publication Data
Anthropologies of Guayana : cultural spaces in northeastern Amazonia / edited by Neil L. Whitehead and Stephanie W. Alemán.
   p. cm. — (Native peoples of the Americas)
 Includes bibliographical references and index.
  ISBN 978-0-8165-2607-9 (hard cover)
 1. Indians of South America—Guiana—History. 2. Indians of South America—Guiana—Social life and customs. 3. Indigenous peoples—Ecology—Guiana. 4. Excavations (Archaeology)—Guiana. 5. Guiana—Antiquities. I. Whitehead, Neil L. II. Alemán, Stephanie W., 1967–
  F2351.A67 2009
  988'.01—dc22
                     2009032640

∞ This paper meets the requirements of ANSI/NISO Z39.48-1992 (Permanence of Paper).

Contents

Series Foreword, by Laurie Weinstein   vii
A Note on Terminology   ix

1   Guayana as Anthropological Imaginary:
Elements of a History   1
Neil L. Whitehead

Part 1
Archaeology and Ecology

2   Pleistocene–Early Holocene Environmental Change:
Implications for Human Adaptive Responses in
the Guianas   23
Mark G. Plew

3   Between Orinoco and Amazon: The Ceramic Age in
the Guianas   36
Stéphen Rostain

4   Points of Convergence—Routes of Divergence: Some
Considerations Based on Curt Nimuendajú's Archaeological
Work in the Santarém–Trombetas Area and at Amapá   55
Per Stenborg

5   Scientific Forestry and Degraded Forests:
The Story of Guiana Shield Forests   74
Janette Bulkan and John Palmer

Part 2
Ethnography and Ethnology

6   *Individual and Society in Guiana* Revisited   93
Peter Rivière

7   The Guayanese Paradox   102
Denise Fajardo Grupioni

8   Imagining Group, Living Territory:
A Kali'na and Wayana View of History   113
Gérard Collomb and Francis Dupuy

9   Historical Perspectives on Areruya Communicative
    Ideology   124
    Susan K. Staats

10 Tongues in Space: Pa'ikwené (Palikur) Language(s), Relatedness,
    Identity   135
    Alan Passes

11 Guyana's Amerindians, Postindependence Identity Politics, and
    National Discourse   145
    Maria del Carmen Moreno

12 Ethnopolitics and Fractured Nationalism in Guyana   154
    David Hinds

13 Postcolonial Policing and the Subculture of Violence
    in Guyana   167
    Joan Mars

Part 3
Theoretical and Imaginative Spaces

14 Guyana as a Literary and Imaginative Space   185
    Lúcia Sá

15 Inhabiting the Imagined Space: Constructing Waiwai Identity
    in the Deep South of Guyana   194
    Stephanie W. Alemán

16 Metaphoric Detours and Improper Translations in the
    Double Field of Waiwai Anthropology   207
    Evelyn Schuler Zea

17 Cultivating a "Culture": Wajãpi Inventions   222
    Dominique Tilkin Gallois

18 Angles of Vision from the Coast and Hinterland of
    Guyana   235
    Alissa Trotz and Terry Roopnaraine

    Bibliography   255
    About the Contributors   289
    Index   295

Series Foreword

The Native Peoples of the Americas series covers the indigenous peoples of the western world. Each volume demonstrates the connections between native peoples to both their past and their environment. At a time when native voices can be easily silenced by the plethora of environmental, economic, and political crises facing all peoples all over the globe, this series proves that native voices resonate with a great deal of wisdom wrought over the millennia. The volumes address both specific and general questions that are timely and instructive: How do societies that have been colonized or nearly annihilated—or both—manage to maintain their cultural identities? What are the forms of native resistance? What lessons can native peoples teach us about how to use and share resources wisely? How do the historical discourses of native peoples versus the discourses of power (namely, the nonnative people who write the histories) vary? What do those variations suggest about *expectations* and the consequent trajectory of problems that can invariably lead from prejudice and exploitation to annihilation? Most important, what do native peoples say about themselves—about their cultural resilience? What is it that they can teach us if we would only lend an unbiased ear?

In the present volume edited by Neil Whitehead and Stephanie Alemán, you will read both the European (primarily British and French) and the native views of northeastern Amazonia. In these contrasting views, the Europeans saw the interiors as mysterious places filled with both gold and cannibals. The natives saw their own landscapes as imbued with sacred spaces and animals. They impeded European perspectives of progress (e.g., mining for gold, reshaping the landscape into "subdued" territories) and were in the way of hegemony building. How convenient, then, for the Europeans to label the native Guayanese as cannibals, less than human, which provided a rationale for their extermination.

Europeans also misunderstood the diversity of cultural groups inhabiting the interior northeastern Amazon. As the contributing authors demonstrate in this volume, many different peoples lived there. Such cultural complexity cannot be reduced to the dichotomy of "Arawaks" versus "Caribs," as Whitehead states in his introduction. Indeed, each Guayanan group created its own *cultural* niche within its own particular environment.

This book provides an in-depth summary of the peoples of Guayana, beginning with a discussion of their complex archaeologies. The evolution of native cultures must be understood within the larger context of the Pleistocene and Holocene environments—also amply described in this text. The volume then moves through a discussion of European contact along with the mistaken perceptions that shaped the history of exploitation of the interior—exploitation that is still taking a toll on the region's ancient forests. Rather than view the peoples as ambivalent actors in their own histories, the volume contributors describe how Guayanese languages, mythologies, social structures, and polities have remained resilient and ever responsive to outside pressures.

This book is not an *easy* read—it is an ambitious volume that covers just about every facet possible of Guayanese culture and history. Neil Whitehead's introduction gives readers background to the history of research in the region. The pages that follow introduce readers not just to the anthropological lens of inquiry, but to native worldviews about their own histories and cultures. In sum, this volume is a much needed and excellent book on northeastern Amazonia.

Laurie Weinstein, Ph.D.
Series Editor

A Note on Terminology

The following terms are used to describe the region discussed in this book:

    Guyana   The independent country formerly known as British Guiana.
    Guianas   The colonial enclaves of British Guiana, Suriname, and Guyane (or French Guiana).
    Guayana   The colonial enclaves known as the Guianas plus the regions of Brazil and Venezuela that lie south of the Orinoco and north of the Amazon.

Anthropologies of Guayana

1

Guayana as Anthropological Imaginary
Elements of a History

Neil L. Whitehead

The national societies of the Guayana region of Brazil, the Guianas, and Venezuela quite overtly construct themselves through a contrast between the historically settled coasts and a still-unexplored or unconquered interior (fig. 1.1). The term *Guyana* refers to the independent country formerly known as British Guiana, and the term *Guianas* is used to refer collectively to the colonial enclaves of British Guiana, Suriname, and Guyane (or French Guiana). Some writers also use the term *Guianas* to refer to the territories of those colonial enclaves plus the regions of Brazil and Venezuela that lie south of the Orinoco and north of the Amazon. The fluvial border created by the connection of the Amazon, Orinoco, and Negro rivers thereby constitute the frontier between the imagined space of Guayana and the historically constituted space of national and postcolonial identity. In the contemporary era, all kinds of development projects, national park and forest preserves, police or military actions in this space can in part to be understood as a sign of the emplacement of the national society in as yet the wild and alien landscapes of the "interior."

This idea of the "interior" thus posits Guayana as the end point of exploration, the counterpoint of modernity, and the obstacle to development. Accordingly, the language of conquest and occupation still suffuses national imaginings of this region, and native societies carry the burden of materializing that alterity.[1] In turn, the encounter with native peoples becomes a token of the traveler's or anthropologist's or missionary's or miner's penetration to that inner mystery.

The Metageography of Guayana

This articulation of the interior, "the bush," through reference to indigeneity becomes culturally grounded, quite literally, in ideas and metaphors of physical space. Some recent work on the cartography of this cultural space in the eyes of colonial travelers such as Henry Bates (Raffles 2002), Robert Schomburgk (Burnett 2000), and Walter Ralegh (1997 [1596]) allows more detailed connections to be made between this peculiarly Guayanese notion of the savage with the broader

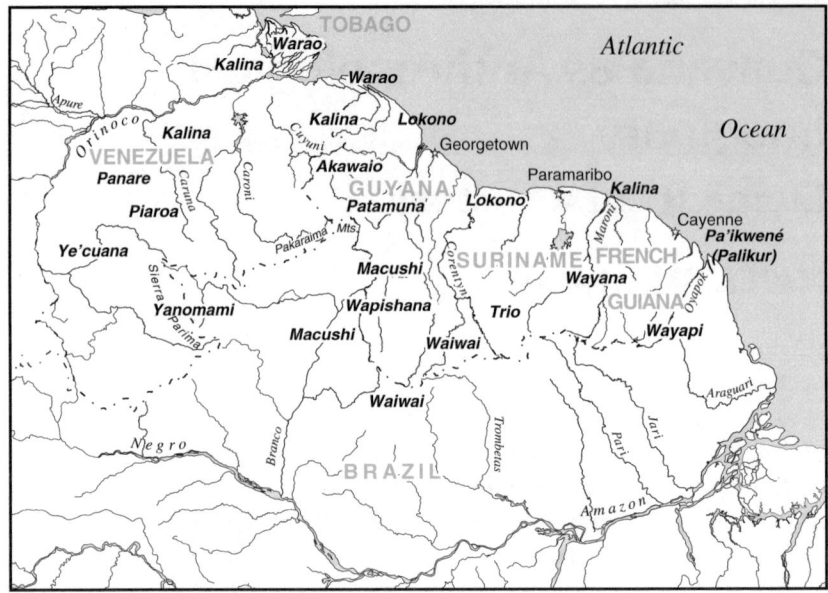

Fig. 1.1 Locations of peoples discussed in this volume.

aims of colonial and national control of this permanently wild interior. This more detailed conjoining of the idea of Guayana with that of native savagery is not just the passing allusion of a few authors or travelers but has proved a fundamental trope to the imagination of "Guayana" from the inception of European exploration through to the present day (Lézy 2000; Whitehead 2002d, 2004). This chapter can consider only some of these materials (but see also chapter 14 by Lucia Sá) and so presents only elements of this history.

Guayana is thus both an intellectual construct and a physical space that comprises the geographical landscape of the region between the Orinoco and the Amazon rivers, defined to the west by the fluvial connection of those rivers via the Rio Negro and to the east by the Atlantic Ocean. In other works (Whitehead 1993, 1994), I have referred to this physical space as "Guayana," using the old Spanish spelling to indicate its epistemological priority over the colonial and national political territories also termed "the Guianas." In the earliest accounts of South America, the land mass south of the Amazon was referred to as the "Island of Brazil," and by analogy the territories of "Guayana" to the north were thought of as forming an island. The fluvial orientation of human connections in this region also underwrites this perception phenomenologically because the rainy season inundates the rivers, creating for the traveler flooded vistas from which the land only intermittently rises as "islands" everywhere. In turn, a political phenomenology of landscape was present in the forms of native topography such that key settlements were often designated using the suffix -*cai*, a native word for "island."

This metageography is also apparent in the continuing experience of place because the approach to the Orinoco from the north is quite dramatic for the way in which it is signaled by pronounced differences in landscape forms (Gibbs and Barron 1993). The flat, hard llanos, composed of grayish shale oil soils, are suddenly replaced by the red earth that is indelibly Guayana. Such red laterite soils also feed ideas about the poverty of Amazon soils because they certainly are a challenge to Western attempts at agricultural productivity. Nonetheless, they are rich in minerals and suffused with the magic of gold. Such contrasts are repeated in the hydrological character of the south-flowing rivers that drain the hard old granitic heart of the Guiana Shield and are filled with deep passages and narrow rapids, unlike the meandering and broad watercourses that flow northward into the Amazon channel. The deep green forest of the northern flanks of the Pakaraima Mountains that form the summit, or the Guyanese Shield, along with the Parima chain, also contrasts strongly with the savannas that cover the southern flanks.

Rooted in these features of the physical landscape, the idea of Guayana as insular is then understood in both colonial and native thought as distinct from its southern counterpart, Brazil. The Amazon River channel is thus a *frontier,* not a center, in such continental systems. The "civilized" chiefdoms to the south and west along the river, such as Tapojoso or Oniguayal, are then in opposition to those of the north bank, such as Arripuna, Conori, or Manoa, which become the wild and exotic lands of "Cannibals," "Amazons," and gold in the early colonial accounts (Whitehead 1994). Indeed, the total space of "America" quickly became identified with two key representational tropes—gold and cannibals—which have persisted as standard reference points in travel writing about South America through to the present day (Whitehead 2002d). Unspeakable wealth in the form of golden cities and unspeakable savagery in the form of cannibalism thus established critical borders in the early colonial world between a penurious but disciplined Europe and a luxuriant but monstrously excessive America.

Eminent among the texts of discovery that established these ideas in the northeastern part of South America was Walter Ralegh's *Discoverie of Guiana* (1997 [1596]), which functions to establish certain kinds of borders between the Old and New World and at the same time to indicate possibilities for the negotiation of those borders as a means of colonial conquest. Outside of the Central American and Andean regions, the European occupation of the Atlantic seaboard of South America and the major rivers of the Orinoco and Amazon valleys was usually hesitant, incomplete, and tentative. In Guayana, European colonial establishment was intimately related to an ability to negotiate the cultural frontiers, not just between Europe and America, but also among native groups themselves. Ethnically discriminatory trading alliances and ethnically based military alliances established by the region's colonial regimes thus necessitated a functional, if not soundly ethnological, basis for policymaking. The relatively more dense human occupation in the Andes and Central America also meant that the effects of European diseases were demographically catastrophic there in a way they were not elsewhere in South America. Along the major rivers and in the coastal regions, local pandemics certainly decimated native populations every bit as effectively as in Mexico or Peru, but demographic collapse was a serial event seen many times in progressively more interior locales right into the twentieth century. Ralegh's *Discoverie of Guiana* has thus had a fundamental and enduring impact on the imagination of the space of Guayana, perhaps most tellingly indicated by the way in which the notions of his account of Lake Parima were not finally dispelled until Richard Schomburgk's geographical exploration of the nineteenth century. Some closer consideration of Ralegh and his text is therefore important, though many other writings contribute to the elaboration and persistence of this way of imaging "Guayana."

Guayana as El Dorado—At the Gates of the Golden Kingdom

In the *Discoverie*, Ralegh refers to the groups at the Orinoco mouth as "Borderers" in precisely this vein and continuously invokes the notion of a "border" to suggest his own proximity, if not direct discovery, of El Dorado. At the same time, Ralegh is quite overtly concerned to deliver a certain kind of impression of the native population's political, economic, and social capacities in order to facilitate the colonial enterprise itself and to negotiate his own position at the court of Elizabeth I. But Ralegh's *Discoverie* also breaks significantly with earlier forms of ethnographic reportage by presenting forms of native voice. This break also establishes the space of "Guayana" as discontinuous with other regions and as penetrable only through a still mysterious native population.

Ralegh's version of the El Dorado legend has sometimes seemed merely fabulous, but the legend certainly refers to a diversity of native cultural practices, and whatever the apparent absurdities of European accounts of El Dorado, that ancient tradition of gold working in northern South America is amply attested to in the archaeological and historical records. These records specifically tell both of the production of native gold work, with all the attendant metallurgical knowledge that this implies, and of the diverse symbolic and ritual uses to which such golden metals were put. Given the vast metallic wealth extracted by the Europeans from both Central and South America, it is not surprising that the notion of El Dorado should have seemed most credible at the time, for although the El Dorado motif was not prefigured in European ethnologies in the specific way that both "Cannibals" and "Amazons" were, it is nonetheless the case that there existed a general expectation, in part deriving from the encounter with Africa, that gold was especially engendered as a geophysical property of the "torrid zone," or equatorial latitudes. In Ralegh's case, his personal interests in and connections with alchemists and mystics, such as John Dee, suggest that he also may have had further reasons to anticipate and seek out a "golden king."

There were plausible reasons for seeking El Dorado in the Guayana region, and these reasons remain valid whatever the cultural rapacity and geographical ignorance of the early expeditionaries who acted on them. The significance of Guayana's uplands as major intracontinental trading crossroads indicates the past ritual and political importance of Guayana in broader networks in northern South America and certainly validates the emphasis given to the upland region in Ralegh's understanding of native politics.

Golden objects circulated in native societies as items of elite, long-distance trade with other native leaders and as items for trade or ransom with the Europeans. The use of exotic gold artifacts, known as *guanin* and *caracoli,* as well as of polished blackwood carvings in the development of elite political structures is well known to the anthropology of the Caribbean and northern South American region. So, too, the myth cycles of both the "Amazons" and El Dorado are key to the interpretation of the archaeological and historical evidence, especially that concerning the production and exchange of *takua* and guanin or caracoli as elite activities in the Guayana region. Ralegh's intuition in this regard is evident from his report of the connection between these myth cycles and the facts of transcontinental trading and elite exchanges of precious objects: "At that time [April] all the Kings of the borders assemble, and the Queenes of the *Amazones,* and after the Queens have chosen, the rest cast lots for their *Valentines.* This one moneth, they feast, daunce, & drinke of their wines in abundance, & the Moone being done, they all depart to their owne Provinces. If they conceive, and be delivered of a sonne, they returne him to the father, if of a daughter they nourish it, and reteine it" (1997:23).

Golden metals had a critical role to play in the validation of political and social authority, particularly where this transaction involved the exchange of persons, whether by marriage or by some other form of contractual relationship. This practice need not imply that gold items were exchanged directly for persons, in the manner of later European slave trading, but the belief systems that supported the valorization of golden objects also signaled the appropriateness of persons as items in a wider cycle of exchange.

This relationship is very evident from the fact that "exchanges" were both commercial and military in form, the distinction between trading and raiding being, as ever, a fine one. The various native beliefs that have been conflated into the European myth of El Dorado clearly testify to this distinction, and although the ritual parameters that went along with such beliefs are unlikely to have been identical in all contexts, as the Europeans assumed, the likelihood of sustained, if indirect, interaction between the elites of these disparate regions is also amply demonstrated by the antiquity and wide dispersion of culturally related archaeological materials from the lower Orinoco to the western Venezuelan llanos. It was these native realities that Ralegh's *Discoverie* of the "Empyre of Guiana" reflected and that, through his political analysis of the borders and borderers of that empire, he held out as accessible to English colonial ambition.

Nonetheless, the emergence of Guayana as an anthropological landscape was only incompletely imagined through the idea of El Dorado, and the possible presence of more threatening cannibals, even *kanaimà* (practitioners of a form of assault sorcery), subsequently comes to inflect various accounts and descriptions of the region and its peoples. The cannibals' core zone actually lay to the north and south of Guayana but was never clearly located within it except as an invasive phenomenon. Cannibals in the Caribbean, the original site of this peculiarly American signifier, border Guayana to the north. Ancient "Cannibals" were hypothesized to have brought their ritual proclivities to the shore of the Barima River as part of a wider invasive moment. The excavation of shell middens in this region by, for example, the missionary William Brett (1881), during which human bones were recovered, apparently anchored this hypothesis with the evidence of archaeology.

Nineteenth-century colonial commentators thus constructed Guayana as resistant to this cultural proclivity until the demon Caribs, plundering and killing their way through the Caribbean islands and delta of the Orinoco, inflicted their warrior disciplines on the indolent indigenes, transforming the local Karinya from farmers of manioc into the "red faces" of Warao legend who ate up the peoples of the Orinoco and the interior. This construction was in itself but a mimesis of a European occupation that had already destroyed the majority of native cultures and had consumed their remnants in the pursuit of colonial development: first, through the system of plantation slavery that induced a dependency on the colonial regime through its payment for mercenary services in policing the interior for runaway slaves; and, second, through the punitive enslavement of certain Guayanese groups themselves, in particular the Makushi and other groups of the deep interior. Slaving then itself became a way of knowing and discovering, and it slipped easily into evangelization as the economic stabilization of the colonial regimes in the region through the plantation economy supplanted the haphazard dependence on individual trade partnerships with native groups.

Likewise to the south, those gourmet cannibals, the Tupi, who so fascinated the French commentators, were singular to their Brazilian location. Although early French ethnology tended to use categories derived from this Tupi encounter to describe the cultures in the Caribbean and even the land of the Iroquois in North America, the attempt to implant such notions in Guayana or to filter the French experience there through this Tupian lens resulted only in various infelicities in ethnological description. It proved all too facile to descry the ethnic dyads of Caribbean experience (Arawak versus Carib) in the dyadic logic of cannibalism and war among French allies in the region of Rio de Janeiro. In this way, Guayana eluded the wider continental categories of conquest and knowledge such that native cultures in Guayana became the marginalia of evolving ethnological schema in the nineteenth-century travelogues and the twentieth-century *Handbook of South American Indians* (Steward 1946–59).

The way in which the colonial regimes of the region occupied and sought to reinscribe their own particular cultural meanings in the context of existing native practices has to be considered alongside the imaginary cartographies of the demonic that orient colonial and national governments in their actions toward and their creation of the indigenous (Whitehead 2002d).

These constructions of the "native" or the "indigenous"—whether in public political discourse, media representations, or anthropological and ethnographic writing—have served to enable and encourage violence against indigenous communities. From the initial charges of cannibalism made against Amazonian peoples in the sixteenth century to descriptions of the Yanomamö's supposed fierceness, there has been a continuous external discourse on native Amazonians' savagery and wildness, most usually demonstrated through their Satanic proclivities (shamanism) and demonic customs (cannibalism). No less relevant to the fate of native peoples today than it was five hundred years ago, this discursive production of "natives" continues to create a broad cultural framework in which violence against indigenous persons can be more easily obscured or justified.

In Guayana, successive waves of spiritual and material development have pounded native communities, leading to the continuous ideological construction of indigenous peoples as obstacles to "progress." This construction is signaled by key cultural practices that have allowed the governmental regimes to separate out the "good" and the "bad" Amerindian. In Guayana, this separation has proceeded along a number of axes, all of which reference spiritual and ritual forms of action as ciphers for the political opposition that given native groups showed toward plans for their redemption and development. Most notorious was the dualistic ethnic typology, originated by Columbus, of Arawaks and Caribs. I have shown elsewhere (Whitehead 1995, 2002a) that this apparently objective ethnolinguistic distinction is in fact highly suspect and refers more to the exigencies of conquest than to native realities. However, this distinction became widespread across the region and in time a component of Amerindian identity itself. Colonial policy enshrined this scheme in legal statute—allowing plunder and slaving of those populations considered Carib. Arawak populations, both through selective alliance and the involvement of key Lokono clan leaders, were then understood as basically tractable and, given a system of raiding and warfare between key Carib and Arawak populations, such as the Karinya and the Lokono, were also considered to be self-interested and thus dependable in their European alliances.

As missionaries began systematic evangelization in the seventeenth century along the Orinoco, this ready-made distinction became self-fulfilling because opposition to the missionaries was defined as "Carib." In this way, the Arawak, who accepted evangelization, were again seen as favorable to colonial development. But this distinction was and still is based on more than these competing representations of Amerindian tractability and intractability. The notions of Carib and Arawak refer also to spatial location and ritual proclivity. Consistent with the demonic nature of the colonial imagination of the space of Guayana, the Carib are pictured as interior, bush dwellers exemplifying the secretive, dangerous, and violent nature of the region's dark heart. The Arawaks, coast dwellers and even urbanites, in turn signal the possibility of indigenous redemption, reform, and development. These competing tropes of the indigenous can then be made to fit varying political and ethnic circumstance using linguistics to bolster the idea of a fundamental difference in the cultural ontologies of Arawaks and Caribs. Despite the fact that linguistic practices do not actually conform to this scheme, it has remained a passionate debate in contemporary anthropology and archaeology (Whitehead 2002a).

Linguistics thus anchors a demonology of development in the ethnology of the region, but this demonology is not just a linguistic distinction correlated with a political opposition but also invokes apocalyptic visions of a threat to all social order—native, colonial, and national—through the linguistically inscribed association of Caribs and cannibalism, the terms themselves being directly related etymologically through European usages. The production of cannibals was thus an economic and political interest, given the legal provisions that allowed special violence against them. It is also a central issue for anthropological interpretation because, as William Arens (1979) rightly indicates, it is the original anthropological question. As a result, the literary and ethnological production of the cannibal has gone hand in hand with the military and political domination of the native population in this region of South America. The violence of conquest in the region mimetically referenced cannibalism as its justification, and representations of the native population suppressed any description of Arawak torture and cannibalism, emphasizing rather the Caribs' barbarity.

Imperial Anthropology and Colonial Culture

In order to understand the subsequent place of Guayana in the emergence of professional anthropology, it is first necessary to set anthropology itself within the broader frame of imperial consolidation in the later nineteenth century. In its early colonial guise, ethnological writing was often indistinguishable from travelogue more generally, being part of the authenticating apparatus of the travel genre as a whole (Whitehead 2002d).

A central element in this imperial gaze was the lens of "Science," which made the otherwise individual and idiosyncratic observer a source of credible and possibly profitable information. As a result, travel writing in this period, even in its ethnological format, is as much concerned with consolidation of empire as it is with the exploration and discovery of new lands and peoples. Indeed, the tenor of some of these writings suggests that such discovery, with all its attendant romantic overtones, must necessarily be supplanted by the stolid/solid work of colonial development. In this context, ethnological writing has a special importance because it represents a conscious attempt to marshal and understand the human resources of the colony.

"Travel" itself, as a concept, also gains a distinct meaning in this period. The major work of exploration having been done, it now remained only to flesh out and precisely delineate the nature of colonial possession. In this way, extended residency abroad became equivalent to the "exploration" of old. The heroic individual, such as Alexander Humboldt in South America or Mungo Park in Africa, was gradually replaced by the government-sponsored expeditionary or field officer, and the tales of close encounter or exotic captivity among wild savages were now echoed in more controlled interviews with pacified or dependent colonial subjects in the making, as was the case for Walter Roth, a key figure in the emergent anthropological imagination of Guayana.

Organizations such as the Royal Anthropological Institute and the Royal Geographical Society played a significant role in promoting a broad but scientifically disciplined interest in ethnological facts, geographical exploration, and natural history. Indeed, interest in natural history was no less linked to imperial expansion than cartography was more obviously to colonial possession, and it was incompletely separated from the "moral" history that in turn comprised ethnology. Plant collecting in particular was an important source of potential profit from journeys otherwise redundant in cartographical terms. The journeys of British botanists to South America—such as Henry Bates, who was to become the assistant secretary of the Royal Geographical Society—were notoriously the source of much economically important information.[2]

Ethnology thus sat uneasily alongside the category of natural science, both because comparative cultural or biological study was itself still limited, but also because the primitive condition of indigenous society was implicitly seen as evidence of its naturalness. In this way, ethnological writing, as much as the better-known botanical and zoological materials, came to be expressive of the imperial scientific gaze.

Walter Roth's cladistic approach to the arts, crafts, customs, animism, and folklore of the native population of Guyana[3] perfectly expresses this intellectual and representational context because, unlike his missionary predecessors, he himself had no particular claim to intimate knowledge of native life or long-term residence in "the bush." For Roth, the veneer of modernity and civilization obscured the still primitive and secretive savage, whose lack of physical hygiene became equated with the absence of moral virtue as well. In contrast, and expressing an ethnic stereotype still very much in vogue today (see chapter 15 by Alemán), Roth saw the Waiwai as "a delightful and charming set of people—clean, industrious, and happy. It was the first occasion that I had come across Indians whistling while they work. The distance of their native haunts from the centers of civilization has so far saved them from being interfered with by the missionary, rancher and balata bleeder: at present they are moral, and during the whole of my stay among them, I saw no drinking. Smoking was unusual" (1929:x).

This aesthetic of nostalgic remorse for the "former savage" is of course evident in colonial writing worldwide (Whitehead 2004). Walter Roth certainly raised ethnological observation from the level of mere travel tale to that of science through his systematic and exhaustive compendia, derived from the works of earlier travelers and discoverers. He also saw the need to combine such ethnological sources with direct experience of native life.

The Cultural Politics of Ethnology in Colonial Guiana

When Roth arrived in British Guiana in 1906, he found an already developed tradition of writing about the native population. In particular, the works of Rev. William Brett, Sir Everard Im Thurn, Charles Barrington-Brown, Richard Schomburgk, and Sir Robert Schomburgk were an established part of the literary and ethnological field into which Roth entered. The earlier writings of William Hilhouse and the Schomburgk brothers were of less contemporary relevance, but Roth's translation of some of the Schomburgks' writings clearly acknowledges their priority in this field. The figure of William Hilhouse makes for an instructive comparison with that of Roth because Hilhouse, too, was appointed "Protector" of the "Indians" in Guiana in the 1830s and his advocacy for them led him into controversy and conflict with the local colonists, as happened to Walter Roth in Australia.[4]

However, Roth's most immediate literary and ethological competitors were the missionaries Brett and Im Thurn and the "field specialist" Barrington-Brown. Although their works were of a previous generation, being published in the period from 1868 to 1883, they effectively set the agenda for at least a preliminary understanding of the character and distribution of the native population. Among the three authors, there were clear differences in literary style and ethnological purpose. Brett (1868, 1881) concerned himself with a spiritual and poetic vision of the "Indian," offering portraits of tribal characteristics and lifestyle alongside extensive recording of folklore and myth.[5] For Im Thurn (1883), providing an analysis of society, politics, and power that would befit a future president of the Royal Anthropological Institute was the principal concern.

In fact, as a fellow government employee, Roth was probably intellectually closer to Barrington-Brown, who himself had parlayed his extensive interior travels into a memoir of indigenous encounters.[6] Roth, however, saw the importance of a systematic approach to ethnological data where Barrington-Brown and Brett did not, and this view made Im Thurn his principal competitor in terms of intellectual legacies in the ethnology of British Guiana.

In order to appreciate the dynamics of such cultural politics, it is appropriate to consider a key topic for both Im Thurn and Roth, the kanaimà complex. Kanaimà received chapter-length attention in Roth's *Inquiry into the Animism and Folk-Lore of the Guiana Indians* (1915), but it is unclear why he utterly ignored Im Thurn's copious discussion in *Among the Indians of Guiana* (1883:328–340), even more so because he relied extensively on all the other key sources, including Barrington-Brown, Brett, Hilhouse, and the Schomburgks. In this context, it is perhaps relevant to note that Roth's works were published by the Smithsonian Institution's Bureau of American Ethnology in the United States, not by the Royal Anthropological Institute or another British institution. Indeed, as Roth explicitly states, his 1926 expedition to southern British Guiana was "on behalf of the United States Government" (1929:v) rather than any British organization. The absent-minded nature of imperialism in British Guiana[7] and the proximity of the United States to Guayana no doubt contributed to this relationship, as did his friendship with J. Walter Fewkes.[8] But Roth's possible disenchantment with the British imperial vision itself may also have played into the decision, silently reflected in his erasure of Sir Everard Im Thurn, future governor of Fiji, from this important aspect of his ethnological compendium on the folklore of the "Guiana Indians." In turn, Im Thurn's presidency of the Royal Anthropological Institute as well as his curatorship of the Museum of the Royal Agricultural and Commercial Society in the 1880s through the patronage of Sir Joseph Hooker (see note 2) reflect this gulf in scholarly credential between the compendia of the medicomagistrate Walter Roth and the field observations and theoretical forays of the politically powerful priest Sir Everard Im Thurn.

These differing orientations to the politics of colonial rule are also evident in the emergence of the Walter Roth Museum of Anthropology. It was the first museum of anthropology in the English-speaking Caribbean and was founded in the year 1974, after independence from Great Britain. Prominently featuring the collections of the Guyanese archaeologist Denis Williams, the museum was so named partly in recognition of (or at least with the suggestion of) a lukewarm regard for the pretensions of imperial rule, if not the potential beneficence of an enlightened colonialism, on Roth's part.[9] It would not have been unusual for a medically trained government functionary to have viewed the missionary effort as somewhat anachronistic in a world where concerns of "public health" and "education," not redemption and salvation, had become the hallmarks of progressive thinking, as is reflected in Roth's account of the Waiwai quoted earlier. Whatever further biographical research might reveal on this issue, it is at least clear that Roth's ethnological compendia suffered for the exclusion of Im Thurn's work, at least on the question of kanaim.

However, Walter Roth's overarching influence in the imagination of the space of "Guiana" remains preeminent not just because of the way in which his compendia make evident the complexity and richness of native life, but also for the way in which that life is given a geographical reality. In fact, this cultural and geographical space was precisely coextensive with the practice of kanaim, which was seen as unique to "Guiana," though it was not quite so restricted as Roth thought when he suggested that it did not occur in Suriname or Cayenne. In other ways, too, Roth was quite overt in creating a "Guiana" space, writing in the preface to *Animism and Folklore*,

As the work progressed, I recognized that, for the proper comprehension of my subject, it was necessary to make inquiry concerning the Indians of Venezuela, Surinam, Cayenne, with the result that the area to be reviewed comprised practically that portion of the South American continent bounded, roughly speaking, by the Atlantic seaboard, the Orinoco, and the northern limits of the watershed of the Rio Negro, and the lower Amazon; and it was not long before I realized that for the proper study of the Arawaks and Caribs I had to include that of the now almost extinct Antilleans. (1915: preface)

Nonetheless, Roth's compendia anticipated and may even have inspired to some degree Julian Steward's editing of the *Handbook of South American Indians* (1946–59) because both were issued by the Bureau of American Ethnology. The *Handbook* is a massive seven-volume collaborative work in which, as in Roth's compendia, the essays synthesize vast quantities of ethnological data ranging over many hundreds of years. However, the same problems with this approach that are apparent in Roth's compendia resurface in the *Handbook,* in particular the conflation of geographical and cultural distributions. Nonetheless, it is notable that "Guiana" is a distinct region in the *Handbook,* and the influence of Walter Roth's work seems undeniable here. It thus transpires that Roth may be rightly criticized with hindsight, but that he very much exemplified the best working methods of his day.

In various ways, then, and through all kinds of ethnological writing and travel memoir, from Walter Ralegh to Walter Roth, the space of Guayana has been an unfolding object of European desire—never quite penetrated but always reinvested with mystery each time a doughty explorer unveils a new wonder. So, too, the modern anthropologist—already conscious of the marginalization of the early Carib and Arawak ethnology of the colonial era by the explosion of interest in the Brazilian Amazon and the northwest regions of Colombia and Peru, exemplified through the *Handbook of South American Indians*—has imagined Guayana as the space of evanescent indigeneity.

The chapters collected in this volume tell a different story of the great antiquity of human presence in Guayana, of persistence and elaboration through time, of innovation and creation in the face of colonial destruction, as well as of recovery and resurgence as the postcolonial modernities of Amerindian, Black, Asian, and Creole peoples themselves become part of global culture in the twenty-first century. They also speak to the particularities of Guayana as a cultural construct in anthropology, history, and local conceptions, underlining the broad historical production of this category through not just colonial knowing but also indigenous tradition and colonial change.

The volume therefore opens with essays by Mark Plew, Stéphen Rostain, and Per Stenborg that serve to situate the notion of Guayana archaeologically and ecologically by providing various levels of regional analyses in conjunction with a temporal schematic extending from first human adaptations in the Pleistocene–Early Holocene era through the emergence of ceramic cultures and a broader consideration of regional interactions among the developed polities of southern Guayana and the Amazon valley. Plew's chapter provides a broad overview of the prehistory of the Guianas with respect to issues and problems that inform our general understanding of Amazonia. In this context, Plew reviews long-term environmental change within the region as a basis for assessing the conditions affecting the varied transitions in food-procurement strategies of early Paleo-Indians, later Archaic hunter-gatherers, and early horticulturalists of the Guiana Shield. Rostain shows that Guayana has been inhabited for a long time. Various types of societies—hunters, gatherers, shifting cultivators, and permanent farmers—coexisted in different environments.

Plew argues that with the available data, the prehistory of this area can be divided into five main cultural stages. The peopling of Guyana began around 8000 BC with the arrival of nomadic hunters and gatherers in the inland savannas. Around 5000 BC, shellfish gatherers and fishermen left shell mounds along the seacoasts at the mouths of the Orinoco and the Amazon. These mounds were the first permanent villages in the Guianas. The first farmers, cultivating with a swidden system, were present in the Guianas around 2000 BC. Their sites are found everywhere, especially along the rivers. Around AD 300, large groups with permanent agriculture occupied the swampy coast, where they built numerous raised fields in the seasonally flooded areas. It is probable that these groups exemplified considerable social-political complexity and hierarchy. Cultural changes occurred around AD 1200 with the arrival of new groups in the interior and on the coast, culminating with the European and African arrivals from the sixteenth century on. Stenborg complements this outline by discussing the Amazon basin region of Guayana. He focuses on the pre- and protohistorical cultural development in the regions of Trombetas and Nhamundá (present Pará) as well as the territory of Amapá. Of particular concern are the links between these areas and the rest of Guayana. In most cases, cultural progress and inventions are assumed to occur inside the domains of discrete sociocultural systems, thereby ascribing certain inherent qualities to particular "cultures." As an alternative approach, Stenborg draws particular attention to the areas of cultural interaction as important scenes of innovation and change. His chapter is based largely on the material revealed through the investigations by Curt Nimuendajú in the 1920s and on his revision of written sources.

This archaeological panorama is complemented by Janette Bulkan and John Palmer's discussion of the environmental history of forest cover in Guayana, reminding us of the significance of human uses in creating the "natural" environment and the way in which the practice of commercial forestry itself needs to be responsive to this condition. Both conservation and development literature describes the forests of eastern Guayana as "frontier forests," one of the four remaining "tropical wilderness" areas in the world (others being Amazonia, Congo, and

Papua New Guinea), marked by low growth rates and a high degree of heterogeneity and endemism. Bulkan and Palmer set out current understandings of the ecology of these forests as well as the local and global political structures that determine the forests' fate. They also outline the socioeconomic context of forest-dependent communities in the various distinct nation-states of Guyana, Suriname, and Guyane (French Guiana).

In part 2, the ethnology of the Guayanan peoples is explored, both in an historical and contemporary frame as well as with regard to indigenous and local conceptions of time, history, and their significance for social reproduction. Gérard Collomb and Francis Dupuy discuss the Wayana and Kali'na—two groups of common Carib cultural heritage and two ethnic identities that have interacted, often in a warlike way, over many decades, even centuries, especially along the Maroni River (also known as the Marowyne). In the colonial context, this long chain of interaction was broken, the Wayana remaining in the interior, and the Kali'na being more directly affected by colonization on the coast. Today, these groups are confronted with a common destiny within the framework of the nation-states of France and Suriname. Collomb and Dupuy's chapter develops a comparative approach to the processes of ethnogenesis, social structuring, and spatial inscription. The chapter by Sue Staats complements this discussion of ethnogenesis and social interaction over the long term by examining the communicative ideologies of Areruya, a panethnic shamanic movement originating in Guyana, as a comparative basis for understanding the regional indigenous perspectives on cultural and social communication. Staats explores the idea of symbolism based on modes of communication. Local forms of communication interrelate attitudes toward personhood and social agency, and, for this reason, communication is a field that both requires and engenders socially effective symbolism. In Areruya, the term *wai* stands for a container for cassava drink, a boom box, and a mythical musical instrument that distributes sacred music to followers of Areruya. As a central image in Areruya cosmology, wai represents a reclamation of communicative principles into indigenous terms, in parallel with and arguably superceding symbolism centered on the Christian Bible and other forms of paper texts. Staats considers comparative perspectives on communication, both in terms of lexically encoded symbols and in terms of communicative relationships that are figured through performance, including Yekuana *ademi* chants, Warao *arebu,* Trio ceremonial dialogue, and Wakuénai *kwepani* (Kuwai dance) ceremonies.

Alan Passes in turn extends our appreciation of linguistic factors in historical and sociocultural terms by showing how ideas of language and relatedness likewise undergird social processes for the Pa'ikwené in eastern Guyana. Passes explores the construction of identity among contemporary Pa'ikwené, an Arawakan "nation" occupying a singular position in the Guyanese space at the heart of a multicultural, multilingual, and multinational nexus composed of four autonomous yet interconnecting elements: the native world, the Creole world, Brazil, and France. Passes looks at how two Pa'ikwené subgroups use language and language choice in order to fashion their own distinct niches in this complex framework, which echoes the Pa'ikwené's traditional multilayered cosmos, and to structure relations with others.

In a similar way, but with emphasis on broader ideas of "cultural revival," Maria del Carmen Moreno explores the connections between Lokono cultural revival and Guyana's national politics. Moreno shows clearly that an understanding of Lokono cultural revival needs both an historical perspective and an appreciation of how issues of cultural and ethnic identity play into the contemporary national politics and institutions in Guyana. Moreno shows that government policies toward Amerindians since independence in the 1960s have emphasized legislation that focuses on the sociocultural appearance of Amerindian communities, thereby creating an alienation from the national political process.

We are also very pleased to be able to include in this part the seminal essay on social organization by Peter Rivière that developed from his monograph on individual and society. The importance of the models proposed in that work are also closely discussed in the chapter by Denise Fajardo, who calls for a more historically nuanced approach in current ethnography, while amply demonstrating the critical importance of Rivière's contribution in developing an anthropology of Guayana. The chapter by Collomb and Dupuy likewise shows how a firm historical sense needs to be brought to any interpretation of social and cultural life in this region. A further important element in the current ethnography and anthropology of Guayana is the attention now being paid to the role of national societies, from the point of view of Amerindian groups as well as Blacks and Asians. The chapters by Hinds and Mars in part 2 thus open up new and vitally important trajectories for ethnographic work, showing the importance of escaping the old colonial counterposition of native/colonial, Indian/Black, and Black/Asian in the categories of anthropology. David Hinds's chapter looks at the relationship between racial competition in Guyana, in particular the competition between African and East Indian Guyanese for control of the political state, and the nondevelopment of a Guyanese nationhood based on shared cultural, social, and political values. It makes three interrelated arguments. First, the persistent drive to marginalize and undermine political opponents, a quality inherent in the elite political culture, has erased the ground for transforming the cultural hybridity among the people into a national ethos. Second, the elite of the race that controls the levers of state power determine the "national" values, leading to "antinational" reactions by the groups outside of the governance structures. Third, unlike some racially plural societies, national space in Guyana does not exist side by side with or in the place of racialized space. Rather, the national is undermined by the racial. The first part of Hinds's chapter examines how the problem was manifested under the African-centered People's National Congress (PNC) government between 1964 and 1992, and the second part looks at how it has been manifested under the East Indian–centered People's Progressive Party (PPP) government from 1992 to the present.

Joan Mars discusses and contextualizes the enduring problem of the excessive use of deadly force and the legitimation of violence in police work in postcolonial Guyana. She argues that an occupational subculture of violence was encouraged and fostered during the colonial period, and to date no concerted efforts have been made to achieve behavior modification, professionalism, and accountability in policing. Using a power-reflexive methodology to provide an explanation for what appears to be a rapid decline of the rule of law in contemporary Guyanese society, she presents and analyzes data showing a sharp escalation of deadly violence by and against the police in recent years. The chapter concludes with suggestions for police reform and the implementation of mechanisms to improve police-community relations and to provide social justice for the increasing number of citizens killed or injured by police. Mars also draws our attention to the way in which the Guayana region itself is embedded in a global system such that the consequences of U.S. domestic policies can be clearly seen on the streets of Georgetown, Guyana.

The critical interplay between the imagination of cultural worlds and the material and physical interactions that such imaginaries may provoke forms part 3 of our volume and thus extends the broad consideration of models for picturing the cultural space of Guayana, as discussed in the chapters by Rivière and Fajardo in part 2, into the particularities of discrete cultural analysis. The opening chapter of this section, by Lúcia Sá, shows how both European and American literatures have actively contributed to the ethnological terrain of "Guayana" as a literary and imaginative space. The Caribs that live in Guayana have kept up literary traditions that date back many centuries and include creation and etiological narratives, trickster stories, war songs, political speeches, and works in other genres. After contact with Europe, these literary traditions were transcribed into alphabetical script and eventually made their way into works by mainstream Western writers, impinging on the novel as a genre. Sá's chapter examines native traditions of Guayana and their impact on novels from Brazil, Guyana, and Venezuela.

Stephanie Alemán discusses the Waiwai of southern Guyana in this kind of context and provides us with very valuable insights into the way in which the iconicity of the Waiwai as forest dwellers and authentic "natives" has been built and reinforced in both popular imagination and professional opinion. The Waiwai are a group of Carib-speaking Amerindians who inhabit the "Deep South" of the nation-state of Guyana. Alemán concludes that the Waiwai cannot escape association with the "Deep South," nor can the "Deep South" be disassociated from the Waiwai. Exploring the many intertwining discourses, including those of the Waiwai themselves, helps us to understand both how places and cultures come to be imagined by others and how a region's inhabitants respond to these imaginings and use them for their own ends.

Complementing this approach to the Waiwai materials, Schuler Zea widens the focus to include the larger image of Guayana as an imagined space, examining notions of imagining and distance from the perspective of the Waiwai. Drawing on research among Brazilian Waiwai villages south of the Acarai Mountains and along the Mapuera and Anaua rivers, she describes how the Waiwai consider imagining as a means of overcoming distance through the dialectical acts of seeing and not seeing. Schuler Zea discusses the reflexivity entailed in seeing and being seen, exemplified through the Waiwai concept of the *yekatî yewru*, which can be glossed as "eye-soul," and examines the creativity of imitating or representing, which involves a summoning or bringing forth (*ñemohkesî*) of what is hidden or distant, such as when Waiwai actors ritually take on the appearance of forest animals. Finally, she examines the reciprocity of not seeing and not being seen, which is most dramatically illustrated through the Waiwai expeditions to search for and bring back the remote *enîhnî komo*, the "unseen" or "uncontacted peoples" in the surrounding region. By analyzing and extrapolating from these concepts, Schuler Zea enlarges the scope of discourse about space and cultural imaginaries very effectively.

Dominique Tilkin Gallois offers a similar demonstration of such process among the Wajãpi of eastern Guayana and shows how it has now been inscribed in global culture through the activities of such organizations as the United Nations. Gallois discusses the "imaginings" of both a Tupi group in Amapá, Brazil, and the public politics developed by different institutions. The concerns here are the process of incorporating Wajãpi verbal and graphic expressions as "Brazilian cultural patrimony" by the Institute of Historic and Artistic National Patrimony; the Wajãpi Villages Council's (Apina) initiative to submit their cultural legacy as a candidate in this ethnological process of legitimization; and the United Nations' ultimate proclamation of these cultural expressions as a "Masterpiece of the Oral and Intangible Heritage of Humanity." Gallois carefully analyzes this process and the political trajectory of the Wajãpi in constructing a notion of "indigeneity" in parallel with their gradual involvement with Brazilian indigenist politics during the past twenty years, paying particular attention to how the appropriation of "indigeneity" is directly derived from the radical transformation of their territoriality as a result of the reduction of their traditional territory into a "reserve." It was during this indigenist movement in the 1980s that members of the different and dispersed groups took on the collective identity as "Wajãpi," enunciating this new category of collective concerns in situations where sociopolitical unity was paramount. Although before this point such collective identities were seldom utilized in the context of the 1980s, the different Wajãpi local groups and many other indigenous groups of Amapá and northern Pará were induced beginning in the 1980s to produce ideas, projects, translations, neologisms, performances, products, and objects that reflected their "indigeneity" and to create a "Wajãpi culture."

The concluding chapter by Alissa Trotz and Terry Roopnaraine grounds such analyses further by intellectually excavating the subtle distinction between "coast" and "hinterland" as a trope of history and ethnology, used to construct and emplace the Amerindian and non-Amerindian in a discrete space, correlated with ideas of progress, modernity, and development. This two-part essay traces and analyzes elements of the relationship between a postcolonial Creole population and the Amazonian peoples and landscape lying to the south. Guyana, 90 percent of whose population makes its home on a strip of coastal land, is a country with a deeply racialized political landscape in which African and East Indian Guyanese continually compete over who is fitter and more deserving to hold the reins of national power. This monopoly, as also discussed by David Hinds in part 2, leaves virtually no space (politically, imaginatively, or materially) for the indigenous peoples who constitute 8 percent of the population and who live primarily and tenuously in what is referred to as the interior or hinterland. For Afro- or Indo-Guyanese "coastlanders," the hinterland constitutes a highly ambivalent space, which simultaneously presents the possibility of great wealth and the grave dangers of the truly unknown. The first part of the chapter shows how the space and peoples of the hinterland, haunting the edges of the coastal imagination and normally an "absent presence" to coastlanders, are rendered visible when they offer redemptive possibilities. The second part turns to a small subsection of the coastal population that has chosen to engage directly and personally with the "bush" and explores how these out-of-place coastlanders make sense of the hinterland and the people who live there.

Taken together, the chapters in this volume strongly demonstrate that a much more positive and complex anthropological agenda exists in the Guayana region than has been appreciated. The *Handbook of South American Indians* created a sense of cultural and geographical space in which "the Guianas" were marginal, and the Venezuelan and Brazilian regions of Guayana were simply assimilated to their national anthropologies or to that of "Amazonia" more widely. Whereas the "Northwest Amazon" in Colombia and the "Central Highlands" and "Xingu" areas in Brazil have enjoyed a degree of theoretical visibility in recent scholarship, Guayana has not. Indigenous peoples of those geographical regions—such as the Gé or Tukano—have formed paradigms for theoretical innovation in a way that, as yet, Carib and Arawak societies have not.[10]

We are not suggesting here that anthropological agendas be driven simply by regional priorities—this was the failing of the *Handbook*'s conceptual scheme—but rather we hope to allow readers to focus on the historically special and culturally unique features of the societies of this region. We also hope to show that the most recent scholarship in and on the Guayana region promises, as it were, a new "El Dorado" of knowledge to be derived from the realm of the still golden king.

Notes

1. This is particularly evident in the term *kanaimà,* which in the regional literature invokes truly strange and troubling acts. The term refers to the killing of individuals by dark shamans through the violent physical mutilation of the mouth and anus, into

which are inserted various magical objects. The killers are then mystically enjoined to return to the victim's dead body in order to drink the juices of putrefaction and thereby to transform themselves on a spiritual plane (see Whitehead 2002b, 2002c). In this way, kanaimà becomes the metaphoric equivalent of Joseph Conrad's (1999 [1899]) "heart of darkness," where there is ultimately nothing but "the horror, the horror."

2. Among such entrepreneurial scientists were Sir Clements R. Markham, botanist and senior official of the India office; Sir Joseph D. Hooker, director of Kew Gardens; and Henry Ridley, director of the Singapore Botanical Gardens. Markham was involved in promoting the cultivation of the rubber plant varieties *Hevea brasiliensis* and *Castilla moraceae,* and in 1875 and 1876 the botanist Robert Cross was sent to Central and South America to collect specimens and report on their requirements regarding climate and soil. The plants and seeds that he brought back, along with the others, were distributed through the botanical gardens at Kew to the colonies of Ceylon, India, and Malaya, and from there throughout the East. *Hevea brasiliensis* proved to be much the most successful rubber plant, and it became the preferred variety, contributing directly to the collapse of the South American rubber industry at the beginning of the twentieth century. This legacy of "biopiracy" is notably still an active consideration in the politics of botanical research in South America today.

3. Roth used the term *Guiana Indians* and understood by that, given his source material, to be the geographical space bounded by the Atlantic, the Amazon, and the Orinoco.

4. Roth's "documentation" of indigenous sexual practices to convince the European scientific community of his credibility as an ethnologist totally discredited him in the eyes of the local and metropolitan white community. The "pornographic photographs" scandal evaporated his claims to represent a higher commitment to the nationalistic goals of moral and eugenicist improvement.

5. Some of these materials became the basis for a volume of poetry by Brett in which he retold them in verse form; see his 1880 volume *Legends and Myths of the Aboriginal Indians of British Guiana.*

6. See *Canoe and Camp Life in British Guiana* (Barrington-Brown 1877). Barrington-Brown was a prominent figure in the life of the colony of British Guiana in his capacity as government surveyor. He was also professionally accomplished as a geologist and well reputed as an explorer. In these ways, he is very much an example of the strength and limits of the imperialist class of his era—literate but not literary, an explorer but not a discoverer, a field geologist but not a scientific innovator.

7. See Peter Rivière's discussion of this topic in *Absent Minded Imperialism: Britain and the Expansion of Empire in Nineteenth-century Brazil* (1995a).

8. In 1895, Jesse Walter Fewkes embarked on various archaeological explorations for the Smithsonian's Bureau of American Ethnology, and in 1918 he was appointed chief of the bureau. He was particularly interested in the prehistoric inhabitants of the island of Puerto Rico, which became a possession of the United States as a result of the Spanish-American War. He excavated a number of sites in Puerto Rico and extended his research to neighboring islands, such as Haiti, Cuba, Trinidad, and the Lesser Antilles, resulting in the work *Aborigines of Porto Rico and Neighboring Islands* (1907). Fewkes retired from the Smithsonian Institution in 1928 and died two years later, just before Walter Roth. In *Additional Studies* (1929:v–xi), Roth mentions Fewkes as a personal friend and quotes his letter to him describing his expedition to the south of British Guiana in January–July 1925, and this connection does much to explain Roth's orientation to the U.S. academic context.

9. This positive evaluation of Walter Roth by the PNC government was also informed by a rejection of more establishment figures such as Im Thurn. After all, Walter Roth came with mildly "radical-liberal" baggage from Australia.

10. However, the edited collections by Ellen Basso (1977) and by Jonathan Hill and Fernando Santos-Granero (2002) provide important exceptions to this generalization.

Part 1

Archaeology and Ecology

2

Pleistocene–Early Holocene Environmental Change
Implications for Human Adaptive Responses in the Guianas

Mark G. Plew

The early peopling and later exploitation of the Guianas are best understood in the context of Pleistocene and later Holocene environmental change. This approach provides a broad context within which to reconstruct the nature of resources available to early populations, particularly in areas where modern conditions do not reflect earlier potentials. Though paleoenvironmental data for northeastern South America are not extensive, a number of general regionally based studies allow for construction of major environmental episodes of change relating to both coastal (littoral) and interior portions of the Guianas (see fig. 2.1). Equally limited are archaeological works that evaluate the relationships between human occupations and environmental change. This chapter summarizes briefly what is known of environmental changes that appear to have influenced human use of the Guiana Shield and discusses the potential adaptive responses to those changes. The chapter does not offer a detailed culture history of the region but assesses arguments relating to the use of biogeographic and cultural-historical models to interpret the archaeology of the area. It assumes economic adjustments to climatic change but argues that Pleistocene-Holocene environmental fluctuations are subregionally more varied and less uniform than assumed. It further argues that environmental alteration led not to instability, but to proliferation of diverse adaptive responses.

Pleistocene-Holocene Environmental Change

Insights regarding Pleistocene environments are based on geoscientific data (geochemical, palynological, lithostratigraphic, and paleoclimatic data [see, e.g., Meggers 2007; Rull 1999] and biogeographic studies [Behling and Hooghiemastra 1998; Haffer 1969; Prance 1973; Vanzolini 1970]). These studies document varying environmental conditions over many thousands of years and suggest the potential for a variety of human adaptive responses. The rapidity of change that seems to

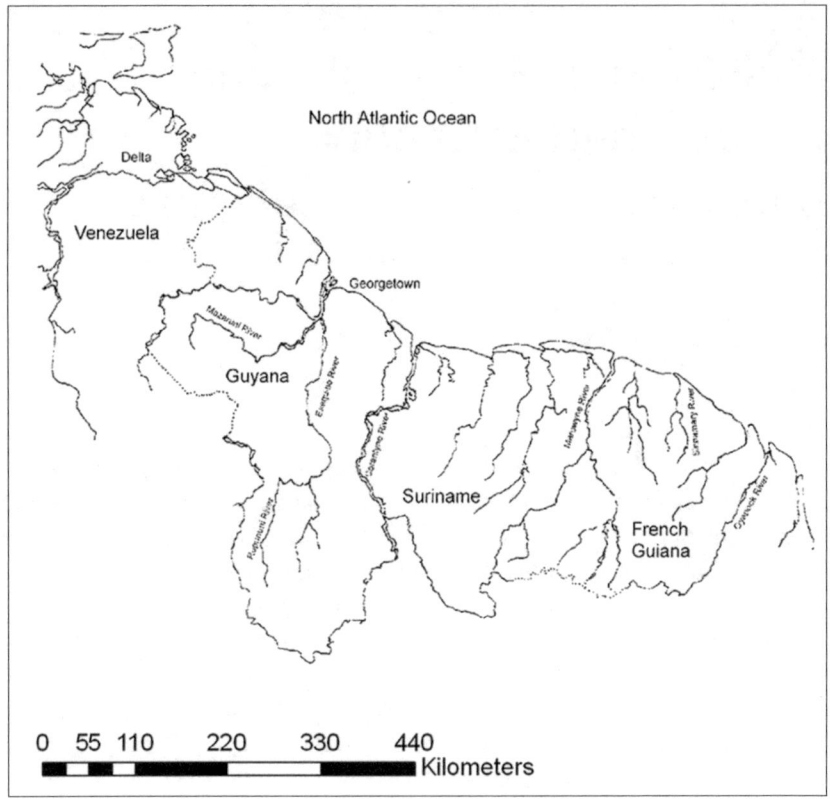

Fig. 2.1 The location of the Guianas.

follow from many analyses argues against models that suggest gradual and relatively uniform human responses (Versteeg and Bubberman 1992; D. Williams 2003). In the Guianas, discussion of human occupations and subsistence has focused on coastal inundations, impacts of mudflats, fluctuations in distribution of mangrove swamps, and periods of aridity influencing decreased forest precipitation and increased expansion of savanna (Boomert 1980b; D. Williams 2003). These discussions follow from an assumption that significant environmental impact is associated with conditions of the later Pleistocene.

Coastal Environments

Following the Pleniglacial period, during which conditions in northern South America were relatively dry, the climate of the Late Pleistocene–Early Holocene (13,000–10,000 BP) became increasingly wet, with the coastline inundated by waters (see Behling 2002; Rull 1999; Tissot, Djuvansah, and Marius 1988; Van Andel

Environmental Change

1967; Wijmstra and Van der Hammen 1966). During drier intervals, as is the case in Guyana, the coast lay considerably seaward, almost one hundred kilometers from its present configuration (D. Williams 2003). In these periods, rivers carried increased water levels and inundated river valleys (Van der Hammen 1963). Indeed, Van der Hammen (1963) suggests that the Demerara River valley was flooded as far up as McKenzie, when waters reached thirty-six meters above the modern land surface at some time during the Late Allerröd interstadial between around 11,500 and 8600 BP (see fig. 2.2). The pattern of high and low sea-level stands associated with glacial and interglacial events is correlated with successions of vegetation types. Pollen spectra indicate that high sea levels are associated with mangrove pollen primarily of *Rhizophora* species, although *Avecinnia*, which produces limited quantities of pollen, is also well represented. In contrast, periods characterized by lower sea levels are associated with low trees and shrubs of the genera *Brysonima* and *Curatella*, typifying savanna conditions prevalent during glacial episodes (see fig. 2.3). Similar conditions existed in Suriname (Roeleveld 1969) and in French Guiana (de Granville 1982; Hoock 1971), where coastal savannas were submerged around 6,000 years ago during the interglacial climatic optimum (de Granville 1982:178). In Guyana between 10,000 BP and 7200 BP, the coastline continued to lie beyond its present configuration and was characterized by open grasslands that are thought to have hosted megafauna (Boomert 1980b; Van der Hammen 1963; see also D. Williams 2003). Denis Williams (2003) argues that the period saw periodically increased sea levels and the emergence of intertidal mud flats. Roeleveld (1969) and Williams (2003) argue for an absolute sea-level rise and the development of a marine-to-brackish coastal zone from 7200 BP until around 6000 BP, followed by a period between 6000 and 4000 BP when mangroves appeared in coastal environments (Brinkman and Pons 1968).

Coastal conditions favoring the development of mangrove swamps and their associated peat deposition created the brackish conditions prevalent today in areas of the northern Guiana littoral. Williams (2003) suggests that between 6000 and 4000 BP highland runoff converted intertidal mudflats to seasonally inundated savannas. Following a warming interval between 4000 and 3500 BP, water salinity increased, and peat deposition ended. During this period, marine shellfish appear to dominate within mangrove estuaries (Absy 1985; Van der Hammen 1974). After 3000 BP, a general warming trend resulted in the emergence of essentially modern conditions.

Environments of the Interior Forests and Savannas

The interior forests and savannas of Guyana were also significantly influenced by glacial climates. Though debate continues about the extent of savannas within the tropical forests of the region (see, e.g., Sarmiento 1984), several dry episodes or

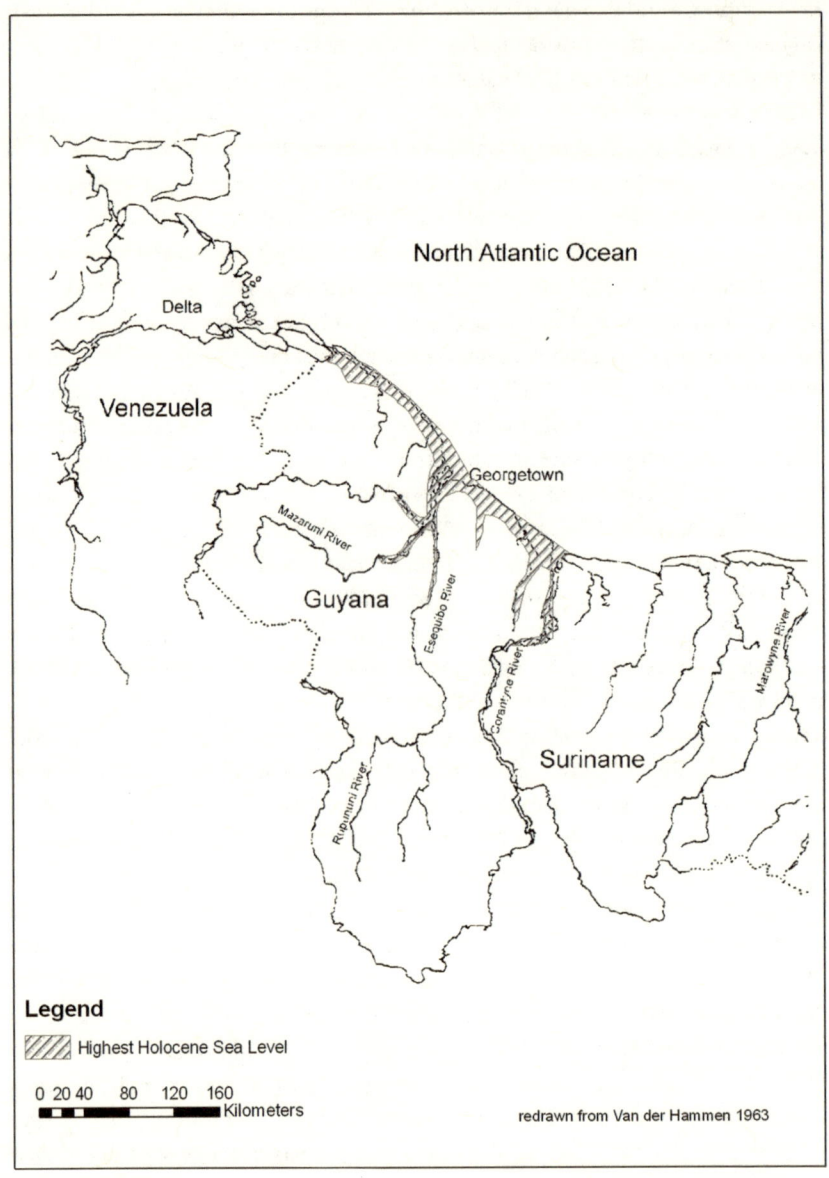

Fig. 2.2 The highest Holocene sea levels along the coastline of Guyana and Suriname. Redrawn from Van der Hammen 1963.

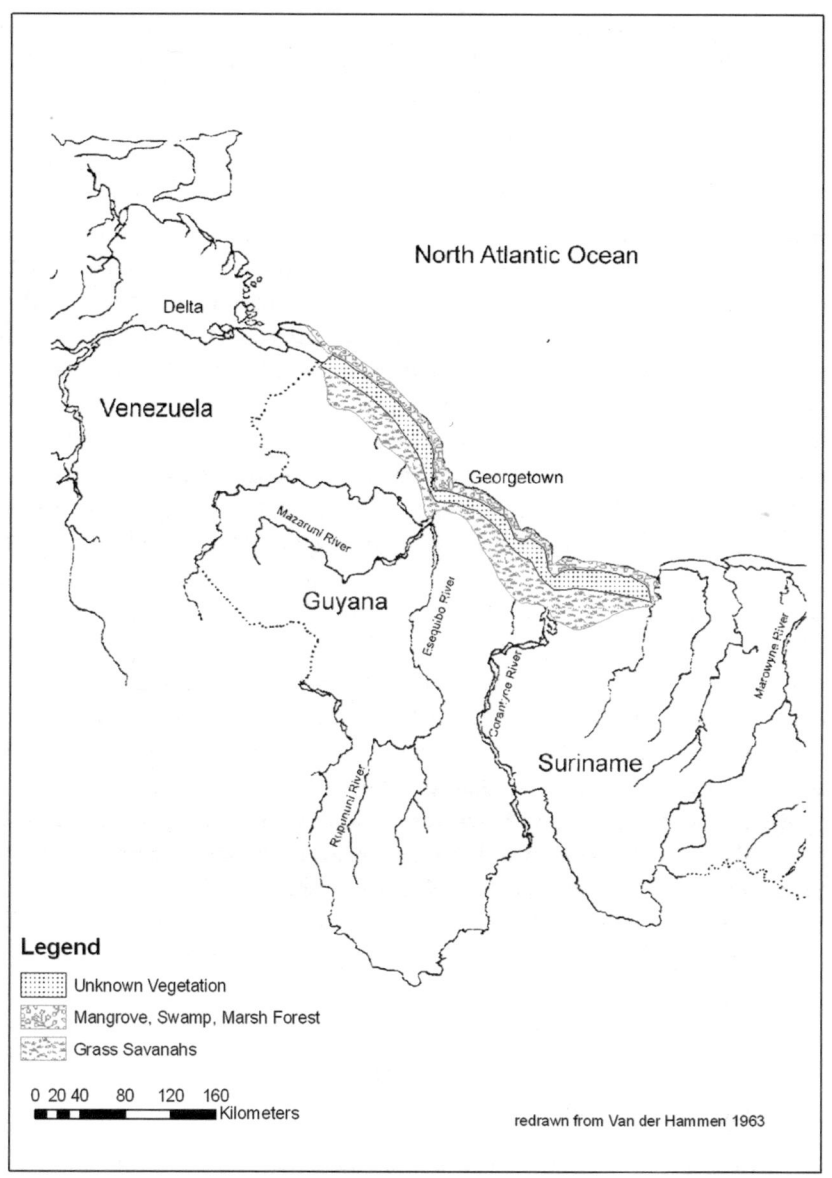

Fig. 2.3 Holocene vegetational zones. Redrawn from Van der Hammen 1963.

warmer periods are known. In the earlier Pleistocene between 26,000 and 14,000 BP, relatively cool and dry conditions prevailed across the Guianas. Following this cooler period, conditions between 14,000 and 10,000 BP became somewhat warmer and were associated with increased rainfall. The emergent conditions of the Holocene or modern period are characterized by several dry intervals between 11,000 and 9,500 BP and also around 4000 BP (Van der Hammen 1963). During these times, there appears to be increased settlement of the interior forests and savannas. Most important in this regard are pollen data recovered from Lake Moreiru in the Rupununi of southern Guyana. A pollen spectrum derived from peat layers dating between 6,000 and 7,300 years ago indicates dense *Brysonima* woodland prior to 7300 BP, with emerging savanna conditions in the Rupununi associated with the most recent glacial period. In French Guiana between 10,000 and 8,000 years ago and again between 6,000 and 4,000 years ago, the diversity of forest species declined, whereas pioneer species increased significantly, indicating a lowering of water levels during these periods (Charles-Dominique et al. 1998). Brown (1977), Brown and Ab'saber (1979), Haffer (1969, 1982), and Prance (1973, 1982) argue for the emergence of refugia, the largest stretching across southern Guyana to the Pakaraima Mountains. Similarly and more recently, Van der Hammen and Absy (1994) argue for a Late Pleistocene (22,000–13,000 BP) dessication, resulting in a large western Amazonian forest and several smaller forests in the eastern shield. Importantly, the desiccation associated with these models would have resulted in significantly greater areas of savanna or mixed forest/savanna of the type associated with Paleo-Indian and later occupations elsewhere in the Amazonian region. Although most models of environmental change pertain primarily to glacial events, Meggers (1994, 1996) provides an interesting review of data documenting the impact of mega-Niño events in the Caribbean and Amazonian regions during the Late Holocene. Meggers (1994, 2007) notes that discontinuities in the archaeological record along the Amazon correlate with drought intervals associated with mega-Niño episodes.

Environmental Change and the Archaeological Record

Archaeologists working in the Guianas have traditionally utilized what K. S. Brown (1977) has described as "refuge biogeography" (see Rostain 1994a; Versteeg 1985; D. Williams 1985, 2003; see also Whitehead 1996) to correlate known environmental events with archaeologically defined economic responses. Archaeologists and linguists (see Migliazza 1982), notably Meggers (1987), have examined discontinuities in the archaeological record and the distribution of ethnographic and linguistic groups with respect to Pleistocene-Holocene refugia. Meggers (1982) appropriately offers a caution regarding inferences made from cultural distributions. New economic pursuits have generally and historically been correlated with what are considered relatively uniform events and conditions resulting from the emergence of new environments. Assertions regarding changing economic regimes have tended to follow traditional arguments regarding the relative importance of *varzea* versus Terra Firme landscapes (D. Williams 2003). Although it remains logical to assume that changing environmental conditions would have precipitated economic adjustments, the scale of the environmental change and the commensurate adaptive responses are not well documented and may have been substantially more varied. Indeed, biogeographic modeling has been the focus of criticism by so-called vicariance biogeographers (Croizat 1958) who reject entirely the argument that Pleistocene climatic fluctuations had significant impact on biogeographic patterns and by population biologists who note that the complex heterogeneity of the neotropic environments might account for biogeographic patterning without alteration of landforms.

The Paleo-Indian Context

Archaeological discussions of Paleo-Indians in the Guianas have assumed adaptations to changing environmental regimes associated with climatic events of the Late Pleistocene and Early Holocene periods:

Years BP	Climatic Conditions	Period
13,000–10,000	Wet	Paleo-Indian
10,000–7,200	Dry	
7,200–6,000	Wet	Archaic shellfishers
6,000–4,000	Dry/Wet	Incipient horticulturists
4,000–3,500	Dry	Horticulturalists

Quite often, the pattern has been described as reflecting a strategy similar to the megafaunal pattern of the North American Clovis (e.g., Boomert 1980b; Versteeg and Bubberman 1992; D. Williams 1985, 2003). In actuality, little evidence of Paleo-Indians is documented in the Guianas. Although sampling remains a troubling problem in the region, the paucity of evidence is striking. Yet in Guyana a total of eight Paleo-Indian points have been reported (see Plew 2005:11–12), including three triangular-bladed quartz crystal points similar to those recovered from other Paleo-Indian sites in the Amazonian region (see Meggers and Miller 2003). The number of Paleo-Indian age sites producing lithics is known, although none is reported in Guyana. Proportionally, however, the number of points found in Guyana is significant relative to the region in general. The eight projectiles are surface finds, none having been radiometrically or geologically dated. Further, they were not found in association with megafauna. It is interesting to note, however, that all were found in interior locations.

The areas from which the artifacts have been collected would have been savannas during the Late Pleistocene, which suggests that Paleo-Indians in Guyana utilized open environments at considerable distances from the interstadial inundations of the coastal region during the Late Pleistocene–Early Holocene period. Similarly, the earliest occupations of Suriname dating to some 10,000 years ago are described for the interior portions of the country (Boomert 1980b; Versteeg and Bubberman 1992). Boomert (1980b) describes two phases for the Sipaliwini Savanna: an early phase in which "big-game hunters" took mammoths, mastodons, and megatherians, and a later Early Holocene phase in which hunters shifted to the exploitation of smaller mammals (see Versteeg and Bubberman 1992 for discussion). Though the shift may reflect changing habitats, it would have most likely led to overhunting (see Alvard et al. 1997). As with many Paleo-Indian sites, few diagnostic tools are present, and little to no faunal materials are found in direct association. Rostain (1994a, 1994b) notes that no Paleo-Indian sites are found along the coastal regions of French Guiana, but he presumes that occupations similar to those described by Boomert (1980b) exist in the interior. More recent investigations in the coastal rain forest of French Guiana at Petit Saut on the Middle Sinnamary River produced nine radiometric dates between 14,900 and 8000 BP. Although no cultural materials are associated with the early dates 14,900 and 12,190, one Early Holocene site dating between 9900 and 8000 BP is associated with lithic flakes and expedient tools. On the basis of meager data, it appears that Late Pleistocene–Early Holocene hunters or foragers were utilizing the rain forests and savannas of the Guianas. The limited data seem to indicate expanding use of the area beginning in the Early Holocene (see fig. 2.4).

Environmental Change: The Archaic and Early Horticultural Context

Between 8,000 and 7,000 years ago, relatively more modern conditions appeared along the eastern and western Guiana littorals. Associated with the eustatic sea-level rises of the previous thousand years, relatively unique conditions emerged along the western littoral west of the Essequibo River in Guyana. These conditions included numerous microenvironments of the estuary ecosystem comprising river mouths, creeks, tidal marshes, and other marine-to-brackish waters in direct interaction with sea water (see D. Williams 2003:76–89). These conditions are in turn associated with emergence of highly productive shellfish resources that were adapted to varying degrees of salinity. Notably, new species—including the Caribbean oyster (*Crassostrea rhizophorae*), fighting conch (*Strombus pugilis*), tulip mussel (*Modiolus americanus*), zebra nerite (*Puperita pupa*), and mangrove land crab (*Ucides cordatus*)—appeared in

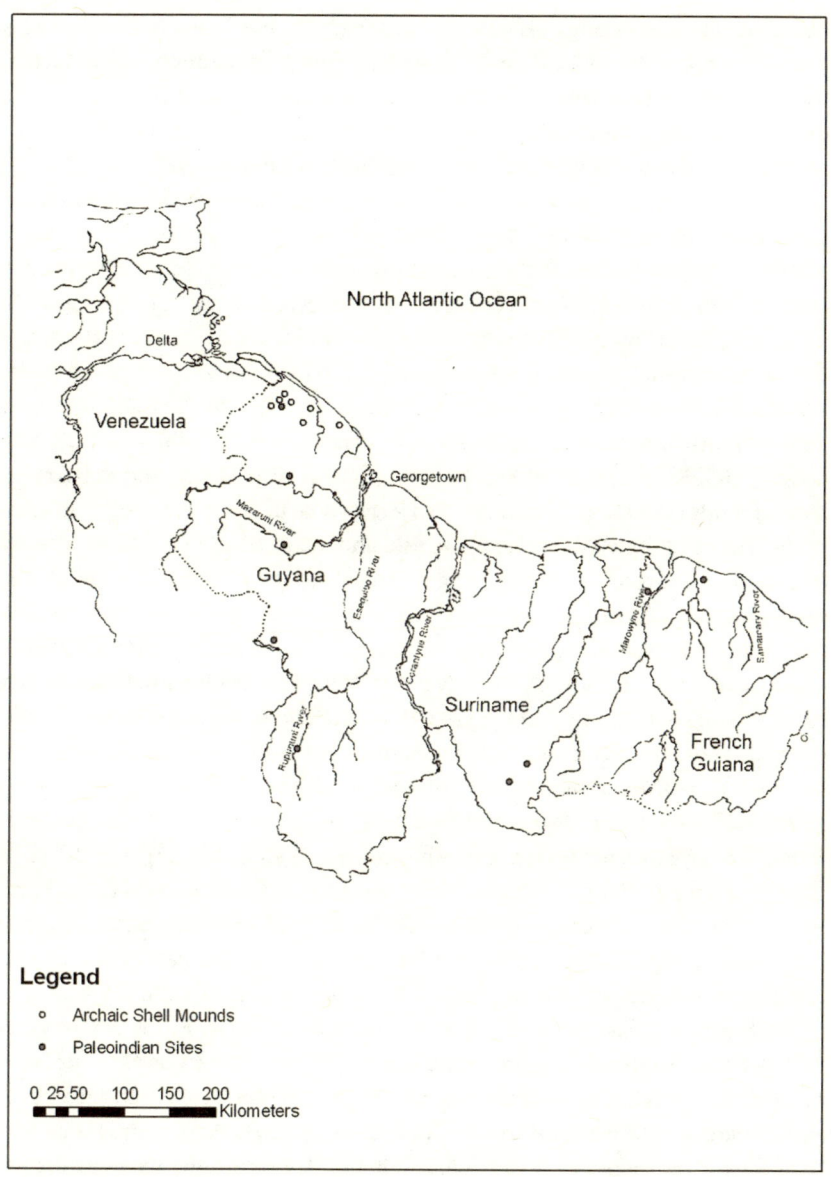

Fig. 2.4 The location of Paleoindian and Archaic shell mound sites.

numerous localities along a salinity gradient that may have extended to distances greater than one hundred kilometers (Odum 1984). In addition to productive fisheries and concentrations of marine mammals and avifauna sheltered by the mangrove canopy, these environments appear to have provided substantial support for Early Archaic (Preceramic) and Early Horticultural populations.

The Archaic occupations of northwestern Guyana associated with extensive exploitation of shellfish are known from excavations of several shell mounds within the region (see fig. 2.4). The mounds, which range up to eighty-by-thirty meters in length and width and between one and fifteen meters in height, provide insights regarding the economic and social lifeway of the early littoral pattern. The earliest known shell mound is the Pirika Mound, which has an uncorrected radiocarbon date of around 7280 BP (D. Williams 2003; see also Plew 2005:205). In addition, early uncorrected dates have been obtained for Akawabi (4020 BP), Barabina (6885, 5965, and 4115 BP), Koriabo (5710 and 6520 BP), and Kabakaburi shell mounds (5340 BP). Subsistence data suggest the periodic use of snail, mussel, oyster, crab, and conch as well as birds, fish, and mammals. Although not directly evidenced in the record, it is presumed that local groups utilized a range of plants, including palm. The toolkit associated with the earliest populations includes simple percussion-made choppers, hammer stones, and picks produced from andesite, quartz, and schist. Associated features of the Alaka Phase culture dating between AD 1 and AD 500 (Evans and Meggers 1960) include fire-cracked rock and concentrations of lithic debris associated with the manufacture of stone tools, hearths, storage pits, postmolds, and burials. Although this phase is generally considered Preceramic, Evans and Meggers (1960:63–64) describe it as a late "incipient ceramic" phase associated with a few rather crudely made shell-tempered sherds of the type Wanaina Plain and recently confirmed by reinvestigation of the Kabakaburi mound (Plew, Pereira, and Simon 2007). The "incipient ceramic" period is associated with groundstone tools that include celts, mortars, manos, pestles, and grinding stones and with the recovery of flexed burials of adults and children.

With regard to the "incipient ceramic" phase described by Evans and Meggers (1960), the Archaic shell mounds of the Northwest have recently become the focus of a debate regarding the early appearance of pottery in Guyana and thereby an early emergence of horticulture. In Guyana, the emergence of horticulture was traditionally associated with large village sites of the Mabaruma Phase dating between AD 500 and 1600 (Evans and Meggers 1960:122). These sites, which range to more than seventeen thousand square meters in area, are associated with coarsely tempered Mabaruma Plain pottery and an assemblage that includes manos, metates, polished celts, and possible hoes. Mabaruma pottery is replaced by sand-tempered Hosororo pottery in the later part of the phase. Denis Williams (1996) assumes the appearance of pottery in the archaeological record to reflect the beginning of the Formative period, and on the basis of early pottery at Barabina and at Hosororo mounds he argues for an early beginning of the Mabaruma Phase at 1600

Environmental Change

BC. Roosevelt (1997) challenges the chronology, noting inconsistencies in data presentations pointing to an early occurrence of pottery in Alaka Phase levels at Barabina. Regardless, the early dates for pottery in Guyana fall within the range of dates from Taperinha near Santarém, Brazil, where dates are established between 5700 and 4300 BC (Roosevelt 1998) for pottery similar in manufacture to the Mina Phase (Simões 1981) and Alaka Phase types (Evans and Meggers 1960).

Environmental conditions similar to those along the coastal regions of the western littoral did not emerge to the east. Although common in eastern Venezuela and Guyana, the shell mound pattern is not found in coastal Suriname (Boomert 1980b; Versteeg and Bubberman 1992) or French Guiana (Rostain 1994a, 1994b). Versteeg (2003) and Versteeg and Bubberman (1992:19) correlate the absence of productive shellfisheries with the clayey sediments of Amazonian origin that dominate the Essequibo-Amazon area. With regard to the interior savannas of Suriname, Boomert (1980b) and Versteeg (1998) argue for the persistence of a Preceramic pattern emphasizing the hunting of smaller mammals beginning at the end of the Pleistocene. Rostain (1994b) assumes a comparable adaptation in the interior of French Guiana. This pattern is equivalent to what Denis Williams (1985, 2003) and Plew (2005) have referred to as the Meso-Indian or Archaic period (Preceramic). The earliest ceramic horizon in Suriname, at the site of Kaurikreek (Versteeg 1978), dates between 2500 and 1600 BC, whereas the earliest sites in French Guiana include Pointe Gravier dated to 1500 BC and sites on the Middle Sinnamary River between 1390 and 1050 BC (Jérémie, Nowacke-Breczewski, and Vacher 1993; Vacher, Jérémie, and Briand 1998). Williams's (1998, 2003) recent reworking of the Mabaruma chronology fits within the chronologies of Suriname and French Guiana. A unique feature of adaptations in Suriname and French Guiana is the use of *cheniers,* ancient sand bars or artificially created earthen mounds, for cultivation and habitation (see Rostain 1994a; Versteeg 1998). In general, it appears that the beginnings of horticulture fit the relatively modern environmental conditions of the coastal and interior portions of the Guianas. Yet these environments were undoubtedly influenced by continental El Niño events and lesser regional events.

Conclusions

Beyond issues of sampling, archaeologists working in the Guianas have struggled to understand variability in human–land use relationships. This uncertainty in large part reflects a continuing reliance on biogeographic modeling based on relatively incomplete data. Although environmental events clearly correlate with the probable use of specific areas and resources during the Late Pleistocene and the Holocene, the body of paleoenvironmental evidence remains inadequate as the basis for interpreting the range of human adaptations in many areas of the Guianas. Until more complete data are available, we should not assume the broad correlates that have driven many archaeological interpretations of the past several decades. In general, anthropologists and archaeologists have assumed broad homogeneity of the Amazonian environment, as reflected in the long-term debate regarding the variable productive values of *varzea* versus Terra Firme environments. Archaeologists should follow the lead of a number of scholars, most notably Moran (1993), who has argued that simplistic characterizations mask the scientifically documented diversity of the Terra Firme. As we recognize the need to account for a greater range of environmental variation, we continue to gain significant insights regarding the rapidity with which ancient landscapes evolved. For example, Blasco Saenger, and Janodet (1996) have demonstrated that the coastal ecosystems of the Guianas and other areas are so specialized that the most minor variations in hydrological and tidal regimes effect noticeable mortality in mangroves. This finding has significant implications for Williams's (2003) discussions of Archaic or Preceramic uses of the northwest coast of Guyana and potentially of other areas inland in Suriname and French Guiana.

Archaeological interpretations of the region reflect a continuing cultural-historical bias toward the view that broad regional environmental change is accompanied by uniform cultural responses. Although presently meager, data appear to suggest considerable variation in the formation of landscapes and associated biotic communities in the Guianas during the past 15,000 years. It is evident even within this small region that marked differences exist in the conditions to which Pleistocene and later Holocene populations were adapted. Rather than assuming that these conditions resulted in an abrupt adoption of new subsistence strategies, it may be useful to consider that Paleo-Indian, Archaic, and many Early Horticulturalists were in fact "broad spectrum foragers" (cf. Lynch 1998; Roosevelt et al. 1996). Recent insights regarding the highly diverse nature of hunter-gatherer adaptations (see, e.g., Kelly 1995) should be considered when thinking about the archaeological record of the Guianas. In this regard, Meggers's observation that biologists (and paleoclimatologists) are rarely forced to confront the archaeological timescale (1987:172–174) is an important one. Equally important are correlations of climatic oscillations with the "differential sensitivity" of hunter-gatherers and agriculturalists (Meggers 1987:172).

If the varied adaptive responses characteristic of hunter-gatherers and agriculturalists are taken into consideration, it may be possible to identify a range of adaptations associated with the ever-evolving microniches of the Late Holocene (see D. Williams 2003). Instead of debating the presence of "incipient ceramics" as a benchmark denoting the emergence of horticulture in specific areas, it may prove more productive to document the full range of environmental events affecting the region, further delineating what appears to be considerable subregional diversity. This documentation must be accompanied by a closer examination of the archaeological record as a basis for determining whether there are—as hunter-gatherer analogies would suggest—many subregional adaptations. Such an examination will necessarily require extensive excavation projects like that at Petit Saut (Jérémie, Nowacke-Breczewski, and

Vacher 1998; Rostain 1994b). Finally and paradigmatically, it will be useful to view episodes of environmental change not as reflecting periods of instability but as events leading to diverse human adaptive responses. Describing the full range of adaptations made by prehistoric peoples of the Guianas will substantially enhance our understanding of the dynamics of all past Amazonian cultures.

3

Between Orínoco and Amazon
The Ceramic Age in the Guianas

Stéphen Rostaín

> We must cut, cut, and always cut, and others must cut when we have gone, felling without mercy, thinning the ranks so that the forest remains sound.
>
> —Anouilh, *L'Alouette*
> (The Lark, translated by the chapter author)

Though more than one-third of the Guianas rain forest has been subjected to clearing by slash-and-burn technique during the past two thousand years (Tardy 1998), knowledge of the first inhabitants is still relatively scarce. However, important advances have been made in archaeological research on Amazonia and on the Guianas in just the past twenty years (McEwan, Barreto, and Góes Neves 2001; Whitehead 1996). Recent publications give a better understanding of the pre-Columbian peopling of the Guianas (Mazière 1997; Plew 2005; Rostain 1994b; Vacher, Jérémie, and Briand 1998; Versteeg 2003; D. Williams 2003). Remaining tasks now include not only defining ceramic typologies, but understanding the interaction between humans and their environment, explaining economical and ceremonial relations, and reconstructing sociocultural developments.

Sedentarism began in the Guianas around 5000 BC with arrival of shellfish gatherers on the coastal area of Guyana, leading later to the invention of pottery and agriculture. Data are still missing to support a drawing of the general panorama of inland archaeology. In compensation, however, the chronology of the peopling of the coastal area over time can be described.

During pre-Columbian times, two large cultural centers influenced the communities along the coast of the Guianas (see fig. 3.1). They were expansion centers. The groups in the western area (Venezuela, Guyana, Suriname, western French Guiana) had their roots in the middle Orinoco area, where subsequently the Saladoid, Barrancoid, and Arauquinoid traditions developed. In the eastern part (Amapá in Brazil and eastern French Guiana), however, the influence of the middle and lower Amazon area was predominant, where subsequently the Incised Rim, the Incised-and-Punctate, and the Polychrome Traditions developed.

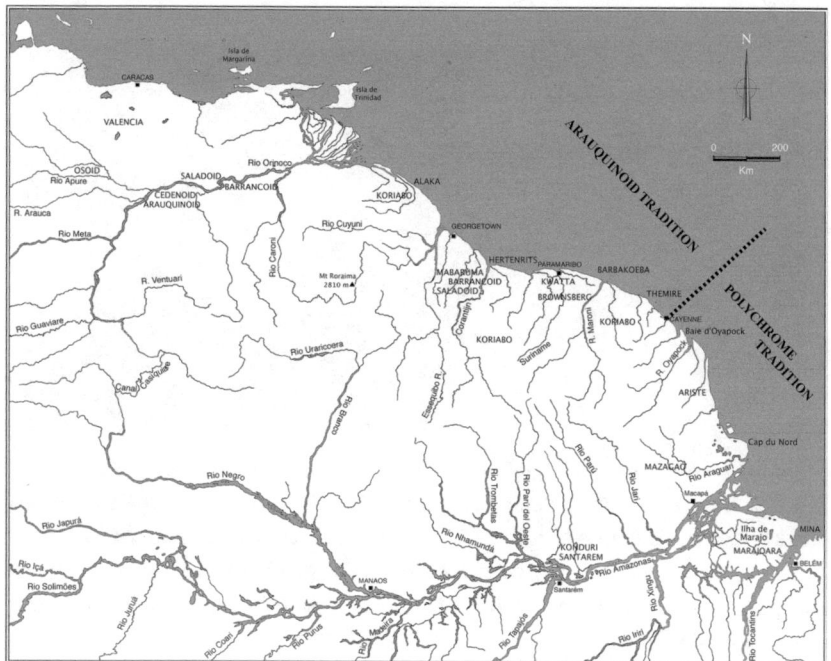

Fig. 3.1 An archaeological map of the Guianas.

The First Ceramists

From 2500 to 1500 BC, elaborated pottery appeared in various sites throughout Amazonia and the Guianas. The earliest sites are located mostly in the floodplains at the bank of the large rivers, such as the La Gruta–Ronquín site (2600–1100 BC) on the middle Orinoco (Cruxent and Rouse 1958–59; Roosevelt 1980). The Saladoid Tradition began in the lower Orinoco before spreading to the north in the Antilles and to the east up to western Suriname, where the earliest ceramics are found in the Kaurikreek site (see fig. 3.2). This site is located along a small creek and dated to 2200–1750 BC (Versteeg 1978). Saladoid sites are found inland in Guyana and in western Suriname. The Wonotobo site, located on the bank of the Corantijn River in Suriname, is dated between AD 70 and 200 (Boomert 1983).

The Saladoid Tradition was later replaced by the Barrancoid Tradition, and in Wonotobo it seems that the Barrancoid influence occurred directly after the Saladoid occupation (Versteeg 2003). The Barrancoid Tradition is represented on the Guyana coastal area by the Mabaruma and Abary cultures (Evans and Meggers 1960; Plew 2005). These first farmers cultivated essentially bitter manioc in small fields cleared by slash-and-burn methods in the forest.

Fig. 3.2 One of the oldest ceramics of the Guianas was found in the Kaurikreek site in western Suriname (2200–1750 BC). At the Taperinha site on the lower Amazon, the oldest ceramics are gourdlike vessels in imitation of former receptacles made with gourds and baskets. The ceramic decoration in Kaurikreek *(left)* is very similar to modern basketry motifs *(right)*.

Chiefdoms from the West

Agriculture developed in the fertile coastal plains to become an elaborated technique on raised fields. From AD 300 to 650, Barrancoid groups built a few mounds in a restricted area in the extreme west of Suriname and eastern Guyana coast. The Guianas coast stayed relatively sparsely inhabited during the initial period, but the situation changed radically from AD 700 on with the arrival of new cultures. The Arauquinoid Tradition appeared around AD 500 in the area between the eastern Venezuelan llanos and the confluence of the Negro and Solimões rivers (Boomert 1980a). The most ancient sites with typical Arauquinoid pottery are located near the confluence of the Apure and Orinoco rivers (Cruxent and Rouse 1958–59). The middle Orinoco Arauquinoid people began to move down the river around AD 500, progressively replacing the old Barrancoid cultures. From this area, new movements went in three directions around AD 600 to 700—to the Venezuelan western llanos, the Antilles, and the coast of the Guianas. The Arauquinoid Tradition formed a specific stylistic group in the Guianas, divided in two chronological phases (Rostain and Versteeg 2003).

The first Guianas Arauquinoid phase seems to be concentrated in residential mounds on the western coast of Suriname. The range of radiocarbon dates shows a gradual rising of the mounds and places the different habitation layers between AD 700 and 950. Long and narrow raised fields were built around the mounds.

Due to a population increase, the cultural distribution of the Guianas coast changed around AD 1000. The coast between the Berbice River in Guyana and Cayenne Island in French Guiana was occupied by four Arauquinoid cultures: Hertenrits, Kwatta, Barbakoeba, and Thémire. All these cultures inhabited specific territories that are delimited by the main rivers. Arauquinoid cultures stayed in the Guianas at least until AD 1250, some of them surviving to 1650. Western sites are older than the eastern ones.

The common aspects of the Arauquinoid cultures of the Guianas are

- settlement in the coastal plain on sandy ridges or on artificial clay mounds, with most sites located less than 20 kilometers from the sea;
- agriculture on raised fields associated with an elaborated water-management system on a territory of approximately 600 kilometers long;
- specialization of specific activities (ceremonial rituals, tools, and artifacts; manufacturing, trade, intensive agriculture);
- transcultural trade of raw materials or finished productions in a commercial net;
- common pottery style (similar patterns in the shapes and the decoration);
- similar ceremonial artifacts (green stone pendants resembling frogs, twin *adornos,* pregnant female figurines).

The oldest Arauquinoid culture of the Guianas is the Hertenrits (see fig. 3.3), found in an area of circa 210 kilometers long and 25 kilometers wide between the Berbice and the Coppename rivers. This spot is the widest part of the Guianas Young Plain, but the absence of sandy ridges and the seasonal inundations render human occupation difficult. For that reason, the Hertenrits groups had to build rounded clay mounds above the water level to settle their villages. Hertenrits is the largest of the mounds, with a diameter of 200 to 320 meters and a height of 2.5 meters. Shallow canals seasonally inundated, interpreted as pathways, run radially, connecting the mound to raised fields and other mounds. Two smaller satellite mounds were built diametrically opposite equidistant from Hertenrits (Boomert 1980a). Hertenrits inhabitants organized and managed with precision their territory in a specific pattern: one main central mound from which pathways ran, crossing raised field areas and connecting secondary mounds.

Funerary activities took place on the mounds, and different types of burials have been found: direct and primary burial, secondary burial in urns, and even mixed burial (primary and secondary). Other ceremonial activities were apparently conducted far from the mounds. For example, the Prins Bernhard Polder site, situated in a peaty area far to the west of the mounds, was probably dedicated only to ceremonial purposes (Versteeg 1985). Many beautiful ceramic artifacts have been found in artificial small hills there (see fig. 3.4). They were probably used during short periods for specific activities, and it can be assumed that the site was not occupied permanently, because of the exceptional quantity and quality of elaborated artifacts and vessels and the absence of a cultural layer and raised fields.

Fig. 3.3 From AD 500 to 1200–1400, groups of the Arauquinoid Tradition settled along the coastal area of the Guianas from Guyana to Cayenne Island in French Guiana. One typical aspect of their ceramic style is the twin adornos, as on this specimen from the Hertenrits artificial mound in western Suriname. The principle of duality was important for the Arauquinoid society. From the collection of the Stichting Surinaams Museum, Paramaribo, Suriname.

The Hertenrits culture is an exception in the Guianas Arauquinoid Tradition in view of its occupation of floodplain without high, sandy ridges. East of the mounds area, the coastal morphology inhabited by other Arauquinoid cultures is different. Here, sandy ridges oriented east to west cut across the coast parallel to the seashore: they are narrow (some tens of meters) and very long (several kilometers). These ridges are remains of old sea beaches confined in the swamps in consequence of coastal evolution. They were very attractive for building villages, and most of the Arauquinoid sites are located on these dry areas. Trade was facilitated by the linear distribution of the villages along the ridges, and products traveled from place to place in an east–west and west–east direction. Three Arauquinoid cultures—

Fig. 3.4 A pregnant female clay figurine from the Prins Bernhard Polder site in western Suriname (height: 5 centimeters). Most of the Arauquinoid figurines represent pregnant women that were most likely fertility symbols for these agricultural societies. From the collection of the Stichting Surinaams Museum, Paramaribo, Suriname.

Kwatta, Barbakoeba, and Thémire—were distributed from the Coppename River up to Cayenne Island.

The Kwatta culture was located between the Coppename and Suriname rivers, which represents an area 92 kilometers long and 30 kilometers wide. Kwatta is the only Arauquinoid culture that is not associated with raised fields. Crops apparently were cultivated on the ridges in a slash-and-burn system because the richness in shells in the subsoil of the ridges in this area is remarkable, providing a good soil for agriculture.

Kwatta people were more oriented to the manufacture of prestige artifacts, managing tradeworks to obtain raw materials and to exchange their finished products. They made elaborate ceramics and a great variety of tools and ornaments with stone, shell, and bone. Their most famous products were the *muiraquitãs,* green stone pendants representing mostly frogs.

The Kwatta groups organized an efficient trade network between the interior and the coast. No rock is found on the Suriname coastal area, so the native peoples there had to obtain their stone from the interior. From AD 1000 to 1500, Brownsberg groups (that were not Arauquinoid) from the central interior of Suriname specialized in the manufacture of cutting tools to export them to the stoneless coastal area of Suriname (Boomert and Kroonenberg 1977). The trade routes were undoubtedly the main river systems, and along the coast the products were traded farther to the west and the east via the settlements situated on the old coastal barriers.

The Barbakoeba culture extends from the Cottica River in eastern Suriname up to the Kourou River in western French Guiana, an area 230 kilometers long and 25 kilometers wide. The Barbakoeba people were not good craftsmen like the Kwatta groups, but they were specialized in agriculture. Near the coastal settlements, enormous areas of raised fields have been found, generally in the swamps to the south of the sites. Three main categories of earthworks can be recognized: raised fields, ditches and ponds, and causeways. Raised fields are rounded, rectangular, or elongated mounds cultivated in the flooded savannas (see fig. 3.5). Drainage was controlled by canals. Ponds served as water tanks or fishponds. Some sites were connected with causeways.

By comparison to the density of other cultivated tropical lowlands and under the assumptions that the western coastal plain of the Guianas was uniformly inhabited and that the raised fields were cultivated permanently, the density might have been fifty per square kilometer (Rostain 1991).

On the French Guiana central coast, the Barbakoeba culture was gradually replaced by the Thémire culture. The Thémire culture's territory extended from Cayenne Island to the Kourou River at least, an area approximately 80 kilometers long by 1 to 5 kilometers wide. The Thémire culture was the most eastern and the latest Arauquinoid manifestation in the Guianas, surviving up to AD 1650 (Rostain 1994b).

Most of the Thémire sites are located on coastal quaternary sandy ridges, but some sites are found in the interior near the most northern rapids of the Sinnamary River in French Guiana, approximately 40 kilometers from the coast. These settlements possibly had a function in the trade between inland groups and coastal communities. The coastal sites contain roughly oval dump areas used for the disposal of refuse outside communal houses and situated around a large space with

Fig. 3.5 (A) Rounded raised fields near Macouria in French Guiana. The organization and the various shapes of raised fields (rounded, rectangular, or elongated) correspond to different adaptations to hydrological conditions.
(B) Elongated raised fields of Piliwa site, between the Mana and the Maroni rivers in French Guiana. This site is located between two sand ridges in a flooded depression and is around 1.2 kilometers long and 50 meters wide at a maximum. The modern Kali'na village of Awala is situated on the southern sand ridge.

few archaeological remains. These "clean" areas are considered to represent a central plaza location in the village.

The Thémire culture is affiliated with the Arauquinoid Tradition, but it includes some Polychrome Tradition influences. It must have had a frontier position on the coast of the Guianas because it had an origin in the Arauquinoid Tradition but absorbed important characteristics belonging to the Late Aristé culture. No Thémire trait seems to occur in the Late Aristé pottery style, which suggests unilateral influence from Aristé on the Thémire culture in prehistoric times. The main difference between the Thémire pottery style and the purely Arauquinoid style of the Barbakoeba, Kwatta, and Hertenrits is the high percentage of painted decorations. Many fragments of pottery show simple typical Late Aristé designs. The Thémire culture is unique in the archaeology of the Guianas by this association of features belonging to two important and distant cultural centers. It forms the pivotal culture between the Amazon and Orinoco cultural influences (Rostain 1994a).

Confederations from the East

If most of the western coast of the Guianas was occupied by Arauquinoid cultures from AD 700 on, the eastern part of the Guianas was dominated by people originating from the middle and the lower Amazon. The Mazagão culture was located in southern Amapá, and the Aristé culture on the northern Amapá coast. In the Ouanary Hills, Aristé culture began around AD 600 to 625 (Rostain 1994a). The close technical and stylistic similarities between the earliest Aristé and Mazagão types suggest a common origin, probably in the lower Amazon, preceding the arrival of two cultures in Amapá around AD 400 (Meggers and Evans 1957).

The territory of the Aristé culture extended along the coast from the Araguari River in Amapá to the Ouanary Hills in French Guiana, an area of approximately 370 kilometers long by 10 to 100 kilometers wide. The villages, smaller than the Arauquinoid ones, were settled on the small hills emerging from the swamps. The large size of the habitation sites, the high density of cemeteries and rock shelters, and the diversity of ceramic innovations suggest that the lower Oyapock River was an important Aristé development center. Coastal hills, which are rare on the coast of the Guianas, obviously were attractive for the native people of this area. During historic times, confederation leaders of Amapá tribes lived in this area, which suggests its function as an important political center.

The Aristé culture in the Ouanary Hills is characterized by two types of habitation sites: villages and rock shelters. Settlements were located on hills or riverbanks. Small sites where a few families could live together are distinguished from larger sites where more extensive communities lived together. Records of the sixteenth and seventeenth centuries describe several nuclear-family homes in this area, definitely suggesting relatively small houses in Aristé villages. Rock-shelter sites have a small surface, on the average 28 square meters. Different people temporarily inhabited these rock shelters at different times, but the main living units were located in the villages. The finds in the Ouanary Hills' rock shelters suggest a ceremonial function for these specific sites in their possible use as retreat locations. Some modern Amerindian groups still use such retreats for isolation, for instance before or after girl/boy puberty rituals and during shaman apprenticeships, chief initiations, couvades, mourning, and specific activities such as the making of stone tools or pottery.

Secondary burial in urns was practiced, and different Aristé cemeteries are recognizable: urns were arranged in a row on the ground or buried, or were generally put against the wall in caves or in shaft tombs dug where caves were absent. The Early Aristé culture is characterized by secondary urn burial—deposition of the bone remains in an urn after decomposition of the dead body. Late Aristé culture, however, presents another type of urn burial: the dead body was cremated before the remains were deposited in an urn. The latter type was predominant in Late Aristé culture, but the former, older type still occurs (Meggers and Evans 1957).

Megalithic sites are found on the central coast of Amapá, generally on hills characterized by large panoramas. These sites consist of vertical granite slabs arranged in lines, circles, and triangles. The megalithic sites were perhaps used for rituals similar to those practiced by the seventeenth-century Arauakí, Tapajó, and Trombeta of the middle Amazon, with wooden and stone idols. They seem to have been used during mourning, fertility, and marriage rituals (Nordenskiöld 1930).

The archaeological record of the Aristé sites notes a considerable number of ceremonial sites. In fact, the majority of the sites have a ceremonial, not a habitation, background. The division might reflect the importance of ceremonial-ritual components in Aristé culture. The specific distribution of the Ouanary Hills sites suggests that the villages were surrounded by different ceremonial spots. The settlements were in the middle of the southern slope and in a central position on the opposite side of the seashore. The rock shelters, slightly above the villages, probably provided covered areas for temporary isolation periods. The dead were disposed of in caves at the top of the hills facing north (Rostain 1994a). The ceremonial Aristé sites in Amapá are megalithic sites or cemeteries in caves or rock shelters, cemeteries that are artificial pits, and cemeteries where urns are on the ground or buried.

Aristé pottery has three different styles that represent an early, a late, and a final phase in the long-standing chronology of Aristé culture. A distinction is made between pottery found in cemeteries (see fig. 3.6) and utilitarian ware that is common in the habitation sites. The intrusive Caripo culture appears in the middle of the sequence. It is similar to the Itacoatiara style on the middle Amazon, which is dated circa AD 1200 to 1500 (Hilbert 1968).

The Aristé confederation is expressed by the uniformity of this culture and the "personification" of the urns, as well as by the precise geographical borders and the extreme scarcity of non-Aristé trade artifacts. Several villages obviously shared a

Fig. 3.6 An anthropomorphic urn with lid of Late Aristé style (AD 1200 to 1750) from Trou Reliquaire cave in Ouanary Hills in French Guiana (height: 45 centimeters). The Polychrome motifs of the anthropomorphic urns reproduce those used in the tribal body painting. Urns are distributed against the wall of the cave as in a meeting of people, a replication in the supraworld of the meetings conducted by living people in this world. From the collection of the Musée des Cultures Guyanaises, Cayenne, French Guiana.

common material culture and participated in a local trade system. The limited number of urns in each Aristé cemetery may indicate that these burials were reserved for persons of high status, such as clan or tribal chiefs. Moreover, the large number of cemeteries, each containing few dead or urns or both, and the variety of the urn decorations may indicate clan divisions. These peculiarities are the manifestation of the different units within the homogeneous Aristé cultural community.

Cultural Changes around AD 1200

During the first millennium of the current era, several sites named *montagnes couronnées* appeared in French Guiana and eastern Suriname. They are located at the top of a low hill and surrounded by a trench. They are oval or round with a diameter between 100 and 300 meters. The ditch is 5 to 15 meters wide and 1 to 3 meters deep. In French Guiana, three sites are dated between the first and the fourth centuries (Mazière 1997), and the only site in Suriname provides a date of around AD 850 (Versteeg 2003). The function of these sites is still unknown, but fortification purposes (Rostain 1994b) or ceremonial function (Versteeg 2003) has been ascribed to these "montagnes couronnées."

Around AD 1200, the Koriabo culture appeared in many places in what are now Guyana, Suriname, and French Guiana. The origin of this culture is still unknown and might have arisen in the middle Amazon or even in the center of the Guiana Shield. The Koriabo groups spread from the south to the north up to the Atlantic coast, where they met the Arauquinoid people. The available data permit a differentiation of inland Koriabo sites, dated between AD 1200 and 1350, and coastal Koriabo sites, dated between 1350 and 1600 (Versteeg 2003). Koriabo trade ware and vessel shape imitations in the Kwatta and Barbakoeba sites suggest at least a partial contemporaneity between the three cultures. The inland sites are located mainly on the riverbanks. However, Koriabo groups often settled on previously inhabited locations, so most of their sites also include traces of the older native culture.

The Koriabo culture is unique because it is the only truly cultural style of the Guianas; it is not found beyond this area. The homogeneity of this pottery style in decoration and shapes is striking given this group's enormous territory between the mouth of the Orinoco and the Oyapock. For example, the same decoration prevailed throughout the region. Variations in the paste occurred according to the availability of local raw materials, but specific shapes such as incised and appliqué decoration are very similar in all the sites (see fig. 3.7).

Colonial "fluvial highways" from the watershed in the south to the sea are probably the same ones the Koriabo people used. It was during these movements that the Koriabo culture occupied the riverbanks in the interior of the Guianas. Specific Koriabo artifacts found in some of these rivers are the silent witnesses of the travels then undertaken (see fig. 3.8).

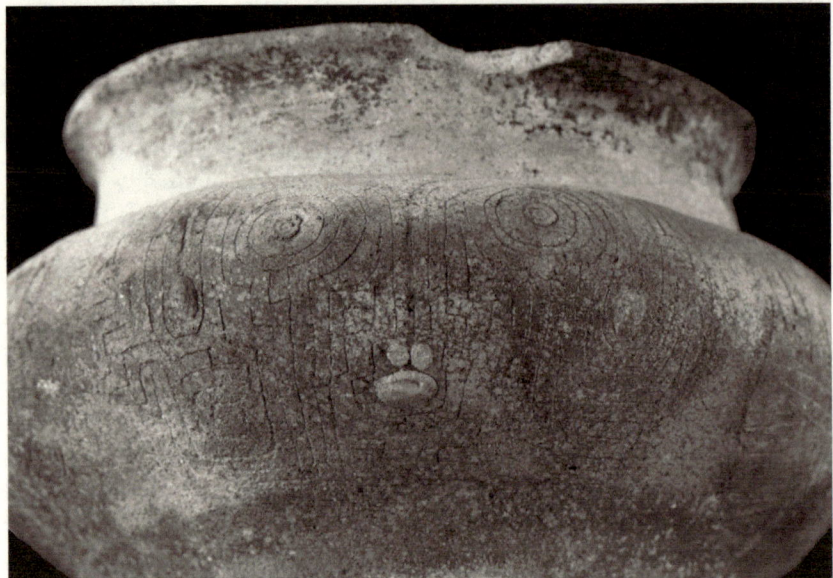

Fig. 3.7 The Koriabo ceramic style is recognizable by the convoluted incised designs and the anthropomorphic or zoomorphic faces. Caricatural animals are very common. Piriform pots with vertical restricted neck and everted rim are also characteristic. Four different human faces decorate the body of this vessel found in the Approuague River in French Guiana (mouth diameter: 19.5 centimeters). From the collection of the Musée des Cultures Guyanaises, Cayenne, French Guiana.

In this way, Koriabo became established in some coastal areas between the Approuague and Barima rivers. The latest mainland Koriabo settlements are located along the coast of the Guianas and in the lower river reaches. Coastal sites of the Barbakoeba, Kwatta, Thémire, and Mabaruma cultures have Koriabo ceramics, indicating that particularly close contact was established between the Kwatta and Barbakoeba cultures. After the Koriabo culture's appearance on the coastal area of the Guianas, it was integrated into intertribal dynamics and participated in a regional trade network.

Although seemingly powerful, the Koriabo culture did not disperse uniformly along the coast of the Guianas. It met resistance from some communities. For example, Koriabo groups never inhabited areas under the domination of the Hertenrits culture in western Suriname (Rostain and Versteeg 2003) and of the Aristé culture in eastern French Guiana and Amapá (Rostain 1994b). The complete absence of Koriabo ceramics in these areas also suggests that little trade existed between these groups and the Koriabo people.

After the sixteenth century, the Koriabo culture lost its powerful position and

Fig. 3.8 An Aristé vessel found in a river west of Suriname, but farther to the west of the Aristé territory (height: 23.5 centimeters). The shape and the painted motifs are typical of the funerary Aristé ware. However, the small size of the pot, the ocelot face (all the Aristé urns are anthropomorphic), and the pot's location in a river (rather than in a cave or buried) differ from the Aristé customs. With respect to the specific treatment of dead shamans in the Guianas today (see Whitehead 2002b), it can be suggested that the urn was a traded one meant for a special person with a particular burial in the river. From the collection of the Stichting Surinaams Museum, Paramaribo, Suriname.

was probably represented only by rare settlements, especially in Guyana and French Guiana. Following the loss of that position, and because of the conditions it created, some migrations back to the inland area may have taken place.

From Prehistory to Colonial Times

Aristé people lived in an area frequently visited by Europeans from the beginning of colonization. These groups were less destabilized, at least initially, by the European Conquest than were the groups in the lower Amazon. The latter area soon became a territorial stake between the Portuguese and other Europeans. Traditional hostilities between native groups became exacerbated over time, and the impact of epidemics was violent at the mouth of the Amazon, where the native population fell more rapidly than in the coastal areas of the Guianas. This difference explains both the disappearance of Mazagão and Maracá archaeological cultures in southern Amapá shortly after the Conquest and the longer survival of the Aristé groups in northern Amapá, located far from Europeans.

Aristé cemeteries were still used during colonial times. In cemeteries, the presence of European trade items (glass sherds, nails, knives, rings, chinaware, small bells, and medals) and of glass beads, melted and sometimes mixed with burned human bones, suggests that the dead were burned with prestigious artifacts. In funerary caves, the presence of chinaware made in the Netherlands between 1670 and 1750 suggests that caves were still used for burial in the eighteenth century. In fact, these historical-period cemeteries seem to represent the latest Aristé culture manifestations, but they also show the absorption of new culture elements.

The Aristé culture lasted up to around AD 1750, and it is the only homogeneous and well-represented archaeological culture of northern Amapá and the Ouanary Hills. Historical records of the same area from the end of the sixteenth century show that several native groups, notably the modern Palikur, were predominant there after the Conquest (Grenand and Grenand 1987; Nimuendajú 1971 [1926]; Rostain 1994b). This finding brings into view one question: Are Aristé people the "ancestors" of the modern Palikur?

The material and cultural homogeneity of the Aristé culture during prehistoric times indicated by the archaeological record differs from what is found in the oral tradition of the Palikur and from the description given by the historical record in early colonial times. What must be stated here is that modern Palikur art differs in style from Aristé expressions present in the archaeological remains.

A comparative ethnoarchaeological study of Aristé utilitarian and ceremonial pottery and the style used by the modern Palikur was conducted to answer such questions (Rostain 1992). The study found that few similarities between Aristé and Palikur styles exist. Only some simple decorative designs and modes are similar, but nearly all the vessel shapes and temper categories used are different. Although the Palikur potters do not use the curved and elaborate lines in designs of the Late

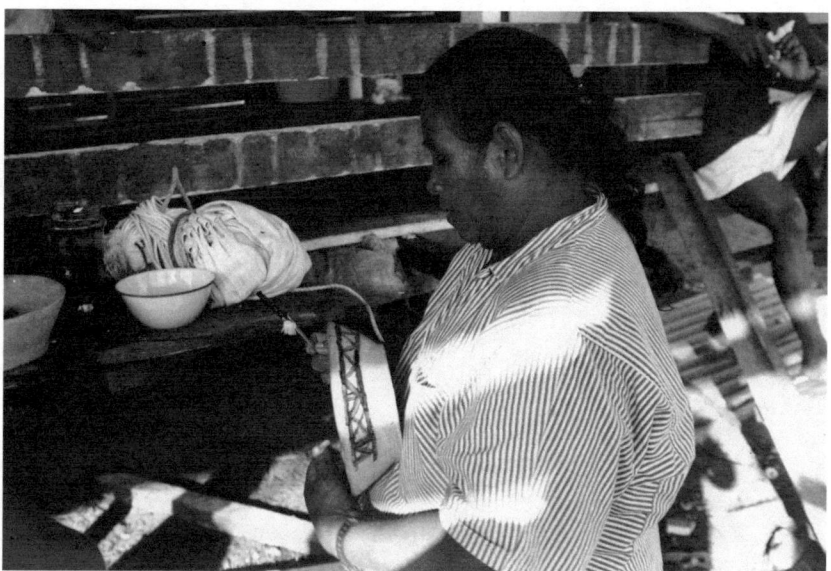

Fig. 3.9 A Palikur woman painting a vessel on the lower Oyapock River in French Guiana. This technique of painting is reminiscent of the local Polychrome style, but the motifs are close to the incised designs of the Arauquinoid Tradition of the western Guianas. Modern Palikur art is the result of the melding of several coastal Amerindian groups' various styles during the colonial era.

Aristé style, they would recognize the linear, triangular, and castellated designs of the Incised-and-Punctate and Arauquinoid Traditions (see fig. 3.9).

It is possible to understand the evolution from Aristé to modern Palikur style by studying the stylistics of Aristé ceremonial ceramics found in the cemeteries. The Aristé funerary pottery shows the emergence of external influences in the Late Aristé style of the historical period. Vessel shapes and decorations began to diverge, becoming more similar to those of the Mazagão and Arauquinoid styles. The modern Palikur style thus originates from a mixture of Aristé, Mazagão, and some Arauquinoid styles that resulted in the evolution of a new pottery style.

This ceramic evolution went hand in hand with abandonment of the typical Late Aristé cremation practices, implying a return to secondary burial after decomposition, which characterized both the Early Aristé and the more recent Mazagão cultures. This evolution agrees with the Palikur oral tradition and with the historical records (Grenand and Grenand 1987). Cremation was still used together with secondary burial by the Palikur at the end of the seventeenth century. During the eighteenth century, however, only secondary burial was practiced before it was finally replaced by Christian burial around 1960.

The changes in Aristé culture are understood as the result of the arrival of new

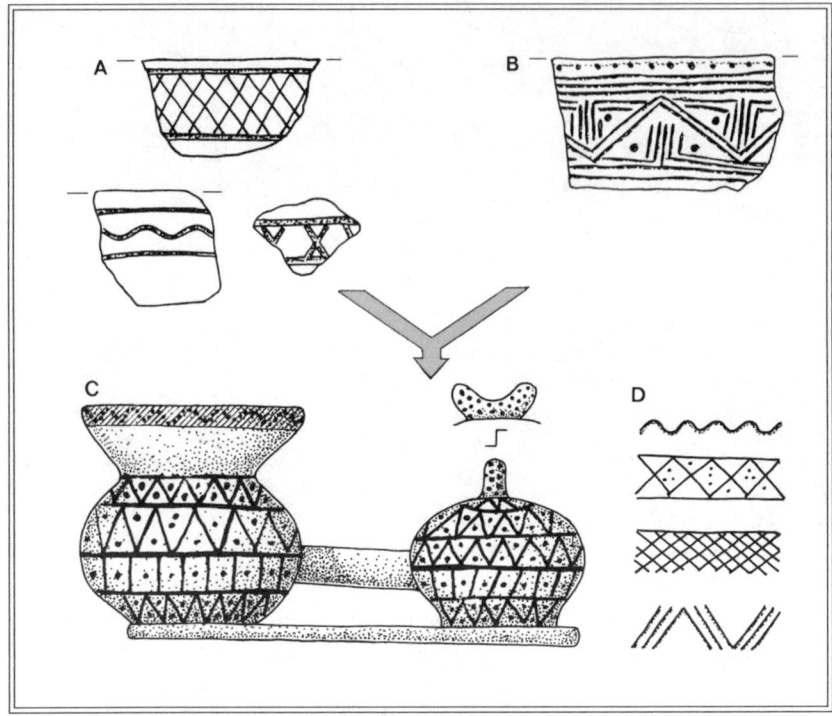

Fig. 3.10 The evolution of modern Palikur pottery from pre-Columbian ceramic styles. Modern Palikur art is characterized by geometrical designs similar to a mixture of Arauquinoid styles from the western Guianas and pre-Columbian ceramic styles from Amapá. (A) Early Aristé incised decorations from Ouanary Hills. (B) Arauquinoid incised motif from Venezuela. (C) Modern Palikur painted vessels. (D) Modern Palikur decorative designs.

groups. Amerindians fled some areas to avoid the European wars and slave hunts. Communities emigrated from the west (refugees arrived from the lower Orinoco/Trinidad during the seventeenth century) to the area between the Maroni and the mouth of the Amazon. Other refugees arrived from the lower Amazon during the seventeenth and eighteenth centuries. These immigrations probably disturbed the stability of Aristé groups.

These emigrating groups, some linked to the Arauquinoid Tradition, which predominated in the lower Orinoco in this period, brought Arauquinoid ceramic characteristics with them, and these characteristics can be seen in modern Palikur pottery. The groups probably also introduced the raised-field techniques that the Palikur began to employ when the population became too large to be supported by slash-and-burn agriculture. In the seventeenth century, the Palikur of northern Amapá still numbered around 1,200 persons and disposed of less than 150 square kilometers of land for shifting cultivation. This surface was too small to provide enough food for the group, so they created large raised fields in the swamp, which they cultivated for several years. As local population declined and consumption needs fell in accordance with that decline, the size of the raised fields became reduced. This technique was abandoned at the end of the nineteenth century (P. Grenand 1981).

Amerindian migration from the lower Amazon to French Guiana is described in the colonial records and in the Palikur oral tradition. The migrating clans had lived previously on the Maracá River, the center of the Mazagão culture. They introduced the Mazagão ceramic traits into the modern Palikur ceramic repertoire. The Mazagão influence may also be responsible for the secondary burial practices discussed earlier. This development and the Arauquinoid influences form the roots of Palikur culture and ceramics (see fig. 3.10).

Although the Palikur seem to be the main heirs of the Aristé and Mazagão communities, other groups participated in the development of this culture. After the European Conquest, eighteen Palikur clans and twenty-three other groups inhabited the Amapá coast. Competition between these groups led to a cultural center's being formed around the Palikur (Grenand and Grenand 1987).

Conclusion

What do we know of the peopling of the Guianas during the millennium before the European Conquest?

From AD 500, the coastal area between the Orinoco and the Amazon rivers was divided into two main territories limited by Cayenne Island. To the west, Arauquinoid chiefdoms dominated the area, with specialized groups living with others in a complementary system. The eastern territory was inhabited by a Polychrome confederation. The frontier of the two territories in Cayenne Island was occupied by a mixed Arauquinoid culture that borrowed characteristics from the Polychrome Tradition (see fig. 3.1). At the same time, various groups such as the Koriabo culture were distributed throughout the interior.

The landing of the Europeans in 1499 dealt a serious blow to the native world as it was prior to the Conquest. That arrival provoked a complete destabilization. Hybrid communities arose due to the interaction of several local populaces. This destruction resulted in a complete reconstruction of the native world and a crossing of territories. A new native panorama with two main coastal territories separated by Cayenne Island came into being during colonial times. Kali'na culture issued from eastern Polychrome Tradition settled between Cayenne Island and Orinoco Delta. Palikur culture arising from the western Arauquinoid Tradition and the cultures of Amapá occupied the eastern area between Cayenne Island and the mouth of the Amazon. The native peopling of the Guianas coast in the colonial period was the consequence of an inversion and a reconstruction of native cultures. After the Conquest, Arauquinoid groups went from west to east in Amapá, and Polychrome groups went from the eastern to the western Guianas. Each therefore went to the other's land. Thus, modern Palikur of Amapá are the heirs of mainly the Arauquinoid Tradition, whereas modern Kali'na of the western Guianas are the heirs of the Polychrome Tradition. The result of this cross-migration is a negative of the pre-Columbian situation.

4

Points of Convergence— Routes of Divergence

Some Considerations Based on Curt Nimuendajú's Archaeological Work in the Santarém-Trombetas Area and at Amapá

Per Stenborg

Curt Nimuendajú

The Germano-Brazilian researcher Curt Unkel Nimuendajú was a central figure of Brazilian ethnography and, to a lesser extent, of archaeology during the first half of the twentieth century. Various previously unpublished texts by Nimuendajú have recently been issued (Nimuendajú 2000, 2004). These publications have provided, among other things, important information about his archaeological research and his collecting of materials. Nimuendajú undertook the greater part of his archaeological investigations as part of his collaboration with the Göteborg Museum in Sweden.

At the time Nimuendajú began his investigations, the knowledge about the archaeological record concerning many parts of the Amazon and Guayana regions was extremely low. The Göteborg Museum established its collaboration with Nimuendajú in 1922 (Rydén 2004) and was at the time becoming an important center for Amerindian studies. Apart from the archaeological collections, the museum also obtained important ethnographical collections from Nimuendajú. In 1924, Göteborg hosted the Twenty-first International Congress of Americanists, an occasion that provided the museum's director, Erland Nordenskiöld, the opportunity to present the material that had up to then arrived at the museum. The Santarém material received particular attention at the time. Nordenskiöld apparently had his doubts concerning the cultural circumstances behind the emergence of the pottery styles from this area, suspecting they might have resulted from postcontact European cultural influences. Nimuendajú, however, assured him—providing comprehensive arguments—that these ceramic styles had, undoubtedly, an entirely Amerindian background (cf. Góes Neves 2004:6; Nimuendajú 2000:73–74, 2004: 151–153). Taken together, Nimuendajú's archaeological collections and reports (most of which remained unpublished until 2004 and are usually referred to as "A Survey of Amazon Archaeology") have provided material for a number of publications by other authors for several decades (e.g., Linné 1928; Linné and Montell 1925; Meggers and Evans 1957; Nordenskiöld 1930; Palmatary 1939, 1960; Wassén 1934).

Nimuendajú usually kept his studies of the written record apart from his discussion of archaeological remains. Nevertheless, his method resembles that of several other early-twentieth-century researchers (e.g., Eric Boman [1908] in Argentina) and might be described as a "direct historical" or "horizontal" approach. In many cases, such an approach ascribed only limited time depth to the archaeological remains, assuming that the vast majority of the cultural traditions the researchers encountered had survived until the time of European contact and that their "bearers" had been recorded by missionaries, early explorers, and representatives of the colonial powers. Given these premises, the researcher could geographically correlate the identified areas of distribution of particular traits of material culture (often pottery styles and complexes) with the early written record and thereby associate these traits with historically known populations (tribes, ethnolinguistic groups, and so on). If we take Nimuendajú's ethnohistorical reading and research into consideration, however, it appears evident that he regarded the populations' mobility, particularly in the postcontact era, to have been relatively high.

Although Nimuendajú was much more of an Amazonian than a Guayana researcher, several of the areas that he investigated are situated inside the area sometimes referred to as the "island" of Guayana (i.e., the territory circumscribed by the Orinoco, the Rio Negro, the Amazon, and the Atlantic). There is the coastal region of Amapá, where he worked in 1923, as well as the border area between Amapá and French Guiana, which he investigated a couple of years later. Between 1923 and 1926, he made several investigations in the Santarém region, including the areas of the northern tributaries of Rio Trombetas and Rio Nhamundá, as well as the regions to the east and west of Santarém. These expeditions covered parts of the areas north and south of the Amazon River.

This text departs from the investigations carried out by Nimuendajú in Amapá and the Santarém region. It focuses on the late prehistoric development, up to the time of European contact, and discusses the results of his work in relation to more recent studies and potential key issues for future research in the areas touched upon.

Amapá

The Brazilian state of Amapá (see fig. 4.1), a region Nimuendajú referred to as "Brazilian Guyana," borders the state of Pará along the Jari River in the west. In the north, the Oyapock River constitutes its limit with French Guiana. To the east, it is bounded by the Atlantic Ocean, and to the south by the northern shore of the Amazon estuary. It was formerly a part of Pará (the territory of Amapá) but since 1988 has been a state of its own.

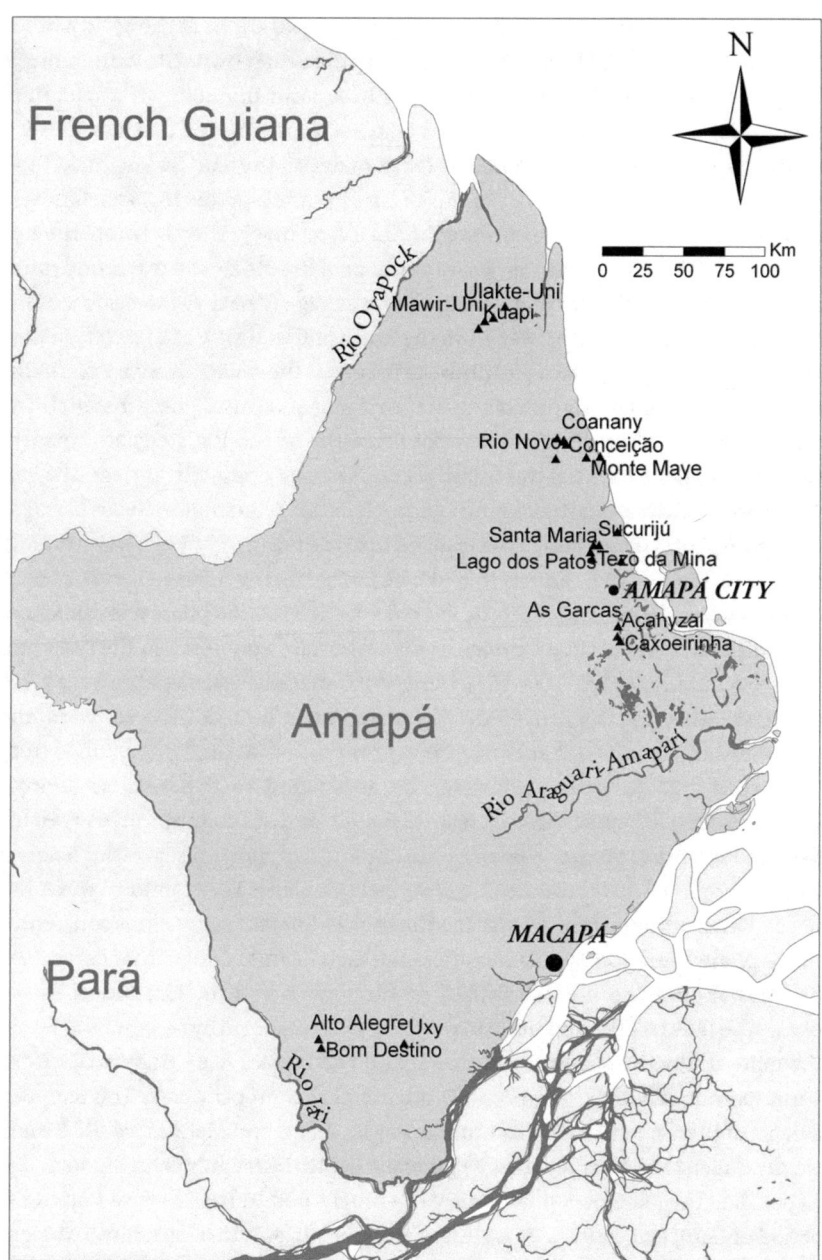

Fig. 4.1 The location of sites investigated and visited by Curt Nimuendajú in Amapá State in Brazil in the early twentieth century. After Nimuendajú 2004 and Meggers and Evans 1957.

In their now classical work "Archaeological Investigations at the Mouth of the Amazon," Meggers and Evans (1957) supplemented their own data with information from earlier research including the at that point unpublished results from Nimuendajú's work in the area, which had been translated and illustrated by Stig Rydén. Based on the composition of ceramic material, the authors identified three phases: Aruã, Mazagão, and Aristé. All of these pottery-producing societies were assumed to be of recent date, arriving in Amapá relatively shortly before the first European contact. The Aruã phase was considered the oldest and was found north as well as south of Rio Araguari-Amaparí. It was suggested that the bearers of the Aruã-phase tradition had arrived from the north and that they at a later stage were driven out of the Amapá area and onto the islands at the Amazon estuary due to the arrival of the populations producing the Mazagão- and Aristé-phase material. The material of the Mazagão phase was found south of the Rio Araguari-Amaparí, whereas the Aristé material was found predominantly north of this river. Meggers and Evans found reasons to assume that the related and contemporaneous Mazagão and Aristé phases did not originate from areas to the north (e.g., French Guiana and Suriname), but had their origins somewhere farther up the Amazon River or one of its tributaries. At a late stage of its development, the Mazagão phase was influenced by traditions of the middle Orinoco, such as the Late Ronquin and the Arauquin (Meggers and Evans 1957:160–167). Denis Williams (2003) suggests, however, that the Aristé phase of the Amapá development was a result of the eastward and southward migrations of Káriban-speaking (or Carib-speaking) populations from the last centuries before the common era on, associating it with the eastern Karinya. Thus, although recognizing Meggers and Evans's claim of a connection between the Mazagão and Aristé phases, Williams finds empirical support for suggesting a northwestern origin of many technical and stylistic elements later found in the Aristé phase. Other authors have nevertheless arrived at different suggestions concerning Aristé-phase sites. Guapindaia mentions the high degree of concordance between the Arawak-speaking modern Palikur oral traditions and the location of Aristé-phase sites (2001:171). In addition to the three phases defined by Meggers and Evans, the quite distinctive material associated with the Maracá (e.g., Guapindaia 2001) anthropomorphic urns have been distinguished as a proper phase. The temporal extents of these four phases (i.e., Aruã, Mazagão, Aristé, and Maracá) are still insufficiently understood, but they are now generally held to be roughly contemporaneous, to postdate the Marajoara phase partly or entirely, and to have survived up to the period of European contact. To a great extent, they appear to be spatially juxtapositional, the Aruã-phase material associated primarily with the northern islands of the Amazon estuary (e.g., Caviana and Mexiana) and southern Amapá, the Mazagão material with the southern part of Amapá, the Aristé material with the northern part of the same territory, and the Maracá material with the area around the Maracá River in the southwestern corner of the Amapá territory (cf. Guapindaia 2001).

Mounds and Stone Settings

In his account of the investigations at Amapá in 1923 (see fig. 4.1), Nimuendajú—as was his wont—began by defusing the importance of the results of his explorations (2004:15). The journey was undertaken in order to investigate the stone settings found in the area. Although he remained uncertain as to the precise significance of these constructions, he considered them somehow related to burials. An important stone setting was that situated at a site called "José Antonio" on the left bank of Rio Calçoene, northeastern Amapá (Nimuendajú 2004:28–31). The partly destroyed stone alignments extended for some one hundred meters. Pottery in low quantities, including an urn without bottom, was found in association with these stone constructions. In addition, large quantities of charcoal were encountered. He found similar patterns at other stone settings, such as at Cachoeirinha, situated south of Amapá City (Nimuendajú 2004:36–37), Igarapé dos Macacos, Rio Novo, Tezo da Mina, and Lago dos Patos. He encountered very little pottery in connection with the constructions. By contrast, at Açahyzal, situated by Rio Frechal between Amapá City and Rio Araguari-Amaparí, he found an abundant ceramic material, albeit in a fragmentary state.

Meggers and Evans interpreted the stone settings found in various parts of Amapá State as being of ritual or ceremonial type and as associated with the Aruã phase (1957:37–44). In the case of Açahyzal, however—basing their judgment on Nimuendajú's account—they came to the conclusion that although the stone alignments at this site had originally been constructed by an Aruã-phase population, the ceramic material encountered in the same context was representative of the Aristé phase, not the Aruã. They suggested that this pattern was the result of a reuse or reoccupation of an originally Aruã site by a population belonging to the Aristé phase (1957:43).

Nimuendajú also investigated a number of settlements but generally encountered little material at those sites. At São Joaquim, situated between Igarapé de Francezca and Rio Cunani, northwestern Amapá, he found fragments of undecorated pottery. From local inhabitants, however, he acquired a *muyrakytã* (also spelled *muiraquitã*, a small, zoomorphous figure made out of stone) and a glass bead. At another settlement site, Bom Jesus de Montana, southeast of Monte Mayé, he obtained a small vessel from a local inhabitant but otherwise found only little material.

Nimuendajú's work at the Monte Mayé site (Linné 1928; Nordenskiöld 1930; Nimuendajú 2004:15–24), situated on a hill near the mouth of Rio Cunani in northern Amapá, revealed three cemeteries, all containing material datable to the period of European contact (see fig. 4.2). Meggers and Evans included the Monte Mayé site in their passage on the Aristé phase (1957:128–130).

At Ilha do Carão, about midway between Rio Amapá Grande and Rio Calçoene, Nimuendajú found a mound situated on a *tezo*, an area resembling an island but

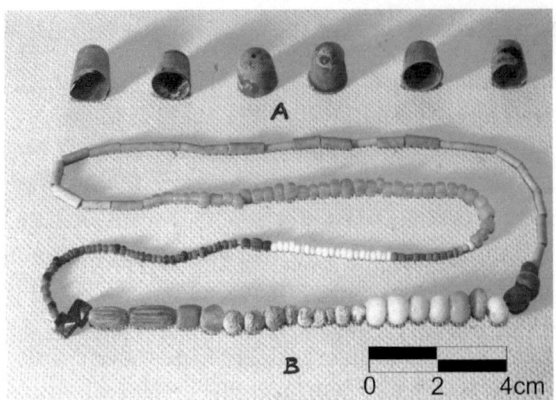

Fig. 4.2 "Thimbles" and glass beads from Monte Mayé. From Nimuendajú 2004.

not reached by the high waters. An irregular stone setting had been constructed on the mound. His excavations revealed a pronounced stratigraphy and high quantities of pottery (Nimuendajú 2004:32–34). According to Meggers and Evans, the Ilha do Carão site may represent a cemetery (1957:130–131). They associated the site with the Aristé phase.

Rio Arucauá

In 1925, Nimuendajú returned to Amapá to investigate sites in the northern part of the state, along the Rio Arucauá and Rio Uaçá, seat of the modern Palikur group. At Kuapi (Nimuendajú 2004:42–44) in the Rio Arucauá area, the Palikur were at this time still using an ancient cemetery. At arrival, he found, to his great disappointment, that the material he had planned to investigate had been excavated in advance by the Palikur magician. The material consisted of urns and other vessels (see fig. 4.3) that, according to the magician's information, had contained beads but no skeletal remains. Based on the Palikur oral tradition as well as on some notable similarities between their historically known material culture and that found in archaeological investigations in their territory (e.g., the so-called grinding bowls), Nimuendajú suggested that the modern Palikur are the descendents of an older population that had been settled in the same area (2004:44–45).

The cave site at Ulakte-Uni (Nimuendajú 2004:47–49) is interesting insofar as the use of natural caves as burial places is a phenomenon found in various parts of the Guayana and Amazon regions, including the Maracá area (Amapá), the Óbidos area (Santarém, Pará), Serpa (near the mouth of the Madeira), and the Orinoco River (Gillin 1948:819–820). At Ulakte-Uni, the chambers contained large quantities of pottery fragments. No burial gifts were found, however. The pottery, probably originating from burial urns, is in several cases decorated with a reddish

Fig. 4.3 Pottery from the cemetery of Kuapi. From Nimuendajú 2004.
Photograph by Ferenc Schwetz.

brown color on a light brown slip. Modeled decoration depicting human faces also can be seen.

At Mawir-Mini (or Mawir-Uni), Nimuendajú acquired an urn that resembled the material he had found at Monte Mayé. At Uakauy-Uné, another modern Palikur village, he obtained a ceramic application shaped like a vulture head that bears a remarkable resemblance to the kind of zoomorphous applications found in the Santarém pottery.

Another cemetery was situated near Coumarouman. According to local tradition, this burial place had been used by a population called the Itoutanes, who supposedly lived there before the Aruãs.[1] The material echoed that of Mawir-Mini as well as some material Nimuendajú had found on Caviana in the Amazon estuary.

Meggers and Evans associated the material Nimuendajú found in the Rio Arucauá and Rio Uaçá areas with the Aristé phase (1957:125–126).

Prior to the investigations mentioned so far, Nimuendajú had visited an area enclosed by the Rio Jari and the Rio Iratapurú by the border between Amapá and Pará in 1915. Because these investigations were undertaken several years before the commencement of the collaboration between Nimuendajú and Erland Nordenskiöld at the Göteborg Museum, the material was not included in the material sent to Göteborg[2] and thus was not depicted by Rydén. However, Nimuendajú sent his own pencil drawings of this material along with a short account of his work in the area (Nimuendajú 2004:93–94; see also Nimuendajú 1927). The sites Nimuendajú mentioned in his correspondence are Uxy, Bom Destino I and II, Alto Alegre, and São João do Iratapurú. The material from Rio Jari/Rio Iratapurú was quite distinct from the material he later found in other parts of Amapá. Meggers and Evans associated it with the Mazagão phase (1957:68–69). Nimuendajú himself found similarities between this material and that of Bacury Alto on the island of Marajó, where he worked in 1922.

Amapá in Archaeological Research

Although the explanative priority of models based exclusively on population movements is unfortunate, the argument nevertheless points to the possible importance of far-reaching relations—for example, in trade—for the late prehistoric development in the region.

Population movements should not be ignored as of potential importance for the emergence of the archaeological patterns outlined earlier, but it may be suggested that an increase in mobility resulting from the early and later European activity in this region—as in many other parts of the New World—have led to an overestimation of the frequency of movement in general among Amazonian populations (cp. Stenborg 2002:16–21, 105–108).

When the compelling archaeological record of Amapá is approached, it seems justified to pay considerable attention to processes such as assimilation and dissimilation. As Guapindaia points out, the distinctive features found in different subregions of Amapá (e.g., the Maracá phase material) may point to contrasting networks of regional and interregional relations as much as to populations' different historical origins or linguistic affiliations (2001:170).

An analysis of how the effects of European contact may have influenced the information documented in the written, ethnohistorical record would probably be helpful in unraveling certain misinterpretations that have become integrated with the archaeological research.

The Santarém Region

From 1923 to 1926, Curt Nimuendajú undertook six expeditions partly or entirely concerned with the Santarém/Trombetas area. Some of these journeys lasted for several months and yielded information on numerous sites. Although his work took the form of surveys rather than profound archaeological research, the impressive coverage of his work in this area gives it a quite unique comparative character.

His first two journeys were carried out from April to August 1923, when he surveyed the area south of the city of Santarém as well as Alter do Chão by the right bank of the Tapajós River, the southern bank of Lago Grande de Villa Franca, and the southern bank of the Amazon between the mouth of the Tapajós River and Lago Grande de Villa Franca (see figs. 4.4 and 4.5). During this time, he was able to locate a total of forty-eight archaeological sites. He did not visit all of these sites personally, however; in some cases, he only acquired information from local inhabitants. The vast majority of these sites were situated on the Terra Firme mainland; in only two cases—Santarém Aldêa and Alter do Chão—were the settlements situated by the river's high-water mark. The settlements were invariably associated with the Terra Preta soils—that is, areas of dark fertile soil characterized by enhanced contents of phosphates, calcium, and potassium. In his account, Nimuendajú discussed the nature of the Terra Preta soils, arguing that they were to be

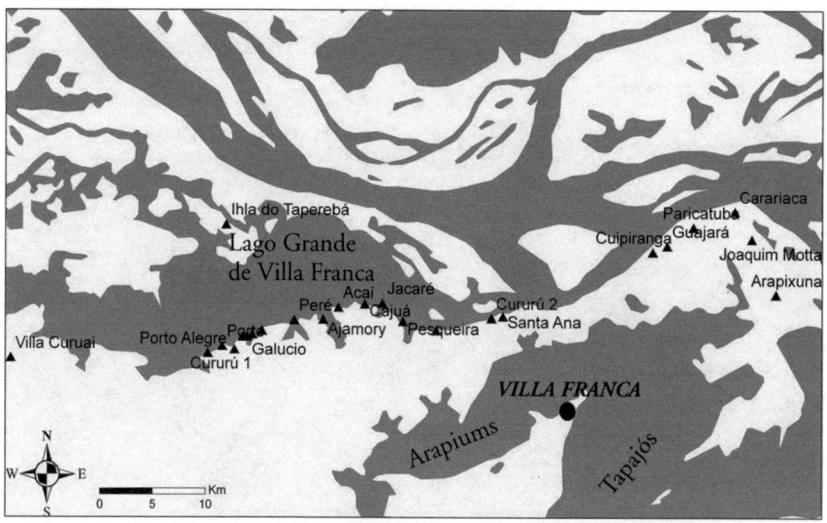

Fig. 4.4 The area of Lago Grande de Villa Franca. After Nimuendajú 2004.

conceived of as Anthrosols rather than as of natural origin. Apart from these settlements, he located a number of wells that he presumed had been dug by the ancient inhabitants of the Terra Preta settlements. He also found a system of roads that had connected the settlements.

Nimuendajú consciously selected decorated pottery and fragments in the shape of figures and applications that frequently occur in the Santarém pottery (see fig. 4.6). He characterized the Santarém pottery as "an abundance of anthropomorphic and zoomorphic motifs, mainly in the shape of heads, but also half and full figures" (2004:124). Plastic décor clearly dominated, although it sometimes occurred combined with polychrome painting (Nimuendajú 2004:130). Apart from the pottery, the material includes lithic objects such as hoes, stone spindle whorls, muyrakytãs, and stone idols. He ascribed the material to the historically known Tapajó and Urucucú populations and particularly commented on the absence of burial urns in this area.[3] Although at this point he had only but begun his work in the region, he nevertheless sketched out the distribution of the Santarém pottery and its relation to other materials. He found the Santarém culture ("the Tapajó culture" in his terminology) to be bordered by another between latitude 3° and 4° south, which he called the Sapupé. The Santarém material was replaced to the southwest by that of the Maué and to the west by that of the Tupinambarana and the Aroagui. To the north, the area of the Santarém material was limited by that of the Káriban populations of the rivers Nhamundá and Trombetas. To the east, material that he held to be that of the Aritú markedly differed from that of the Tapajós/Santarém area (Nimuendajú 2004:125).

His work in 1924 revealed additional sites in the Santarém area. He also found

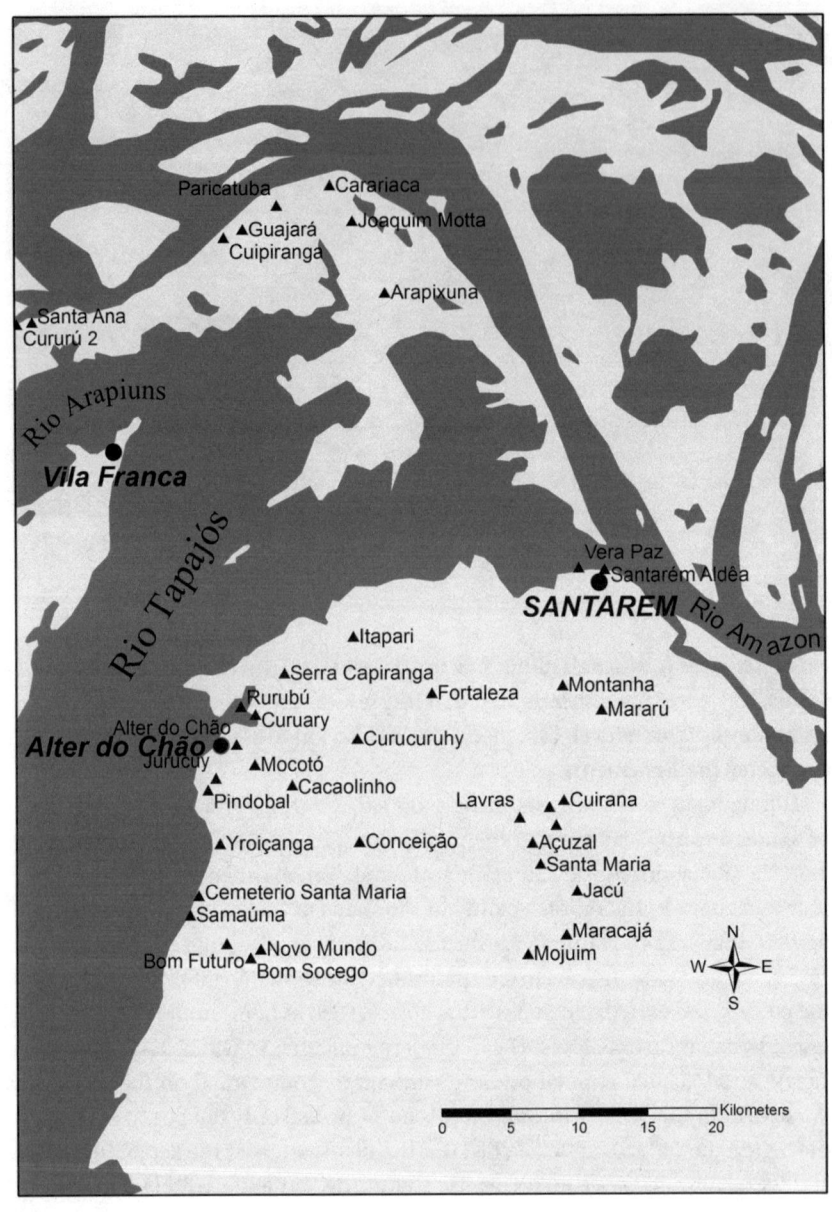

Fig. 4.5 The area of Santarém and Alter do Chão. After Nimuendajú 2004.

Fig. 4.6 Pottery from the Santarém area. From Nimuendajú 2004. Photograph by Ferenc Schwetz.

indications of contact between this area and that of the Kondurí (the area of Rio Nhamundá and Rio Trombetas) to the north. Some pottery resembling that found farther west—along the Rio Arapiums, which meets the Tapajós River from the west some distance above the mouth of the latter—was found. He also carried on work in the Lago Grande de Villa Franca area, where the material was very similar to that of the Santarém. On a shell bank at Ilha do Taperebá, he found pottery fragments. According to local information, material such as muyrakytãs and stone idols had previously been found at the site. The layers were quite different compared to those of the Terra Preta sites in the same region, indicating a different use of this location. At Serra Bananal, west of Lago Grande de Villa Franca, he encountered what appeared to be the limit between the distribution of the Santarém pottery and that of the Kondurí pottery on the southern side of the Amazon. He later specified this limit as situated at longitude 56° west (Nimuendajú 2004:155). To the south, he found Santarém pottery as far as Aramanahy, but he was convinced it was to be found also farther south, along the Tapajós River. He thought the similarity between individual items of the Santarém pottery quite remarkable. This "standardization" of particular types indicates a highly specialized craftsmanship.

In discussing the existing information on the languages spoken in the Santarém area, Nimuendajú found it most reasonable to suggest that the carriers of the Santarém pottery spoke a Káriban language (2004:120).

The Trombetas/Nhamundá area

Nimuendajú continued his work in 1924 by crossing the Amazon River to survey the areas of two of its northern tributaries: Rio Trombetas and Rio Nhamundá (2004:135–140) (see fig. 4.7). The Trombetas River debouches into the Amazon from the north, about ninety kilometers west of the mouth of the Tapajós River, near the town of Óbidos. Another one hundred kilometers farther west, the lower

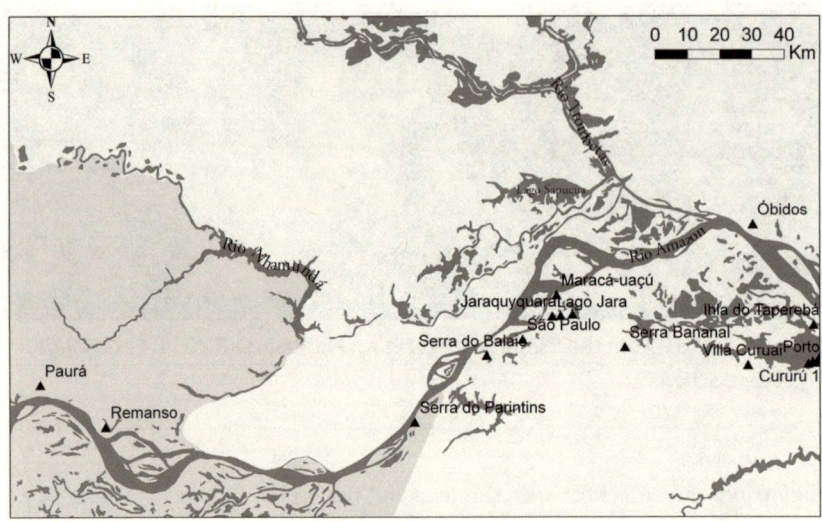

Fig. 4.7 The lower Rio Trombetas and Rio Nhamundá. After Nimuendajú 2004.

reaches of the Nhamundá River form the limit between the Brazilian states of Pará and Amazonas. He described the area west of the Trombetas River as an extensive swamp where archaeological sites could be found on the mounds or plateaus rising above the wetlands. On such mounds by the left bank of the Rio Nhamundá (Paraná do Bom Jardim), he encountered a number of sites of the Terra Preta type (e.g., at São Benedicto). He followed the waterways back and forth between the various parts of the area. He investigated sites by the Lago do Sapucua and Serra Uajará.

The pottery found in the Trombetas-Nhamundá area was very similar to that which he had found earlier at Serra do Bananal, south of the Amazon. In some cases, he found small pieces of Santarém-like pottery, muyrakytãs, and stone idols. In 1926, he concluded that the Kondurí pottery extended as far west as the Serra Parintins. South of the Amazon River, then, the Kondurí pottery was found in an area extending from the western margins of Lago Grande de Villa Franca in the east to Lago Selé and Lago Curumucury in the west. Occasional finds of Santarém pottery (vulture heads) also occurred almost as far west as the Kondurí pottery.

On the northern side of the Amazon, he found the western limit of the Kondurí pottery at Remanso. Nearby, at Paurá and at Terra Preta, Catanhal, and Santa Cruz on the opposite, southern side of the Amazon, he found distinctive and, among themselves, related types of pottery. An additional difference was that he came across burial urns in this area.

The population of the Trombetas-Nhamundá area is sometimes referred to as being Kondurí—after "Queen Coñorí" mentioned in Carvajal's account (1942:55).

It appears this population was Christianized by the mid-seventeenth century and disappeared as an ethnic and cultural unit by the early eighteenth century (cf. Nimuendajú 2004:140).[4]

Nimuendajú was quite uncertain concerning the language spoken by the Kondurí population—whether it belonged to the Káriban, Tupi, or Arawak linguistic family. He nevertheless indicated that it might have belonged to the Káriban linguistic family (primarily owing to the presence of Kárib place-names in the area).

To the East: The Areas of Monte Alegre and Rio Curuá

East of Santarém, Nimuendajú investigated areas north (Monte Alegre) as well as south (Rio Curuá) of the Amazon River. The material at Monte Alegre (see fig. 4.8) clearly differed both from the Trombetas-Nhamundá material and from the Santarém material. A distinctive feature was pottery with imprints from leafs, fabrics, and straw mats. Little information could be found concerning the population living in the area in historic times, the reason probably being that they withdrew inland after conflicts with the Portuguese in the early seventeenth century. Crossing the Amazon by Monte Alegre, the Rio Curuá constitutes a minor southern tributary, meeting the Amazon some seventy kilometers east of Santarém. Here, the pottery most closely resembled that of the Santarém area. There were also, however, elements that he had met at Monte Alegre, such as various types of imprints to the west.

At Bom Futuro by the Paraná Urariá–Paraná Arary confluence and at Correnteza (see fig. 4.9), he encountered a pottery complex related to the Amazonian Polychrome Tradition. Only in exceptional cases did he find incised or plastic décor. Somewhat farther west, however, the latter kind of ornamentation appeared again at Conceição—probably an indication of a diachronic relationship between these sites. A few fragments signaled some form of linkage with the Kondurí and Paurá materials (Nimuendajú 2004:158–159).

Nimuendajú's work in the Rio Madeira area yielded little result, although the material he did collect clearly differed from that found in the other areas. In the Rio Autaz area (Rio Apipica and Rio Mutuca), the material appeared to be related to that which he had found at Parana do Ramos and at Paurá.

North of the Amazon, by the Urubú River, opposite the mouth of the Madeira River, the Bocca de Xavier site constituted a typical Terra Preta settlement. Nimuendajú came across dots, lines, and painted décor as well as broad, incised lines, and he noted that this kind of ornamentation was found also at the southern side of the Amazon. At Lago Saracá (Mocajatuba), he found figures and bases of vessels somewhat resembling those of the Santarém area.

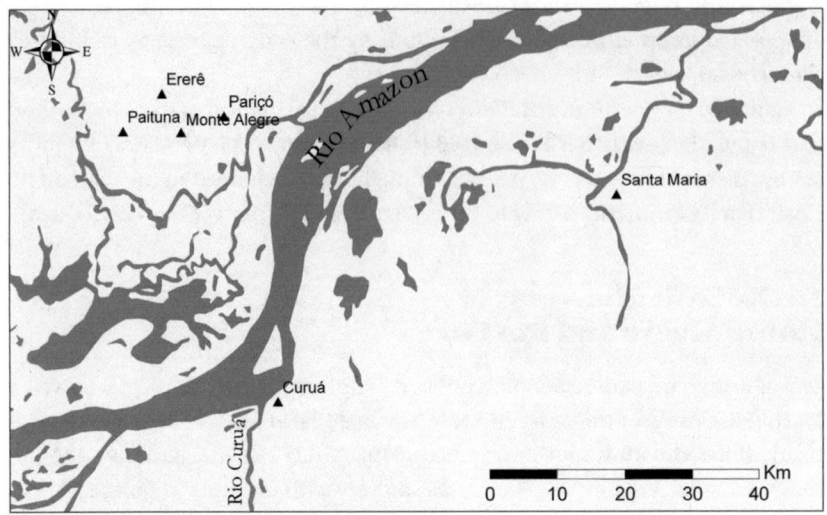

Fig. 4.8 Monte Alegre and Rio Curuá. After Nimuendajú 2004.

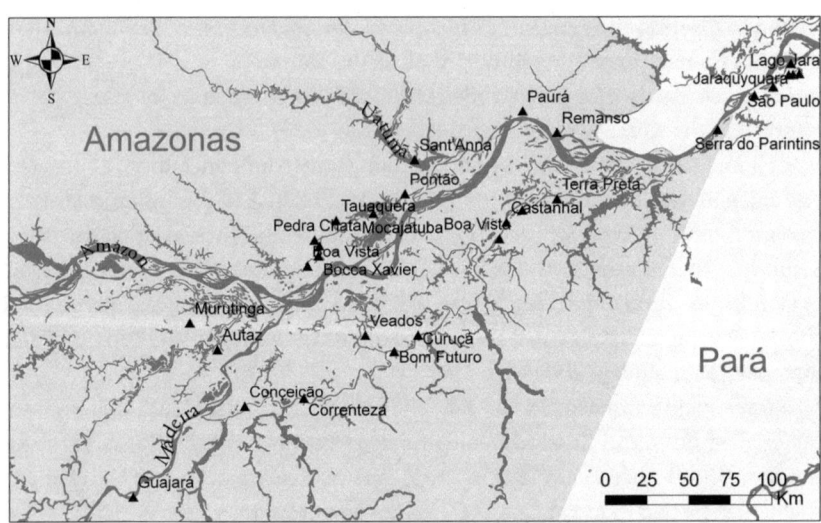

Fig. 4.9 Sites investigated by Nimuendajú in western Pará and eastern Amazonas, Brazil. After Nimuendajú 2004.

Some Implications of Nimuendajú's Work in the Santarém and Trombetas-Nhamundá Areas

Although marred by many failings—such as an almost complete lack of stratigraphic documentation; a selectiveness concerning the collection of material, which has resulted in a heavily biased representation of the composition of the archaeological record; and, in some cases, poor information concerning the material's precise provenience—Curt Nimuendajú's work has provided an invaluable mapping of the varied and challenging archaeological landscape of this region.

It is certainly no exaggeration to claim that the Santarém region, albeit constituting an unusually rich archaeological environment, has attracted surprisingly little scientific interest (a fate shared by most of the South American continent outside the central Andes). The existing "archaeological map" (see fig. 4.10) thus provides us with data from a number of unevenly distributed sites, primarily concentrated in the southern part of the region. Similarly, concerning the existing data from the Guayana region in general, the coastal regions and the areas adjacent to the major rivers are clearly overrepresented. The present archaeological map probably more accurately reflects modern use and exploitation of the region than the prehistoric distribution of human populations.

Despite these problems, archaeological data do indicate that far-flung connections have existed, at least from the early first millennia BC onward. Contacts are revealed through the appearance of similar stylistic traits in the pottery produced in both regions. These traits, jointly referred to as Barrancoid (also known as the Modeled-Incised or Incised Rim) Tradition, have a wide distribution in tropical lowland South America, thereby indicating that relations had emerged, which somehow allowed the spread and merging of cultural elements. The later distribution of polychrome pottery, referred to as the Amazonian Polychrome Tradition, over large portions of lowland South America again displays the existence of ties linking together enormous areas. The mechanism behind these distributions of traits remains a subject for debate, where the suggestions involve processes such as migration (e.g., Lathrap 1970, 1977),[5] the spread of agricultural techniques (Lathrap 1970, 1977), and the development of trade relations (Hornborg 2005).

The different "areas" Nimuendajú identified represent chronological differences as well as differences concerning material culture between contemporaneous societies. The lack of stratigraphic documentation and classification of the material he collected considerably complicates any attempt to evaluate the local chronologies of the sites. The majority of the material from the Santarém and Trombetas-Nhamundá areas may nevertheless be associated with the last millennium BP and with the so-called Incised-Punctate (or Incised-and-Punctate) Tradition (Meggers and Evans 1961). The related Konduri and Santarém complexes are held to cover temporally the period from AD 1000 to 1700. There are, however, so far very few radiocarbon and luminescence dates from the Santarém and Trombetas–Nhamundá

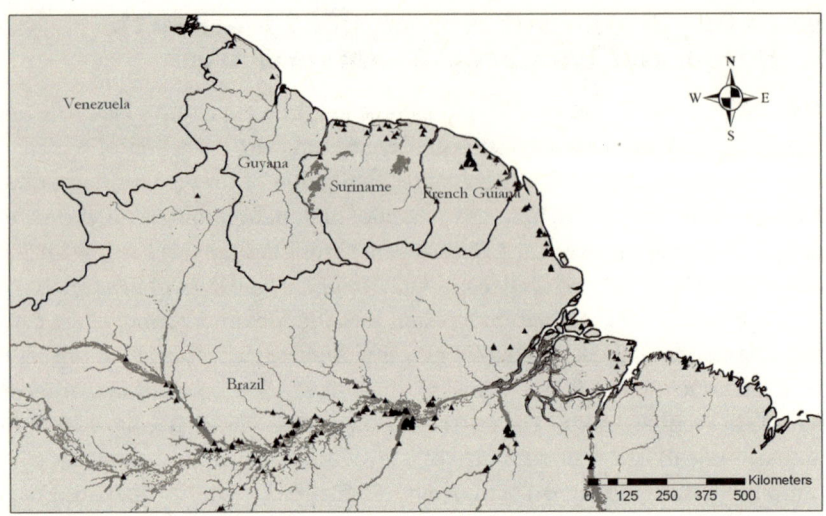

Fig. 4.10 The location of the greater part of known archaeological sites in the northwestern Amazon and the Guianas (sites in Venezuela are not included on the map). After Heckenberger, Petersen, and Góes Neves 1999; Nimuendajú 2004; Pouguet 2002; D. Williams 2003; and others.

areas, which is why the more precise temporal extension is yet to be established. Luminescence dates on Santarém material from the Museu de Arqueologia e Etnologia of the Universidade de São Paulo undertaken by Denise Maria Gomes (1999, 2001, 2002) ranged from AD 900 to 1200. One radiocarbon dating from a Kondurí context gave 490 ± 130 (Hilbert and Hilbert 1979:448), calibrated to AD 1260–1630 (Pouguet 2002). It is interesting to note, as did Nimuendajú, the limited influence of the so-called Amazonian Polychrome Tradition visible in the Santarém and Kondurí material (cf. Petersen et al. 2004:21). Polychrome material is found west (e.g., at Guarita and Paredão in the central Amazon/Rio Negro areas [Góes Neves 1998; Heckenberger, Petersen, and Góes Neves 1999; Hilbert 1968; Lathrap 1970; Petersen et al. 2004]) and east (e.g., at Marajoara [Meggers and Evans 1957; Schaan 2001]) of the Santarém and Trombetas–Nhamundá areas. The pottery styles held to belong to the Polychrome Tradition are considered coarsely contemporaneous, their similitude held to reveal direct or indirect contacts over large parts of the Amazon. The divergence from this general pattern (also involving the absence of burial urns in the Santarém and Trombetas–Nhamundá areas) may indicate that contacts along the tributaries (Trombetas and Nhamundá) were of particular importance. Several authors have pointed out (usually from a diffusionist standpoint) stylistic similarities between the Santarém pottery and pottery found in, for example, Venezuela and Suriname (e.g., Corrêa 1965; Palmatary

1939, 1960). Trade routes and networks for communication may directly and indirectly have linked enormous areas together. These routes of communication along waterways would have involved key points, particularly in the junctions between north–south and east–west connections. If these assumptions are correct, interruptions of the reasonably homogenous pattern of material culture found along the Amazon may reveal the positions of particularly important routes of communication along the tributaries.

Nimuendajú found materials that markedly differed from the Santarém and Kondurí complexes only some seventy kilometers to the east (Monte Alegre) and some fifty kilometers to the west (Rio Arapiums) of Santarém. He also discovered little-known pottery complexes farther west (e.g., at Remanso, Paurá, Catanhal, and so on). The existence of a number of different ceramic complexes within a relatively limited area poses important questions concerning the development of precontact intercultural relations in these regions. As stated earlier, the chronological relations between some of these materials are yet to be established. It should be remembered, however, that societies of quite different socioeconomic organization are likely to have existed side by side in late prehistoric Guayana and Amazon. Long-distance contacts and trade have undoubtedly been of critical importance for the overall cultural development in lowland South America. It should also be pointed out that the areas of cultural interaction—that is, the borders between sociocultural units—have largely been overlooked as scenes from which innovation and change originate. An enormous challenge awaits archaeologists when it comes to analyzing aspects such as land use, economy, and settlement structure and their variation in space and time. The emergence of distinct, although related ceramic complexes, such as Santarém and Kondurí, needs to be analyzed and related to earlier material—for example, Pocó—in the same areas. It is highly gratifying that several research projects[6] have recently been initiated in the Tapajós and Trombetas areas that will substantially improve our knowledge concerning the issues mentioned here.

As noted, Nimuendajú discussed the Terra Preta phenomenon as early as 1923 (2004:122–123). In recent years, these Anthrosols, or "cultural soils," have received increasing attention from scholars in a number of disciplines (e.g., Glaser and Woods 2004; Lehmann et al. 2003). Nimuendajú's discussion is also somewhat related to the recent view of the Amazon as a cultural landscape, where human activity through time has come to modify the environment.

In spite of propositions regarding long-distance relations—such as those mentioned earlier—the intercultural contacts and relations on the more limited scale of the Amazon basin and neighboring regions, such as the Guianas, may be considered more vital for our understanding of cultural processes and cultural development not only with respect to the regions in question but also at a more general level.

Curt Nimuendajú's work penetrated several areas of crucial importance for our understanding of the prehistory of the Guianas and the Amazon. It reinforces the impression of the border areas between the Guianas and the Amazon as regions highly suited for studies of the unfolding intercultural processes and relations through time.

Apart from the frequently discussed issues of large-scale phenomena, such as the emergence of related pottery complexes over extensive sectors of lowland South America, topics such as the establishment and implications of boundaries between different sociocultural systems also deserve attention.

Notes

1. It may be worth noting that the name "Aruã" was, according to Nimuendajú, first mentioned in 1596. The Aruã were later on to become one of the principal opponents of Portuguese colonialism in the region. The relation between the Aruãn ethnolinguistic group and the so-called Aruã phase is, of course, impossible to assert. Apart from the islands in the Amazon estuary and adjacent mainland to the north, there is also information on Aruã populations settled in the Rio Uaçá area (northern Amapá) (Gillin 1948:802; Nimuendajú 2004:51) by the time of European contact. Their increasing importance during the contact period may well have been a consequence of the development of the relationship between Europeans and natives, which at the same time heavily reduced the importance and size of previously significant populations, such as the Tapajó, in the Santarém area (Whitehead 1993:287).

2. The material from Rio Jari and Rio Iratapurú form part of the collections of the Museu Paraense Emílio Goeldi in Belém, Brazil.

3. Urn burials seem to have been uncommon in the Santarém area. Ethnohistorical information suggests that rituals including mummification and ceremonial consumption of decarnated remains of deceased occurred in the region (cf. Quinn 2004:45ff.). Gomes, observing similarities with Maracá-phase funerary urns from Amapá, nevertheless suggested that the large anthropomorphic vessels found in the Santarém area may have served as funeral vessels as well as containers for storing liquids.

4. In many areas along the Amazon River, the natives withdrew their settlements from the immediate surroundings of the river as a response to early European activity in these areas. Already in 1542, Francisco de Orellana received reports that large settlements and densely populated areas were to be found farther inland (e.g., Carvajal 1942). It is reasonable to assume that in general the increasing interaction with the Europeans in the decades that followed Orellana's voyage implied a process of resettlement of villages and people and a depopulation of the interface for this interaction (i.e., the riverbanks and their environments). As European–native relations evolved, trade and other activities motivated native groups to settle once again in the vicinity of the rivers.

The populations by the mouth of the Tapajós River had made themselves respected by the Europeans, who feared their poisonous arrows; for this reason, they were initially left in peace to a greater extent than were other native populations (Acuña 1891 [1641]: 181). These circumstances should be kept in mind when we compare the information on population numbers and sizes of settlement in various parts of the region dating from the period following the initial contact period. After these populations were defeated by the Portuguese in 1639, their numbers rapidly declined, and they apparently vanished entirely within less than a century (Nimuendajú 2004:118, 132).

5. Discussions of long-distance contacts and relations were common in the early-twentieth-century research. Based on the theoretical premises of movements such as the *Kulturkeislehre* and the culture-historical tradition, cultural change was preferably explained as the outcome of either population movements or diffusion (e.g., P. Schmidt 1913). Works such as that by Herbert J. Spinden, where early cultural "archaic" forms in both North and South America were interpreted as having a common origin, have impinged on later research in more than one way. According to Spinden's model, elements of this early culture (e.g., stone and clay figurines) were spread over vast regions as a side effect of the diffusion of early agriculture (1922:43–65). He placed the cradle of New World agriculture in the Mexican highlands, suggesting that maize was first domesticated there. This archaic horizon had once extended from northern Mexico to the Peruvian coast and eastward all the way to the island of Marajó at the mouth of the Amazon. Concerning the Santarém region, Palmatary (1939, 1960), who made detailed studies of existing Santarém material in museum collections, also adhered to the idea of cultural contacts on a large scale, possibly reaching as far as the Mississippi region. In Lathrap's model (1970, 1977), the suggestion that population movements played a role in both material culture and languages was entirely associated with particular ethnic groups: the distribution and extension of traits of material culture, such as pottery styles and languages, could be perfectly explained as the outcome of population movements. Although such a simple model of the relationship between populations and their material culture is evidently untenable, the possibility that population movements (as well as various forms of exchange and interaction) were somehow involved in establishing an initial homogenization of material culture on a regional scale cannot be ruled out.

6. Among others, the Museu Goeldi in Belém, the Universidade Federal do Pará, the Universidade de São Paulo, the University of Illinois, and the University of Göteburg are involved in archaeological fieldwork in the Tapajós and Trombetas areas.

5

Scientific Forestry and Degraded Forests
The Story of Guiana Shield Forests

Janette Bulkan and John Palmer

> Dah wood kyan done (The forest is inexhaustible).
> —A traditional Guyanese saying

Guyana and Suriname, located at the center of the Guiana Shield, are countries that have experienced forestry projects with significant technical innovation but remarkably little durability and internalization after the end of donor-funded projects. Forests cover about 163,377 square kilometers (17 million hectares) or 80 percent of Guyana; 148,550 square kilometers or about 90 percent of Suriname; and 75,000 square kilometers or 90 percent of French Guiana. The majority of these forests in all three countries are legally owned by the state, which in theory should make the attainment of sustainable forest management more achievable. This chapter focuses on Guyana because of the limitations of space.

The standard narratives of national forest services portray setbacks and declining trends as bolts from the blue or irrational opposition, generally from the private sector and especially from the locally owned loggers and sawmillers. Reading economic and political records alongside forestry reports, however, suggests that the adversities encountered by forestry plans have both endogenous and exogenous explanations. We have chosen three periods in the life of the national forest service of Guyana when considerable technical improvements in forest management were beginning to be made or were demonstrated to be possible, but internalization or upscaling nevertheless did not occur. We examine circumstantial evidence as to why the advances did not gel and suggest that a narrow focus on technical solutions will continue to fail until donor-funded projects or national forestry programs take notice of the wider economic and sociopolitical landscapes in which forestry is embedded.

The Poor Soils of the Hinterland

The natural forests of the Guiana Shield remained, until some fifteen years ago, relatively unaffected by the industrial-scale logging that has degraded so much of the perhumid forest in the tropics. The forests grow on very infertile soils derived by in situ weathering from the Proterozoic metamorphic and igneous rocks of the Guiana Shield (Gibbs and Barron 1993). This region has been marked by its geologic stability: it has not been transformed by tectonic uplift or downwarping or by periods of marine or fluvial incursion (except on the narrow coastland reclaimed from the sea during early colonial times) or by vulcanism. So the original rocks have been slowly decomposing into lateritic Cambisols, Ferralsols, and Leptosols in the inland areas, and into the brown and white sandy Arenosols, Ferralsols, and Podzols on the White Sand plateau nearer the coast. For eons, the rain has been eroding the ancient rocks in the hinterland and forming these soils, washing out the bulk of plant-feeding nutrients (Ek 1996).

The northwesterly flowing ocean current brings waves of brown mud from the Amazon River and has deposited the alluvium that forms the Cambisols, Fluvisols, and Histosols on and just behind the coast. During the colonial period, these geologically recent soils were reclaimed through empoldering and draining by slave labor (Rodney 1981:2–3).

Tree Adaptations to Poor Soils

Not surprisingly, many of the trees and other plants that can survive and grow on such weathered soils are specialized, resulting in a high degree of endemism (Berry, Huber, and Holst 1995). About 50 percent of an estimated eight thousand species of vascular plants are endemic to the Guiana Shield (Lindeman and Mori 1989: 377). Compared with other tropical moist forests, trees of the Guiana Shield are relatively short and thin and have relatively hard and heavy timber adapted to cope with the low levels of plant nutrients and the low water-storage capacity in the soil. These forests also display the usual wide range of tropical tree-growth habits and life strategies. Small canopy gaps favor species that have larger seeds dispersed by birds and mammals (van Roosmalen 1985), longer periods over which germination can occur, and the ability to grow slowly under light shade. However, the "slow but sure" strategy carries the penalty of constant attack by insect pests and pathogenic fungi (Hammond and Brown 1991, 1993). Toxins formed in the heartwood, however, help to reduce insect and fungal attack, making some timbers from the Guiana Shield especially valuable where durability is important, such as in naval constructions.

Also not surprisingly, forest-management methods developed for tropical forests elsewhere are unsuitable for these forests. Yet, even so, both the timber industry and government administrations in Guyana and Suriname tend to disregard a century of forestry research and fail to exploit the special opportunities of Guiana Shield timbers (ITTO 2003). It is this paradox that the chapter explores.

The sparsity of the human and animal populations and the lack of permanent agriculture in the Guiana Shield forests are further indications of the infertile soils.

Gold was dispersed in the alluvial sands and so worth extracting only in low-cost, scattered artisanal operations. Nevertheless, the colonial governments were always aware of the forests' revenue-raising possibilities and of the geopolitical value of loyal outposts of the empire (Burr 1897). Grants were awarded to riverine lands and for extraction of forest produce, with authority derived from the charter of the Dutch West India Company, incidentally sidestepping preexisting Amerindian land rights (Menezes 1988). Grants to cut wood were issued in Berbice from 1741 and in Essequibo from 1803. In 1803, at the time of the transfer of power to the British, the incoming lieutenant governor issued a prohibition on the export of any timber from the colony (*Essequibo and Demerary Gazette* 1804). Unfortunately, the reasons for and duration of this embargo on timber exports are now unknown.

Anatto, the natural food colorant scraped from the seeds of *Bixa orellana,* was barreled under crabwood tree oil (*Carapa guianensis*) and exported from the Guianas in the early colonial period (A. Benjamin 1993). The rare letterwood (*Piratinera guianensis*) was dominant in timber exports between 1624 and the 1770s (Welch 1975) and was explicitly mentioned in the British capitulation of Suriname to the Dutch in March 1667 (Record and Hess 1943:393). The durable woods, in particular greenheart (*Chlorocardium rodiei*) in Guyana and basralokus (*Dicorynia guianensis*) in Suriname, were used locally as framing timbers in civil construction and exported consistently from the 1880s.

Amerindians' complaints about the destructive nature of uncontrolled timber harvesting were recorded from 1815 (Menezes 1977), and written expressions of government concern were recorded in 1882. The absence of an Amerindian polity able to insist on original rights to natural resources made it easy for the colonial governments to declare that resource access was a privilege, not a natural right. In Crown Lands Ordinance Number 2 of 1871, the governor of British Guiana defined the forest privileges of the Amerindians, admitting no recognition of endogenous "rights."

Regulations protected at least one commercially valuable forest product against destructive harvesting—the bulletwood (*Manilkara bidentata*), whose balata latex was used in vast amounts for proofing submarine telegraph cables and for industrial power transmission belting from the mid–nineteenth century. The government in British Guiana was not slow to pass legislation and regulations, with associated revenue taxes, on this valuable product, which is now mostly a curiosity. Later regulation provided for royalty payment on forest produce extracted for trade and for minimum squared log size. These regulations were administered by the Department of Lands and Mines (DLM), a precedent that would have far-reaching consequences for Guyana's forests.

The mercantilist attitude to the forests began to be modified in 1895–96, when the first observations were recorded of shortages of market-size greenheart after repeated logging of the most accessible areas (Sandbach Parker chapters in Rodney 1981:252 n. 14). However, not until 1903 was there a conventional legal basis for government forest administration, with the passage of Crown Lands Ordinance Number 32. This ordinance, essentially to put the revenue gathering onto a less arbitrary basis, continued in force with little modification until 1953. In 1903, forest products were second in exportation value after sugar.

The first opportunity for systematic forest management began in 1908, when the Forestry Branch was set up in the DLM. The impetus was science, not revenue or trade. Revenue administration was already under DLM control, where it remained until 1960, except for the period from 1927 to 1931. "The survey modality" characteristic of British imperialism (Cohn 1996:4) then expanded from mapping and minerals to trees. Yet the lure of the interior continued to lie in the promise of gold. From the colonial period on, mining has taken precedence over forestry, but both, in turn, are peripheral to the country's coastal focus.

In 1908, DLM's Forestry Branch began a systematic evaluation of the forests' production potential, with emphasis given to collection of samples and scientific identification. These forest-valuation surveys were continued annually until 1963. Thirty-four expeditions from 1908 to 1916, for example, covered twenty-five forest districts defined by river boundaries, including the upper Essequibo and the Rupununi. An initial report in 1912 (Anderson 1912) was followed by a second compiled up to 1916 and finally published with updates in 1928 (Haman and Wood 1928). Crown Lands Regulations in 1919 enabled the DLM to issue wood-cutting leases, but the valuation surveys apparently did not influence the locations or terms of those leases.

A status report on British Guiana forests was provided to the second British Empire Forestry Conference in 1923, following which the Forest Department, based on the Indian Forest Service (IFS), was established in 1925. However, the administrative and revenue control remained with the DLM, institutionalizing the schism between technical advances and forestry practices that has endured to the present.

Former IFS conservator of forests B. R. Wood recognized the importance of administrative control over forest lands. His presentation in 1926 to the notoriously conservative Combined Court, well known for its tight-fisted approach to spending beyond the coastlands, was apparently convincing. Forest Ordinance Number 29 for protection and control of forests and forest products was passed in October 1927. Management of Crown Forests was vested in the independent Forest Trust, which funded the operational activities of the Forest Department. The ordinance provided for legal constitution of forest reserves in the Permanent Forest Estate (PFE) and effectively guaranteed an operational budget for the Forest Department.

Wood planned three phases of forest administration: first, exploration-inventory, mapping, volume estimation, utilization, and stimulation of overseas capital into the local commercial timber industry; second, legislation to set up the PFE; and third, forest management with working plans and regeneration of forest post-logging (Welch 1975). Wood envisaged that selected forested areas would be reserved by law as the PFE, with the DLM continuing to administer forests deemed to be not of sustainable value. These phases accorded exactly with the technically effective scheme of the first IFS director general, Dietrich Brandis, from 1856 in lower Burma (Dawkins and Philip 1998).

However, presaging the shape of future relations, the local timber industry evinced little interest in taking up Forest Department suggestions, such as controlling wood-boring insects by painting the logs with cheap diesel oil. The Forest Department, in turn, could enforce no penalties for wasted logs while negligible royalties were paid through the DLM only on logs delivered at the mills.

The Forest Department demonstrated that air seasoning of sawn lumber gave as good results as imported North American conifer timber, the "New York boards," which had been used traditionally for house walls since the 1880s (Welch 1975). Samples of many forest products had been sent to overseas laboratories since 1908, and the Forest Department used extracts from laboratory reports to stimulate overseas interest, but the local timber industry was not interested or was not capable of responding to the resulting orders. The Forest Department itself participated in major exhibitions and trade fairs but was apparently not accompanied by private-sector enterprises, which did not appreciate the trading opportunities.

The Forest Department also participated in the Oxford University expedition to Moraballi Creek for fifteen weeks in 1929. This pioneering synecological study in tropical moist forest was published in two influential papers (Davis and Richards 1933, 1934) and served as a baseline for the first major synthesis of tropical forest ecology (Richards 1952). A preliminary demarcation of the Bartica-Kaburi area of 49,800 hectares, the intended first reserve in the PFE, was under way in 1931 (Troup 1939:410).

However, this halcyon period of technical advance and secure budget ended in 1931, when Crown Forests were placed back under the DLM's administrative control, where they remained until 1953, with revenue accounting going on under the DLM until 1960. The Forest Trust was downgraded to an advisory board, and the special provision of the Forest Trust fund was removed.

The conservator of forests moved the Forest Department headquarters from Georgetown to His Majesty's Penal Settlement on the Mazaruni River above Bartica, at that time a day's travel from Georgetown, where it stayed until 1937, continuing its research program. Although forest harvesting was concentrated in the Bartica area, the physical withdrawal of the department from the capital effectively reduced its influence within governmental circles. In addition to forest-valuation surveys, silviculture studies began, and plantation trials with local and exotic species were also undertaken. Methods for successful greenheart regeneration were applied from 1937, with heavier canopy opening from 1943. However, lacking administrative control of the forests, the Forest Department could not legally control loggers, systematize logging spatially, or prevent damaging reentry into previously logged

Scientific Forestry and Degraded Forests 79

areas. Forest Improvement Operations, as they were called, were stopped in 1946 (Clarke 1956), by which time only 9,000 hectares had been improved.

During the time at His Majesty's Penal Settlement, the Forest Department had started its own small-scale logging, sawing, and secondary processing. Importers of Guyanese timber pressed for the 1937 Export of Timber Ordinance to control export quality for compulsory inspection and certification of exported timber, except for exports to the Caribbean region. Two years after the Forest Department's return to Georgetown, it moved into a new headquarters building that was a showcase of local timbers. The building included workshops for preparing timber test samples and for continuing the air-drying and preservative work.[1] The wartime ban on import of timber (from September 1939) enhanced the importance of the Forest Department's timber-seasoning yard. However, the increase in wartime demand for sawn wood of any quality guaranteed the private sector a continuing market for green, unseasoned timber. Today, more than half a century later, the national timber markets in Guyana (lumberyards) and Suriname (*houtmarkts*) continue to offer only green, unseasoned timber for sale.

In this first phase of developing forest administration, from 1925 to 1944, the Forest Department had built usefully on the annual forest-valuation surveys since 1908 and had undertaken pioneering ecological and silvicultural studies in natural tropical moist forest and plantation trials. And it had begun to constitute the PFE. In hindsight, one may decry the biophysical emphasis. Even during the period from 1927 to 1931, when the Forest Department had autonomy and control, there seems to have been little focus on financial sustainability or the cost of implementing the three-phase plan. It is not surprising, then, that the autonomy and guaranteed budget were taken back from the Forest Department when the general slump in world trade combined with low prices for cane sugar, and British Guiana's economy became precarious. In addition, there was a retrenchment of staff throughout the British Colonial Services. Although the Combined Court was replaced in 1928 by more conventional fiscal-control systems, the antipathy toward spending government money outside the coastal zone continued.

The return of administrative control to the DLM in 1931 meant that the national logging enterprises could in effect cut whatever they wanted in order to fulfill individual orders, wherever and whenever they wished, for derisory royalties paid to the DLM, not to the Forest Department. There were no controls on the quality of logging, and the system of paying the tree cutters on piecework only for solid timber had two pernicious outcomes that are still around. First, much useful timber was left standing, leading to damaging reentry into logged stands. Second, the traditional way of determining tree soundness or defect, by knocking the tree with an axe, was later found to be only 60 percent accurate, so many trees were felled and then left on the ground (de Milde 1969).

The confinement of the Forestry Department's role to research unconnected to Crown Forests or forestry practices also facilitated the entrenchment of the small elite that had historically monopolized the State Production Forests for private gain. Today, only the composition of that elite group has changed, with Asian tycoons and their local surrogates replacing the predominantly Portuguese and later East Indian national large-scale logging and sawmilling enterprises.

The unsuitable legislation and administrative arrangements for forests continued into the 1950s. The drafting of a forests act was completed by Conservator W. A. Gordon, who was also a barrister and, later, the author of the first major textbook on tropical forest law (Gordon 1955). The main barrier was the need to revise legislation for other sectors to eliminate overlaps and contradictions. Even after the passage of the Forests Act in 1953, it took until 1960 for the DLM to relinquish control of production statistics, revenue collection, and accounting for the Crown Forests. New lease agreements for the four largest national timber operations, located in the Bartica Triangle, were concluded in 1954 and required harvesting in conformity with a forest-management plan approved by the Forest Department. But even systematic block working was not enforced (or legally could not be enforced while the DLM retained administrative control).

With the passage of the Forests Act in 1953, 2.8 million hectares of Crown Forests were placed under Forest Department control, but the PFE was not advanced. Indeed, the intended Bartica-Kaburi reserve of 1931 was abandoned. An indication of the narrow vision for forestry is borne out by a World Bank development mission's recommendation in 1953 to restart silvicultural treatments in logged greenheart forest to improve growth rates. The technical feasibility of doing so had been indicated by 1936, and the possibility of doubling diameter growth rates was later shown by sample plots established in 1963 and assessed in 1971 (Prince 1973; Steege et al. 1994). With no visible forestry constituency present, however, foreign technical expertise had no need to extend its recommendations beyond the few valuable tree species accepted commercially on world markets—to see the wood for the trees, as it were. Guyana has more than 1,000 tree species, but only about 120 are cut for commercial sale, and of the latter only 14 were exported in volumes exceeding 1,000 cubic meters of logs in the first ten months of 2006 (Guyana Forestry Commission 2007).

The Neglect of Small Lease Holders and the Elite's Dominance of the Forestry Sector

Forestry activities in British Guiana were predominantly small scale until the 1960s. In 1935, a mere 370 square miles were held under harvesting concessions—"only 0.02 percent of the estimated area of the merchantable Crown Forest." "[Four] Leases over an area of 191,508 acres" and "136 Wood-cutting licenses covering an area of 45,052 acres" had been issued (British Guiana Forest Department 1935). In other words, the forestry permissions held by 136 or more small loggers (given the practice of many persons working on a single lease) totaled less than one-quarter of the area allocated to four leases. The division of the State Production Forests between small and large lease holders has remained the same, reflecting continued domination by the elite over every aspect of economic life in Guyana, including forestry. Fifty years later, the major difference is the substitution of Asian companies in place of Guyanese-owned companies.

Up until the end of the Second World War, "small grant-holders, Aboriginal Indians and others" were the majority suppliers of logs to the Forest Department and the downstream processing sector (Welch 1975:52). Ironically, the small-scale national logging and chainsaw milling sector continues to fulfill this role even while state and multilateral support have focused on the large concessions to the relative neglect of the small-scale sector.

It has often been remarked that the national loggers and sawmillers in both Guyana and Suriname pay scant attention to marketing the unique Guiana Shield timbers. Their approach has always been to wait for orders to be placed and, even when that happens, to choose to fail to meet an order rather than share it out among other timber suppliers. Part of the explanation may be that niche markets existed in Europe and North America for the prime timber species. But the national large-scale logging and sawmilling enterprises were in the main coastal, family-owned businesses that approached forestry as a capital-generating investment. These businesses concentrated their efforts on monopolizing as much of the production forests as they could, either directly or indirectly, using "sprinters" (subcontractors without their own harvesting licenses) to cut logs to meet specified orders. Few would ever set foot in the forest or spend any length of time there. Their refusal to read or use technical reports on the characteristics of Guiana Shield timbers, including the rapidity of localized extinction following high grading (that is, highly selective logging) of commercial species, continues into the present. It comes as no surprise, then, that these large-scale national loggers and sawmillers would quickly be transformed into clients of the Asian multinationals who entered the timber sector in the early 1990s. Within a decade, the Asian companies distorted forestry into an enclave sector supplying prime hardwood logs to Asia for transformation into high-quality expensive flooring and furniture for export to Europe and North America.

Guyanization of the Forest Department (1946–1966)

In preparation for independence, the ten-year development plan for forestry was drawn up for the period from 1954 to 1964 and funded through extrabudget Colonial Development and Welfare (CD&W) funds. The plan provided for expanded training so that all senior Forest Department staff would be Guyanese by 1960. CD&W funds also allowed the expansion of the small-scale Forest Department venture into secondary processing of timber, so useful during the Second

World War, in the Central Timber Manufacturing Plant (CTMP). Although the CTMP was commercially unsuccessful under civil service management, it demonstrated that more than thirty local timbers were perfectly adequate for construction and furniture if suitably seasoned or preserved. Nevertheless, this information did not seem to stimulate investment or technical improvement in the commercial timber industry.

Although aerial photography had been used for forest mapping in other tropical countries from the 1920s, it was not until the 1950s that CD&W funding enabled Dutch experience to be brought in from Suriname. The forest-valuation surveys since 1908 had been ground inventories, but interpretation of aerial photographs and associated cartography permitted much greater and faster coverage. The government commissioned various aerial survey firms from 1949 to 1960 to produce black-and-white panchromatic photos mostly at a scale of 1:30,000. A little later, from 1962 to 1965, the Royal Air Force photographed the more remote areas for pictures at 1:60,000, and this military coverage was later declassified. Preliminary work on photo interpretation was undertaken by N. G. L. Guppy (1951, 1952), better known for his writings on the Waiwai Amerindians (1958, 1973). A. T. Vink and E. J. Swellengrebel carried out the initial large-scale interpretation and forest type mapping from 1956 to 1959, and I. A. Welch followed them beginning in 1961 (Welch 1966; Welch, Sampson, and Bell 1972). The 1:30,000 photos were used to classify forest areas into broad cover types based on canopy appearance and topography. Swellengrebel (1959, 1960, 1961a, 1961b) carried out some of the first attempts to identify individual tropical tree species and estimate individual tree trunk diameters from crown size. More than half a million hectares were mapped to a scale of 1:500,000 by the end of 1964, and some in more detail. Selective ground control was established in the Bartica Triangle, the upper Essequibo area, and the North West District.

These world-class forestry studies, however, took place against a backdrop of increasingly intense and fraught preindependence politicking and in a powerless Forest Department. The "scholarship boys" had only limited field experience but were pitched into senior positions on return from training. From 1959 to 1964, the Forest Department was shifted between ministries and lost its own administrative support staff, especially from 1963 onward. Revenue administration began to dominate the Forest Department's work, a pattern that continues today.

Forest Industries Development Survey

From 1960, the small and new Guyanese senior staff in the Forest Department submitted applications to the Food and Agriculture Organization (FAO) for United Nations Development Program (UNDP) Special Fund assistance in forest resource inventories in primary and logged forest, and for United Nations Technical Assistance Board help with new inventory techniques, including aerial photographs

Scientific Forestry and Degraded Forests 83

and random sampling. Applications were resubmitted in 1965 after preliminary FAO consultancies from 1962 to 1964.

The major FAO agency at this time was the Forest Industries Development Survey (FIDS), which undertook extensive aerial photo interpretation of soils, vegetation, and forest types and carried out reconnaissance-scale inventorying from 1966 to 1970 (Gross-Braun et al. 1966 for soils; and De Milde 1969, De Milde and de Groot 1970a, 1970b, 1970c, 1971a, 1971b, Huss 1971, Welch and Bell 1971 for inventory). The FIDS took full advantage of the mainframe computers then becoming commercially available. Technical backup for inventory design was provided by K. E. Haller at the Bundesforschungsanstalt fuer Forst-und Holzwirtschaft, Reinbek bei Hamburg, in Germany. FIDS included advanced aerial photo interpretation, renewed attempts to identify tree species on large-scale infrared aerial photographs, innovative and statistically efficient sampling schemes for ground-level inventory, new ways of quantifying the taper of tree trunks, and the reliable identification of defective trees and estimation of the extent of internal rot and other defects. Electronic computation, although extremely limited compared with our current abilities, enabled the reliable checking and processing of much larger quantities of tree measurements and numbers of trees than ever before in the tropics. Reconnaissance-level inventory from February 1968 to May 1969 covered 14.9 million hectares out of a total forest area of 16.9 million hectares. For preinvestment studies from November 1968 to December 1970, 435,000 hectares in three main inventories were covered in more detail, including the Great Falls area (Welch and Bell 1971), which was later awarded to the government-owned Demerara Woods Ltd. (DWL).

Hundreds of trees were bored with portable electric drills during the study on defect. This study showed conclusively that the traditional sounding methods for determining defect were at best only 60 percent reliable and that consequently many nondefective trees over the cutting girth limit were being bypassed. Logging costs were thus higher than they needed to be (De Milde 1969; Grayum 1971).

Conversion from Manual to Mechanical Harvesting

In parallel with the forest resource assessments, FAO facilitated the introduction of chain saws, a change that the larger logging companies received well. Within just a few months, axe felling was almost entirely replaced by chain-saw felling, and the costs of felling and cross-cutting were halved. The demonstration skidder was sold locally, and the local timber industry ordered more skidders and other mechanized equipment before the end of the project because it was demonstrated that skidding costs could be reduced by 40 percent (Grayum 1971; Vieira 1967, 1980).

A succession of FAO specialists had worked at the CTMP and had demonstrated and made recommendations about improvements in forest products processing and marketing (for example, Mueller-Eckhardt 1969; Palmer 1969; Roejkjaer 1967a, 1967b). The FAO specialists in Guyana recommended economies of scale, with low-intensity, low-cost, low-impact logging at long intervals and with value added through efficient industries. FIDS envisaged large-area concessions managed with much greater technical understanding and marketing skills than the local timber industry then possessed. It also suggested provision for small-scale operators having limited capital, but the main emphasis was on economy of scale.

Thus, by the early 1970s the Guyana Forest Department had been swept to the forefront of (static) tropical forest resource assessment, and a mass of well-summarized and statistically reliable information had been gathered about the forest resources in accessible areas and displayed in map form as well as on marked-up aerial photographs. In addition, the Forest Department had accumulated a considerable body of technical knowledge since 1908 and especially during the 1950s, before the FIDS's entrance to the scene. A notable proportion of the Forest Department technical staff had been involved in FIDS and had received external in-service training. FAO recommended strongly that this new knowledge should be used for a comprehensive forest-development plan, with management units configured according to sustainable industry requirements. FAO recommended that existing wood-cutting leases should not be renewed on expiry in 1974, a policy initially stated in 1954 or 1956 (Vieira 1980). It also recommended that instead of the haphazard arrangement of leases given out in response to requests, the Forest Department should use the new data to make a formal plan for the sustainable use of the commercially accessible Crown Forests and only then issue new forest-harvesting permits. It suggested that the Forest Department should be seen to take charge and not simply respond passively to the commercial operators. None of these recommendations were taken up.

Given the Forest Department's accelerating accumulation of technical knowledge and its regaining of administrative authority over the Crown Forests in 1960, one may well wonder why it did not surge ahead in sustainable forest management. Its accessible records are silent on this issue. However, the ensuing stagnation in forestry is indicative of the economic and political convulsions of the postindependence era. There was little external interest in investment in Guyana. In forestry, only the United Nations through FIDS and post-FIDS projects provided support to the processing and marketing of Guyana's forest products. What UNDP did not provide was training in business skills or insistence on the need to depoliticize the forestry concession award process.

The kinds of investment for value-added processing anticipated by the FIDS (Grayum 1971) were beyond the vision of the monopolistic timber industry in Guyana and beyond its financial resources after the mid-1970s. Even before the FIDS closed, the warning signs appeared. The government announced in 1970 its intention of taking control of the "commanding heights of economic production" and marketing (Baber and Jeffrey 1986:32, 129). In the same year, external trade was nationalized. The thirty-two major private-sector companies were nationalized with mortgage-type arrangements for compensation from 1971 to 1976, and the country entered upon a period of autarchy. In this era, the holders of large forest concessions entrenched themselves with the political directorate and extended their forest holdings.

Postindependence Developments

The joint public- and private-sector Timber Marketing Board was created in 1970, and the associated act and regulations were passed in 1973 and became operative in 1974. The UNDP Special Fund provided a specialist on timber grading, devised rules, and gave training in 1972–73. Also in 1973, the CTMP was converted into the Forest Industries Corporation (FIC). The FIC was an economic failure, however, with the industry run by noncommercial civil servants. A number of factors—including shortage of spare parts, lack of foreign-exchange and import licenses for their purchase, the difficulty of securing bank credit, and the loss of key staff through emigration—adversely affected all aspects of the economy, including forestry.

The Forest Department was converted into the Guyana Forestry Commission (GFC) in 1979 through an act that dwelled more on corporate banking and insurance functions than on the administration and promotion of sustainable forest management. Most of the trained staff emigrated during the years immediately after FIDS closed, and the local timber industry, like the rest of the private sector, hunkered down to wait for better days. It was a long wait, with the political nadir perhaps in 1980, when a new constitution was passed in a heavily rigged ballot. In this constitution, Article 15 (2) stated that the "national economy will be based on social ownership of the means of production, distribution and exchange" (Baber and Jeffrey 1986:84, 87). In that year, the People's National Congress or its supporters controlled more than 80 percent of the economy. In the following year, 1981, the gross domestic product per head, US$629, was the lowest in the Caribbean Community and Common Market (CARICOM), and external debt per head was one of the highest in the world.

The economy was opened to external investment after the death of President Forbes Burnham in 1985 and gradually freed of government's heavy hand. It was thus an unlucky coincidence of timing that the technical knowledge built up so strongly during the FIDS period could not propel Guyana's forest sector into the modern era. So ended the second opportunity.

The lack of domestic and foreign direct investment during the 1970s and 1980s forced the government of Guyana to seek loans from the international finance institutions. At least one World Bank loan included earmarked funds for the government-owned DWL to increase greenheart exports, but that injection of funds failed to overcome the gross mismanagement of DWL. Highly selective channeling of aid failed to secure improvements and further entrenched the large-scale logging and sawmilling sector. From 1984 to 1989, only seven companies took 94 percent of Official Development Assistance to the forest sector, underlining yet again the elite's domination of the sector. The prevalent "crony socialism" continued into the Desmond Hoyte administration.

When the Hoyte political administration was seeking investors to complement the provisions of the structural adjustment program accompanying loans from the international finance institutions, there was a feeling that southern investors would be less opportunistic and predatory than northern investors. In July 1988, the liberal Investment Code overturned much of the cooperative socialism in effect and provided for privatization of state-owned enterprises. Unfortunately, the Investment Code was not accompanied by detailed regulations or guidelines, so several different kinds of incentives were offered for foreign direct investment, but with weak or no details concerning criteria or trade-offs or concerning penalties for noncompliance. Much was left undefined, in practice leading to a lack of transparency in negotiation, at least the suspicion of corruption, and some extraordinary one-sided deals in favor of the foreign investor (Colchester, Rose, and James 1997), with little or no oversight by the rarely sitting Parliament or by a weak and disorganized civil society from the 1980s to the present.

Both main political parties promoted the idea of unexploited riches in the hinterland—as expected, considering that some 80 percent of Guyana remains under a forest canopy, albeit degraded over large areas by almost uncontrolled selective forest harvesting of prime commercial species. At this time, highly capitalized Asian forest products companies were beginning to look to nontraditional source countries and were finding that weak governance and weak economies often coincided. Foreign investors were thus stimulated by the "give-away" sale of Government of Guyana Timbers Ltd. (formerly Commonwealth Development Corporation, sold to the government in 1973) to Colonial Life Insurance Company of Trinidad for the low price of US$2.7 million in 1989.

The weaknesses in governance led to the now notorious and poorly considered investment agreement in early 1991 with the Korean/Malaysian Barama Company Ltd. The conditions of most foreign direct investment deals are not made public, but at least some of the arrangements for Barama have been published (see Colchester, Rose, and James 1994, 1997). Barama enjoys a twenty-five-year renewable Timber Sales Agreement over 1.6 million hectares, fixed royalties denominated in Guyana dollars and not adjustable for inflation or any other economic change, and a range of freedoms from taxes and import duties. The lack of skill on the part of the government negotiators and weaknesses in corporate law in Guyana have allowed Barama to extend these privileges to its new front companies and partly owned subsidiaries and contractors, thus providing an economic advantage over locally owned enterprises. Barama's freedom from import duty on fuel gives it a large comparative advantage over Guyanese companies in the fuel-thirsty business of logging tropical forests where commercial trees are far apart.

Scientific Forestry and Degraded Forests

Other donors approached for aid to the economic recovery program begun by the Hoyte administration were alarmed at the ease with which such unbalanced South–South deals were concluded. Similar alarm was voiced by donors concerning Suriname (Sizer and Rice 1995). A three-year moratorium on the allocation of new large concessions and the introduction of nonbinding no-harvest State Forest Exploratory Permits were conditions for a U.K.-funded project to support the institutional reform of the GFC. This project ran from 1995 to 2002 and did much to aid reform of the GFC into at least the beginning of a modern service-focused government agency.

Unfortunately, this project was negotiated between technical staff and never really had the support of the political staff of the bilateral donor or of the real decision makers in the Guyanese state. On the contrary, political interference and harassment undercut the GFC's efforts to reform and carry out its mandate. Such political interventions are justified under the unwritten political philosophy of democratic centralism, which overrides valid legislation and regulations at the direction of cabinet officers on the grounds that implementing such laws would not be in the national interest. No criteria are ever provided for what that overriding national interest might be.

Continuing Exodus of Trained Staff

With such heavy-handed political direction, it is not surprising that the best of the GFC staff trained during the period from 1995 to 2002 turned from "gamekeeper to poacher" by joining the Asian-owned logging companies or continued the exodus of the well educated and entrepreneurial from Guyana. The historic privileging of "scientific forestry" also meant that training was disproportionately skewed to the tertiary level, thus neglecting front-line forestry staff. The principal beneficiaries of state-sponsored scholarships are invariably the first to leave.

The end of the colonial era also meant in practice the beginning of the short-term, project-based approach of bilateral or multilateral aid, with its consequent lack of continuity. Asian forestry companies and traders soon filled this vacuum, consolidating their control over state forests through a variety of contractual arrangements, including covertly controlled subsidiaries. This control extends to one-sided log harvest agreements with land-titled Amerindian communities, whose forest resources are by definition not part of the state forests under GFC administration. Such arrangements are either illegal or certainly against the spirit of the Amerindian and Forests acts.

The GFC support project from 1995 to 2002 had concentrated very largely on institutional reform, but technical knowledge did advance in the late 1980s and through the 1990s even if that knowledge was not then applied to sustainable forest management or better fiscal administration of Guyana's forests. A joint project between the University of Guyana and the University of Utrecht in the Netherlands was centered at Mabura Hill beginning in 1988, in the then DWL Timber Sales Agreement area. In 1989, the interuniversity program was rolled over into the Tropenbos Guyana Program, one of Stichting Tropenbos International's (TBI) country programs. TBI's science-based knowledge developed in Guyana aimed to support the government objective of sustainable and more equitable utilization of forest resources. By the end of 2005, more than eighty publications had been produced.[2] Subsequent studies on reduced-impact logging and the long-term effects of reentry in greenheart harvesting have been used in the Guyana Forestry Training Centre Inc. (van der Hout 1999; van der Hout and Marshall 2004).

However, as in the two previous periods of potential advance, the national forest service has limited leverage. The revised Forests Act first drafted in 1995 (Toppin-Allahar 1995) and widely circulated in 1996–97 remains in draft, so industry compliance with the GFC Code of Practice for Timber Harvesting (Guyana Forestry Commission 2002, the second edition) remains voluntary. It would not be difficult to improve the draft of the revised Forests Act to close the loopholes currently being exploited by Asian logging companies and to respond fully to the constructive comments offered by the World Bank in July 2005. Although not difficult, such an improvement was astonishingly not made anytime during the course of a decade (1995 to 2005) when the spatial scale and intensity of logging of the prime commercial species threatened to wreak irreversible damage on the fragile unique Guiana Shield forests.

In conclusion, for the third time in eighty years, Guyana's national forest service finds itself unable to implement coherently and equitably a set of technical advances that would carry Guyana to the frontier of tropical forest management. Are all the proposals for improvement a step too far, too fast? Available documentation suggests that the proponents of such advancement have been at pains to present technically feasible and economically rational suggestions whose implementation would raise the net social value of forests and forestry in Guyana. Lack of donor coordination means that there is no shortage of advisory reports. There is general concurrence between reports covering the same subject area. It is generally easy to recommend technological answers, but political and cultural factors have been more intractable. What is notable is how little seems to change.

State forests are largely treated politically as plums reserved for the favored in disregard of official forest policies and procedures. The World Resources Institute (WRI) report on forestry in Guyana is a case in point. Following WRI's warning report on the "fire sale" of forest resources in Suriname (Sizer and Rice 1995), President Cheddi Jagan of Guyana invited the institute to make a comparable study in Guyana and publicly launched the ensuing report, *Profit without Plunder* (Sizer 1996). Ten years later, however, none of the seven WRI recommendations has been implemented.

Almost all of the forestry consultancy reports, internal and donor driven, have suffered the same fate. In most cases, the diagnoses were reasonable, the options well identified, and the initial progress promising. Then enthusiasm waned, and the task of battling with intersectoral communication and coordination seemed not worth the isolated effort in the absence of an effective parliamentary system of oversight or a civil society able to call Parliament to account. Sustainable forest management is not impossible when democratic centralism has the last word, but the nontransparent crony capitalism associated with weak governance and near-failed states is only too evidently alive and well in the forest sector of Guyana. This weakness extends to the supine role generally played by the GFC board, contrary to the legal requirements of the GFC Act (1979) and of corporate law in Guyana (Haraksingh 2002; Ramjattan 2002).

One common thread connecting this history of failure are the narratives of change that, in spite of all evidence to the contrary, focus on initiatives from the center (the state) or the large-scale logging and sawmilling sector. It can be argued that both the FIDS in the 1960s and 1970s and the GFC support project and the International Tropical Timber Organization in the 1990s produced such a welter of documents that the absorptive capacity of weak institutions and local decision makers was overwhelmed. It is usually not up to the individual consultants to demonstrate how the proposed advances can be "rolled out" from the existing policies and procedures. More pertinently, the lack of political will to change the system of using forest concessions as patronage relegates proposed technical and other innovations to the scrap heap.

It is evident that the kind of control of the land exerted by the state in Guyana and Suriname provides only another means for consolidating economic and political power. The beneficiaries of the country's natural wealth are not the citizens, but only a small elite. One should not wonder at those who emigrated through the open door into North America and the international agencies. Instead, one should wonder why anyone would stay and keep trying for improved and sustainable management of the national patrimony—the 80 percent of Guyana that is covered in forest.

Notes

1. At the time of writing (2007), this historically significant building, refurbished at donor expense in the 1990s, was due to be demolished to make way for a casino resort. The GFC building has not been razed. In January 2009, President Jagdeo reportedly said that "the global credit crunch impacted on the Kingston hotel project. . . . Many big projects also took a hit as a result of this. . . . The sources of capital that had been identified for the hotel deal were simply no longer there" (quoted in "Kingston Hotel Project Not Dead—Jagdeo," *Stabroek News*, 8 January 2009).

2. See http://www.tropenbos.nl/sites/site_guyana.php and http://www.tropenbos.nl/scripts/dsp_listdoc.php?country=103.

Part 2

Ethnography and Ethnology

Individual and Society in Guiana Revisited

Peter Rivière

It is now more than a quarter of a century since *Individual and Society in Guiana* (Rivière 1984) was delivered to the publishers. Since then it has appeared in a Portuguese version, *O indivíduo e a sociedade na Guiana* (Rivière 2001a), published by the University of São Paulo Press. I was asked to write a new foreword for that edition, which was included as "Prefácio à edição brasileira." The English original of the foreword has not previously been published, so its appearance in this volume permits the opportunity for it to be. It is reproduced here as it was submitted, with minor changes to allow for the fact that it is here divorced from the original work. For example, references that occurred in this preface that had appeared in the 1984 edition were not included in the bibliography of the Portuguese preface; here they are.

It should also be noted that there are some differences between the typescript I submitted and the published Portuguese version. For example, the three endnotes included in the typescript were, for no obvious reason, omitted. They have been reintroduced here, although with some changes. The original note 1, which explained the bibliographical arrangements referred to in the previous paragraph, has been replaced by one regarding spelling with respect to the present volume. It might also be observed that my typescript was dated "Oxford, August 1997"; in the published version, this became "Oxford, agosto de 1998."

It would have been useful to have looked at some of the developments in Guianan[1] ethnography and anthropology over the past eight years, but the pressure on space prevents all but the most superficial comment, which is to be found in a postscript to this chapter.

Foreword to the Portuguese Edition

It is a great honor to find this work, first published in 1984, now available in an excellent Portuguese translation. Not only do I appreciate that honor, but I am also grateful to have the opportunity to express some retrospective thoughts on a work that was sent to the press fifteen years ago. It is probably true to say that by the time it was published, I was already dissatisfied with what I had written and would have written a different book. Although that is the way it should be and any other reaction would have evinced intellectual stagnation, I still stand by large parts of what I wrote then, even if I would express my ideas in a more nuanced manner now, especially perhaps in my discussions of gender relations, which today look rather dated. My rethinking of parts of the book are not entirely the result of my own efforts, but have been assisted by discussions with colleagues and the comments of reviewers who were mainly more than kind and fair. The one exception would probably not have been satisfied whatever I had done because he seemed to hold to the position that any attempt at generalization is wrong, and clearly no comparative endeavor can hope to succeed if it is tied to the level of each ethnography.

A fair amount has happened in the intervening years since the original publication, in terms of the development of both my own ideas and those of my colleagues working in Guiana and elsewhere in Lowland South America. Interestingly, one thing that I do not need to take account of is any great increase in the ethnographic literature relating to Guiana. In the second paragraph of the English version, I commented on the monographs that had been published in the 1960s and 1970s, and predicted a lull in this output (Rivière 1984:1). My prediction has proved remarkably accurate, and with the exception of a few works, such as David Guss's 1989 book *To Weave and Sing* on the Ye'cuana (or Yekuana), relatively few major ethnographic works relating to the region have appeared in the past decade and a half. However, even if there is not a great deal of additional information to take into account, there has been considerable change in the attitudes toward it and the interpretation of it. What I propose to do is to pick up certain themes and reconsider them in the light of more recent thoughts.

A start may be made with the comparative method that I employed and that I considered in the second section of the first chapter (Rivière 1984:6–9). There I used the analogy of a "mosaic" and argued that each population group represents a piece in the Guiana mosaic and that the Guiana mosaic itself forms part of the wider tropical forest picture. I now find this metaphor far too static, and there is some evidence to suggest that I did so even at the time of writing the book. In the final chapter, I suddenly introduced the idea of the kaleidoscope (Rivière 1984: 102), and certainly this is the image I have used in recent years when talking about variation within Lowland South America.[2] A kaleidoscope contains a finite collection of assorted colored and shaped pieces that form different patterns depending on these pieces' relationship to one another. If the kaleidoscope is shaken, a radically different pattern occurs between each viewing, whereas if the viewer holds the kaleidoscope up to his eye and turns gently, it is possible to watch one pattern dissolve into another. Another possible and even more modern analogy might be the shifting screen-saver patterns that are created by computer software.

In terms of sociocultural comparison, the pieces within the kaleidoscope are the elements out of which Lowland South Americans construct their social and cultural worlds. The same elements recur again and again, but their relationships to one another vary, thus giving rise to different patterns. However, like all analogies, this one has its limitations, and one of them is that the kaleidoscope is sealed and does not permit the entry of any new pieces, whereas in practice there is every reason to believe that new cultural elements will appear and others disappear as the viewer brings different groups into focus because the Lowland South American culture area is not some bounded entity. Even with this limitation, the kaleidoscope analogy does provide a way of representing both the invariance and the variance within the area in a more dynamic and relational manner than the mosaic analogy. The limitation to the computer analogy is rather different. Whereas there is no difficulty in introducing new elements to it and eliminating others, someone has to write the program to do this. Furthermore, the order in which the patterns change is also programmed; in other words, there is a sort of "big brother" behind each pattern. The patterns do not have the degree of randomness they have in the kaleidoscope. There is here a further question, and that is whether any particular cultural form is randomly put together. In a recent study of the historical relationship between the Arawakans of the upper Rio Negro and the Tukanoans to their southwest, Jonathan Hill (1996a) seems to be suggesting that the latter consciously selected their form of social organization to mark themselves off from their neighbors.

Because in many ways *Individual and Society* was an exercise in ground clearing, I chose to concentrate on the invariants and managed to locate them at the sociological rather than the cultural level. As several reviewers pointed out, I rather overdid this so that I made it appear as though society was divorced from culture and cosmology, although, within the Amazonian context, it quite clearly is not. The problems were two. First, I was unable find a way of handling the high level of cultural variation in matters such as style of haircut, funerary practices, and dietary preferences that exists throughout the region. On this matter, I am not certain that I would be able to do any better today. Second, and the fault here is certainly mine because I cannot have been clear and full enough in my account, there is a remarkable fit between the sociological ideas characterized by, on the one hand, consanguineous, endogamous, and autonomous residential units and, on the other, the metaphysical and cosmological ideas dominated by a conceptual relationship between inside and outside, associated respectively with security and danger, similarity and difference. I know now how I would overcome one of the deficiencies my reviewers identified: I would combine the presentation of social, cosmological, and metaphysical ideas by using the notion of the "house," as introduced into anthropological theorizing by Claude Lévi-Strauss, as the armature on which to construct the comparison. Furthermore, as Janet Carsten and Stephen Hugh-Jones have pointed out, the "house" may provide an appropriate vehicle for a pan–Lowland South American comparative study (1995:35–36).

If I were writing *Individual and Society* today, certainly chapters 2 and 3, perhaps the whole study, would be informed by attention to the house. An idea of the direction I would take is provided by my article "Houses, Places, and People: Community and Continuity in Guiana" (Rivière 1995b). It is worth looking at aspects of my argument from that piece and especially at the part that relies on Guss's Ye'cuana material. I make the point that ethnographers of Guiana have always needed to focus on the settlement and coresidence in the absence of other social formations on which to hang their descriptions. Throughout the area, the ideal settlement or house is seen as consanguineous, endogamous, and autonomous. In practice, it is nothing of the sort. This contrast between ideal self-sufficiency and practical dependency is clearly illustrated in my book by reference to Nelly Arvelo-Jiménez's 1971 work on the Ye'cuana, much referred to in the following pages. Guss has provided further support to the earlier description of Ye'cuana ideals: "The Aschano caadi ceremony that accompanies the application of the last mud to the outer wall [of the roundhouse] lists the name of every foreign spirit and tribe, commanding that they stay away or face destruction. The circle of the house is thereby sealed both physically and symbolically, reinforcing the autonomy and self-reliance that is the ideal of every Yekuana community" (1989:26).

That the Ye'cuana house is a microcosm has been recognized for a long time, but Guss adds a new dimension to the description of it. The original, prototypical Ye'cuana house was built by the culture hero Wanadi and is still visible today in the form of a conical-shaped mountain near the center of these people's homeland. But this visible representation conceals an inner nonvisible reality. This is equally true of the present-day roundhouse, or *atta*. "As with all other forms, the atta is the result of two interlocking realities—an illusionary and material outer one encasing a more powerful and invisible inner one" (Guss 1989:32). It is the invisible reality that endures and provides continuity, whereas the external form is ephemeral, and this is true whether one is speaking of settlements or people. The information on the Ye'cuana house is particularly rich, but I make the point in my 1995 article that similar principles and ideas seem to be operating throughout the area, and to a large extent they support the conclusions that I reached in 1984.

Guss's account of the Ye'cuana house has also allowed me to reassess and understand in a different way Jean-Paul Dumont's comment (cited in Rivière 1984:99) that for the Panare, the shaman is conceptually related to permanence and the headman to impermanence (1978:73). Dumont himself does not explain what exactly he means by this remark, and I, with the aid of J. A. Morton's (1979) reanalysis of Waiwai ethnography, took it to refer to the nature of "spiritual" or "mythic" nonlinear time as opposed to the episodic time of events and, I would now add, life cycles. I still think I am right on this point, but Guss's remarks have allowed the addition of a new dimension: the ephemerality of the visible world's phenomena (the world of settlements and headmen) as contrasted with the perdurance of the invisible world's noumena (the world of origins and essences). The latter now seems to me to be a crucial component in the idea of continuity within the region and as such fits well with ideas reported from other ethnographic regions of Lowland South America. At the same time, I would reiterate my opinion (1984:100) that the relationship terminology, the main idiom of social relations, also provides for orderly continuity in that its categories, which cover the totality of the social world, reproduce themselves from generation to generation.

The focus on the house would have also provided a further advantage by introducing a spatial component into consideration. I have insisted for a long time on the importance of concentric dualism in the ordering of the Trio and other Guiana cosmologies, and no evidence has been forthcoming from the region to make me change my mind on this point. Indeed, Eduardo Viveiros de Castro's (1998) proposal that Dravidianate terminologies of Amazonia are concentric in nature reinforces my view. Crudely and simply, this concentricity has to do with kin on the inside and affines on the outside. The association of coresidence with consanguinity has been repeated too often to require any further elaboration here. More complex is the idea of affinity, if for no other reason than that marriages may be either internal or external to the community, and the term *affinity*, defined as "relations by marriage," is inadequate to describe the features of marriage in Guiana and elsewhere in Lowland South America. In *Marriage among the Trio* (1969), I had introduced the idea of "related" and "unrelated" affinity, aware that this distinction involved a spatial as well as a genealogical aspect. In chapter 5 of *Individual and Society*, I more explicitly drew attention to the importance of the spatial component in understanding the notion of affinity and to the relativity of the notions of consanguinity and affinity. In the same chapter, I proposed that a further useful distinction to be made is that between the terms *affinity*, referring to those who are related by marriage, and *affinability*, referring to the potential for becoming an affine. I confess that I am less convinced today of the value of this particular distinction than I was and regard Viveiros de Castro's formulation of "virtual," "actual," and "potential" affinity as analytically more useful (1993:167–168; see also Viveiros de Castro and Fausto 1993:145). I do not wish to discuss these ideas at length here, but one aspect of them is worth considering in the Guiana context. It has to do with the argument that actual affinity is an impure—contaminated by consanguinity and other factors—and impoverished, localized form. Potential affinity is global and generic and underpins ideas of cosmological exchange through practices or images of warfare and cannibalism—in other words, Viveiros de Castro's "political economy of predation." Bruce Albert (1985) has demonstrated with great clarity and detail how the Yanomami articulate their world in these terms, but I purposely excluded these people from a central role in *Individual and Society* on the grounds that the apparent variation within the group deserved a study of its own, and I sensed them to be sufficiently different from their neighbors to make it difficult to incorporate them in the study. The point I wish to make here is that whereas the other groups of the region clearly have ideas about exchange and interaction with peoples, real and imagined, beyond the confines of kin relationships, they do not seem to form the elaborate cosmological schemata that, for example, characterize the Tupi speakers.

Perhaps one of the disappointments of the past decade has been the relative absence of further regional comparative studies. It is not difficult to point to certain areas, such as the Northwest Amazon or the upper Xingu, where the richness of the ethnography calls out for studies showing internal variance and invariance and their position in the wider Lowland South American scene. Evidence for these sorts of variation has continued to accumulate. For example, Jonathan Hill's (1996a) discussion of the variation as one moves from northeast to southwest across the Northwest Amazon region—from the Arawakan peoples of the upper Rio Negro to the Eastern Tukanoans of the Vaupés region, with the Cubeo and Wanano representing intermediate forms—is highly suggestive and deserves far more attention. Furthermore, it might well be possible to extend this cline farther in both directions. To the east, into the Orinoco basin, the Arawakans are adjacent to Guiana and the near neighbors of the Yanoama. As just mentioned, although I excluded detailed consideration of this latter group from my study, in the final pages I brought certain aspects of these people into play because they had featured in Kaj Århem's (1981) comparative study of the Makuna, Cubeo, Yanomamö, and Piaroa. These four groups lie along the cline just mentioned, and although this new foreword is not the place for detailed examination, I cannot but be struck by the move from types of social and political arrangements characteristic of the groups described in this book through the shallow patrilines found among some of the Yanoama groups, to the strongly hierarchical patrilineal phratries of the Arawakans with their linguistic endogamy, to the linguistically endogamous, phratrically exogamous Tukanoan Cubeo and Makuna, to the linguistic exogamy of the Eastern Tukanoans. There is still much to be done in the arena of regional comparison in Lowland South America.

At the same time as intensive comparison at the regional level has been in a sense shunned, attention has been given to the identification of more abstract metaphysical principles. In some way, these studies have their origins in Joanna Overing's 1981 review article and her proposed "elementary structures of reciprocity." Since then, we might note two further approaches, one of which has already proved influential and the other of which has signs of being so. The first is Viveiros de Castro's "political economy of predation," which I mentioned earlier and which has at its heart the global interactions of potential affinity. That the world ordering of most Lowland South American peoples involves communication across a wider range of peoples and entities, real and imagined, than those involved in marriage, food, and ceremonial exchanges now seems generally accepted. These wider interactions include communication with beings of the invisible world, but we have to ask to what degree this communication inevitably involves predation rather than other types of relationship.[3] The question is implicit in Philippe Descola's (1992) hypothesis, which is the second approach. He has proposed a distinction between "totemic" and "animic" systems; in the former, the differences in nature are used as a model for understanding and organizing relationships with nature. Whereas tropical forest South American systems seem mainly to be animic (although mixed animic and totemic ideas also coexist [see Århem 1996], and the Jê clearly have totemic arrangements), the character of the relationship with "nature" or the "outside" or the "other" varies among these systems. Descola concentrates on those arrangements involving what he calls reciprocity and predation,[4] although in fact predation often involves reciprocity of a "negative" form. In other words, animic societies typified by reciprocity are those that base their social and cosmological theories on the idea of exchange, whereas those societies characterized by predation interact with the outside world in terms of war and revenge. Descola's main ethnographic examples are the Tukanoan and Jivaroan peoples, respectively reciprocal and predatory, although he accepts that both practice the opposite form of interaction in some circumstances (such as wife capture among the Tukanoans).

If today I were to add a chapter to *Individual and Society*, it would be to look at the Guiana material in the light of these ideas.[5] Here only a few perfunctory comments can be attempted. First, the Guiana material does not fit well with the proposed political economy of predation. At first sight, the most promising case is that of the Piaroa. Overing (1986, 1993) has described for them a discourse of predation, cannibalism, and revenge. For example, the Piaroa's relationship with the outside world is metaphorically cannibalistic—both a safe, logically acceptable exocannibalism that involves the consumption of beings different from oneself (affines, fish, and plants) and a dangerous, morally unacceptable endocannibalism that involves the consumption of beings like oneself (kin and forest animals) (Overing 1986:93–94). This relationship reflects Overing's earlier argument (1981) that the dangerous outside is necessary for the safe inside if there is to be a productive and reproductive world. But this discourse is narrow in range (that of Viveiros de Castro's virtual and actual affinity), and if we look at predation on the wider scale (that of potential affinity), we can see that it involves a world separate from that of the living community of people. Overing specifically contrasts the Piaroa case with that of the Araweté, the *fons et origo* of the political economy of predation: "Thus, the world of the social for the Araweté—a people for whom truth and desire always lies [sic] with the Other and in their future afterworld life with and as cannibal gods—is marginalized, and society becomes a precarious space.... In contrast, the desires of the Piaroa are directed firmly toward *this* world which they view as the privileged space within the cosmos, and when in it, unlike the Araweté, they want no contact whatsoever with *their* dangerous and non-social dead" (1993:193, italics in the original).

Among the Piaroa's Carib neighbors, there is even less evidence of the existence of a political economy of predation. This does not mean that ideas about cannibalism and revenge are absent, but merely that they do not form part of the neighbors' cosmological constructs involving humans, animals, and transcendental entities. For example, among the Trio, spirits and wicked shamans are understood to prey on people, whom they then devour (see Myths 49 and 50 in Koelewijn and Rivière 1987). Likewise, death is often explained in terms of sorcery and entails revenge, and even if the spirit world is harnessed for this purpose, sorcery acts and accusations occur between people, although not necessarily those directly known to one another. At death, the soul's path to "heaven" may be beset by dangers and difficulties, but it is not cannibalistically consumed so that it may achieve immortality. Rather, soul matter, which exists in a finite quantity, is recycled (see Rivière 1997). At the same time, it is clear that the Trio relationship with the outside world depends on a nonpredatory reciprocity, even if the reciprocity on occasion turns sour as a result of default or misunderstanding. The first affinal relationship, entered into by the culture hero Përëpërëwa, resulted in the acquisition from his wife's father, the Giant Alligator, of a whole range of cultural elements, including tools, a house, hammocks, gardens, and cooked food (Koelewijn and Rivière 1987: Myth 1). The agreement between the ancestors and the Master of the Peccary, the stereotypical Master of Game Animals, was peccary in exchange for garden produce, and the relationship is explicitly that between trading partners (Myth 17). Similar themes occur among the Waiwai. There is no evidence among the Waiwai for a political economy of predation, but reciprocal exchange is very evident. The first culture heroes received their wives from an aquatic creature, the Anaconda people in this case, to whom the heroes failed to make proper return and to whom the Waiwai thus remain in eternal debt. The exchange between the Master of the Peccary and the shaman is equally unpredatory, involving tobacco for meat, although under certain conditions the Master may exact revenge (Fock 1963:26–31, 42).

A full exploration of the nature of the Guianan symbolic economy must await another occasion, but on first inspection there seems to be no equivalent to the political economy of predation that exists among the Tupi-Guarani peoples. The Guiana peoples, however, are undoubtedly, in Descola's terms, an animic society, and the social life of animals and spirits parallels that of humans. The people's exchanges with the "other" are marked by reciprocity rather than by predation, but at the same time one can recognize a slight unwillingness to fulfill their side of the bargain. In other words, although the outside is essential for the existence and reproduction of the inside, it is still dangerous, and dealings with it should be kept to a minimum.

These new ideas about the metaphysics of Lowland South America, of which I have provided a cursory sketch here, form part of the subject's recent development. I have selected them for a brief consideration because it seems to me that any future studies in Guiana, whether individual ethnographies or wider comparative studies, will need to take them into account. The high level of generalization in both approaches needs to be tested against the specificities of Guianan ethnography. If I am right (and I think I am) that Guiana contains the logically simplest form of Lowland South American social organization, the Guiana evidence will be an essential ingredient in our understanding of the elaborations found elsewhere.

Postscript

If the space were available, I would very much like to have dealt with some of the criticisms of Guianan ethnographers of the 1970s and 1980s advanced in a volume entitled *Redes de relações nas Guianas* (Gallois 2005). In fact, I did have an exchange with the contributors to that volume in 2007 (see Rivière et al. 2007). Simplified, the position taken in this volume is that these previous Guianan ethnographers placed too much stress on the settlement as an autonomous, self-sufficient, inward-looking unit, whereas, in fact, it is enmeshed in networks of external relationships. A straw man lurks here in that virtually every one of those earlier ethnographers stresses the point that the latter is the native model and that, in practice, every unit is demographically, economically, and ritually dependent both productively and reproductively on other like units. Indeed, there are some rich and detailed accounts of how outsiders' involvement is essential for the reproduction of the social person (see, for example, Henley 2001). Furthermore, the readiness to dismiss the historical reality of that earlier period of research is curious considering that Arvelo-Jiménez (1973) had already documented the rapid changes in Ye'cuana social and political organization in response to upheavals of external origin. Thirty to forty years ago the situation across the interior of Guiana was significantly different from what it is today. The ethnographies on which *Individual and Society* relies should now be seen and treated as historical records.

Notes

1. Consistent with the presentation in *Individual and Society*, I have retained the spelling "Guiana" and "Guianan" in this foreword rather than using the present volume's spelling "Guayana" and "Guayanean."

2. I cannot now recall how I came on the image of the kaleidoscope—whether I thought it up for myself or borrowed it from someone else. B. J. Isbell uses the notion in a rather different way in her study of the Chuschi in the Peruvian Andes (1978:11–12), but I doubt that I took it from her.

3. Later changed to the more appropriate "symbolic economy of alterity." For my earlier questioning of the use of the term *predation*, see Rivière 1993:513.

4. Descola draws attention to other possibilities, such as the Arawakan peoples of the Andean foothills of Peru, whom he characterizes as having a Manichean worldview (1992:121). Their world has two domains, one with which they interact and one with which they do not.

5. Since 1997, I have done this and looked more closely at Descola's thesis and its applicability to the Guiana region (see Rivière 2001b). Perhaps the easiest thing to do here is to reproduce the abstract of my article:

> This paper is based on Descola's argument that there is an homology between the way in which people treat nature and the way in which they treat each other. He contrasts the Jivaroan peoples with the Tukanoans; the former organizing the relationship in terms of predation, the later reciprocity. A third contrast in the form of the Guiana region is introduced and it is hypothesized that a degree of self-containment, an isolation from nature, will be found there. In fact it is, but it is also possible to identify, depending on data and context, predatory and reciprocal relationships with nature or the outside. It is suggested that this is likely to be generally the case.

7

The Guayanese Paradox

Deníse Fajardo Grupíoní

A paradox derives from the confrontation between the minimalist image of the Guayana region constructed by Peter Rivière (1984) and Joanna Overing (1983–84), on the one hand, and the extensive historical literature about the region rich in descriptions of intense networks of intermarriages, migrations, commerce, and war, on the other. However, ethnographic studies carried out in the 1990s (namely, the Guianas Project) are closer to the image produced by the historical literature about the region.[1]

These studies were searching for a new format for the old challenge of developing adequate models for the Guayanese Amerindians' social forms that had previously been described mainly in a negative way, as lacking something. As a starting point, these studies examined the description of networks of multilocal relations in the region and analyzed social relations in space articulated with social relations in time.

In this chapter, I discuss the possibility of establishing some continuity between sociopolitical units in the past and the present by using historical and ethnological works. I propose that the discourse of "lack" in Guayana be reviewed—such as the lack of moieties, producing the ideal of local endogamy and the subsequent atomism of the residential units; the lack of corporate groups, producing fluidity and amorphism; and the lack of segmentary organization, producing an individualism and minimalism in social forms. My aim is to show that it is only in contrast with other regional models that such "lacks" appear for the Guayana region.

The Basis for the Production of a Regional Synthesis

The ethnographic material produced about the Guayana region until 1950 consists mainly of texts written by European colonists and travelers since the sixteenth century. Among this earlier material are texts produced by Sir Walter Ralegh (1596), Cristóbal d'Acuna (1641), Joseph Gumilla (1745), Sir Everard Im Thurn (1883), Henri Coudreau (1886 to 1899), Olga Coudreau (1900 to 1903), Alexander von Humboldt (1907), William Curtis Farabee (1918, 1924), Lodewijk Schmidt (1942), and Richard Schomburgk (1836, 1848), among others. Additional important materials are the Jesuit and Franciscan documentation as well as the archives of the Boundary Commissions formed by the governments of Brazil and Venezuela and by the British, Dutch, and French colonies mainly in the early twentieth century—for example, the Anglo-Brazilian Boundary Commission. This material is not uniform and can be called "ethnographic" only in a very generic way. Professional ethnographic works date mostly from the beginning of the 1950s, when studies in increasing quantity and quality were based on intensive and specific fieldwork. Pioneer work as such can be found in the monographs of Napoleon Chagnon (1992 [1968]), Neils Fock (1963), Jean Hurault (1968), and Rivière (1969).

This proliferation of anthropological monographs that brought new approaches to the region, especially in the 1980s, resulted from the publication of a number of works in which anthropological knowledge fed on historical knowledge and vice versa through a confrontation of both the old historiography and the modern ethnological material. Distinguished here are studies by Simone Dreyfus (1993), Nádia Farage (1991), Dominique Gallois (1986), and Neil Whitehead (1992 [1989]), among others.

Just as the so-called set of regional complexities emerged from this kind of material, so too the idea of a "Guianese region" had resulted from earlier works such as "Guayana and Tribal Carib Names" (Goeje 1924) and the surveys published by Walter Roth (1924, 1929) about symbolism, material culture, and customs. The idea's most important source is the *Handbook of South American Indians* (Steward 1946–59), in which John Gillin published "Tribes of the Guianas and the Left Amazon Tributaries" (1948, 3:799–860) and where the Guayana region appears definitely as a "cultural area" (Steward 1946–59, 5:670) within a larger set of ethnographic subareas in South America.

Guayana as an "Ethnographic Area"

Four decades had passed since the publication of the *Handbook* when in 1984 Rivière published *Individual and Society in Guiana* and Overing published the article "Elementary Structures of Reciprocity."

Both works represent important landmarks in Guayanese ethnology. Rivière's work produced the first ample comparative study about the region, and Overing's inserted Guayana in a larger comparative scene alongside central Brazil and the northwestern Amazon.

At the same time, these comparative works launched the basis of contemporary Guayanese ethnology. In their basic formulations, they highlighted a paradox that emerged from the confrontation between the emphasis given to the value of the endogamous ideal, considered a characteristic of the Amerindian peoples of the Guayana region, and the historical literature about the region—rich in the description of intense networks of intermarriage, migrations, commerce, and war—that opposes the picture these authors propose.

Such a paradox intrigues those who study both works mainly because newer ethnographies are closer to the image produced by the historical-ethnological literature about the region than to the image produced by the Guayanese ethnology between the 1960s and the 1980s.

One might question if this contrast arose out of the impact caused by the increasing process of depopulation that hit the region throughout the colonial period until the middle of the twentieth century, when a series of assistance policies began to be implemented by governmental and nongovernmental institutions, thus starting a period of demographic recovery.

The impact of depopulation leads one to assume that the image of "atomism" was the result of a historical coincidence: just as the Guayanese ethnographic corpus was being consolidated with the production of a number of monographs about the region's Amerindian peoples, conditions became adverse to external relations, configuring a social and political landscape significantly distinct from the one we had known until then.

In this case, the atomism recorded in contemporary ethnography was a direct result of a specific but transient historical context. But even if we take the image of atomism as a parameter for comparative analyses with the past or even with the present (after the 1980s), it is an unconvincing picture of ruptures and discontinuities in the social forms that have characterized the region. Rather, it is only when we look at the analytical priorities predominant in these studies, centered in the sociospatial relations, and try to establish a critical distance from African social models that we fully understand what is behind them.

Sociopolitical Units in Guayana

Carrying out fieldwork in the Guayana region is not politically or logistically easy, but there is an even bigger challenge in dealing with the available terminologies for the description of the region's typical sociopolitical units.

The current Amerindian inhabitants of the region are recognized generically under no less than twenty different ethnic denominations. Among them, I highlight those that the Guianas Project has studied—from east to west: Palikur, Galibi of the Oiapoque, Karipuna, Galibi-Marwono, Wajãpi, Wayana and Aparai, Tiriyó and Katxuyana, Zo'é, Waiwai, and Yanomami.

This current picture dovetails with the one that emerges from the historical sources available from the sixteenth century—the stories of the first chroniclers of the region certify the profusion of names—to the first half of the twentieth century, with works such as the one by Protásio Frikel (1958), who identified about 144 groups with distinct denominations in his incursions into the center-south of the Guayana region in the 1940s and 1950s.

In order to understand such disparity in naming, it is necessary to acknowledge that a vast disparity of sources and informants aggregated in many ethnological descriptions. It is rarely clear if one is considering demographic data or rather the changing parameters of naming and cultural ascription.

The complex task of sorting through the naming problems goes beyond this chapter's parameters. That said, however, it is difficult to supply a better analysis of Guayanese Amerindian societies without at least differentiating between two types of circumstances that historically have contributed to modifying the sociodemographic composition of these societies and to constantly redesigning the boundaries between the groups in the region. Processes that underscored the depiction of fluid social boundaries in Guayana—where depopulation was caused directly or indirectly by the European settlement throughout the past centuries and by the installation of assistance policies in Brazil and in the Guianas (French, Dutch, and British) from the beginning of the twentieth century—produced fundamental changes in the extant forms of social aggregation in the region. Alongside these colonially induced changes, processes of fusion, separation, and disappearance of Amerindian groups as a consequence of alliances and wars between different groups have to be factored in to any evaluation of core social logics in this region.

In the modern anthropological literature about the region, we can distinguish two moments of Americanist ethnology: the first used conceptions that appear in the *Handbook,* such as "nuclear family," "extensive family," "lineage," "clan," and "tribe," which presuppose the existence of some constructs based on descent among Amerindian peoples; in the second, such units practically disappeared from the ethnographic texts produced in the 1960s. In the latter period, marked by the criticism regarding the influence of African models in the Americanist ethnology, notions of "local group," "society," and "ethnic group" gained eminence in the description of the social organization of native societies in Guayana.

Images of Guayana's Amerindian Peoples

In *Société contre l'etat,* Pierre Clastres (1974) announced a challenge for Americanist ethnology: to find proactive components in the social forms of the peoples of the tropical forest, and it was exactly in taking up this challenge that Rivière (1984) and Overing (1983–84) focused their comparative efforts.

Nevertheless, in both works the authors came to a definition by negation of the ideal type of Guayana's social organization. In *Individual and Society in Guiana,* Rivière states that in the region there is a lack of corporate groups, a scarcity of human resources, and a lack of sociological mechanisms to manage this scarcity, in addition to other "lacks" that have led him to put Guayana in an elementary position vis-à-vis other ethnographic regions.

And in "Elementary Structures of Reciprocity," Overing states:

> When compared to the highly ritualized social organization of the Central Brazilian societies and with the well-conceptualized layout of the North-West Amazon villages, the endogamous kinship groups of Guayanese Amerindians appear fluid and amorphous in shape. In the Guianas there exists no complex

spatial figuration reflecting the order of social life; there are no naming groups, no moieties in ritual exchange with one another acting out ceremonially a particular vision of cosmological ordering or expressing an eternal ordering of "another world" from the mythic past. There exists no ritual to declare the elaborate interlocking of the units of which society is comprised. To sight [sic], Guayanese social groups are atomistic, dispersed and highly fluid in form. (1983–84:332)

Thus, the northwestern Amazon and the central Brazil models supply the comparative parameters.

But how is it possible that the positiveness of the Guayanese model has been found exactly in the absence of institutional and ceremonial forms present in other ethnographic regions? In other words, how is it possible to find positiveness in absence and in its own negativeness?

This vision is based on two notions reiterated in the ethnographic Guayanese literary corpus since the 1960s: on the one hand, the economy of the organizational and institutional forms of the regional sociological landscape, from which come the reputation of "Guayanese minimalism"; on the other, an implicit positioning in crediting such parsimony and attitudes to a native ethos inherent to such societies, without taking into consideration other possibilities, such as those given by the historical dynamics that all societies display.

Here we return to the question of knowing whether the image of Guayanese atomism and minimalism corresponds to a native structural form and to historical circumstances or is a result of anthropologists' analytical focus and theoretical biases. Once more, however, it is necessary to leave this discussion on hold, with the promise of addressing it in the future.

Rivière's and Overing's comparative works made possible the systematization of a kind of "ideal type" for Guayana, constructed from the rich harvest of ethnographic studies about different groups of the region produced between the 1960s and the early 1980s.

The two authors make a crucial divergence regarding the structural principle of Guayanese groups; for Rivière, that principle is the ties of consanguinity, whereas for Overing it is "alliance-based groups," even though both models emphasize the endogamous ideal for local groups.

Rivière synthesizes his model by highlighting the following characteristics common to the region: cognatic descent, two-line prescriptive relationship terminology, preferred settlement endogamy or uxorilocal residence or both, emphasis on coresidence in ordering relationships, and small and impermanent settlements (1984:4).

Overing, in turn, although not opposing Rivière's model with regard to the analytical use of the cognatic, refers instead to the prescriptive character of the forms of marriage and to the uxorial tendency, given the supposed importance of relations of affinity in the constitution of the local groups. This view inspired a shift in the analytical focus from the internal level to the local group and to the relations among local groups.

This analytical perspective can be found in the work of other authors, such as Bruce Albert (1985) and Eduardo Viveiros de Castro (1986), as well as of a later generation of researchers dedicated to demonstrating the sociocosmological dominance of affinity over consanguinity and of the exterior over the interior in the Amerindian social systems.

This critical perspective allowed a wider appreciation of excessive focus on kinship and emphasized the need to give account of the networks that articulate the local groups. However, the Guayanese ideal type was not questioned, and most authors continued to accept the minimalist image of the region despite the fact that they disagreed with the highly local focus it entailed. The starting point of the Guianas Project was the need to reveal the multilocal networks found in the region, and it resulted in a number of principles that contrasted with those previously postulated.

Openness and Closure in Amerindian Guayana

The Guianas Project research shows evidence of the impossibility of reaching an understanding of the socio-organizational structure of the Guayanese Amerindian peoples without correlating social relations established in space to relations established through time. Lack of correlation makes it difficult to take the local group, as defined by Rivière (1984), as the basic unit of analysis because according to this model one analyzes such a social unit only in its synchronic aspects.

Therefore, the local group is synonymous with "village" and "settlement." It possesses a physical and social reality circumscribed to a place and a given period of existence. Each one is unique in its configuration and its sociodemographic composition; and the time it lasts is highly susceptible to internal or external circumstances—leading to abandonment for political reasons, such as conflicts between families, or for ecological reasons, such as plagues or the exhaustion of resources nearby, or, within a certain length of time, for reasons of another order, such as the death of its founder.

Seen from the perspective of the local groups, the basic unit of this system does not ensure social continuity. Because of the impermanence and inconstancy of their existence, local groups appear temporary. The image of them that emerges is one of loose social ties and the constant meeting and dispersion of individuals. One might say that, given the ephemeral nature of local groups, the sociological unit is questionable with regard to its capacity to produce social groups worthy of sociological analysis.

From another point of view, such a unit is not just a spatial phenomenon but also an historical one. In the perspective adopted in the analysis of the Wajãpi by

Dominique Gallois (1988) and Flora Cabalzar (1997) and of the Zo'é by Nadja Havt (2001), the local group is not synonymous with a "village" or "settlement" composed of a localized and predominantly endogamous bilateral kindred, as conceived of in the majority of monographs on the region. Rather, it is synonymous with a group that cannot be defined only territorially because it is self-constituted through time and exists only in relation to other groups. In this way, it is not circumscribed by a limited temporality or to a delimited space, as is the space of the village as a physical settlement.

The problem is that in working with different conceptions, we run the risk of talking about different things under the same name and then of comparing incomparable things. It is impossible to come to a solution to this problem here, but it is important to highlight such distinct conceptions so that we may move ahead with the argument that when the local group is conceived synchronically, the image that emerges of the social organization is one of dispersion of individuals in groups without sociological consistency due to their high degree of impermanence.

In the Tiriyó case, with which I work, however, I attempt to replace this vision. To do so, I focus on the native category *itïpï*, which means "continuation"—not exclusively, but in a genealogical sense.

Each itïpï has its own denomination, which is followed by suffixes such as *-yana, -koto, -yo,* and *-so*. Thus, among the current Tiriyó, for example, are the following itïpï: Aramayana (Bee People), Okomoyana (Wasp People), Akuriyo (Agouti People), Aramiso (Pigeon People), Maraso (Eagle People), and others. From this perspective, the notion of itïpï is connected to the notion of *pata,* which in the Tiriyó language means "living place" in the sense of a physical unit, such as a settlement located in the space where individuals live who consider themselves mutually *imoitü*, or relatives among themselves. Both notions concern the basic coordinates with which the Tiriyó place themselves in space and time.

Through each of these units—pata and itïpï—we have access to differentiated prisms of the social relations system. The pata favors synchronic frameworks, and the itïpï diachronic frameworks. Both units constitute inside them collectives of distinctive yet complementary natures. An individual has no alternative but to be part of both at the same time: it is not possible to live in a given place and at the same time not *belong* to a continuation in the genealogical sense. That is to say, Tiriyó individuals place themselves in space and time in a nonexclusive way.

Thus, it can be said that a person lives, locates herself or himself, is born, dies, or currently lives in a pata with a set of bilateral relatives. Not only the Tiriyó but also other beings that are part of the cosmos—as it is conceived—live in their respective patas. Humans as well as the animals and spirits that populate the universe are conceived as beings that inhabit places called "pata" and that likewise relate with their respective *pataentu* (literally, "owner of the place").

The itïpï, for its distinct nature, cuts the social set not in space, but in time. Thus, in a synchronic vision of the system, it is impossible to map the set of people

The Guayanese Paradox

who compose an itïpï: first, because the itïpï possesses a historical depth that exceeds any synchronic plan, and, second, because from a spatial point of view, although the members of an itïpï are associated with a place of origin, they circulate throughout their lifetime among the different pata that compose the social relations system in which they are inserted.

And here we get to a point recurrent in our research in the Guianas Project: the dispersion of groups of brothers in search of marriage alliances out of their places of origin. In this sense, different studies demonstrate that the dispersion of siblings and local exogamy in Guayana—that is, the marriage with someone from another village—are not exceptions, but rather a recurrent movement, complementary to closure and local endogamy.

In effect, closure and endogamy are tendencies that stand out when we analyze relations that are limited to the lifetime of a local group. However, as demonstrated by Gallois and Havt (in Gallois et al. 1999), among the Zo'é it is the exogamous alliances that are at the base of the constitution of the local groups, and it is the continuity of the exchanges between them that generates local endogamy. This preference will prevail until the village goes through some kind of split. Among the causes for such a split are the death of an important member, conflicts that for some reason produce disruption of marriage alliances, and the quest for new alliances.

The Karipuna case, in turn, demonstrates the way in which, after decades of intense contact with non-Amerindian peoples, a Guayanese group that is highly heterogeneous from the point of view of its social composition can be an example of the model that the Guianas Project has identified as typical of the region. The Karipuna present a large number of extremely closed alliances of the avuncular type, but at the same time they also present a significant number of marriages with "outsiders," whether Amerindian or not. According to Antonella Tassinari, "The two tendencies of marriage of the Karipuna—the one of closure, manifest in the endogamy at the level of the extensive family, and the other one of openness, evident in the valuation of unions with outsiders—constitute two movements, apparently opposing, but that are complemented in the construction of a proper pattern of social organization" (1998:179–180).[2]

The movement of openness to others in the region is made the moment a man leaves his village in search of a marriage alliance either for himself or for his children or, as occurs more frequently, for his grandchildren. It can be a search for the replacement of a previous exchange or for an alliance with a group with which his family had never exchanged wives.

When one focuses on the local group, the relations established, whether between members inside the group or between members of different local groups, appear from a synchronic point of view to be relations of an interindividual character. However, when we shift the focus to the history of the relations that each individual carries with himself, we see that because this individual is someone's son, grandson, or great-grandson, he is not a neutral individual in space, but carries in himself an accumulation of previous relations that act toward both favoring old or new alliances and making difficult old or new alliances with others.

Thus, despite the often reiterated absence of corporate groups in Guayana and the proclaimed absence of any construct of descent in this region, the Guianas Project research shows that we cannot deny the existence of some type of social distinction tied to descent, which makes it possible for individuals to classify themselves not only as close or distant, but also as equal or different among themselves, and to give this distinction some type of operation in the social structure.

For the groups studied in the Guianas Project, ethnographic data on the Palikur and the Tiriyó point in this direction because in these groups it is possible to identify units to which individuals say they belong as being based on some filiation criterion. Other groups—such as the Wajãpi, the Galibi-Marwono, the Zo'é, the Waiwai, and the Wayana and the Aparai—also show indications, in one degree or another, of precisely this aspect.

In the Tiriyó case, the term *itïpï* returns us to a notion of the "continuation" of a people who succeed one another through time. In order to ensure such continuity, the members of one itïpï must marry members of another itïpï. This prerequisite for marriage among the Tiriyó is not so evident because they do not usually verbalize it.

In order to understand this movement of the itïpï, or subgroup, toward exogamy that is parallel to the inverse movement of the pata, or local group, toward endogamy, it is necessary to have in mind that neither in a hypothetical point of view nor in a historical and concrete point of view can an itïpï be thought of as an independent unit. An itïpï exists only in relation to another itïpï. Such relation, independent of being peaceful or warlike, has among its purposes the establishment of ties of marriage alliance.

The stage for this relation between differentiated itïpï is the physical and social space of the pata (i.e., of the village). It is in this space that the alliance purposes of the itïpï materialize. Descent and exogamy no longer make the same sense they make in the itïpï stage. The pata is logically the result of an initial exogamic alliance, and its movement is to reiterate previously established alliance ties among individuals belonging to different itïpï that came to share a common life.

In this sense, the movement of the pata is logical and ideally endogamous, and, according to this perspective, the importance of descent gives way to the importance of alliance, and the exogamic ideal gives place to the endogamous ideal.

Thus, it can be said that the logic of the itïpï is one of openness to the exterior, and the logic of the pata is one of closure. So the itïpï moves to create ties of interdependence with other itïpï, whereas the pata, which is really the fruit of these ties, moves toward autonomy.

The Guianas Project studies have demonstrated that among Guayanese Amerindians there exists a great diversity of native conceptions as to how to designate collectivities of people—conceptions that do not coincide with the village boundaries or with its ethnic boundaries, but that cross such boundaries and introduce

The Guayanese Paradox

difference. In this sense, the Galibi-Marwono "race," the Wajãpi *wan,* the Palikur clan, as well as the Tiriyó itïpï reveal the importance of the social distinction tied to temporal depth in the region and point to the need to work with the notion of "network," as suggested by other authors (e.g., Dreyfus 1993; Farage 1991; Gallois 2005; Viveiros de Castro 1993).

From a wider point of view, such notions seem to come close to the Shuar notions of "people" and "tribe," discussed by A. C. Taylor (1985, 1993), and to the Piro's conception of "classes of people" or *razas,* as described by Peter Gow (1991: 85). They also suggest comparisons between the Carib suffix *-yana* and the Pano suffix *-nawa* (cf. Erikson 1993; Sáez 2006).

Because of their nature, such notions point to the "character of flux" that Viveiros de Castro (2002:105) suggests with regard to Amerindian Amazonians' collective identities, which makes problematic not only the use of the classical conception of "tribe," but also the use of the conceptions of "society" and "ethnic group" to describe the Amerindian Guayanese peoples.

In a general way, our studies through the Guianas Project have not produced yet another ethnographic reality guided by other principles. Like the Guayanese ideal model, our research points to similar aspects among groups such as the predominance of the prescriptive marriage between bilateral cross-cousins and of the avuncular marriage, the cognatic descent, and the uxorilocal tendency. However, in our analysis, such social forms assume distinct contours. Thus, if on the one hand we recognize cognatism as a form of descent typical of the region, as the Guayanese ideal model proposes, on the other hand we do not consider that the Amerindian peoples used this form to neutralize filiation and make it undifferentiated. Our research demonstrates that among the studied groups, a descent, in spite of being conceived as cognatic, invariably reveals patrilineal or matrilateral biases depending on the specific dynamics each group assumes in relations between filiation and residence because both generate some kind of unilinearity by reaffirming the strengthening of ties—at times in one direction, at times in another. The point leads us to agree with Clastres (1977:36–55) in his stance that even though one cannot speak of lineage when descent is bilateral, one also cannot speak of neutral or undifferentiated filiation because the very rules of residence by themselves are already responsible for a certain degree of unilaterality and therefore for attributing differential values (or weights) to the *patri* and *matri* lines.

We are not "discovering" new things, but rather identifying some formulations previously suggested in the historical and ethnographic regional literature. Therefore, we should also take into account that when we shift the focus of the analysis, we are able to question a number of points in previous characterizations of the typical Guayanese social unit, such as the assumptions that the prescriptive alliance is not based on a descent scheme, that the local endogamy in the region is supposedly strong, and that the character of interlocal marriages is statistically residual.

Some nonvariables emerge from our comparative approach in addition to the ones mentioned earlier, regarding the marriage exchange networks that come into existence through the dispersion of groups of brothers, the operationality of the patri or matri inflections in the scheme of bilateral descent, and the construction of social relations on the basis of alliance and descent.

Thus, the image of the Guayanese social system that emerges from our research is one in which the constant imbalance between openness and closure, dispersion and isolation, exogamy and endogamy, and descent and residence reveal an open system and a living world in an eternal process of construction, where "the openness to the other"—as Claude Lévi-Strauss (1991) proposed for Amerindian thought —appears also as a structural aspect.

Notes

1. When studying both works, one is intrigued by this paradox, as happened with the members of the research project Indigenous Societies and Its Boundaries in the Southeastern Region of the Guianas (known as the Guianas Project), coordinated by Dominique Tilkin Gallois at the Nucleus of Indigenous History and Indigenism of the University of São Paulo, which serves as a base for this chapter.

2. The original text in Portuguese is: "As duas tendências de casamento dos Karipuna —a de fechamento, manifesta na endogamia no nível da família extensa, e a de abertura, evidente na valorização de uniões com pessoas de fora—constituem dois movimentos, aparentemente opostos, mas que se complementam na construção de um padrão próprio de organização social."

8

Imagining Group, Living Territory
A Kali'na and Wayana View of History

Gérard Collomb and Francís Dupuy

On the occasion of the publication of *The Maroni River Caribs of Surinam* (Kloos 1971), Peter Rivière (1973) observed that, in spite of having been transformed by several centuries of colonial presence on the Guianese coast, the Kali'na society studied by Peter Kloos showed characteristics that linked it to other Carib societies. This remark presumed the construction of a social model common to those societies (Rivière 1984).[1] The Kali'na and, not surprisingly, the Wayana essentially relate to this model where the pertinent social unit is the residential settlement (as proposed by Rivière) that revolves around a man (who is usually elderly), his nuclear family, his married daughters, and his sons-in-law. His sons and their wives can also be added to this unit (however, this is rare because residential rules are, in principle, uxorilocal), as well as other nuclear families who may not be directly related to him as founder of the settlement, but who enjoy a clientelist relationship with him. Productive activities are conducted, goods are circulated, and collective work forms are organized from within this residential settlement. It is also from here that manioc beer (*cachiri*) celebrations take place, celebrations that nourish a rich social life and provide a meeting point for kin groups and allies living far away from the village.

In these societies, the political locus (in the sense that it defines the institutional form of "being together") is closely associated with the person of the founder of the residential settlement (the *tamusi*) and the relationship he establishes with surrounding people, who are his dependents, his *peito*. The actual social unit thus stems from relationships of alliance, uxorilocal residence, and bride service (temporary, in principle) to which sons-in-law are submitted, but which they can try to avoid in order to reinforce the residence (and the filiation) on the patrilinear side.[2] Alliance is thus the structural dimension of kinship, which models residential units and creates social dynamics, compelling the regular rebuilding of kinship relationships through frequent relocation to other villages: nuclear families are susceptible to leaving the settlement because of cohabitation difficulties, ultimately either establishing a new village or joining another.

The strength of this model undoubtedly lies in its capacity to embrace the diversity of situations in the Guianas and to render a comparison with models relevant to other societies in the Lowlands. It nevertheless has its drawbacks. Although it is able to account for group morphologies, it is unable to explain the dynamic almost permanently at work in their formation and functioning, and it does not allow understanding of the fluidity and continuous recomposition that characterizes the very logic of these social ensembles (Whitehead 2003a). A dynamic reading, complementary to a functionalist approach, thus requires an historical analysis of the processes constructing collective identities in order to consider jointly an important Amerindian social fragmentation and the existence of large regional ensembles—such as how history makes these identities appear and how they have survived up to today in the indigenous social representations and practices. In this endeavor, following propositions made by Marshall Sahlins (1985), it seems useful to replace these societies, as far as possible, into their proper time and space to see how history (or events) and structure have interacted to create a state of becoming.

Two Carib Groups—Two Contexts

The border zone between the former French and Dutch colonies and Brazil where these different powers played out their territorial rivalries is the implantation site of the Wayana[3] (on the upper side of the Maroni River, or the Litani) and the oriental Kali'na, the Kali'na *tilewuyu,* whom Europeans called "Galibis" for a long time.[4] The former group, coming from the Brazilian side, is quite recent in the region, whereas the latter has been well established for a long time on the coast.

The Wayana today are divided into three subsets: in one, they live on the Paru River (a tributary on the Amazon's left shore); in another, on the upper Tapanahoni (a tributary on the Maroni's left shore in Suriname); and in the third, on the Litani.[5] Since the eighteenth century, this ensemble has been slowly moving from the south side to the north side of the Tumuc Humac Mountains. Previously established near the Jari and Paru rivers, the Wayana have gradually been expanding to populate the area over the upper Maroni basin. During this process of expansion, they have grown closer to the world of the Maroons, in this instance the Aluku, with whom they have managed to establish a pacific relationship and a complex for exchanges of goods between personalized partners.

The history of the Kali'na tilewuyu unfolds in a different space, inscribed for five centuries in the east of Suriname and the west of French Guiana, in a zone where they have been forming since the eighteenth century, and are, by far, the most important Amerindian population in the region. Throughout the second half of the nineteenth century, the Kali'na tilewuyu became more and more limited in their collective mobility, and their economy became even closer to the colony's activities. From then on, they had only occasional relationships with other Amerindian groups, and in that half of the century they ended up in a new world that they had to share with allogenic populations—Creoles, Europeans, and Maroons from the lower Maroni. They had now fully entered the colonial universe (Collomb and Tiouka 2000).

The Maroni River has formed a historical link between these two populations, but their relationship mostly seems to have been belligerent. The Wayana tradition records many wars against the Taira—the name that the Wayana themselves gave the "Galibis." The Taira appear to have tried to control the river in the eighteenth century and at the beginning of the nineteenth century.[6] The Kali'na tïlewuyu, however, appear to recall vaguely the memory of this river-dominating period: after stepping back into the region of the mouth of the river, they have not had contact with the Wayana, who are themselves established south of the Tumuc Humac or on the northernmost fringe—upstream on the Litani and mostly on the Marouini.[7]

The nineteenth century and the beginning of the twentieth century reinforced the separation between the two groups. France was only marginally interested in the hinterland and abandoned it to long-distance administrative control—the border between French Guiana and Brazil was definitely established only in the years between 1950 and 1960. The "Inini statute" contained the entire hinterland and protected it from coastal influence (between 1930 and 1969), thus accentuating this partition: on one side the Wayana living away from the world of the Whites and Creoles in a strictly Amerindian universe,[8] on the other the Kali'na tïlewuyu having entered a process of progressive cultural and economic assimilation to a dominant society that controlled only the coastal region. The gap between the situations that these two populations have encountered during four centuries of colonial history reveals interesting contrasts: the Wayana until recently (1970s) seem to have conserved a relative economic, cultural, and political autonomy, whereas the Kali'na tïlewuyu have seen their fate constrained to a certain extent by colonial influence since the eighteenth century. Today, both groups have found a status, according to specific modalities and to a varying degree, in the ensemble that constitutes the Guianese society and in the French institutional space (Collomb 1997).

An Indigenous Political Philosophy

Among the symbolic productions through which the Wayana and Kali'na represent their history, both groups readily put forward some narratives when notions of their collective identity are challenged. These stories, which we touch upon here, organize the important elements and references of an "indigenous political philosophy"; they have in common the ability to depict simultaneously the singularity of a group through its attachment to a place (and to create the legitimacy of a primo-occupation) and its indefinite extension through an interconnection of reference levels.

The Wayana Myth(s)

The Wayana discourse places the Wayana ensemble as the result of a fusion of several autonomous groups and their inscription in a certain space; this discourse unfolds in two large versions, more or less competing, but partly in agreement, that account for the group's ethnogenesis.⁹ The first version emphasizes segmentation and assemblage by defining the founding groups as the "true Wayana," thereby reinforcing their position as first occupants of space, which has consequences to this day on the Litani. The second version insists on the fusion process and constructs Wayana identity by reducing the hierarchy between subgroups. In reality, rather than competing, these two versions appear complementary in the sense that they allow a spectrum of legitimacy in the Wayana political interplay.

A first set of narratives identifies two founding groups, the Kumarawai and the Kukuyana (considered the "true Wayana," the Wayana-hle), and hypothetically a third one, the Araguayana. The members of the first group, described as fearsome warriors with exacerbated cannibalistic practices,¹⁰ were neighbors of the Tiriyó and originated from the sources of the Paru. They migrated eastward, allied with the Tiriyó, and warred against the Taira. Then, on the other side of the Tumuc Humac Mountains, they moved northward along the creeks of the upper Marouini, where they were joined by the Kukuyana coming from the upper Jari; it is there that the first French explorers met with the "Roucouyennes" (Tony 1843 [1769]). The Kumarawai would in fact get absorbed by the Kukuyana,¹¹ who would end up constituting the only "true" Wayana, the stock onto which other groups would later graft: the Okomëyana, Opaguana, and Upului (belatedly), to cite only the most important ones. The Kukuyana, as a founding group, despite their extremely reduced numbers today, still enjoy strong prestige, and, as the first ones to settle on the Litani, they are considered the "owners" of this river.

In other narratives, several warrior or civilizing heroes intervene, the most important being Kailawa.¹² Coming from the upper Jari, Kailawa is said to have spent his life making war in the entire region of the Tumuc Humac, notably around Temomairem and Talwakem (two inselbergs situated in the junction zone between the upper Jari and the upper Litani). He waged many wars against neighboring peoples (the Tiriosan, the Pianakoto, and so on), but also against many semihuman and semianimal (*itupon*) "peoples" as well as against monsters. During these wars, he gathered around him young men, all excellent warriors, originating from several groups that had been separated until then. It is through this warrior story and the incorporation of these warriors that Kailawa accomplished the fusion of the groups in a constituted ensemble, the Wayana, to whom he also delivered a series of gifts: plants for feeding (banana), weaving (cotton), and doing magic (the *hemit*); a safe territorial seat (free from enemies and mapped by pathways); and an anthropomorphized space inscribed with references (by giving names to several places). To complete his work, Kailawa killed *tulupele* (an aquatic monster) on the upper Litani, thus unlocking the river and allowing his people to settle down progressively. This story of Kailawa—quickly summarized here—strongly states a principal idea: it is for and through war that the Wayana were constituted as an entity.

But the fusion came with an inverse movement, one referred to as *ëtakpapïtpë* in the Wayana myth, which we translate as the "division" or the "sharing." This "event," which could have happened on several occasions, consisted of undoing what had been agglomerated: in order for remaining wars between subgroups to subside, a decision was taken to gather the peoples' dignitaries: chiefs, great warriors, shamans. At the end of a day and a night of talks and negotiations, a geographical distribution of the groups was decided, the only guarantee to establish peace. In addition, women were exchanged between groups in order to seal the peace.

This logic is not at all obsolete; on the contrary, it continues to operate. For example, on the Paru, the Apalai, considered by the Wayana as a foreign group against which they say they warred much, are today on the verge of being absorbed into the Wayana through intermarriages and the everyday relations of cooperation in the villages; the linguistic difference has not prevented the fusion from happening.[13] The same holds in French Guiana for the Emerillon subgroup (Teko) installed near the Wayana on the Tampok and Litani rivers, whereas the most important section of the same Emerillon lives on the Camopi and the Oyapok rivers, near the Wayãpi (or Wajãpi). It must be emphasized that in this case the linguistic difference is much more important because the Emerillon are Tupi-Guarani.

The Kali'na Tïlewuyu Myth

The Kali'na discourse contemplates history and builds a collective being in a comparable mode through a story that today holds an important place in the oral tradition of the Kali'na tïlewuyu of the Maroni region between French Guiana and Suriname. Stemming from a shamanic thought marked by Jesuit evangelization of the seventeenth and eighteenth centuries, this story recalls the efforts made by the shamans of the village of Ulemali Unti, on the Mana River, to bring back the dead to the earth by realizing what is called *epa'kano:*[14] "Epa'kano was what Whites called a miracle. . . . Everything was ready for what was going to happen, people from the village came and went, and they were all restless: those who are above were coming down." But the transgression of a taboo by a woman from the village impeded the shamans' powers, and epa'kano failed: "Those from the sky then left. . . . That is how everything stopped forever. Then people dispersed" (Collomb 2001:152).

The different versions of this story insist on the fact that this event was the occasion of a gathering of "all the Kali'na," several families coming from the "west" for the occasion, from farther beyond the Maroni. Proceeding through aggregation, the story mentions the maximum extension of the social, linguistic, and cultural space of the eastern Kali'na in a time when, to a large extent, the political, economical, and cultural continuity with the groups from the west of French Guiana and Venezuela had vanished. However, the story also insists on the fact that the persons who left the village of Ulemali Unti after the failure of epa'kano formed the villages on the Mana and the Maroni that we know today or knew in the recent past.

As a background to its spiritual and symbolic dimension, the epa'kano story thus describes a refounding of the Kali'na tïlewuyu world from this historical heart that represents the Mana River, the point of origin of the families occupying the current villages. Moreover, it establishes a discrimination and hierarchy between autochthonous families who took part in this dramatic shamanic enterprise and those who progressively came from Suriname to join them beginning in the second half of the nineteenth century: the latter, according to the epa'kano story, "came when everything had already come to an end" (Collomb 2001:152).

But if the story is indeed a narrative about the past, it is recalled today only to shed light on the present. The memory of the dichotomy between the families who can claim superior status because they took part in the epa'kano ceremony and those who are said to have come "too late" still contributes toward legitimizing the preeminent status claimed by the autochthonous families in those villages, as evidenced by the political challenges experienced by the Amerindian district of Awala-Yalimapo. One further witnesses from individual strategies and political matchmakings, alliances and alliance overthrows, that the structural influences of the local political life still follow quite precisely the shape of the great family constellations but also the division between autochthonous families and "foreign" families (Collomb 2001).

The progressive entry of the Kali'na society from Guiana and Suriname into an institutional order and into political spaces that had been foreign till then cannot be analyzed solely through this autochthon principle or through the preeminence claimed by founding families, but this dimension unarguably continues to play a role in the contemporary Kali'na political dynamic and its ideological frame.

The Components of a Segmentary Logic

The Kali'na, like the Wayana, thus elaborated their history as ensembles who saw themselves as being intersected by processes of fusion and disjunction, adjunction and dispersal: this dynamic is readable in the myths through which these societies mark their inscription in time and space. For that reason, it appears that none of these ethnic entities can be held as definitive and finite, and that no association can be thought of as perennial. In this regard, we can support the analysis of Audrey Butt Colson (1983–84:120), who speaks of a "segmentary system" to describe the social and political dynamic that she observed in two other Carib groups (the Kapon and the Pemon).

If we take away from this "segmentary" model, put forth by Africanist anthropology, its rigidity and its reference to lineage and unifiliation, we will then have a tool that enables us to think a strongly dynamic social reality from this dimension of social groups, a reality that E. E. Evans-Pritchard called "structural relativity." We can then try to identify a group of factors that play together in these dynamics. These factors are of a different nature and of unequal relevance and effectiveness in the two groups' lives; three of them are illustrated by the material presented earlier, and the last one refers to the groups' social forms.

The Reference to the Primo-occupant

A primary factor in these social dynamics is spatial distribution or assignment of territories (i.e., the institution of appropriated spaces). For the Kali'na, as for the Wayana, every subgroup is associated with a place, in general a river, and that subgroup is considered its legitimate occupant. However, even when legitimacy plays into account, the primo-occupant does not consider this place a permanent residence because there are many occasions when the need arises to settle elsewhere.[15]

Other subgroups know and respect these associations between the nuclei of individuals and places. In the case of the Wayana as a constituted ensemble, other ensembles are recognized as having proper territories—even if their definition is subject to debate. This logic is clearly contained in the idea of "sharing" mentioned earlier, which pleads in favor of a definition of those ensembles as full ethnic entities who live, recognize, and identify themselves as such—even if, here again, recomposition is frequent.

War: The Interplay of Fusion/Separation

Another element contributes to this "segmentary" logic: it is what is designated as "war." Even today, war is omnipresent in the Wayana discourse that glorifies the elders' exploits. As a normal, if not ordinary, state of the social relationships in the Wayana society whose image is rendered by myth, "war" is not only the consumption of enemies through which the "social production of persons by persons" is achieved, as Carlos Fausto points out (2001:456), but also inseparably a social fact that allows groups to form against a common enemy or, inversely, that provokes breaks and separation between these groups. In the Wayana memory, it is war that inscribes a territorial claim against those previously established in that territory: space seems infinite in these countries, but that is not always the case, and competition to claim a territory can be strong.

This process has lost some of its importance for the Kali'na because the European presence progressively changed the relationships that had traditionally been established between Amerindian peoples on the Guianese coast. If collective memory preserves the representation of great chiefs and a warring past, the interplay of the colonial powers gave wars a powerful stake through political and military alliances with newcomers, the control of the slavery networks, and the capture of slaves for European slave merchants. Some peoples in the inner Guianas, such as the Tiriyó from Suriname, remember the fear inspired in their ancestors by the Kali'na expeditions seeking slaves to sell in Paramaribo, where Amerindian women and children represented a workforce valued for domestic chores. Such *razzias* were conducted in Guiana and Suriname until the second half of the eighteenth century among the Tiriyó, the Wayana, and the Emerillon, with encouragement by Dutch colonists.

Alliance. Alliance is usually the inverse figure of war. The establishment of peace is generally accompanied by matrimonial alliances that contribute to the fusion of groups. Similar to war, alliance facilitates the absorption of the other or allows absorption by the other—that is what happened, for example, between the Kumarawai and the Kukuyana. Matrimonial exchange and political alliance seem, in this logic, intimately linked and closely complementary, moving toward the same objective. Both conjointly offer the possibility of reaching the same goal as war—that is to say, the incorporation of or the separation from the "other." In other words, war and alliance, or war and exchange, are two social and political actions more or less interchangeable.

It must be added that neither war nor matrimonial exchange nor political alliance is able to abolish the initial affiliation: everyone remembers their association with a precise subgroup (Kukuyana, Upului, and so on) and knows how to situate others in the same fashion. In other words, the fusion that can be accomplished by one or the other mode (war or alliance/exchange) is never definite or closed; it always refers to this "segmentary" logic and to its different levels of embeddedness.

Centrifugal Forces. In the case of the Wayana, as in the case of the Kali'na, the contrast with the world of the neighboring Maroons (Aluku and Ndjuka) reveals two characteristics that have arguably been insufficiently emphasized in terms of their consequences on the functioning of these two Amerindian societies. On one hand, the Wayana and the Kali'na do not possess a cult of ancestors—in the classical sense of this expression that implies a permanent and necessary relationship with the "world of the dead," regularly invoked and questioned to confirm the order imposed on the living.[16] Rather than constituting the dead a grounding force, these two Amerindian societies are preoccupied by the forgetting of the dead and express the desire to flee from them (Taylor 1993).[17] On the other hand, they are not equipped with institutions for conflict resolution—there is nothing here that resembles the *kuutu* (council) found in the Maroon societies. Wayana and Kali'na individuals and families remain at the mercy of interpersonal or interfamilial rivalries, all of which have a potentially dangerous shamanic side: when a conflict exists between rival factions, the only way to solve it is for at least one faction to move on.

These two factors "in negative" ease the regular movement of villages and groups, which does not contradict the fact that the right of primo-occupants is recognized: the Wayana insist on the rule according to which every newcomer must ask the predecessor in the place for permission to settle in turn, which is the condition for an understanding and the basis for exchanges to come.

Exchange Networks

In the end, it must be recalled that these societies are, of course, embedded in social, economic, and cultural spaces operating at a much larger scale. A final factor to consider in this regard—this list is not intended to be exhaustive—are exchange networks. We know how old these networks are and how they are joined together, step by step, throughout the inner Guianas (Butt Colson 1973; Dreyfus 1992; Hurault 1972); we also know their amplitude and importance in terms of establishing a relationship between groups (Gallois 2005). We know, too, that through these networks, ordinary but also precious goods circulated, such as "green stone" figurines (Boomert 1987), as well as goods from trade with Europeans along the coastal area. These exchanges, accompanied by celebrations and sometimes long-distance and lengthy visits, are particularly prominent in Wayana stories and are remembered in Kali'na memory, even if the practice of having such networks is much more ancient. Similarly, these occasions are often invoked to justify movement by subgroups from one region to another, movements that can result in new settlements.

These networks contribute to individuals' and groups' mobility and enable both a cultural proximity and a certain kinship in social forms between the large ensembles present in the greater Guiana region.

Conclusion

The experience of history delivered in the stories of the Wayana and the Kali'na thus emphasize that these ensembles do not present themselves as closed, self-centered entities, but on the contrary as "nebulae" constantly recomposing themselves, either by the incorporation of foreign groups or by scission and differentiation. The different factors identified earlier have modeled these ensembles, deploying them through circumstances, whether provoked or endured, on territories whose boundaries are fluid. Myths recall them, thus explaining how these groups are inscribed in time, in a history—even if chronology is often lacking in this matter. In turn, this history refers to a space, a lived space, invested and codified. Time and space are thus inextricable, as Rivière suggests.[18]

These ways of thinking about history continue to organize and shape the social and political interaction today: just as in the Kali'na a kind of division persists between families who can claim an anteriority of occupation of the lower Mana, in the Wayana of the Litani there is still a marked distinction between the first settlers (Kukuyana) and those who came from the Jari (*jari warikpë*). The colonial experience, however, resulted in the divergence of the history of the Wayana and the Kali'na tilewuyu. For the latter, the dynamic that we have roughly delineated seems to have been challenged on the coast by a particular context, which established a one-on-one relationship with colonial society beginning in the nineteenth century. Therefore, in order to capture—or reconstitute—an explicative model, how should we organize the comparison with the former? In other words, can the groups from the inner Guianas offer material for a social and political "archaeology" of coastal societies?

Notes

1. Laura Rival and Neil Whitehead provide a critique of this model, summarizing its five premises as: (1) a settlement core constituted through cognatic descent; (2) kinship expressed by a two-line prescriptive relationship terminology; (3) an emphasis on coresidence in ordering relationships; (4) uxorilocality as the preferred residence rule; and (5) endogamous, small, and impermanent settlements (2001:3).

2. The practice of bride service encourages mobility and interaction between factions by obliging young men to leave their filiation group in order to join their affine group. This is all the more true because the practice of marrying the cross-bilateral cousin is inconsistently followed, despite the fact that the Wayana still impose it as a rule. The affine relationship is undoubtedly prevalent over the consanguine relationship as a structural force and as a dynamic force within (and between) subgroups.

3. Whom the Europeans formerly called "Roucouyennes."

4. The eastern Kali'na—established between the center of French Guiana and eastern Suriname—call themselves "Kali'na tilewuyu" in opposition to "Milato," a name given to Kali'na populations that were considered mixed with Maroons in the center and the west of Suriname (Collomb 2001).

5. The total Wayana population numbers roughly fifteen hundred persons, the majority (approximately nine hundred) of them gathered around the Litani.

6. Rare European sources on this region from this time period attest to a Taira military presence on the upper Maroni in the eighteenth century (Mentelle 1821; Tony 1843 [1769]). The Wayana themselves recount that the Taira planned to colonize the country and that they were fearsome because they had boats, which the Wayana lacked. Today, the Wayana are capable of identifying the sites of old Taira villages all the way to the Tumuc Humac Mountains and the sources of the Litani. They also report how one day, during a large meeting, peace was established with the Taira and that the Taira then freed the river and settled downstream. See also Chapuis and Rivière 2003:490–505.

7. It is there that Jules Crevaux (1883) in the 1870s and Henri Coudreau (1893) in the 1880s found them.

8. The Wayana have also been in a face-to-face situation with the Aluku (or Boni) Maroons since the end of the eighteenth century, which constitutes an important aspect of this history.

9. One can observe that in this instance, as in many others, the Amerindian voice is rarely unitarian or univocal.

10. "There were many human bones in Kumarawai villages," recall the Wayana.

11. The Kumarawai and Kukuyana are said to have waged a tiring war against the Taira, to the extent that the first of those founding groups lost large numbers of its members and was then absorbed into the second group.

12. Two other lesser heroes are often mentioned: Wapotoli and Sikëpuli.

13. This current incorporation of the Apalai by the Wayana is a reminder of the incorporation of the Upului by the Jari, although more ancient, which historical accounts indicate.

14. From a Kali'na verb form meaning "to extract."

15. Today, despite some infrastructure (health centers, schools, water supply systems) that tends to fix villages settled on the Litani, subgroups or families continue to move for diverse reasons.

16. Such a cult of the ancestors goes hand in hand with the lineage principle (ancestors being a full part of lineage), which is not found in Amerindian social forms.

17. This forgetting in part explains why movements by the Wayana groups often follow a general direction, so that they do not have to retrace their steps for fear of meeting with the realm of the dead.

18. "Time is embedded in and represented by space" (Rivière 1984:99).

9

Historical Perspectives on Areruya Communicative Ideology

Susan K. Staats

Across the Guiana Shield and in nearby regions, many indigenous peoples incorporated paper into their fields of religious action and discourse as a spiritually potent substance or as a token of social power. Edmundo Magaña (1993–94) writes that the Trio of Suriname sometimes apply a Bible to the body of a sick person during curing rituals and (following Bruce Albert) that the Yanomami sometimes keep protective bits of paper in metal boxes. A Wakuénai chant owner told Jonathan Hill that Europeans' dream souls are made of paper: "The missionary's soul is a Bible, the merchant's soul is a financial record, and the anthropologist's soul is his notebook" (Hill 1993:6). Yekuana tell the creation story that Europeans were given paper by the culture hero Wanadi: "They immediately wrote three requests with three words that only Wanadi understood: iron, silver and horse" (Barandiaran 1979:20–21; see also Guss 1986), an appeal that accounted for European economic strength. Just as paper held fascination for indigenous people, these tales hold equal fascination for Europeans. Stories about paper resonate with Europeans' historical self-image, that civilization is conferred upon those who write, but they also further restore Europeans' appreciation of the substance of this power, the paper itself.

In similar fashion, Areruya, one of the major religious traditions in the circum-Roraima region of the Guianas, holds that Paba, the deity shared with Christians, gave an Amerindian Bible to the Kapon founder of the religion. This material object was lost over the years, but hymns tell of another book, *Paba kareda* (God's book or God's paper), in which the deity writes the deeds of each person's life. Another hymn likens Areruya dancers' movements to the turning pages of a book. In this chapter, I outline a potential pathway through which paper became a significant image in Areruya discourse. I argue, however, that other images, like paper, are also associated with modes of communication and are more central to Areruya concepts of spiritual power. Musical instruments known as *wai, iga riga,* and *arawera* that are thought to reside in heaven are the fundamental mechanism of Areruya power because they transmit music and texts to followers during Areruya performances. Thus, as significant as paper seems to be in historical documents on early preaching and missionization in the interior, Areruya prophets embody the central concepts of sacred communication using images of purely indigenous provenance.

Prophets, Piaichang, and Communicative Practice

Areruya is one of the major indigenous religious practices in the circum-Roraima region of the Guianas. In 1998, Areruya leaders in the central village Amokokupai in the upper Kukui River basin in Guyana had ceremonial relationships with thirteen villages in Guyana, Venezuela, and Brazil. These villages maintain church buildings that require periodic blessings from Areruya leaders; the building allows the village to sponsor weekly dance ceremonies. Even without a church to dance in, many families in villages dominated by missionary churches or those living along rivers far from villages sing Areruya *eremu* (hymns) and repeat the spoken genres of *esegungang* (prayers) and *maiyin* (memory verses) daily. Areruya in its present form developed after the emancipation period in British Guiana from 1834 to 1838 as annual distributions of trade goods ended and missionization and logging in the interior took hold. From the ethnography of Audrey Butt Colson (1954, 1960, 1973, 1985, 1998), we know that Areruya practices probably took shape in the latter half of the nineteenth century when *piaichang* (shamans or spiritual curers) learned to use the technique of soul flight to reach the most powerful place in the cosmos, the center of the sky near the sun. This technique represented a broadening of the domains of sacred power: other types of spiritual action in the region, *piai* (spiritual curing) and *tareng* (magical blowing), relied primarily on the relationship between people and spiritual beings in the forests, savannas, rivers, and mountains.

A series of Makushi (Macuxi), Kapon, and Pemon *epugenak*s (prophets) received hymns and spoken texts from God that form the contemporary Areruya corpus. As Areruya was shared across ancient trade networks (Butt Colson 1985), the texts were performed in the language of the original singer, so the tradition has been actively preserved as multilingual (Staats 1996:175). Areruya discourse is a reservoir of historical, ethnic, and linguistic consciousness in an area that is otherwise dominated by social integration through the village or the family compound. The epugenak's position blends elements of other leadership roles: the spiritual contact of a piaichang, the regional renown of a long-distance trader, and the local authority of a village leader. Given that a new social position developed through the authority imparted by new speech forms, it is not surprising that principles of communication are richly elaborated in Areruya discourse and metadiscourse.

In this chapter, I view the musical instruments wai, arawera, and iga riga as symbols that are transformations of communicative ideologies associated with piai and contrast them with the semiotic capacity of paper as a sacred medium. Communicative ideologies can take many forms: explicit commentary on the meanings of speech forms, the ideologies implied by named speech genres, unnamed habits of communication that allocate power differentially, and so on. Communicative ideologies are, as Kathryn Woolard puts it, "implicit and explicit signaling about language-in-use" (1998:4) that both responds to and initiates social changes.

More generally, I draw attention to the possibility that locally recognized forms of communication can be the basis of resonant, multivocalic symbols that are powerful precisely because they unite local concepts of the body and personhood with specific forms of social agency.

Communicative Principles of Piai

Contemporary Mazaruni Areruya people draw a strong distinction between Areruya and piai practices, saying that the original Kapon prophet, Abel, taught that "piai work" is wicked and that Areruya people should have nothing to do with it. Nevertheless, the relationship between piai and Areruya is a complex one. Many of the early prophets underwent piai training in their youth and transformed the spiritual techniques into abilities that allowed them to fly to the sky and learn Areruya texts there, and there is evidence that the two practices coexisted compatibly until recent years (Butt Colson 1954; Henfrey 1964; Staats 1996). Indeed, Neil Whitehead reports that contemporary Patamona Kapon consider Areruya to be a type of shamanism (2002b:150). Some Areruya hymns speak of "Areruya spreading far away," as if the performances of one community can dispel the negative spirituality of neighboring peoples in a somewhat less aggressive manifestation of the piaichang's long-distance attack on other communities.

Very few piaichang openly practice on the Mazaruni River today, but the sense of piai performances that Butt Colson gives from the 1950s is that of highly interactive, often humorous community conversations that relied on revoicing the intonational patterns of the language of spirit beings and ethnic others. Maiongong, Spanish, and English were represented intonationally if not lexically in the performances that she observed (Wavell, Butt, and Epton 1966:45–46). Similarly, Magaña observes that piaichang must learn to speak in the voices of animals in order to communicate with them. The performance of piai is a continuation of earlier conversations with villagers that often produce conflicting speculations on the cause of an illness. Spirits who assist with soul flight are summoned, such as the piai's teacher-partner *uladoi*, *kuwai* (tobacco), *kumalak* (swallow-tailed kite), and Kalawali (ladder spirit), along with the spirits of dead relatives, who discuss the events in the lives of their relatives (Wavell, Butt, and Epton 1966:154).

> As the various spirits and ghost spirits arrive they will, in many instances, ask questions and probe deeper and deeper into the life of the patient. They will also interrogate his relatives and people of the village about their affairs. Sometimes the spirits converse with each other as a number of them assemble about the shaman's bench or possess his body. . . . The continual probing by means of spirit inquiry in a séance allows for an unusually frank confrontation between interested persons. (Wavell, Butt, and Epton 1966:159–160)

Revoicing generally occurs in Areruya performances in only the most prescribed ways—for example, when prayers are spoken line by line by a single church leader and echoed by the participants. The piaichangs' spontaneous revoicing of the language of spirit beings contrasts sharply with current Areruya performance expectations on the upper Mazaruni owing to the intense efforts there to maintain purity of texts and to understand precisely the origins of words. Areruya leaders are deeply suspicious of novel visions or hymns because they are uncertain of the visions' or songs' origins or authorship. To sing a hymn, for example, that might have originated among spirits of the landscape—the forest, savanna, water, and mountains—rather than in the sky would be ineffective and would invite these beings into the village, where they may cause illness and social discord.

In other respects, however, principles of piai communication are elaborated in Areruya performance and ideology, specifically considering the piaichang as a vessel that is filled with spirits interacting with community members. Areruya hymns generally have two or more verses in which lexically similar phrases are exchanged in parallel position. The phrase *iga riga maimu* (iga riga's speech) in the first verse of a hymn might be exchanged for *arawera maimu* (arawera's speech) in the second verse. At the moment when the hymn leader switches to the second phrase, the song's message is said to flow out from the leader's heart to the other singers' hearts. When the leader returns to the first verse near the end of the hymn, the message returns to his or her heart (cf. Hill and Staats 2002). The interactive shamanic séance has in Areruya become a metacommunicative performance principle. Areruya people also say that at the end of time, the *ewang*, or motivating force of all beings, will return to heaven. The husk of the being that is left on earth will be rendered ineffectual: fire will no longer give heat, and food will no longer provide strength. The notion that spiritual power requires a hollow location to contain it is also reflected in beliefs about the body: different parts of the body contain hollows in which spiritual fractions of the person reside. Although Areruya restricts the spiritual revoicing of piaichang, it retains the principle that communicative mediation is interactive and that it depends on understanding a spiritual being as a vessel, a signifier.

Preaching in the Interior and the Trade in Paper

The earliest missions in British Guiana were the Anglican bases established at Bartica at the confluence of the Mazaruni and Essequibo rivers in 1829, at Pirara in Makushi territory in 1837, at W. H. Brett's mission on the Pomeroon from 1840, and at Great Falls and Muritaro on the Demerara. Because the missionaries understood the role of the Kapon as trading intermediaries, the Kapon were the long-hoped-for population of converts. Nevertheless, the impetus for the Kapon to appear in the northwestern district missions and at Bartica came not from the mission work itself, but from several episodes of millennial preaching in the interior (see Whitehead 2002b:142–147 for a fuller account). On separate occasions, informal preachers drew hundreds of people from their home communities, with results ranging from disillusionment to tragedy. These events suggest the development of interest in paper as an exchange object.

A Creole man named Smith who spoke Kapon positioned himself twice as a prophet in Kapon villages in 1844–45 and attracted a large audience with promises of cassava fields that would grow from one cassava stick. After the food supply failed, however, families returned home, only to suffer hunger there, too, because they had neglected their fields. According to Brett, the privations the Kapon faced led them to raid other tribes and set off a series of reprisals by indigenous assassins known as *kanaimà* (Brett 1881:202; Whitehead 2002b). Smith's second endeavor was based along the Kako River, a tributary of the Mazaruni, in Kapon and Pemon territory. This episode contributed in an indirect way to the first wave of Kapon to seek contact with the Pomeroon mission from 1853. Among the many Kapon families who traveled to hear Smith preach in 1845 was one headed by "Capui" from the northwestern district. As food ran out again and families began to return home, Smith gave Capui a "commission written in hieroglyphic characters" authorizing him to assemble others once again at a certain date (Brett 1881:202). The leader discarded the paper and had nothing more to do with Smith. His son, however, came to Brett's mission some years after his father's death and was baptized with the name "Phillip." By this time, Brett had already begun to translate key scriptures into Carib, and Phillip encouraged Brett to do the same into Kapon. After 1863, Brett began to send cards that bore the Lord's Prayer and the Apostle's Creed written in Kapon, accompanied by margin illustrations, to distant communities. The false prophet Smith's strategy of sending written but unreadable letters therefore was an indirect model for Brett's own Christian "hieroglyphic" invitations. Large groups began to visit the mission, including some who targeted Phillip for kanaimà attacks. Those who stayed provided cassava for visitors until 1866, when the mission crop failed and visits subsequently dropped off. Whitehead reports that a decade later the Patamona were using Phillip's pamphlets to study mission teachings (2002b:149, based on Pierce 1881).

Again in the 1840s, Awacaipu, an Arekuna man, drew a large audience with a message centered on gaining superiority over whites. He called people to meet in the Kukenaan Valley in a land that he called "Beckeranta," a Dutch-based name understood as "Land of the White" (Appun 1893:342–343). Those who came to hear him speak gave Awacaipu trade goods and received paper in exchange: pages of books and newspapers. The German naturalist C. F. Appun heard the story in 1864 and recorded that

> [Awacaipu] sent messengers inviting all of them to a great assembly which he intended to hold at the commencement of the dry season, at which he told them they would hear wonderful things and obtain the means of putting themselves on an equality with the white people. They must engage to forget all their quarrels and bring offerings to the mighty Piaiman. . . . Thus it happened in this

Kukenaan valley at the time appointed nearly a thousand Indians of all the Guiana tribes were gathered together. Here they erected huts and waited the pleasure of the great Piaiman and the fulfillment of his magnificent promises. Every family brought presents of knives, scissors, looking-glasses, beads, salempores, ammunition, needles and other articles of value to the Indians, receiving in return, as charms to protect them from the evil spirit, three small pieces of printed paper. These consisted of leaves of books and newspapers, including the *Times,* which had been used by SCHOMBURGK for drying his plants, and were left behind at Roraima when that gentleman wanted to reduce the bulk of his luggage as much as possible. (1893:342, original emphasis)

Awacaipu explained that all those who died on the spot would return within weeks from Mount Roraima with white skins and firearms (Brett 1881; Butt Colson 1954: 81–82), and he set audience members to fight against one another. When the dead did not return after a few days, Awacaipu was killed.

As Neil Whitehead and Silvia Vidal observe, transforming the consumption of human bodies into spiritual and social power is associated with kanaimà assault shamanism (2004:61). At the same time, the exchange of newsprint prefigures preoccupations with paper among practitioners of Areruya, so that the Awacaipu episode can be seen as an unstable mediation of the two major spiritual orientations of the time, Areruya "modernism" and kanaimà "traditionalism" (Whitehead 2002b; Whitehead and Vidal 2004).

Sir Everard Im Thurn (1883) commented on several indigenous churches that he visited on the eastern side of Mount Roraima that had newspaper clippings and pages from novels displayed prominently. Theodore Koch-Grünberg visited the Taurepang Pemon community led by the Areruya adherent Jeremiah in 1911 and found that the leader had great stores of papers from the Muritaro Anglican mission, some written in (Koch-Grünberg assumed) Kapon (1979 [1917]:114). Im Thurn also wrote of a Makushi church in which papers were displayed above what seemed to be an altar: "over this was stuck up a portrait, from the Illustrated London News, of Mr. Gladstone and the first page of a cheap American edition of Mr. James Payn's novels" (1934, qtd. in Butt Colson 1954:86). William Ewart Gladstone, the former British colonial secretary and celebrated prime minister, seemingly kept watch for the Amerindian transformation into white-skinned people that Awacaipu foretold.

In 1921, on his second trip to the upper Mazaruni, Father Cary-Elwes discussed the origins of Areruya with the chief of a village near Amokokupai: "He told me he had the Alleluia on a piece of paper that came from heaven. 'How interesting,' I said. 'Do show it to me.' He brought a small box, full of cotton wool, in the midst of which was a piece of white paper with nothing written on it, about half an inch square. He also brought a bottle in which was a drop of quick-silver 'also from heaven.'" The conversation continued later: "'Tell me,' I said, "who gave you that piece of paper you said came from heaven?' 'Kosari.' he replied, indicating a man standing by. 'How can you do such a thing,' I said to the man indicated. . . . 'Why have you lied to this man?' I said. 'A man from Kamarang gave the piece of paper to me,' he replied, 'and assured me it had come from heaven'" (qtd. in Butt Colson 1998:106–107). This piece of paper had exchanged hands at least twice.

Regardless of the would-be leader's ethnicity, paper became associated with novel bids for spiritual and political authority. At times, it was clearly a communicative medium, as in Smith and Brett's written invitations and in the Amerindian Bible and *Paba kareda*. In other cases, paper became an exchange object that acted as a token of spiritual power, particularly through the preaching of Awacaipu, but apparently also among Areruya people as well. Whether paper was a medium of authorship or an exchange object, it tended to represent unidirectional authority in the spirituality of the interior of British Guiana as Mazaruni people experimented with more authoritarian and regionally integrated forms of leadership (Hill 1984). Indigenous valuation of paper as a medium of unidirectional, authoritative communication is a semiotic representation of the sense of "modernity" that millennial movements, including Areruya, expressed (Whitehead and Vidal 2004). Furthermore, the semiotic capacity of paper, as it was developed in the Mazaruni, contrasted with the communicative ideologies of piai and Areruya performances. Incorporating paper as a communicative symbol into Areruya practice probably reflected a developing concern with the authenticity of sacred teachings and with the uncontrolled revoicing of spirit languages. Indeed, spiritual interaction appears to be a point of philosophical conflict in the development of Areruya. Paper, at least as it was used in Mazaruni spirituality, could be exchanged and could present spiritual authority, but it could not be erased and rewritten. It lacked the potential to mediate human relationships with the spirit world.

Cassiri Bowls as Linguistic Sign: Learning the Language of Heaven

The images that Mazaruni people instead use to understand sacred interaction are the musical instruments wai, iga riga, and arawera,[1] which distribute music and texts to prophets and to the people who repeat their words. Like many Areruya terms, *wai, iga riga,* and *arawera* have an everyday meaning. All of these terms, but most commonly *wai* and *arawera,* can refer to tape recorders and stereos that distribute music to people, a usage that immediately resonates with the sacred meaning of the terms. In everyday life, though, *wai* also refers to a small container for serving the cassava drink known as *cassiri*. Wai is a warm and domestic image, the passing bowl that family and friends drink from, the container that mediates the distribution and sharing of sustenance. In this sense, it fulfills the promises of the early preaching and mission experiences that instead ended in hunger. Like the Creole preacher Smith's miraculous cassava stick that could produce an entire cassava farm, wai expresses spiritual replenishment through the metaphor of physical satisfaction.

Wai also represents one of the region's economic strengths. Clay pots known as *oini*[2] were one of the major items of local manufacture that the Patamona contributed to the indigenous trade system, so that wai also allowed for regional economic integration (Butt Colson 1973; D. Thomas 1972). Like paper, wai was an object of exchange, but it resolves the issues of spiritual communication that paper cannot. It is a hollow vessel that contains life-sustaining substance—a vessel that is drunk from, shared, drained, and refilled. As a musical instrument, it preserves sacred authorship and mediates the performance of these texts in multiple contexts.

Unlike images of books and paper, references to wai, iga riga, and arawera are almost obligatory in Areruya performances. Hymns referencing these instruments often occur near the beginning and end of singing and dancing ceremonies to remind people that the music that they are singing originates in heaven and represents the deity's authentic teaching. Wai, iga riga, and arawera also occur in a genre known as *maiyin*, translated as "memory verse," that closes every Areruya performance. Maiyin texts have a standard core of some fifty ordered words, segmented into stanzas, that express images fundamental to Kapon life. These words start with foods such as water, fish, bird, meat, meat broth, cassava bread; items of clothing; sacred music instruments, including wai, iga riga, and arawera; powerful implements such as axes, shotguns, and shotgun shells; and Areruya prophets and spirit beings. They finally pass into the church in heaven to end at the throne in the center of heaven. Maiyin words are folded into particular maiyin texts by associating the words with a repeating phrase, as in a maiyin that tells of the events at the end of time:

tuna ewang mokaning (water spirit leaving)
morok ewang mokaning (fish spirit leaving)
torong ewang mokaining (bird spirit leaving)

Taken together, maiyin words trace the pathway of a soul from an earthly to a sacred domain (Staats 2003), and as we see in the following list of words, wai, iga riga, and arawera introduce this shift in setting in the fifth stanza:

tuna	water	*kiari*	food
morok	fish		
torong	bird	*maming*	apparel
ok	meat	*arika'*	scissors
tuma	meat broth	*sarai jarai*	hair comb
egi	dry cassava bread	*wanamari*	mirror
		mawasa	razor
pïzau	cassiri bowl		
wai	cassiri bowl	*sabado*	shoe
wa'nok	drink	*puküru*	trousers

pokiri	belt	*keyapo*	cap
awüni	beaded pectoral	*arakapiza*	shotgun
arok	hat	Jise Kulai	Jesus Christ
keraba	hair oil	Pregomang	Pregoman/Elijah
wai	musical instrument	Mochi	Moses
iga riga	musical instrument	Epurï	Abel
arawera	musical instrument	*enjeru amuk*	angels
sedumba	musical instrument	*apaji*	sister
sambana	musical instrument	*megabaji*	megabaji
kurak	clock	*anjijiria*	anjijiria
aibiribing	God's power	Richabek	Elizabeth
kompas	compass	Remangbaji	Mary
maming	apparel	*pada*	heaven
kazurü	bead	*proroi*	churchyard
kamichang	lap cloth	*sochi*	church
maria	knife	Kad	God
waka	axe	*wii*	sun
kurupara	gunpowder	*abonok*	throne
piroto	shotgun shell		

Areruya people say that besides describing the final movement of a person's soul, maiyin words form the language that people will use in heaven—when people speak, they will need only the terms *tuna, morok, torong,* and so forth, but in heaven the current meanings of words will detach themselves, and new meanings unknown to living people will inhabit the lexicon. The link between the signifier and the signified will be dissolved. That Areruya requires a Saussurean concept of the sign derives from the sense that spiritual substance, motivating power, and now linguistic meaning need a vessel within which to reside—a belief that is echoed throughout Kapon concepts of empowering mediation: the piaichang who is the vessel for multiple spirits, the drinking bowl wai that holds cassiri, the spiritual entity that loses its ewang at the end of time, and the Areruya leader who sings a message into dancers' hearts and takes it back again for safekeeping.

Conclusion

New forms of leadership and spirituality in the Mazaruni were supported by reconsiderations of sacred communicative processes. Religious leaders in the interior—European, Creole, and indigenous ones—all sensed that paper possessed the communicative potential for a single author to engage many others and so to make possible new forms of social relationships. Areruya shared this interest in developing symbolism and metadiscourse that allowed for an increased degree of centralized spiritual authority; the communicative potentials of paper and writing influenced attempts to remake Kapon communities in both pre-Areruya and early Areruya movements. The genius of the figure of wai, however, is that it allowed Areruya leaders to co-opt the authoritative, unidirectional elements of writing but at the same time to preserve indigenous spiritual positions that writing and paper could not fully express. The figures of wai, arawera, and iga riga relied on indigenous concepts both of the body as a vessel of spiritual power and of spiritual agency. Areruya prophets reinterpreted the communicative practices of piai so that leaders could mediate between the spirit world and the community, but only through the recognized words of the prophets.

Ironically enough, diminishing the importance of paper as a metacommunicative principle in Areruya ideology and performance led to an unexpected correspondence in indigenous and Western philosophy. The indigenous view of the interdependence of the spirit and the quotidian worlds found expression in wai, the vessel that encloses spiritual power and that metonymically represents the entire sacred lexicon formed by maiyin words. The Mazaruni interpretation of the sign, like Saussure's, takes vocal sound as essentially linked to meaning but inverts their roles. The vessel wai plays the role of the sound vehicle, and the musical power that it projects is the essential meaning and nourishment that it provides. This indigenous take on Saussure's sign allows Mazaruni people to prepare for life after death as they memorize the language of heaven.

Acknowledgments

I gratefully acknowledge the support of the Wenner-Gren Foundation and the Graduate School of Indiana University, which supported my research in Guyana in 1997–98.

Notes

1. None of my consultants has been able to offer a physical description of the three musical instruments or define a functional difference among them. They collectively are the single, authentic source of the word of God.

2. It may be worth considering the sound /wai/ as a morpheme in northern Carib languages because we have many examples of it in words that seem to connote roundness, containment of transformative substance, sometimes social integration, sometimes social transformation. In Kapon, there is *waiakapiapï*, the stump of a great tree reaching between heaven and earth from which grew all the plant foods of the world (Butt [Colson] 1954:58). The cutting of the world tree allowed great torrents of water to flow, forming all the rivers known to other circum-Roraima people (Civrieux 1980). In Taurepang, there is a conch shell trumpet called *uayi-kulu:* Erich Hornbostel writes that the original owner of piai knowledge, the mountain spirit Pia'ma, was killed by a conch shell trumpet (1955–56:139). This mythic triumph of sacred music is incorporated into upper Mazaruni Areruya ceremonies, too, which are usually opened by blowing a conch

or cow horn shell. In Yekuana, there is the *waijama*, ritual singing that celebrates the construction of a roundhouse, first performed by Wanadi "in a ceremony of thanksgiving and joy for having completed the first replica of the universe ever built on earth" (Arvelo-Jiménez 1971:192). Among the Yekuana, too, there are ritual specialists called *jowai* as well (Arvelo-Jiménez 1971:182).

10

Tongues in Space
Pa'ikwené (Palikur) Language(s), Relatedness, Identity

Alan Passes

> In heaven we'll speak one language; here we speak many.
> —Pa'ikwené villager

The Pa'ikwené,[1] an Arawakan clan society of northern Brazil and French Guiana, occupy a singular position in the Guayana region comprising four interconnecting elements: the native world, the Creole world, Brazil, and France. Following extensive missionizing by fundamentalist Protestant sects, they have recently tended toward large multiclan communities affiliated to particular denominations (Capiberibe 2001, 2007; Musolino 2006; Passes 1998), a fact relevant to the following discussion with regard to the part played by ideological differences, concomitantly with linguistic differences, in the contemporary creation of ethnic and national identity. Expanding my earlier writing on the subject (Passes 1998: chaps. 3–5, 2003, 2006), I focus on the linguistic behaviors and choices (and their link with history and place) of the younger members of two adjacent French Guianese Pa'ikwené villages near the town of St. Georges on the Oyapock River, the frontier between French Guiana and Amapá State in Brazil. The communities, Premier Village Espérance and Deuxième Village Espérance, hereafter Espérance 1 and Espérance 2, share clan ties but are split over religion and language use.

My premise is that the two subgroups use language not only to mark out, but also to "activate" their own distinct niches, or homes (Ingold 1995), in the wider Guayanese space; this space and the Pa'ikwené's situation within it are to be seen in the social rather than the geographical terms of an "activated place" (Certeau 1984)—a lived relational and cultural space created and sustained by human agential practice (cf. Corsín Jiménez 2003; Ingold 1995; Munn 1990; Overing 2004; Raffles 1999). Such practice, interactive and dialogical (Tedlock and Mannheim 1995), is embedded in an Amazonian understanding of sociality predicated on a system of values that stresses sociability and inclusivity (Overing and Passes 2000a, 2000b).

The Pa'ikwené are long conversant with a stratified universe in their relations with nonindigenous others and in their cosmology. Living Pa'ikwené and other "real humans" inhabit the social surface world, Minika or Maywak, which is interlinked with four supernatural spheres: Wainpi (Underworld), Ëna (Highest Sky), Mikené (Middle Sky), and Inúgik (Lowest Sky), which Pa'ikwené Evangelical-Pentecostals have reinvented as heaven (Green and Green 2003; Nimuendajú 1971 [1926]; Passes 1998:chap. 9). Such a configuration fits Joanna Overing's profile of a "multiverse," whereby Amazonian space is activated by the interpenetration and interaction of a multiple-world landscape of mythic beings and practices with the human landscape of social practice (2004:81–84). I suggest that the Pa'ikwené also dwell in another multiverse, a coinhabited territory in which multiple national, ethnic, and cultural entities as well as subgroups and individuals construct their particular spaces, each of which is simultaneously historical, societal, political, linguistic, and ideological.

Historical Context

The Pa'ikwené's location on the northeasternmost edge of Brazilian Amazonia, one of Guayana's outer limits, spares them being tagged as thoroughly wild and uncivilized, as the peoples of the interior "at the end point of exploration" are (Whitehead 2003b:68). Yet in nonindigenous representational terms generally and in expansionist political-economic terms particularly, the Pa'ikwené, etymologically the "People of the Middle," are terminal and "peripheralized" (Passes 2002; Santos-Granero 2002b), despite their centrality to the region's history.

Archaeological and narrative evidence places the Pa'ikwené in Amapá and what is now French Guiana before the Conquest. Western awareness of the Pa'ikwené (in south Amapá) and the appearance of their name (in various forms) on maps date back to the beginning of the sixteenth century CE. They virtually dropped off the Western radar for the next 150 years, but Pa'ikwené oral history recounts their presence in northern Amapá, where they consolidated into a powerful confederation that played a key part in a panregional macropolity, with extensive ties to fellow Amerindians throughout Amazonia. The Pa'ikwené were influential in the Arawak coalition that fought a protracted war against the Caribs across northern Amapá and the wider Guayana region, which was recorded by various Europeans, including Dutch, English, and Irish settlers on the Oyapock. Hard contact with the Pa'ikwené was finally made in 1653–54 (Biet 1664). In colonial times, they had an instrumental and better-documented role (see, e.g., Fauque 1839) in the Franco-Portuguese conflict over control of Amapá, in which, to defend themselves against Portuguese slave raids and deportations, they sided with the French (Dreyfus 1981; Green and Green 2003; Grenand and Grenand 1987; Nimuendajú 1971 [1926]; Passes 2002, 2004a).

When Brazil gained possession of Amapá in 1900, numerous Pa'ikwené opted to join those of their group already established on the lower Oyapock in French Guiana. When the group was depleted by disease by the 1920s, most survivors returned to the homeland in Brazil, Aúkwa (Uaçá River region). Over time, the culture and language of those who stayed in French Guiana became increasingly influenced by the Creole world (with which the Pa'ikwené had long enjoyed economic relations). Their descendants, together with more recent incomers, compose today's French Guianese Pa'ikwené population (roughly half the total population of some 1,800 Pa'ikwené). Perhaps the memory of the old alliance with France may explain an apparent pro-French tendency, for many contemporary Brazilian Pa'ikwené choose to settle in French Guiana.[2] They are also prompted by the perceived superior benefits and rights of French residence such as social-welfare entitlements, health care, state education, and, for Amerindians born on French soil, citizenship.

Identity by Language and Creolization

Pa'ikwené articulation and interaction with the nonindigenous world, then, involves creolization, a process with far-reaching implications for native sociocultural and linguistic practices. Although present-day Pa'ikwené are generally multilingual, using Creole, Portuguese, and (increasingly) French as well as the vernacular, Pa'ikwaki, many inhabitants of Espérance 1, including the younger ones, tend to speak Creole not only to non-Pa'ikwené outsiders, but among themselves as part of their community's ongoing creolization. At the time of my field research in 1993–95, Espérance 2 people (old and young) in contrast still favored Pa'ikwaki. So set were the Espérance 1 youths (male and female) on effectuating a full language shift[3] and so hostile to it were the Espérance 2 youths that the situation led to friction and even blows (Passes 2003). Creolization is, of course, a matter not just of language, but of cultural and behavioral change, lifestyle, and "identity"—or, as Espérance 2 people see it, loss of identity. Indeed, most Pa'ikwené would agree with my informant, who maintained that the neighboring Karipuna people were not "real Indians"[4] because they had lost their own language, whereas he, having Pa'ikwaki, was an Indian (Amerindian) and a Pa'ikwené. Many Amazonians share this logic,[5] which ostensibly validates claims about the interchangeability of language, culture, and nation (Herder 1986 [1772]) and the essentialist viewpoint whereby language determines identity, be it ethnic (Saussure 1966:20, 223–224) or racial (Brinton 2008 [1891]).

However, identity can exist independently of language, as Edouard Glissant argues (1990, 1996, 1997, n.d.; see also Kulick 1992:10 and Santos-Granero 2002a: 25–27). For Glissant, identity neither equates with language nor derives from it. Instead, identity is relationships and, as such, is created through the inclusive and dynamic intersubjectivity integral to Caribbean-type "poetics of relations" from which creolization unfolds. In Glissant's model, which I extend to the circum-Caribbean, creolization embodies a nonabsolutist, nonexclusivist, open-ended "archipelagic" style of thinking, sustained by a relativist aesthetics of diversity and formed by free-flowing movement (of languages, discourses, ideas, images, relationships) from locality to locality, subject to subject (cf. Hannerz 1987).

On Language and Pa'ikwené Construction of Identity

Espérance 1, a largely Seventh-Day Adventist community of some 200 inhabitants at the time of my fieldwork, is composed of Brazilian Pa'ikwené who in the 1960s hooked up with the creolized descendants of the Pa'ikwené migrants of 1900. Espérance 2, with a population of around 160 people, was founded in the 1980s by Evangelical-Pentecostal (Assembly of God) Pa'ikwené from Aúkwa. The youths of this village privileged the vernacular in order explicitly and self-consciously to reproduce and affirm their identity as Pa'ikwené and "Indians" vis-à-vis the multipartite nonindigenous world. They were offended, therefore, that their Espérance 1 peers spoke Pa'ikwaki less and less and were shifting to Creole as a means of apparent self-incorporation in the Creole "nation." Some shifters said this was indeed their intention (cf. Gow 2003), but others that they would remain Pa'ikwené nonetheless. Espérance 2 youths were not antagonistic to Creoles and were attracted to certain elements of their lifestyle (e.g., foods, dress style). Nor did they repudiate the Creole language per se; it was both one of their several imported codes and a lingua franca used by local outsiders and other Amerindians. They reasoned, however, that if one's own language endows identity, then replacing it with someone else's language signifies a forfeiture of identity, a betrayal of ethnic integrity.

Language shifters would not necessarily concur. The aforesaid Karipuna continue to identify themselves as Karipuna rather than as Creole or Brazilian, even though they now speak a Creole-Portuguese hybrid (cf. Hill and Hill 1986; Kulick 1992, 1998). In fact, many of today's Pa'ikwaki-speaking Pa'ikwené are descended from non-Pa'ikwaki speakers. For the Pa'ikwené, entity is the outcome of constant ethnogenesis, involving fusion with and the pa'ikwenéization of various outsider groups, some of them non-Arawakan, by the original Pa'ikwené core clans (Grenand and Grenand 1987; Passes 2002, 2004a).

When Espérance 2 people apply their essentialist logic to Espérance 1 language shifters, they are condemning the failure to speak one's own language rather than the speaking of another language as such. On the contrary, they consider speaking other languages a positive thing as long as one also continues speaking one's own language, and they routinely code-switch between Pa'ikwaki and the other codes (Creole, Portuguese, and French), sometimes combining all four in one utterance (Passes 2003:100). Many Espérance 1 people also code-switch. At the same time, however, a significant number of them do not use Pa'ikwaki either because it is their language of first choice or, as is often the case with villagers of mixed Pa'ikwené-Creole parentage, because they do not know it.

According to an Espérance 2 teenager who had fought with the youths of Espérance 1 over their language shift, many of the latter did in fact know just as much Pa'ikwaki as he, but pointedly chose to speak Creole instead when Espérance 2 youths addressed them in Pa'ikwaki. From his standpoint, it was a matter of "attitude," a feeling shared by many older Pa'ikwené anxious for Pa'ikwaki's future and regarding the Espérance 1 youths' conduct toward it as disrespectful and shameful (Passes 2003:103; cf. Kulick 1992:13–14). The issue was so contentious in the early to mid-1990s that, as mentioned, it sometimes drove the two groups of youths to physical aggression.

Fueling the Espérance 2 youths' consternation was the perceived threat not only to their native language, but also to their sociality and sense of relatedness. Pa'ikwené exclusivist thinking on language and identity coexists with a more inclusivist approach, in which identity through language is in practice unbounded. Native-born Pa'ikwené or not, whoever uses Pa'ikwaki as his or her tongue and as part of a Pa'ikwené lifestyle can become Pa'ikwené. As for many other Amazonians, ethnicity for the Pa'ikwené is ontologically not an innate part of one's identity but is generated, like personhood, in the daily performance of sociality through acts productive of mutual care and sociability, or "conviviality" (Overing and Passes 2000a, 2000b; Passes forthcoming). Typical acts include sharing the same tasks, eating the same foods, practicing the same skills, and speaking the same language (see, among others, Belaunde 1992; Overing 2003; Passes 2000; Rosengren 2002; Storrie 2003).

A horizontal and potentially infinite social universe in which identity is coupled to a notion of "community of similars" where people "different in kind" and therefore dangerous can become "of a kind" and safe through the process of a shared life (Overing 2003:300) occurs elsewhere in Amazonia (see, e.g., Overing and Passes 2000a; Rosengren 2002; Storrie 2003). The paradigm, sometimes named "rhizomic" (see, among others, Glissant n.d.; Rosengren 2002), posits identity based not on ethnicity, but on mutual history. Ethnicity stresses incompatible differences in people's cultural origins; history emphasizes shared experience, relatedness, and complementary differences (Rosengren 2002; cf. Gow 2002).

Pa'ikwené inclusive identity is conceptually present in the words *Palikur*, a generic term signifying all Amerindian peoples, including the Pa'ikwené, and *naoné*, meaning "my other" and "nation." The latter expression is bestowable on an ever wider social field, radiating from one's immediate community and clan to other communities and clans, to an aggregation of clans, and ultimately to non-Pa'ikwené native Amazonian nations.

The Pa'ikwené line on language, language use, and identity seems, then, ambiguous and inconsistent. It alternates between the essentialist, exclusivist position of metalinguistic discourse (language gives ethnic identity) and the inclusivist one of social practice (neither language nor ethnicity is a natural given of identity; rather, all three are products of intersubjective social life).

Languages, Religion, and Nationality

For Adventist Espérance 1 at the time of my fieldwork, Creole was not just the language of the local French Guianese population and a desirable modern lifestyle, but the one in which religion was practiced. In Espérance 2, the Evangelical-Pentecostal services were held mainly in Portuguese by non-Pa'ikwené Brazilian officiants[6] and with many Brazilians attending. Yet it was Pa'ikwaki, not Portuguese or Creole, that Espérance 2 people determinedly continued to use as their language of preference, or their "solidarity code" (Hill and Hill 1986), for everyday relations, village politics, and ritual performance, including nonformal Christian activity. There was also another, so far unmentioned language associated with religion, the "Language of the Angels," which Pa'ikwené Evangelical-Pentecostals believe is spoken by everyone in heaven (Passes 1998:225)—a language shift they would presumably welcome. Each of these languages did not serve just as the means of religious expression but was also socially constructive of place.

To the religiolinguistic factor may be added that of nationality. The Pa'ikwené, who consider themselves a nation (Passes 2004a), often refer to French Guiana (Guyane)[7] as "France," recognizing it as another nation on the basis of, among other things, the language spoken by French people. The Pa'ikwené consider the Creoles, the majority population in French Guiana and probably the most contiguous of the Pa'ikwené's non-Amerindian coinhabitants in the region, a distinct nation, too, the cultural entity formed by its Creole and creolophone members. Creole can be described as the de facto national language of French Guiana, and French as the language of the state. In the eyes of Espérance 2 villagers, the younger Espérance 1 inhabitants were thus not merely influenced by the Creole nation and appropriating one of its most distinguishing traits, language, but also, more radically, deliberately detaching themselves from the Pa'ikwené nation in order to join or become a foreign nation.

Relations, Codes, and Linguistic Representations

A brief look at the two villages' relations with French Guiana and Creole people will help to elucidate Espérance 2's reading of Espérance 1 attitudes. As the older settlement, with some members descending from the 1900 wave of immigration, Espérance 1 had socially closer links, including intermarriage, with Creoles and consequently a greater knowledge and a probably more social (and even intimate) experience of their language, whereas for the Pa'ikwené in Brazil during the same period Creole was essentially a trading language.

Creole also had political utility. However, Espérance 2 villagers were disadvantaged because, as later arrivals, they had weaker ties than Espérance 1 with the local Creole political establishment. Accordingly, they attached great importance to their children's learning French to enable the community in the future to deal directly with the national authorities.[8] The Pa'ikwené's most recent code, French is taught to the young of both villages, who attend state school. Macropolitically, Espérance 2 tended up till now to be less proactive than Espérance 1, some of whose members had stood in local and even national (i.e., French) elections. Most Espérance 2 people, being Brazilian nationals in the 1990s, were ineligible to take part in elections.

Pa'ikwené tend not to think of languages, or codes, in terms of intrasocial status so much as of values. As Don Kulick (1992:11, 17, 78, 112–113, 1998) and others reveal, code-switchers accord positive or negative values (e.g., authority, selfishness, solidarity, friendship) to each of the codes at their disposal. Switching to a code lets one tap into the value(s) it incorporates. The question, then, is one of linguistic representation. Like many Amazonians, the Pa'ikwené believe in the "magical power" of words, immanent in the utterances of spirit beings and transmittable through chiefs and shamans. For Pa'ikwené, this magical power is also accessible to "ordinary" men and women, manifest in the efficacy of their everyday words to reproduce the community as a sociable, peaceful, and healthy entity (Passes 1998, 2000, 2004b, forthcoming). In the next four sections, I consider the different codes and their embodied values, or powers, as perceived by Pa'ikwené speakers.

Pa'ikwaki

Originally the language of a particular clan that all the clans eventually adopted, Pa'ikwaki is linked to various other Arawakan languages throughout Amazonia (Grenand and Grenand 1987:29–31; Passes 2002:176–177).

If we accept language as dialogical practice and a process of human agency and creativity, we can conceivably further our understanding of the way code-switchers combine old and new lexical items, ideas and values, both native and imported, in the construction of meanings and social life. Old native terms, ideas, and values can be rethought and assimilated in new social and cultural contexts, and imported or borrowed terms, ideas, and values can be integrated into the preexisting context (see, e.g., R. Williams 1976). Thus, to give an example, Pa'ikwené converts will use the Pa'ikwaki word *ihamwi*, "healer" or "shaman," to describe Jesus, who is sometimes spoken of as "the greatest ihamwi."

Preexistent or appropriated, such keywords (R. Williams 1976) can embody the community ethos. For Espérance 2 villagers, the very name "Pa'ikwaki" represents being a Pa'ikwené person, living a Pa'ikwené life. As well as marking identity, both the name and the act of speaking Pa'ikwaki invoke a chain of positive values, states, and practices such as sociability, sociality, solidarity, morality, beauty, tradition, community integrity, and continuity. As noted, Pa'ikwaki is also associated with (informal) religious practice. Against this view, for many Espérance 1 people, notably the youths, Pa'ikwaki (its name, the speaking of it) connotes negative values such as backwardness, tradition, being "uncool," being "uncivilized," and following the wrong religion or no religion.

Creole

Pa'ikwené knowledge of Creole is longstanding in view of the historical relations between the two peoples. Espérance 2 villagers' perception of this language is ambivalent. It has the negative connotations of wrong religion and danger (because capable of damaging Pa'ikwené integrity), but the positive connotations of pragmatic usefulness (as a trading language) and friendship, both with Creoles and with others for whom it is a lingua franca.

In contrast, Espérance 1 people's estimation of Creole seems entirely positive: in addition to the last two attributes just indicated, it embodies the desirable values of modernity, "coolness," "Guyane-ness," local political power, and right religion.

Brazilian Portuguese

Being first- and second-generation migrants from the homeland in Amapá, most Espérance 2 people know Brazilian Portuguese. As the principal language of public (Evangelical-Pentecostal) worship, the prime values it represents are religion and divine authority. For both Espérances in general, its other values are mostly negative because they reflect a nation the Pa'ikwené have historically often experienced as oppressive (Passes 2002, 2004a).

French

For Espérance 2 people, the French language incarnates the power of the French state and the asymmetric relations inferred from it. In the context of community life, where power relations tend to be symmetrical (and there is a typical Amazonian rejection of direct orders), code-switchers sometimes employ French interjections and imperatives[9] in order to suspend the customary egalitarianism by appropriating, however briefly, the authority that this language is seen to contain. Consequently, French as a "power code" has a certain (micro)political value not possessed by Pa'ikwaki and unmatched by Brazilian Portuguese and Creole (Passes 2001; cf. Gumperz 1982, Hill and Hill 1986, Kulick 1992, 1998, and McCallum 1990). Other values deemed to inhere in French and connected with its political power are "civilization," education, and law.

Thus, Espérance 2 adults place an emphasis on their children's acquiring French. Mastery of the language, they argue, will allow their community to better fight for its interests and rights and to prevail in the courts. Learning French is thus a means of countering local Creole hegemony and engaging in the wider political process of their region.

Notwithstanding the tactical benefit of particular codes, Espérance 2 people consider that, outside heaven, the commitment to the single foreign-code option and thus its values (language shift) is an abandonment of Pa'ikwené values. Such a shift is notionally a swing from inclusion to exclusion inappropriate for social life and for the continuation of sociable relations with others, Pa'ikwené or not. However, although many Espérance 1 youths declare assimilation with Creoles to be the objective, some hold it possible to creolize while staying Pa'ikwené. Indeed, as Peter Gow (2002) demonstrates, what looks like assimilation may be the reverse in Amazonia. A group can adopt foreign things (goods, skills, practices, languages) not in order to assimilate, but to be itself: self-definition being achieved not in relation to others, but in relations with others.

Conclusion

As Overing states, "[Social] [p]ractices make space. . . . In the Amazonian context; hunting creates one landscape, gardening yet another" (2004:71, following Munn 1990), and, I would add, so does speaking.

Thus, I have explored indigenous theory and social practice with respect to language use, identity, and relatedness in order to suggest the capacity of language —or, rather, of people speaking it together (be it Pa'ikwaki, Portuguese, French, or Creole singly or jointly)—to construct Pa'ikwené social space as a domain of agential, meaningful, and effective intersubjective acts (cf. Corsín Jiménez 2003).

As discussed, in the period I did my fieldwork, the early 1990s, some younger generation French Guianese Pa'ikwené opted for language shift, but some for code-switching while continuing to privilege the vernacular. It seems to me that both groups were using their languages of choice to engage or not to engage (even when the latter provoked disputes) with others on a basis of social inclusion and relatedness, and, in doing so, to build their social and sociable spaces in the local area, French Guiana and greater Guayana. Shifters and code-switchers alike similarly humanized and socialized—in short, activated—their overlapping spaces by the relational practice of language: the choice of a language, the speaking of it, the speaking of it with others, and their speaking it with us.

Acknowledgments

I thank the editors for inviting me to contribute a chapter to this volume, as well as Joanna Overing, Dan Rosengren, Isabella Lepri, Javier Carrera, and Artionka Capiberibe for discussions on issues contained in it. This chapter was developed from my article "You Are What You Speak, or Are You? Identity, Language, Sociocultural Change, and the Pa'ikwené (Palikur)," *Estudios Latinoamericanos* 23 (2003):91–108.

Notes

1. *Pa'ikwené* is an autonym, *Palikur* the ethnonym.
2. Around St. Georges and at Macouria, Régina, and Roura.

3. On the determining instrumentality of youngsters in a language shift, see Kulick 1992.

4. A positive term for Pa'ikwené.

5. See, for example, D. Thomas 1982:19, J. Jackson 1983, Santos-Granero 1991:87–88, and Rosengren 2002 on the Pemon, Tukanoa, Amuesha, and Matsigenka, respectively.

6. Although this was the case at the time of my fieldwork in the early to mid-1990s, services are now run by the Pa'ikwené themselves and in their own language.

7. Technically not a colony, but a French overseas department.

8. Dealing with their respective national authorities particularly requires the leaders of Brazilian and French Guianese Pa'ikwené to be good Portuguese or French speakers.

9. For example, "Ça suffit!" (That's enough!), "Arrête!" (Stop [it]!), "Donne!" ("Give [me that]!") (Passes 2001).

11

Guyana's Amerindians, Postindependence Identity Politics, and National Discourse

María del Carmen Moreno

"Government's Underhanded Role in Amerindian Cultural Revival"

Scholars of South America and Caribbean Amerindians recognize the growing number of Amerindian communities that are asserting their political identity and becoming politically organized and active.[1] In Guyana's coastal areas, we can see this phenomenon occurring among the Lokono. To understand Lokono communities and their emphasis on cultural revival, the connections and complexities between Lokono communities and institutions at the national level need to be explored. Guyana's postindependence governments have, through their policies, contributed to perpetuating the image of Amerindians and their communities as cultural rather than political entities, thus further alienating them from the political process.

Racialized Politics in Postindependence Guyana

Historically, the national governments largely ignored Guyanese Amerindians and marginalized them from the larger society. The latter years of British colonial rule saw no change in this marginalization; however, there did surface within Guyanese society an Afro- and Indo-Guyanese elite. These two divergent and antagonistic groups, headed by Forbes Burnham and Cheddi Jagan, respectively, became the focus of attention during the latter years of British rule. "In an attempt to articulate and organize discontent with the colonial policies, the East Indian Cheddi Jagan and his . . . wife Janet Jagan set up a Political Affairs Committee (PAC) in 1946" (Gibson 2003:23). The PAC became Jagan's People's Progressive Party (PPP), with Burnham as its chairman. Accusations that the PPP had Communist leanings led to the party's losing national support, which contributed to a split within the party and resulted in Burnham's organizing the People's National Congress (PNC) along political and racial lines.

The political and racial politics that surfaced with the PPP and the PNC were not necessarily new to the country (B. Williams 1991). One only has to delve into the colonial literature to see conflicts between the different ethnic groups within colonial Guyana (see Whitehead 1988). For example, the fact that Amerindians served in the colonial administration still infuses tensions between Amerindians and Afro-Guyanese. Racial tensions arise when people speak of the importation of East Indians as indentured labor to replace the emancipated slaves. Feelings of resentment and animosity fed by colonial racial politics were evident during my fieldwork in the summer of 1994 and from September 1997 to May 1998. In discussions of land demarcation, non-Amerindian Guyanese still question Amerindian land rights with respect to Guyana's cooperative image and the political discourse of "one land, one people."

Although there was a discourse of racial politics at the national level in postindependence Guyana, the Amerindian population was not part of the political landscape and was not viewed as a major "threat."[2] In Guyanese history, several national efforts have been made to direct, or at least to influence, the social and cultural progress of Guyanese Amerindians. In most of these efforts, however, each government has treated Amerindians as cultural rather than political beings.

In the postindependence period, minimal interest was paid to Amerindians primarily because members of the government were far more concerned with their own survival than with acknowledging the least politically active and least visible social group in Guyana. As such, Amerindians and their needs did not initially become part of the national discourse. By the latter part of the 1960s, the government promoted the assimilation of Amerindians into national society and Western culture as part of its efforts at presenting a diverse but unified nation.

Lands Commission Report, 1966

After independence, the national government made a concerted effort to assimilate and acculturate Amerindians and their communities. The *Lands Commission Report* (*LCR*) of 1966 suggested how the government could better understand and influence the dynamics of Amerindian life and culture.[3] The Amerindian Lands Commission, as its name implies, was created to deal with lands in relation to Amerindians and with the limits and extent of the lands' functions. More important, it was to provide a declaration of intention by the government to grant legal ownership of lands to Amerindians:

> The question of adapting the Amerindians to Western civilization has proved to be possible and generally desirable and the long-range policy of Government should be based upon this fact. There must be no question of permanent segregation of these people and reservations should be looked upon as temporary sanctuaries and tribal Amerindians should be left alone only until such time as

it is considered that they have reached a standard of civilization which will enable them to take their place in the general life of the Colony. (Amerindian Lands Commission 1966:no. 40, 14)

With such patronizing and grand plans so soon after independence, we need to ask: What happened to this proposal? As Sister La Rose, the Amerindian welfare officer under the PNC government during the 1970s, explained to me in April 1998, the national government shifted this policy of assimilation to one of promoting and showcasing the uniqueness of "Amerindian" culture. The importance of the Lands Commission was its clear delineation of what needed to be accomplished at the local level to incorporate Amerindians into the nation-state.

Sister La Rose's job required her to *"look into the state of culture in Amerindian communities"* (her emphasis). "During the 1970s, the main focus was on the country's need to understand its different communities in order to become a stronger nation. It was also important for each community, or each nationality within [the] Guyanese nation, to appreciate and understand each other." At this time, the challenge facing the national government was how to forge a unified country composed of a diverse ethnic population that had minimal positive encounters among the different groups. According to Sister La Rose, "We had been a colony, and now we [were] a nation, and we were trying to bring all the people in the country into one, and to acknowledge the fact that we were a nation and to be integrated into this nation. So, like that, when the revival of the culture started, it was not only in the Amerindian communities, it was in all the peoples in the country."

Sister Rose Magdalene's work in the Ministry of Culture ran very much in tandem with and was supportive of the work being done by Sister La Rose. According to Sister Magdalene, during our conversation in April 1998, her unit in the Ministry of Culture was started in 1975 and by 1977 was responsible for the Guyana National Festival for the Arts (Guyfesta). The focus of her unit was to collect folklore and legends and make them accessible in book form to Guyanese society.

The minister of culture was very explicit about Guyfesta's objectives.[4] It was to encourage and highlight Guyanese culture—a culture that is strictly their own. However, this emphasis on Guyanese culture revealed a significant shift in the political consideration of Amerindians. As Sister Magdalene explained, "During the British occupation, English was the only topic taught and talked about in school. The missions came and were a great influence; however, the focus and emphasis was on English tradition and language." Thus, Guyfesta sought to promote a more authentic culture "that is ours and ours alone" rather than the English culture, which was "a culture of deprivation which alluded to the past."

In essence, Guyfesta sought to encourage the Guyanese people's active participation in their nation and to strengthen their sense of national identity, pride, and unity. In Guyana's changing political landscape, the national government's efforts at presenting a positive image of cultural plurality had partially shaped the content and direction of the country's cultural revival. In contrast to policies of the 1960s, the different governments since the mid-1970s have sought to showcase and revive Amerindian traditions and to glorify Amerindian contributions to the nation. In this effort, although Amerindians have not been viewed as a political entity or even as a future political threat, they are still viewed as largely a passive and malleable people.

Sister Magdalene noted that she encouraged Amerindian communities to participate in Guyfesta in order to rectify the "culture of deprivation" she found in these communities. During her visits to them, she instructed teachers in how to support the national emphasis on traditional culture. She also collected Amerindian legends and folklore for publication. The Ministry of Culture eventually used this folklore compilation to teach Guyanese students in the schools about their history.

Sister Magdalene acknowledged that there was a problem with the communities she visited in terms of people's knowledge base and interest in their tradition. According to her, Amerindians in the communities she visited "did not know about their culture." In response to this lack of awareness, she selected individual Amerindians to serve as "cultural animators" in their communities. These cultural animators were to motivate others and maintain an interest in reviving local culture and traditional practices by and for local communities.

The Lokono community of Kabakaburi is a great example of the cultural and material benefits derived from contact with individuals such as Sister Magdalene and Sister La Rose. When Sister Magdalene spoke of "cultural animators," she was speaking of individuals such as Canon John Peter Bennett, Horace and Gloria Lowe, and Victoria Robert—individuals who have become prominent through their involvement in Lokono cultural revival at the local, national, and international levels.

Lokono Voices and Identity Politics

The Lokono are Arawak speakers and number around fifteen thousand people. They compose nearly 2 percent of Guyana's population, which also includes Indo-Guyanese, Afro-Guyanese, Brazilians, Asians, and a number of other Amerindian groups (Forte and Melville 1990). All Lokono communities are located along the Atlantic coast of Guyana. Their proximity to larger population centers has allowed for contact, intermingling, and adoption of other cultural practices (see Friedman 1994; Hill 1996a, 1996b; Sider 1993; Whitehead 1992 [1989]).

After European contact, many Lokono converted to Christianity, learned to read and write, and served as catechists in Kabakaburi and other missions. Even today, Lokono educated in mission schools continue to serve the southern part of Guyana as catechists, teachers, and, in the past decade, development workers. Although the popular image of the Lokono has been one of an inherently passive and nonviolent people, both historical documentation and recent cultural revival activities dispel this myth. Thus, when speaking of Lokono, we are not speaking of isolated communities, but rather of communities that have historically had contact with a host of external players, including government officials, nongovernmental organizations (NGOs) and development agencies, tourists, researchers, other Amerindians, Afro-Guyanese, Indo-Guyanese, Brazilians, and others (Greene-Roesel 1996; Whitehead 1988). Lokono oral tradition features a proud people who distinguish themselves from other Amerindians based on their level of education, ability to speak English, and manners of dress, as well as evolving standards in dwellings, food consumption, and hygiene.

Lokono leadership and activism at the local level are best exemplified in the villages of Kabakaburi and Wakapao. According to Mr. Colin Klautky, secretary of Guyana's Organization of Indigenous People at the time of my conversation with him in July 1994, intellectuals in the capital and leaders of other Amerindian communities throughout Guyana consider "the Lokono of Kabakaburi to be articulate and politically active." Horace and Gloria Lowe, the most prominent couple in Kabakaburi, are aware of their community's history and its cultural place in the national spectrum. When asked to identify key informants on Lokono culture, non-Amerindians in the Ministry of Culture and Education always directed me to Kabakaburi and particularly to Auntie Gloria. The Lowes were identified as the premier cultural representatives of Lokonoism and of Kabakaburi in Guyana and overseas.

The Lowes are recognized for having facilitated cultural activities in Kabakaburi during Guyfesta during the 1970s and 1980s. Auntie Gloria was the Amerindian cultural leader who took students from Kabakaburi to the capital and overseas—specifically, Barbados and England—to "perform culture." Uncle Horace, a gifted musician, played an important role in Lokono musical revival beginning in the 1970s. He, along with other Lokono from the Pomeroon River, performed traditional music in the rural and urban centers of Guyana as well as overseas. One can still obtain recordings and photos of these musicians playing their traditional instruments at Guyfesta.

Sister La Rose praised the work done by Gloria Lowe in the cultural revival. She admired Gloria's ability to generate interest and maintain momentum during live cultural performances of cassava making in Georgetown and overseas. Gloria is also credited with introducing and making Lokono cuisine during these cultural performances. In Kabakaburi, Auntie Gloria formerly taught home economics at the local school. She also happens to be one of the few Arawak speakers still alive in Kabakaburi and is credited with introducing Arawak-language classes to adults in Kabakaburi, with materials written by Canon Bennett. She also attempted to introduce Arawak-language classes in the local school.

Uncle Horace credits his sister-in-law, Mildred Lowe, the assistant minister of culture in 1998, with maintaining Kabakaburi on the cultural map. According to Horace, she "always thinks of Kabakaburi for cultural activities" (author's field notes 1997-98). Thus, it seems that the choice of Kabakaburi as a major center of Lokono cultural revival was due not only to its proximity to Georgetown, but also to family connections in the Ministry of Culture and urban intellectual sphere. It is important to highlight this connection because, in many ways, it goes to the heart of how Lokono have dealt with outsiders and opportunities that have assured the survival of their community over the past two centuries. Apart from Horace and Gloria Lowe, the other most prominent Lokono voice in Kabakaburi is that of Canon Bennett.

Although today Canon Bennett has slowed down due to age and illness, at the time of my fieldwork in 1997-98 he was eighty-four years old, and the publication of his Arawak-English dictionary had established him as a premier Lokono intellectual. Canon Bennett embodies the intellectual possibilities for Amerindians at the local, national, and international levels. To Lokono and Amerindians in general, his dictionary legitimizes Lokono history, tradition, and language. Its publication demonstrates how Amerindians can contribute to their own heritage by passing on their language to the next generation. It also demonstrates that each group within the country can make a contribution to the nation-building process of a "diverse yet united" Guyana.

The village of Wakapao, similar to Kabakaburi, has its share of political activists. One of them is Auntie Mabel Sanday, eighty-six, a feisty, articulate Lokono woman who was captain of the village during the 1980s and served as a PNC government appointee. In recognition of her service and prominence, the government named the elementary school of Koria, Wakapao, in her honor. She is cynical about politicians and noted in my conversation with her in the spring of 1998 that they take an interest in Amerindian communities and trek through rivers, creeks, and forest to visit them only in the hopes of garnering their votes during election time.

Mabel Sanday believes in local organization and action rather than in waiting passively for what government and companies will bring. She is a big supporter of the village councils as advocates and arbiters of villager interests. In addition, she believes it is important for communities to take the initiative by vocalizing their needs and concerns to whoever will listen—NGOs, politicians during elections, and government ministries that claim to serve Amerindian communities. Today, to counteract the marginalization of Amerindian communities, Amerindian organizations are voicing their concerns, lobbying for and against legislation, and becoming engaged in political and social activism.[5]

However, tensions have developed between local and national actors involved in the discourse of "Amerindianness." Increasingly, Lokono resist the urban depiction of them as a humble and passive people living in harmony with nature. Auntie Gloria reflected this resistance in her comment, *"We Lokono are children of the forest no longer. Amerindians are finally articulating their rights and voicing their concerns for their people"* (author's field notes, July 1994, Gloria's emphasis).

The tensions Auntie Gloria alluded to are prevalent and visible in Lokono communities and underscore how Amerindians are increasingly claiming their rights and asserting their identity at the local and national levels. In making her assertion, Auntie Gloria was challenging the limitations placed on them by government and others. Clarence Roberts, a Lokono from Kabakaburi and member of the village council, commented, "We Amerindians are being exploited, we do the hard work, and another gets rich destroying the environment without being held accountable" (personal conversation in Georgetown, 26 July 1994). Clarence's comment parallels Auntie Gloria's concerns and assertions and is important not solely because of what it says, but because it verbalizes criticism of larger power structures.

Similarly, the tensions between the national and the local discourses is again apparent in a comment made to me by Victoria Robert in July 1994: "First the British told us we had to learn English, dress in western clothing and live in western houses. Now, the national government is pushing us to speak our native language [Arawak] and live the life of our ancestors. Well, the reality is that we don't speak the language and have never lived that way."

The tensions between the national and the local discourses are precisely at the root of elders' fears for the future of their community. It is not only their community's viability that concerns them, but also the very essence of "Lokonoism."

Gloria and Horace Lowe view language learning as a crucial factor in identity politics. They are very vocal and opinionated regarding the place of Lokono in the national spectrum. They acknowledge that the government originally introduced Amerindian Heritage Month in order to yield political dividends from Amerindians. However, they also consider Amerindian Heritage Month an opportunity for Amerindians to celebrate their culture and to preserve the Lokono's dying traditions.

According to Sister La Rose, with the PPP in power, the 1990s saw an ideological shift in Guyana's national politics that opened it to the rest of the world. During this time, Guyana also experienced the drying up of public funds that had been plentiful in the 1970s and 1980s as well as a shift in politics toward Amerindians. In 1995, the PPP focused its attention on Amerindian Heritage Month as a way to showcase Amerindian culture and traditions, and, more important, as a possible public-relations venue for ecotourism. This view was apparent in 1996 when Guyana's Ministry of Tourism billed 1996 as "the Year to Visit Guyana" in an effort to promote ecotourism to "pristine" Amerindian communities. Ecotourism was praised as a sustainable-development strategy that "balances development and economic gain . . . [and] can benefit both the mature and developing destinations" (Scace 1993:64). The government and development organizations posited ecotourism for poor Amerindian communities as a way to generate and sustain development without dependency.

Concluding Remarks

I contend that Amerindians in Guyana were and are not marginal to national politics (see Friedman 1994). The mere fact of being Amerindian—identifying as a

Lokono, for example—is a political act with assumptions and consequences beyond the individual. At the national level, the concerted effort to treat and portray Amerindians as a cultural entity diminished their potential to be a political force in Guyana's postindependence politics. In efforts to diminish the potential threat posed by Amerindians, the national government portrayed them as apolitical, outside of the mainstream, and uninterested in postindependence national politics in Guyana.

However, as we know from recent experience and research, Amerindians are not apolitical and have made significant political strides. In the past decade, a number of developments have galvanized Guyanese Amerindians to focus their attention on national affairs, including the institutionalization of Amerindian Heritage Month and the promotion of ecotourism as a source of revenue and "folklorization of Amerindian identity" (J. Jackson 1991; Price 1998:173). Also, just prior to my arrival in Kabakaburi in September 1997, two significant cultural and political events set the stage for my research on Lokono cultural revival. These events revealed and in a more personal way reinforced my perception that one cannot understand contemporary Lokono culture revival in isolation from their historical experiences and more specifically from their connections to external influences.

First, in July 1997, a group of Caribs from the island of Dominica came to Guyana to reestablish cultural ties with the Carib communities in Guyana's Pomeroon River region. During the visit, Amerindians in Kabakaburi and other communities along the river were keenly aware that the Dominican Caribs did not "speak" the Carib language or have the physical appearance of "being Carib," yet identified themselves as such and were seeking cultural ties with their "lost brothers" of the Pomeroon. The second significant event, which also occurred in 1997, involved changing the name of the Guyana airport from "Timehri International Airport" to "Cheddi B. Jagan Timehri Airport" in honor of the late president Cheddi B. Jagan, a Guyanese of East Indian decent. The renaming generated strong opposition from Amerindians, who perceived it as an affront to the historical significance of the word *timehri* (referring to petroglyphs) and its connection to Amerindian history.

Both of these events led the Lokono to wrestle with defining what constituted Amerindian identity and Amerindian rights, and, more specifically, with what it meant to be Lokono in the face of a changing political landscape. In addition, these events and many others like them spawned in the Lokono a renewed interest in their history and a cultural revival that sought to impart in young people a sense of identity, pride, and understanding of what constituted "being Lokono" in contemporary times.

As the Lokono enter the twenty-first century, the discourse on Lokono identity still wrestles with the following questions: What is Lokonoism, and *who are* the Lokono in contemporary times? I contend that by emphasizing cultural revival and pushing Amerindian Heritage Month and even ecotourism, the national government's efforts have in effect frozen Amerindians in time in the display of a traditional way of life that is at odds with the current Lokono community's reality.

However, the politicization process of Amerindians in Guyana has local, national, and global dimensions. For example, although the Lokono continue to be part of the "diverse but united Guyana"—a land of six races, each with its own unique history and tradition, all participating in *marshramany,* the Amerindian version of cooperative work—they are also forging connections with Amerindian activists and organizations at the national, regional, and international levels. Not surprisingly, these connections induce more activism at home and a louder, more concerted Amerindian voice on Guyana's political stage.

Notes

1. The quotation used in this section's heading comes from a personal conversation, but see also Terry Roopnarine, "Small Scale Gold Mining and Environmental Policy Challenges in Guyana: Protection or Pollution," *Stabroek News,* 6 May 1998.

2. Unrest regarding land demarcation and self-determination was the impetus of the Rupununi uprising of 1969 that involved a number of Lokono from Kabakaburi (see Farage 2003).

3. Maurice Bennett was the Amerindian representative on the commission. He is the son of Canon John Peter Bennett, a prominent Lokono intellectual and originally from Kabakaburi whom I describe more fully later.

4. Based on the back cover of the pictorial review *GUYFESTA '77: The Guyana National Festival of the Arts. Theme: My Community, My Nation.* (Georgetown: Department of Culture, Ministry of Education, Social Development, and Culture).

5. Amerindian People's Association and Guyana's Organization of Indigenous People are the two prominent Amerindian organizations in Guyana.

12

Ethnopolitics and Fractured Nationalism in Guyana

David Hinds

This chapter presents an overview of ethnicity and politics in Guyana, one of the most ethnically divided societies in the world. In particular, it looks at the sources of the problem and how it is manifested in the sociopolitical process. The central contention is that the fierce political competition for control of the government between the two major ethnic groups has shaped relations between them and in turn frustrated the evolution of a sense of shared nationhood. There has developed instead a fractured nationalism whereby the two groups function more as ethnic enemies than as conationals.

The prevalence of ethnic conflict is one of the most enduring features of modern politics. So pervasive is this phenomenon that very few countries have managed to escape its clutches. Donald Horowitz hits the nail on the head when he says that "ethnic conflict is a world-wide phenomenon . . . [and], of course, a recurrent phenomenon" (1985:3–4). With the collapse of colonialism in the so-called Third World and the attainment of independence, most of the hitherto dormant conflicts erupted into open warfare. Colonial rivalry in Africa had led to the creation of colonies, which evolved into independent states where different tribes were cramped together within the same borders. In the Caribbean, in particular Guyana and Trinidad, East Indian indentured servants were imported to fill in the labor gap when the African slaves were freed. Today tribal conflicts rock Africa, and East Indians and Africans are locked in a constant struggle for political power in Guyana and Trinidad.

At stake in most cases is control of the state. As Horowitz states, "Control of the state, control of a state, and exception from control by others are among the main goals of ethnic conflict." He contends with considerable justification that "decolonization set in motion a chain reaction. . . . [W]ith some exceptions, ethnic differences tended to be muted until independence was achieved. Following independence, however, the context and the issues changed. . . . [T]he question was to whom the new state belonged." He further asserts that "the language of ethnicity is the language of kinship." Central to this contention is the key role of the family. According to him, "The ethnic group is dependent on the family. A strong sense of ethnic identity is difficult to maintain without strong family ties. These [ties] include, most prominently, marriage within the group, for completely free choice of

Ethnopolitics and Fractured Nationalism

marriage partners would undermine the birth bases of the ethnic group" (1985:5, 4, 57, 61). It is this strong "blood bond," therefore, that explains the deep-seated commitment to ethnic solidarity as opposed to the important but sometimes fickle class solidarity, which is only socially derived. One is not born a worker or a peasant or a bourgeois in the same way one is born an African or an Indian, a Youruba or an Ibo or a Jew.

The problem of ethnic conflict is very pronounced in Guyana. Known also as the "land of six races," Guyana has one of the most multiethnic populations in the Americas. Descendants of African slaves constitute 30.2 percent of the population; those of East Indian indentured laborers make up 43.5 percent; and Amerindians, Portuguese, Chinese, Europeans, and individuals of mixed ethnicities make up 9.2, 0.2, 0.2, 0.1, and 16.7 percent, respectively. Guyana first attained self-rule in 1953, gained its independence from Great Britain in 1966, and became a "cooperative republic" in 1970. Britain had colonized the country since 1814, when the Dutch surrendered it. And before this point, the territory had rotated among the British, Dutch, and French, circumstances that affected the country's ethnic composition. The ethnic diversity of Guyana has had serious implications for politics in the country. The two major groups, Africans and East Indians, have historically found themselves in constant conflict—the roots of which initially lie in the colonial rulers' deliberate divide-and-rule tactics and later in the Cold War machinations by Great Britain and the United States.

Guyana's political history can be divided into four broad periods. First, the colonial period spans the time from European contact up to 1955, when the races, despite mutual distrust and tensions and deliberate divide-and-rule tactics by the colonizers, united in the face of a common enemy. The high point was the formation of the multiethnic working-class-oriented People's Progressive Party (PPP), which in 1953 won the first election held under universal adult suffrage. After 133 days, the British overthrew the PPP government and suspended the Constitution on the grounds that the PPP was a Communist Party. In 1955, the PPP split into two ethnic factions—one led by the African leader Forbes Burnham and the other led by the East Indian leader Cheddi Jagan.

The second period covers decolonization and early independence (1955–64), beginning with the split in the nationalist movement and culminating with the coming to power of the African-dominated People's National Congress (PNC). In between these two developments, there was another split in the original PPP in 1956 when the remaining African leaders left the party as it moved toward a ethnic-based politics. The East Indian–dominated PPP governed from 1957, when elections were reintroduced, to 1964, when the PNC came to power in a coalition with a right-wing party, the United Force (UF). Cold War machinations by Great Britain and the United States as well as competition between Africans and East Indians for control of the government led to racial disturbances between 1961 and 1964 and the PPP's loss of power.

During the third period (1964–92), the PNC developed the most authoritarian government in the Anglophone Caribbean, and Walter Rodney and his new party, the Working People's Alliance (WPA), were instrumental in building a multiethnic movement against the African authoritarian regime. In the spirit of the Cold War, the Americans made it quite clear that under no circumstances were they going to tolerate a Communist PPP government.

In the process of transforming the colonial state into a neocolonial authoritarian state, the PNC used several techniques such as nationalization, militarization, and control of the judiciary. Although it often used naked force, it also manipulated the legislative process, which enabled it to legitimize a number of undemocratic practices. The end result was the institution of the "paramountcy of the party," whereby the party and the state became indistinguishable. Electoral fraud, denial of civil liberties and civil rights, political assassination, and economic underdevelopment were the norm. Elections in 1968, 1973, 1980, and 1985 were rigged.

The first serious challenge to the PNC regime came in 1979, when the WPA, led by Walter Rodney, succeeded in bringing thousands of people to the streets in what is popularly referred to as the Civil Rebellion. Rodney, who had remained in Guyana despite being denied a job at the University of Guyana, had emerged as the leading opposition. His message of multiethnic class solidarity, self-emancipation, and people's power captured the imagination of the masses on both sides of the ethnic divide. In addition, he was able to expose the regime and its leaders and in the process to remove the awe and fear that surrounded them. Under pressure from a united opposition movement and the changed international situation occasioned by the end of the Cold War, the PNC yielded to free and fair elections in 1992, which the PPP won.

The final or postauthoritarian period (1992–present) is characterized by the return of free and fair elections, but also by the simultaneous return of political instability and ethnic conflict, which have combined to push the country to the brink of disintegration. Elections in 1997 and 2001 were accompanied by violence as the African-based PNC refused to recognize the PPP governments. In this regard, the PPP's victory in the 1992 election was more a catalyst for political instability than the anticipated transition to democracy. As the ruling party has sought to use its control of the executive and legislative arms of the government to consolidate its hold on the state, the PNC has resorted to extraparliamentary tactics, and the police, the army, and the civil service—all of which are dominated by PNC supporters—have refused to cooperate with the government.

The government has struggled to establish its authority, which has hampered its ability to push through its programs and to maintain law and order. This serious political crisis in the country has paralyzed the political institutions. In other words, already shaky institutions have collapsed under the weight of the political competition for power. Extremism has grown to such an extent that any discourse between African and East Indian advocates degenerates into fierce shouting matches, with each side claiming victimization and in the process demonizing the other. Attempts at dialogue between the two major parties have failed to put a dent in the situation. In fact, all three rounds of "dialogues" have floundered, leading to increasingly hardened positions. In the meantime, a swift rise in crime has threatened to reduce the country to a killing field. Although most of the killings have been related to drugs, there is also evidence that the gangs called "freedom fighters" and "phantom groups" have direct and indirect ties to the two major parties.

Economic development has stalled as investment and productivity—scarce commodities in the best of times—have dried up. Although there were some signs of economic buoyancy in the early years of the new government, they soon dissipated as the instability increased. From 1998 to the present, there has been negative growth. Foreign investments have been reduced to a trickle, and local enterprises have been folding up at an alarmingly high rate.

The Roots of the Problem

One root of ethnic conflict in Guyana lies in both its colonial past and its postcolonial rivalry for control of the state. According to Eusi Kwayana, the conflict began when the colonial state levied taxes on the freed slaves to finance indentureship. He said that this "social injustice" was the work of the plantocracy "using the power of the purse to secure its profits." He also points out that "there was not a single Indian in the law-making machinery in those days, nor was there any African" (1988:2). The problem also has to do with the fact that two different ethnic groups were ripped from their original homes and transplanted in a hostile and alien environment. Whereas the colonialists destroyed the Africans' cultural values, they tolerated the other group's values. These factors combined to create the deep suspicion and distrust that exist between the two. Kwayana refers to this development as the "interracial dynamic," which strikes at the heart of the problem:

> There has long existed an interracial dynamic in Guyanese society. In the absence of forward planning to contain racial rivalries, it could not be avoided. There are dynamics in social life in any case. And in areas where there are ethnic groups and where there is no forward planning or thinking for mutual security and for solving problems which arise, what can be called "the interracial dynamics" come into play. The fact that Guyana was becoming and had already become the home base of a population of inhabitants, most of whom were laborers or farmers, but who were defined by time, right of occupation of time of arrival, and to a large extent by ethnic-type corresponding with these, gave rise to the need for management of the more important differences and conflicts of interest among these groups. Time of arrival, as well as what can be described as social progress, like the village movement, kept them mainly separate, with the exception that minorities [sic] of Africans lived in the major

estates and later a minority of Indians lived in the new villages. They lived separately but were visible to one another and within earshot of one another. It was to be expected then, that at least after a lapse of time, the action of one group would call forth consideration or response from other groups. . . . The interracial dynamic is a fact of multiracial societies depending on the formation of each society. It proceeds from the first development, that is, the consciousness of a racial, religious, or language group itself. (1988:15–17)

The second source of the problem is the postcolonial competition for power. As Horowitz contends, political power is most often at the root of ethnic conflict. He argues that power is sought both to secure benefits for a given ethnic group and to prevent domination by another group (1985:185–187). The ethnic conflict in Guyana generally fits into this paradigm. Africans in Guyana have historically felt that because they arrived in the country long before the East Indians, they are the legitimate successors of the British colonialists (Horowitz 1985:206). Further, because they are better versed in the British system of government, they are better equipped to be good statesmen. In contrast, the East Indians have felt that their larger numbers entitle them to control of the state, particularly in light of their universal support of democratic principles. It is this difference over who should control the state that motivates ethnic conflict in Guyana. Because each ethnic group fears domination by the other, each tries to gain control of the state as a means of preventing this domination.

Kwayana identifies the struggle over the choice of political leadership since the 1950s as the most prominent issue. He sees ethnic insecurity as a part of the dynamics of a multiethnic society. According to him, "People have a right to seek living assurances of non-racialism before dropping their 'ethnic guard' and reservations in a society with a history of both positive and negative experiences, especially when the negative experiences held center stage in the propaganda" (1988:10).

Ethnicity and Class

Class has become almost extinct in the national discourse. Although class discrimination is alive and well, class consciousness is manifested more among the middle classes than among the working classes. The consequence has been a primacy of racial solidarity whereby the East Indian and African working classes seek solidarity with the middle and ruling classes of their own ethnic group rather than with the working class of the other group.

Despite sharp socioeconomic differences between working-class Africans and their upper-class counterparts, both groups have been united in their support for the PNC. In fact, after Burnham broke with Jagan, he merged with his former foes in the African middle-class party to form the PNC. Shortly afterward, they were joined by Eusi Kwayana, a working-class leader and African nationalist who left the

PPP because of what he perceived as the party's racial turn. Thus, the PNC included Blacks across the class-ideological spectrum. Members of the East Indian commercial class were also admitted into the upper ranks of the socialist-oriented PPP.

As Kwayana (1988) argues, insecurity is the major issue for both Africans and East Indians. In Guyana, a culture has developed where each major ethnic group, African and East Indian, see domination of the government as the best defense against bullying by the other group. The two parties' respective leaderships share this critical view of the intragroup convergence of expectations, thus cementing a political culture that is resentful of cooperation, consensus, and notions of equivalence and united governance. Although other factors such as ideology, external intervention, corruption, mismanagement, and authoritarianism have contributed to the woes, racial fear and insecurity have always been central. Whenever the African-dominated PNC has been in power, East Indians' fear and insecurity have increased, and the same is true for Africans whenever the Indian-dominated PPP has been in power. The end result has been permanent instability.

East Indians' fear and insecurity result from the understanding that although their party can win any free and fair elections, it will not be allowed to govern because of Africans' control of the armed forces and the public-service sector. The threat of physical attacks on both poor East Indians and East Indian businesses increases whenever the PPP is in office. These attacks seem to be premised on the view that they will force the East Indians' party, the PPP, to respond to the Africans' demands. East Indians have also not been able to rely on protection from the armed forces given the predominance of Africans in those forces. In the final analysis, the PPP cannot guarantee security from the state even when it is in power.

Africans' fear and insecurity spring from the knowledge that given their numerical minority status, their party cannot win free and fair elections. Although they dominate the armed forces and the public-service sector, they cannot hope to control political power under the winner-take-all system. Because the administrative arm of government holds legislative power and the power of resource allocation, Africans are excluded from the crucial councils of national decision making. East Indians' dominance of the business sector, in which African participation is negligible, completes the Africans' dilemma.

Ethnicity, Governance, and the Political Economy

Given the nature of politics in the Caribbean, the state has emerged as the most powerful entity. It has almost unchecked monopoly of power in all spheres of life. The government of the day therefore wields immense power over both state and society. The key here is the Westminster Model, which in the Caribbean has been transformed into the opposite of its democratic original. Rather than promoting liberal democracy, it has served as a catalyst for liberal authoritarianism at best and for dictatorial authoritarianism at worst. When one party wins, it wins all power and shares none; checks and balances as well as accountability are at a bare minimum or totally absent. Guyanese politics, therefore, is largely an exercise in consolidating power and marginalizing the opposition.

In these circumstances, the burning question is, How can there be a truly democratic flowering in a state that consists of majority and minority ethnic groups? The modern state, with its strong historical tradition of individualism, comes into conflict with ethnic affiliation. As Horowitz puts it, "The institutions of the modern liberal state—institutions such as democratic elections—tend to be biased against birth. These institutions have their roots in the ideological heritage of the post-Enlightenment West, and that heritage is individualistic in its assumption" (1985:87).

In ethnically segmented societies such as Guyana, the adversarial politics takes on an added dimension. Control of the government and domination of state and society amount to domination and control by one race. Similarly, marginalization of the opposition leads to the out-group's perception of ethnic discrimination. This correspondence has been the central problem in Guyana's political economy since 1955. The winner-take-all model has been unhelpful in both the democratization of governance and the encouragement of ethnic harmony. It has instead tended to encourage ethnic disharmony and authoritarianism. Ethnicity and democracy, therefore, are inseparable in Guyana's case.

Governance in Guyana has evolved into an exercise in political witch-hunting, party domination, marginalization of the losing faction, plunder of state resources as a means of personal enrichment, and maintenance of state clientelism. Opposition has meant destabilization of the government. This brand of adversarial politics is inconsistent with Westminster culture, which puts national unity above partisan considerations. A key point here is that whereas in Westminster terms opposition means "government in waiting," in the Caribbean's "adapted Westminster" it means marginalization of nearly half of the populace, possibly permanently.

Once in power, each ethnic party has used state power to channel tangible benefits to its respective group. These benefits generally take the form of jobs such as top positions in the government and other sectors of the state, but they also include economic programs that are beneficial to the particular ethnic group in power (Desperes 1967). During the reign of the East Indian party from 1957 to 1964, the government implemented various programs in the agricultural sector, which was dominated by East Indians. The mostly East Indian rice farmers were paid better prices for their produce, and the government undertook extensive drainage and irrigation projects. State lands were also distributed to mostly East Indian supporters of the party, and several new schools were erected in East Indian communities. Many East Indians were appointed to the top positions in the civil service sector, which was dominated by Africans. Most of the government ministers were East Indians, and despite the fact that the police force was predominantly African, the cabinet minister in charge was East Indian (Hinds 1998).

These developments caused great concern among the Africans, who felt shut out of power. Those who hitherto had not supported the African party now rallied to its call for ethnic solidarity. Africans began overtly to sabotage the government. They used their strategic location within the civil service to initiate political strikes, which continuously crippled the economy. Finally, with the collusion of British-U.S. imperialism and a small capitalist party, the African-dominated PNC rose to power in 1964.

The situation was then quickly reversed. Many of the previous government's programs were either scrapped or "reformed," and most of the political appointees were relieved of their positions. Africans now dominated the top echelons of the various government branches. Many Africans were placed in jobs for which they were not qualified because ethnicity became the criterion for employment in the state sector (Desperes 1967:144). As noted, the PNC government, which reigned for twenty-eight years, eventually became the most authoritarian in the English-speaking Caribbean (C. Thomas 1984)

Ethnicity and Electoral Politics

As mentioned earlier, despite a mutual mistrust between Africans and East Indians, there were instances of united anticolonial action. This unity reached its peak during the first election held under adult suffrage in 1953. The PPP, at this time a new multiracial party with Cheddi Jagan as leader and Forbes Burnham, an African lawyer, as chairman, won the contest with eighteen out of the twenty-four seats and 51 percent of the popular vote. This victory was significant for the ethnic situation in the country for three main reasons. First, the PPP, even with an East Indian leader, won the majority of African votes. J. E. Greene (1974) estimates that 80 percent and 46 percent of working-class and middle-class Africans, respectively, voted for the PPP. Among both categories, the PPP did better than the African-dominated middle-class party, the National Democratic Front (NDF), which received 12 percent and 34 percent of the working-class and middle-class African vote, respectively. Among the upper-class Africans, the PPP received 25 percent and the NDF 55 percent of the vote.

Second, and related to the first observation, is that race, not class, played the major role in the voters' choice, at least among the Africans. Although there is no empirical evidence to show that the East Indians would have voted overwhelmingly for the PPP had its leader been an African, one can assume they would have, given the weakness of the two East Indian parties that contested the elections and the apparent unity of the PPP top brass.

Third, the 1953 election represented the last time that the two races voted overwhelmingly for the same party. In 1955, the party split into two factions—one led by Burnham and the other by Jagan—following the suspension of the Constitution and the landing of British troops after only 133 days with the PPP in government.

Thus, 1953 represents both the peak of multiethnic solidarity and the roots of the consequent ethnic conflict. According to Kwayana, who was the PPP's assistant general secretary and one of its government ministers, some East Indian supporters of the party had expressed their unhappiness at the large number of African candidates on the party's slate during the campaign (1992:6). Some African supporters also questioned the African leaders' supporting role in the party. Kwayana further claims that the development of such feelings was due to "the perils of a hastily built party, resting on a hastily built unity and entering the race for office in an ethnically competitive situation" (1992:7).

The split in the PPP, therefore, decisively polarized Guyana along ethnic lines. With independence imminent, efforts at reconciliation became fewer. Each group expressed fears of domination by the other in an independent country; hence, each wanted its party to be in power. As Horowitz (1985) contends, the imminence of independence foregrounded the central question of who would control the state. So polarized had the country become that ethnicity took precedence over Guyanese nationalism. East Indians and Africans began referring to themselves in ethnic rather than national terms.

This attitude is vividly demonstrated when East Indian and Pakistani cricket teams tour the West Indies: the Indo-Guyanese openly and proudly support the touring teams over the local team. The strong ethnic bond is also reflected in the fact that despite the historical religious differences between Hindus and Muslims, they find a common home in the PPP.

The results of the next three elections after 1955 and the ethnic conflict that ensued demonstrate that ethnicity had at this point overtaken class as the dominant political factor in Guyana. The elections held in 1957 were won by the PPP with 47.6 percent of the popular vote, compared to the PNC's 39.4 percent. These figures generally corresponded with the racial breakdown of the population if one considers that the section of the population that is mixed is usually classified as Black and identifies itself as such.

The ethnic trend continued during the 1961 and 1964 elections. However, in these elections there was a third party, the UF, led by Portuguese businessman Peter D'Aguiar. This party emerged as the representative of the Amerindian, Chinese, Portuguese, and European sections of the population. It was able in the 1961 elections to pull away about 10 percent of the PPP's usual vote. These votes came from among the more wealthy East Indians, who were fearful of Jagan's Communist leanings. However, in 1964, when the racial conflict was intensified, many of these wealthier East Indians returned to the PPP. The results of the 1961 elections were as follows: PPP 42.6 percent, PNC 41.0 percent, and UF 16.3 percent. In 1964, the PPP received 45.8 percent of the vote, the PNC 40.5 percent, and the UF 12.4 percent.

After the PPP's victory in the 1961 elections, relations between Africans and East Indians took a turn for the worse. The next three years witnessed violent clashes between the two groups, which culminated in a civil war in 1964. The Africans perceived the policies of the PPP government to be overwhelmingly in favor of East Indians and, given their minority status, feared permanent domination by the latter. It was against this background that the African party, the PNC, with the aid of the British and the Americans, persuaded the UF to join it in a coalition in 1964 to oust the PPP from office.

Ethnicity and Political Mobilization

Over the years, much of the rhetoric of the two oldest political parties in Guyana has been characterized by commitments to independence, multiracialism, and socialism. In the early period of the independence movement up to 1955, when the leadership was united under the same banner, the major mobilization strategy was directed toward harnessing the people's anticolonial sentiment, which cut across racial-ethnic lines (Desperes 1967:221; Hintzen 1989:46) and as such formed the basis for a united, multiethnic movement. This strategy proved successful in the 1953 elections, and the united PPP won a majority of the votes, gaining support from both major ethnic groups.

After the split in the movement in 1955, the mobilization strategy of the two factions reflected to a large extent the ethnic rupture among the people that resulted from the split at the leadership level. Though not abandoning the anticolonial appeal, both parties sought to consolidate their respective bases among the two ethnic groups. According to Leo Desperes,

> By 1958 the East Indian and Afro-Guianese cultural sections appeared to represent the only bases of mass power accessible, respectively, to the People's Progressive Party and the People's National Congress. In order to integrate these cultural sections politically, however, adjustments in organizational strategies were needed. Specifically, particularistic appeals had to be made to the groups contained within each cultural section. Accordingly, the two major political parties devised and implemented plans to achieve this effect. (1967:221–222)

The same method of mobilization continued after independence in 1966. Both parties advocated socialist construction but continued to direct their appeal to the consolidation of their ethnic bases (Hintzen 1989:65–73). The major mobilization tools both parties used over the years were ideology, religion, race, and clientelism (Hintzen 1989:56). When operationalized collectively by the PPP, these tools were dubbed "*apanjat* politics." *Apanjat* is a Hindi word that in English means "vote for your kind." Given the social structure inherited from the colonial period, wherein the majority of the people, mainly Africans, East Indians, and Amerindians, occupied the lowest sector of the social ladder, and the minority, Europeans and Mulattoes, occupied the highest sector, race and class have always been intertwined in Guyanese political history. The political parties have used this situation to appeal to the people's class instincts while simultaneously soliciting their support based on ethnic identification. Thus, the PPP and the PNC can simultaneously be both "socialist" and ethnic.

During its term in office from 1957 to 1964, as noted, the PPP implemented extensive programs in the agricultural sector, ostensibly to improve the conditions of the working class. However, because East Indians dominated agriculture, the party was able to steer benefits to its base in the name of national development. In the PPP's five-year development plan of 1959, for example, 52.5 percent of government funds was allocated to agriculture, whereas only 3.6 percent was allocated to industrial development—a sector dominated by Africans (Desperes 1967:246). Most of the funds allocated for agriculture went toward the extension of the existing rice acreage, an area in which African participation was almost nonexistent (Desperes 1967:246).

During the 1961 election campaign, the major plank of the PPP's platform was its agricultural plan (Desperes 1967:247). Central to this thrust was a land-development scheme located on the Correntyne Coast in the heart of the PPP's stronghold. Of 150 families settled on the site of the project, 147 were East Indians. The heads of the three African families there were PPP members (Desperes 1967:248). Desperes also observes that between 1957 and 1961, the PPP's mobilization strategy among sugar workers in particular consisted of "fomenting labor unrest on the estates and utilizing the PPP's apparatus in association with Janet Jagan's position as Minister of Labor as an unofficial union in opposition to the anti-Jagan Man Power Citizen's Association" (241).

Another aspect of the PPP's mobilization strategy was its appeal to religion and consequent infiltration of religious organizations. Both the Dharmic Maha Sabba and the United Sad'r Islamic Anjuman, the main Hindu and Muslim associations, respectively, were connected to the PPP. The president of the Maha Sabba, Sase Narain, had close ties to the PPP, and its secretary, Repu Damam Persaud, was a PPP member of Parliament; the Anjuman's president, Yacob Ali, was also a PPP assemblyman (Milne 1981:34). These officials used their influence in the temples and mosques to steer the memberships to the PPP. Desperes concludes that apanjat politics held out the following promises to the East Indian community: (1) hope for a new and more prosperous way of life; (2) new markets and economic power for East Indian businessmen; (3) new opportunities and access to the prestigious civil service positions for East Indian teachers and other educated East Indians; (4) better representation and a larger share of the profits of their labor for East Indian sugar workers; (5) more land for the Indian peasants. In short, the PPP's mobilization "symbolized Indian nationalism" (1967:251–252).

The PNC's strategy was originally a mixture of ethnic appearance and anticommunism, with "reverse racialism" being the central component (Desperes 1967:260). This "reverse racialism" meant that the PNC, although not openly calling for an African vote, could mount a campaign to "inform the African people of how the PPP was practicing apanjat politics in order to mobilize the Indian community for

Ethnopolitics and Fractured Nationalism 165

the purpose of bringing Guyana under communist rule" (Desperes 1967:261). As in the PPP's strategy, we can observe the convergence of race and ideology in the PNC's strategy. In the African villages, the PNC told the farmers of Jagan's plan to settle East Indians on African "ancestral" land. This strategy was successful among the Africans because East Indians were already indeed squatting on lands historically occupied by Africans, and the PPP had merged some "African land" into the agricultural development schemes (Desperes 1967:262).

After the PNC assumed power in 1964, patronage became the major mobilization tool as the government sought to woo support with promises of jobs and other prestigious appointments. This form of clientelism was, however, directed more at PPP cadres and the African elite than to the African masses. The PNC maintained the latter group's loyalty through a combination of authoritarian measures and the perceived threat of the return of East Indian domination (Hintzen 1989:70–73.) Percy Hintzen also notes that "the [PNC] regime continued to maintain control of the black mass organizations through communal mobilization directed by the party. Such mobilization, however, came to be channeled to the goals of statism and away from the particular interest of the black population" (96).

Although both parties used similar organizational strategies, the PPP's leadership sought to maintain the loyalty of its constituency through programs and policies that catered to their particular interests. The PNC leadership, in contrast, sought to advance its own class hegemony and as a result did not provide the same kind of security for the African masses as the PPP did for the East Indian masses.

Conclusion

Since the return of electoral democracy in 1992, the adversarial zero-sum politics has reached tumultuous proportions, with both sides of the political divide refusing to make any significant concessions. Although the PPP continues to be elected by fair elections, half the population refuses to accept its authority. A clear example of this behavior is the army's refusal to carry out President Bharrat Jagdeo's orders to crush an African-supported political-criminal insurgency in 2002. He was forced to plead publicly for political space to govern the country, thus accepting that the opposition PNC had succeeded in making the country ungovernable. His plea was similar to that of another PPP leader, Dr. Cheddi Jagan, who said during the 1957–64 PPP tenure that although the PPP was in office, it was not in power.

The end result of these political battles is that the underlying poverty of postcolonial Guyana, accumulated from centuries of economic exploitation, has become chronic, leading to an unprecedented escalation of social problems and mass migration. It is manifested in overflowing unemployment, squalid social conditions, and their attendant social ills. Such a development has served as the perfect breeding ground for the narcotics trade that is fast compromising the health and integrity of the populace. This combined economic and political crisis has engendered a prolonged period of uncertainty that has transformed the country into a time bomb that goes off at the slightest irritation. When a country teeters on the brink of anarchy and disintegration, the temptation to use coercive means under the guise of law and order is real. Resort to such means in a situation of racial animosity can have two consequences: increased ethnic hostility and the institution of a police state, the latter being the first step to full-blown dictatorship. The thin line between legitimate protest and criminal activity is just the kind of breeding ground for the use of state force. In the circumstances, the threat of a return to authoritarianism is a real one.

Such a condition would invariably lead to the use of undemocratic means by the minority in a bid to gain power or by the majority to protect its hold. As ethnic conflict increases, the state must invariably confront the question of whether it is violating the people's right to association as it moves to curtail their activities. How does a democratic state deal with the threat of secession by an ethnic group within its borders without violating the right to self-determination? How does the state reconcile an ethnic minority's right to equal representation in a majoritarian democracy?

13

Postcolonial Policing and the Subculture of Violence in Guyana

Joan Mars

The implementation of a military model of policing, with the attendant reliance on coercion and violence as a means of communication, was an important component of colonial rule for the dependencies of the British Empire in the Caribbean. In the case of Guyana, notwithstanding the achievement of political independence in 1966, this model has remained firmly in place for more than a century[1] and may have played a role in shaping the current occupational subculture of aggression and the excessive use of force, resulting in the frequently unnecessary infliction of personal injuries, the destruction of human life, and the alienation of the public. In the face of sharp increases in serious crime, however, the police have recently also found themselves facing unprecedented levels of violence from suspected criminals in their attempts to conduct arrests and to maintain order. In this chapter, I trace the historical development of military-style policing in the context of an authoritarian colonial state and the promotion of an occupational subculture of violence in police work. I examine the current crime situation in Guyana and argue that the reliance on unwarranted aggression and violence is a double-edged sword and that an understanding of the escalation of violence by and against the police in Guyana requires more than an examination of the challenges of day-to-day police work.

Violence was an integral part of governance during the long history of colonialism and remains embedded in the cultural conditioning of a militarized police force in Guyana. After independence was achieved, the police continued to function as an arm of a self-indulgent, postcolonial authoritarian state in an ethnically polarized, economically stratified society, which is now facing not only a crisis of legitimacy, but also organized crime, violence, and lethal assaults by private death squads that have resulted in the extrajudicial killings of citizens and frequent murders of police in the line of duty. Although police cannot successfully combat the current crime wave without earning the trust and confidence of the law-abiding public, changing the police culture will require much more than improved police-community relations and police reform.

Theoretical Perspectives

Beginning with William Westley's (1970) identification of police culture with the coping mechanisms needed to deal with negative aspects of police work, many scholarly attempts have been made both to explain the determinants of police culture and to determine meaningful ways to bring about behavioral reform. Much of this research has focused on the development of attitudes and behaviors occasioned by the stressful organizational environment, the occupational milieu, and the day-to-day dealings with a potentially dangerous, hostile, and unappreciative public (Bittner 1974; Broderick 1977; M. Brown 1988; Cain 1973; Crank 1998; Drummond 1976; Kappeler, Studer, and Alpert 1998; Manning 1995; Paoline, Meyers, and Worden 2000; Reiner 1985; Skolnick 1994; Van Maanen 1974). Notwithstanding the fact that individual officers cope with the strains of police work in various ways (Broderick 1977; Muir 1977; White 1972; Worden 1995) and a significant degree of variation exists in each officer's degree of adherence to traditional attitudes and values (M. Brown 1988; Jermier et al. 1991; Muir 1977; Worden 1995), there is some evidence to suggest that the internalization of the salient features of police culture—loyalty, secrecy, solidarity, distrust of the public, social isolation, and aggression—can translate into unwarranted coercive and violent behaviors against citizens (Terrill, Paoline, and Manning 2003). Further, it appears that some police subcultural norms such as the illegitimate use of force or the administration of "street justice," as it is sometimes called, are also reinforced by internal social control mechanisms. In a recent study of officer peer retaliation, Jeffrey Cancino and Roger Enriquez found that deviant officers who used illegitimate force against the public were protected from internal police disciplinary mechanisms by adherence to the code of silence. Officers who violated this subcultural code and reported on peers guilty of street justice could be ostracized as well as penalized in more serious ways, such as through the withholding of backup support in dangerous situations (2004:331).

I endorse these findings with reference to the traditional perspectives on police culture and the link between cultural values and coercive behaviors but argue that an understanding of the resilience of negative subcultural values and behaviors in postcolonial constabularies requires the inclusion of a new set of variables that have hitherto received little attention in the scholarly literature. Police culture in Guyana is shaped from a broad spectrum of historical, social, and political factors that encompass much more than the usual organizational and occupational strains, challenges, and dangers that officers deal with in their work environment. The complexity and resilience of cultural norms require an understanding of the coexistence of multiple competing cultures in a single police agency (Wilson 1989) and of the institutional and societal context in which police operate (Chan 1996). Janet Chan (1996) argues, for example, that in the case of the New South Wales Police Service, a reconceptualization of the occupational culture to include the social and political context of police work was necessary in order to craft solutions to a range of negative behaviors, including the normalization of the use of violence and the enforcement of the internal code of silence to shield deviant officers. According to Chan (1996, 1997), understanding the resilience of police culture requires acknowledgment of the interdependent and dynamic relationship between "field" and "habitus" as well as of the importance of social, legal, and organizational variables in shaping police behavior.

I suggest that in the case of the Guyana Police Force, explanatory variables for police cultural conditioning should also include the authoritarian legacies of the colonial state and an increasingly ethnicized and politicized postindependence Caribbean state. The historical derivation of the state from a typically authoritarian colonial tradition, despite that state's pretensions to democratic standards, predisposes it to seek coercive or authoritarian solutions to recurring internal legitimation crises. This internally "weak" state is characterized by the unequal distribution of power and resources as well as by entrenched divisions along class and racial lines, so it becomes increasingly dependent on its police force to maintain the status quo. Against this background, an informal police culture that encourages aggression, coercion, force, and the threat of force is fostered and becomes resistant to reform efforts.

In my examination of these issues, I first discuss the historical development of the colonial authoritarian state, the legacy of police violence, and the structural conditions that support and foster the police occupational subculture of aggression and coercion in the postcolonial period. I then analyze data on the excessive use of force by and against the police during the postindependence period, in particular the breakdown in public security and the rule of law during the past decade. Finally, I discuss the possibility of reducing police violence in the context of the unprecedented growth in organized crime and violence, a rapidly expanding drug trade, and the unfolding crisis of governance in Guyana.

The Caribbean State and the Legacy of Police Violence

The authoritarian legacies of the colonial state in the English-speaking Caribbean are derived not only from British colonial policy and the arbitrary and often violent impositions by its colonial governors, but equally from the dominant planter classes that were eager to extract cheap labor from a reluctant working population, to deny the latter access to the political process, and ultimately to maintain the existing unequal social order. In response to the demands and protests made by the subject population, alliances between colonial governors and the planter classes were almost always complete, despite moments when planters and colonial authorities argued over financial and administrative matters. From its inception, therefore, the Caribbean state (particularly in its colonial mode) was conceived not as a social contract involving all of the people, but as an alliance in opposition to potentially rebellious subordinate groups that were held in check primarily through force and class domination.

The importation of indentured labor from Madeira, China, and India after emancipation in 1834 brought to the region different cultures and ethnicities, which introduced greater complexity to a social structure already differentiated along class, "color" ("pure" Africans versus Mulattoes), and racial lines. This complexity necessitated a somewhat more sophisticated strategy on the part of the colonial Caribbean state, for whom "divide and rule" (the cultivation of alliances along "color" lines and with particular ethnic groups) became most useful as a complement to the earlier coercive strategies.

Under the colonial system, the legitimacy of colonial authority and the maintenance of social order have always been problematic. Caribbean slave and early peasant support for the British Crown was usually highly selective and related mostly to expectations of the fulfillment of the peasants' material self-interests rather than to conscious consent to or validation of their own domination. The same transient type of loyalty to colonial authority is applicable to the laboring classes on plantations and elsewhere in the colonial economy, in which the quest for autonomy, whether in the form of wage-gang bargaining or the demand for trade union organization or even self-government, was paramount and paralleled the earlier Black peasants' quests for "free villages" and independence from the plantation system (Marshall 1996; Young 1958).

It is also notable that the main value-oriented affiliations of the subordinate classes in the Caribbean—whether they be Africanist religious beliefs or emancipation in slavery and colonial times or nationalism or socialism during the decolonization and postcolonial periods—tended to be rebellious, reflecting in the main antiplantation, anticolonial, or anti-imperialist sentiments and therefore constituting a crisis of legitimacy on the part of the state or dominant classes in the region. At the same time, the demands implicit in these value-oriented commitments (to freedom, land, autonomy, economic betterment) tended to be rather pragmatic and realistic, reflecting the need for tangible entitlements or fundamental improvements in the mass population's material well-being.

Because subordinate groups have consistently sought to share in the distribution of political and economic resources traditionally denied them, the political legitimacy of Caribbean regimes would seem, therefore, to be bound up with the capacity for distribution of such resources relatively equitably and widely across classes and ethnic categories in the political system. In the absence of such capacity, however, whether because of the regime's failure to access or acquire the necessary economic resources or to give adequate political representation to the various ethnopolitical groupings in the system, the perceived alternative for such a regime is usually a reversion to naked force to control inevitable mass discontent, with serious consequences (Toland 1993).

Postcolonial Policing and Violence

Under the colonial rule, another disturbing practice in the quest for subordination of the underclass was the manipulation of racial groups under the "divide-and-rule" policy, which created entrenched racial hostilities and divisions that were historically exacerbated by both the composition and the operations of the security forces. In most cases of slave revolts, for instance, the White population was mobilized to augment often Black or mixed (Mulatto) militias. During the 1823 and 1856 riots in Guyana, Amerindian or East Indian elements of the population were used to reinforce White troops in the capture, incarceration, mutilation, and execution of Black rebels (Craton 1996; Rodway 1891; Weber 1931; E. Williams 1964). During the 1905 riots in Georgetown, a predominantly White officer corps of the Guyana Police Force ordered the use of deadly force against unarmed Black workers who were engaging in a strike for better wages and working conditions. Eight people were killed and thirty wounded by police ("The Riots in Georgetown" 1905). In the Enmore riots of 1948, the colonial authorities used mainly Black police officers to help suppress East Indian strikers on the sugar plantations. Five sugar workers were killed and fourteen wounded (Enmore Enquiry Commission 1948).

Racial preferences were always reflected in the composition of the police force and the militia, which maintained an overrepresentation of Africans and Mulattoes in preference to East Indians. Recruitment formulas were purposefully designed to ensure that the force would be an effective deterrent against challenges to the existing political and social order. The dependability of the Mulatto population corresponded with the creation of special accommodations, life opportunities, and social roles based on lightness of skin color resulting from blood ties with the dominant planter class (R. Smith 1962). During the slave period in Guyana, Mulattoes were counted as Whites for the purpose of fulfilling the British Crown's security requirement that a ratio of one White to every fifty slaves be maintained on the plantation (Demerara Ordinance of 1784). They served in the regular slave patrols that existed during the slavery period, and from around 1822 they were allowed to take up commissions in the militia (Shahabuddeen 1978; R. Smith 1962). The Mulattoes' proven dependability and loyalty to the colonial masters was reflected in the supervisory positions they held throughout the colonial administration and in the security forces, especially the police force.

The situation was more ambiguous in the case of the descendants of African slaves, but a certain degree of confidence developed over time with respect to expectations of obedience from the Black rank and file in the force in preference to East Indians. The destruction of the African family, language, and culture under the slave system, the extensive work of Christian churches, and the requirements of a social order where opportunities for upward mobility were enhanced by the assimilation to British culture and values—all played a role in the preference for Africans. East Indian contract laborers and their descendants remained insulated from British culture for a longer period, and immigration regulations prevented the destruction of their families and cultural practices. East Indians also faced a language barrier because most of them spoke Hindustani upon their arrival, whereas by the beginning of the indentureship period former slaves and their descendants had become fluent in English.

Occupational specialization among the racial groups also helped to produce an overrepresentation of Africans in the police force. Blacks who were practically driven off the land that they tried to farm independently after emancipation tended to seek positions in the civil service, whereas East Indian contract laborers were initially given their own plots of land to farm and were encouraged to remain on the estates after the end of their period of indenture (Moore 1987). In addition, entrance requirements for the police force, such as those for certain height and chest measurements and for unmarried status, operated to exclude East Indians, who tended to be more diminutive in stature than Blacks and adhered to their cultural tradition of arranged marriages at an early age (British Guiana Commission of Inquiry 1965).

East Indians have always been significantly underrepresented in the police force when compared to their numbers in the general population. In 1965, one year before independence was achieved, East Indians composed only 18.4 percent of the force, although they accounted for about half of the country's population. Meanwhile, Blacks composed 74.9 percent of the force, although they made up only about 30 percent of the population (British Guiana Commission of Inquiry 1965). This significant underrepresentation has continued throughout the postindependence period, and no attempts have yet been made to take affirmative action to increase the number of East Indians in the force.

The role that racial imbalances in the force can play in generating violence and undermining the ability of a democratically elected government to govern was demonstrated during the preindependence period of colonial "self-rule" in Guyana from 1953 to 1966. During this period, the democratically elected People's Progressive Party (PPP) ruled the country under constitutional arrangements that permitted the colonial authorities and, ultimately, the British Crown to retain operational control of the police force.[2] In 1953, concern about the Communist ideology of Premier Cheddi Jagan (the leader of the PPP) resulted in the suspension of the Constitution by the British government and the removal of the elected ministers' portfolios (Jagan 1997). During the state of emergency that followed, the predominantly African Guyana Police Force—under the command of White expatriate officers and with expanded powers of arrest, detention, and search designed to neutralize and contain the PPP's Marxist revolutionary potential—openly participated in coercive, intimidatory, and in some cases violent acts against the members of the East Indian–dominated PPP government. In other cases, the police failed to act to prevent race-based attacks during the political disturbances that took place in 1962 and 1963 as well as during the 1964 race riots. In all these cases, the police force's loyalty to the colonial establishment and its willingness to act in the furtherance of the British Crown's political agenda took precedence over its duty to act to protect the public (Jagan 1997).

Historically, therefore, it seems that police violence was never an isolated, work-based, purely occupational phenomenon, but part of the British Empire's governmental strategy for controlling the complex and diverse ethnopolitical challenges that resulted from colonization.

In the postindependence period, several factors continue to reinforce the preference for coercion and violence on the part of the police. First, the force has retained its position as an important arm of a weak and self-interested state apparatus facing the challenges of maintaining the status quo in a racially polarized society, especially during national elections, which are constitutionally due every five years. Much like its predecessor, the postcolonial state in Guyana is largely a class state controlled by a middle-class political elite that superseded the old planter classes and the Crown of the colonial period. Thus, not unlike the earlier planter classes, the middle-class political elite of the postcolonial period suffers from a similar crisis of legitimacy, as reflected in what appears to be their primary preoccupation with security issues. Although the planter classes' concern for security may be understood from the fact that they were everywhere significantly outnumbered by the excluded, oppressed, and therefore potentially rebellious majority classes, the insecurity of the present-day middle-class controllers of the postcolonial state seems to derive from their weaknesses and dependence vis-à-vis foreign aid agencies and monetary systems and not least their increasing lack of control over national economic and material resources (given massive foreign ownership and current International Monetary Fund structural adjustment policies). As a result, the state is unable to fulfill its own promises of material advancement to the Guyanese masses.

Second, the police force has remained the only mechanism for controlling a growing underclass that was left out of mainstream society in the development of policies and programs for nation building. Conflict explanations of violence have tended to support the view that the exclusion of these economically marginalized groups or the closure or total absence of access to economic or political resources can inevitably lead to law breaking, criminality, and violence both as a form of protest against what is perceived to be an unjust social order and as a way to alleviate the consequences of relative or absolute deprivation (Jenkins and Schock 1992; Tilly 1978). Similarly, social disorganization and the decay and destruction of communities have been linked to increased criminality among the disadvantaged (Sampson 1987). More recently, research has linked injurious assaults and the felonious killings of police to variables measuring economic inequality and the political subordination of racial minorities in the United States (Jacobs and Carmichael 2002).

During the postindependence years, Guyana has experienced a declining economy, increasing racial polarization, the unequal distribution of economic resources resulting in extremes of wealth and poverty, and high rates of unemployment. The political system is dominated by two main parties, the PPP and the People's National Congress (PNC), which are divided along racial lines, with the former consisting mainly of East Indians and the latter of Africans. The "winner take all" result of governance under the Westminster parliamentary system inherited from the British has resulted in the economic and political exclusion of supporters of whichever party is unsuccessful at the polls. A history of racial voting and of racial cleavages and hostilities resulting from the divide-and-rule policies of the colonial period has resulted in charges of economic and political subordination by supporters of the major opposition party—a problem that has never been seriously addressed. As a result, a sizeable percentage of the population always feels victimized by the racially unequal distribution of political power and economic resources in the society. The drug trade has firmly established itself, and the state has failed to grapple with the changing social and economic landscape or to craft solutions for those who feel politically and racially excluded and economically marginalized.

Police Violence in the Postindependence Period

Concern about police violence first surfaced openly with the publication of the *Guyana Human Rights Report,* an annual exposé of the human rights situation in Guyana by the Guyana Human Rights Association (GHRA), which was incorporated in 1979. The GHRA receives complaints of human rights abuses from the public residing mainly in the capital city of Georgetown and other urban areas (lower East Coast Demerara, East Bank Demerara, and Linden), For many years, the association also gathered information regarding police use of force from the local newspapers to arrive at accurate figures for the entire country. Using data on police-caused homicide collected for the period 1981 to 1986 and data provided by the Guyana Police Force for the period 1991 to 1994, the GHRA researched and analyzed a total of 150 cases (Mars 2002). For the period 1981 to 1986, a police-caused homicide rate of 2.2 per 100,000 of the population was computed and compared with other countries in Latin America (Costa Rica 0.70, Venezuela 0.85, Canada 0.07, and the United States 1.14). Guyana's police homicide rate was found to be closer to that of countries with well-known records of human rights abuses, such as Argentina (2.03) and Brazil (4.06) for a comparable period. Police-caused homicide is a relatively rare event, and the frequency of the use of lethal force may indicate a predisposition to abuse the power to use force (Chevigny 1995). In the case of Guyana, the evidence indicates that many of these deaths represent the excessive and illegal use of deadly force by the Guyana police (Mars 2002).

An investigation of the circumstances surrounding the use of fatal force revealed that it took place mainly during the process of apprehending criminal suspects, most of whom were unarmed, and that the majority of police shootings during these encounters resulted in fatalities. It was also noteworthy that most of the deaths occurred during the years when the level of violence in the community, as reflected in police official records of serious crime, was declining (Mars 2002). In other cases of police-caused homicide, death resulted from injuries allegedly inflicted during the interrogation process while the criminal suspects were in police custody (Amnesty International 1985–95; GHRA 1980–2000; Mars 2002). The circumstances of these deaths in custody have added a new dimension to what was previously known regarding the police occupational subculture of violence in Guyana. In a handful of these cases where relatives of the deceased were able to bring civil actions for compensation for wrongful death against the attorney general and the Guyana police, examination of the court records and, in particular, autopsy reports indicated that gruesome injuries had been inflicted on the suspects allegedly during the interrogation process. The types of injuries inflicted left no doubt that there is no legal justification under domestic law for the extreme violence employed by police in the interrogation process and that such violence is a grave violation of Guyana's human rights obligations under international law. The cause of death stated in the autopsy reports of two suspects is representative of the medical examiner's findings in such cases.

In the first case, the deceased was an eighteen-year-old male who was arrested and taken into custody by police for questioning in connection with a report of property crime, in this case "break[ing] and enter[ing] and larceny." After five hours of interrogation, he was taken to the Georgetown hospital by police in an unconscious state and bleeding from the mouth, where he died shortly thereafter. The cause of death as stated on the autopsy report was: "Asphyxiation due to oedema of the larynx and vocal cords. Extensive internal hemorrhage, multiple abrasions on forehead, right forearm, right clavicle, subcostal region, abdomen scapula, dislocation of left shoulder joint" (qtd. in Mars 2002:180).

In the second case, the deceased was an adult male who was arrested by police along with four others and taken into custody for questioning in connection with a robbery and murder. He died while in police custody. The cause of death as stated on the autopsy report was: "Pneumonia of left lung and pleurisy of left lung. Left and right eyes swollen with subconjunctival hemorrhage present; puncture wounds on right eyelid upper; abrasions on forehead, eyes, neck, earlobes, right and left shoulder, forearm, elbows, ankle, knee, upper limbs, instep; body greenish discoloration, grass and sand on genitals, mud on buttocks; haematoma present on scrotal sacs; bleeding from both nostrils" (qtd. in Mars 2002:181). In both of these cases, police denied responsibility for the infliction of the injuries that caused death, but the cases were settled for modest sums of money as compensation for wrongful death.

These injuries represent a disturbing escalation of unlawful behavior whereby not only excessive force was used, but apparently also methods of interrogation that amount to torture or to cruel, inhuman, or degrading treatment or punishment that is prohibited under the Constitution of Guyana as well as under international law: the Universal Declaration of Human Rights (1948), Article 5, to which Guyana is a signatory. Guyana is also a signatory to the International Covenant on Civil and Political Rights, which, in addition, requires state parties to take measures to prevent the arbitrary deprivation of life by their own security forces, to respect the presumption of innocence in criminal proceedings, and to render humane treatment during arrest and detention by the state (Articles 6, 9, 14). There is also credible evidence that the use of nonlethal violence by police against suspects in their custody is widespread and continuing in Guyana. The U.S. Bureau of Democracy, Human Rights, and Labor's annual assessment of human rights practices in the country, entitled *Guyana: Country Report on Human Rights Practices* for the period 1999 to 2005 routinely confirms that police brutality and the abuse of force is continuing in Guyana and that the government does not fulfill its responsibility to address this problem. The 2001 *Country Report* for Guyana indicated further that from 1995 to 1997 the GHRA was sent around twenty complaints per year from victims for the use of violence by police against them (U.S. Bureau of Democracy 2001). The physical abuse was sometimes serious enough to result in fatalities, as suggested by the autopsy report of a suspect who died in police custody on June 8, 2001, from a fractured skull and hemorrhaging (U.S. Bureau of Democracy 2001).

Allegations of extrajudicial killings and the use of excessive force have continued to plague the Guyana Police Force, and it has become increasingly difficult to gather information regarding the actual number of police-caused homicides from police or other local sources. The GHRA no longer publishes its annual *Guyana Human Rights Report* with tallies of persons killed or injured by police, although it apparently provided the U.S. Bureau of Democracy, Human Rights, and Labor with such tallies until the year 2003.[3] After that year, no specific number of killings is reported in the bureau's *Country Report on Human Rights Practices* for Guyana. In February 2002, the GHRA published a report on extrajudicial killings in Guyana for the period 1980 to 2001 and has since then commented on police violence only in press releases. In this 2002 report, titled *Ambivalent about Violence,* the GHRA recorded a total of 239 deaths caused by police during the period 1995 to 2001, 102 of which were deaths by shootings—thus noting a significant increase in police shootings. The GHRA also reported that 18 of the 239 deaths occurred while the suspect was in police custody.

The only other independent and external entity receiving complaints about the police is the Police Complaints Authority (PCA), which was established by the Police Complaints Authority Act of 1989 to inquire into complaints of misconduct on the part of any member of the force. The PCA publishes an annual report, but until recently it received complaints only in the capital city of Georgetown, where its headquarters are located. There is no mandate for the PCA to collect national data on police use of force, but complaints of misconduct include unlawful killings and the use of unnecessary violence by police; there were eleven and eighteen such complaints, respectively, for 2004, the most recent year for which the *Police Complaints Authority Annual Report* is available. Taken together, these complaints of the abuse of force amount to 12 percent of the total number of complaints received for the year (*n* = 239) (PCA 2005:12). It must be noted, however, that the complaints received annually represent only a fraction of the actual incidences of police violence that take place throughout the country. Under the Police Complaints Authority Act, the PCA receives complaints from members of the public and is then required to refer the complaints to the commissioner of police for investigation (sec. 9[1]); it may make recommendations regarding findings of misconduct only to the director of public prosecutions, the minister of home affairs, and the commissioner of police (sec. 15).

Contemporary Police Violence and the Postcolonial State

During the past decade in Guyana, police violence has steadily escalated, and corruption and scandal, including the allegation of a "black clothes" death squad, have rocked the Guyana Police Force (*Stabroek News*, 23, 25, 30 January 2004). There are also reports that private death squads and a "phantom" police force with links to the official police force have engaged in extrajudicial killings sanctioned by a government minister (U.S. Bureau of Democracy 2004). The minister was also accused of approving the issue of gun licenses to persons involved in extrajudicial killings (GHRA 2004). According to the *Stabroek News* (31 January 2004), the British and Canadian High Commissions joined in the concerns expressed by the U.S. ambassador, who received a report from an informant who had been a member of the death squad colluding with the minister. On 4 April 2005, the minister was exonerated by members of a Presidential Commission of Inquiry, who cleared him of allegations that he was directing a killing squad, although he admitted to having interactions with some members of the death squad (U.S. Bureau of Democracy 2005). He was subsequently appointed Guyana's high commissioner to India after both the political opposition and local human rights organizations protested against his continued tenure as minister of home affairs (GHRA 2005). An alleged drug baron who is wanted for cocaine trafficking in the United States and is currently a fugitive from U.S. justice recently confessed (through the media) to having conducted crime-fighting activities to benefit the government, with the assistance of police officers and others on his payroll, resulting in the killing of several alleged criminals (*Stabroek News*, 12 May 2006).

The racially polarized PPP government and a weak judiciary have also been linked to a thriving drug trade that has converted Guyana into a major transit point for drugs entering the United States and the rest of the Caribbean from South America (Joint Press Release 2006). In 2005, the *International Narcotics Control Strategy Report 2005* by the U.S. Congress painted a grim picture of the proliferation of drugs in Guyana and the resourcefulness of those involved in the drug trade when it noted that cocaine is shipped out of the country in anything Guyana exports. According to the U.S. Drug Enforcement Administration, joint U.S.–Guyana narcotics operations were constantly stymied by corruption allegedly in both the Guyana Police Force and the Customs Anti-Narcotics Unit. Although at least twenty to twenty-five metric tons of cocaine pass through Guyana annually, no drug trafficker has been indicted in Guyana. Drug barons have been granted duty-free privileges, timber concessions, and access to remote airstrips and have allegedly successfully infiltrated the official agencies for democratic governance and security in Guyana (GHRA 2004; Joint Press Release 2006). Over the past three years in particular, execution-style murders, usually associated with the drug trade, have become commonplace and remain unsolved. Violent and gun-related crimes have escalated; weapons, especially AK-47 rifles, proliferate; and police are frequently killed by criminals, a new feature in law enforcement in Guyana. Although no official data are available, and it is difficult to ascertain the numbers of police killed in the line of duty, the GHRA provided a 2003 figure of nine murders of police officers during that year in its press release on International Human Rights Day (10 December 2003; see GHRA 2003).

In the past decade, the apparent escalation of fatal police violence against criminal suspects allegedly either "while attempting to arrest them or while a crime was being committed"[4] is revealed in the number of reported police killings:

1997	27
1998	11
1999	9
2000	13
2001	16
2002	28
2003	39
Total	143

(U.S. Bureau of Democracy 1999–2003)

As can be seen, the number of deaths caused by police increased significantly during the years shown. Although the data on which the U.S. Bureau of Democracy relied are only a partial count and by no means representative of the "true" figures (which are likely to be much higher), there is sufficient basis for concern about what appears to be a preference for street justice on the part of police. It is noteworthy also that this trend developed in spite of declining rates of indictable[5] or serious crime. On 5 September 2002, the police released a document summarizing its initiative for crime reduction in which it noted that reports of indictable crimes had decreased from 12,003 in 1996 to 9,233 in 2001 (Guyana Ministry of Home Affairs 2002:13).

It must be noted, however, that since this report was published, there has been a significant escalation of violent crime in Guyana following a jail break in 2002. In addition to criminal suspects killed by police and reported to the media over the

Postcolonial Policing and Violence

past three years,[6] numerous alleged criminal suspects, mainly young males of African descent, have been killed "execution style" by unknown assailants, and none of these murders has been solved. Although media reports of violent crime, particularly against businesses owned by East Indians, continue to proliferate, few criminals are apprehended and brought to justice. Instead, alleged drug-related death squads continue to operate with impunity. In May 2003, calls by the political opposition and human rights groups for an investigation of the local security situation resulted in the National Assembly's appointment of the Disciplined Forces Commission to inquire into the disciplined services (police force, army, prison service, and fire service) and to make recommendations. The commission submitted a final report in 2004, which contained 164 recommendations for improvement of the disciplined services, but the document has not been made public or the recommendations acted upon.

Conclusions

The breakdown of civil society in Guyana in recent years and the escalation of violence by and against the police are occurring within a complex framework of governmental and judicial incompetence and corruption, ethnic polarization, the proliferation of illicit drugs and drug barons, a declining economy, and high levels of unemployment. In 2001, a United Nations Development Program survey revealed that 35 percent of the population was living in poverty (cited in U.S. Bureau of Democracy 2005). The PPP-dominated government has been implicated in sponsoring death squads to exterminate criminals, and an alleged drug baron who is a fugitive from U.S. justice (having been indicted in the United States for cocaine trafficking) has confirmed that he paid and directed contract killers who are responsible for an undetermined number of brutal murders of criminal suspects and others over the past three years. A prominent opposition political figure as well as a minister of the government, his security guard, and several members of his family were also recently slain.

The same alleged drug baron is currently challenging the police commissioner's authority and integrity through the use of taped private conversations between the commissioner and various persons in order to secure his removal from the force. This breach of national security is receiving little attention from the minister of home affairs (who is responsible for national security) and the government, who are instead acting on the alleged contents of the tapes and have demanded an explanation from the police commissioner (*Stabroek News*, 5 June 2006). The alleged drug baron, who owns several businesses, has poured scorn on a wanted bulletin issued for him by the police, gone into hiding, and is currently attempting to carry on a dialogue with the police commissioner and the government through almost daily statements released to the media by his attorneys. The pervasive and destructive impact of the drug trade on Guyanese and Caribbean society was prophetically captured sixteen years ago in a report by the West Indian Commission (1993), which was quoted in the *Stabroek News* on 29 March 2006:

> Nothing poses greater threats to civil society in CARICOM[7] countries than the drug problem and nothing exemplifies the powerlessness of regional governments more. . . .
>
> It is a many layered danger. At base is the human destruction implicit in drug addiction but implicit also is the corruption of individuals and systems by the sheer enormity of the inducements of the illegal drug trade in relatively poor societies. On top of all this lie the implications for governance itself. The damage to the people, the economies, the system of government—to democratic society itself—from the drug problem is as great a menace as any dictator's repression. CARICOM countries are threatened today by an onslaught from illegal drugs as crushing as any military incursion.

This prediction aptly describes the current breakdown of democratic systems of governance and the rule of law in Guyana, as well as the organizational meltdown that seems to be occurring in the police force, which is finding itself increasingly at odds with the government. The operation of private drug-related death squads with impunity and the frequency of public execution–style murders underscore the police force's inability to provide for the safety and security of citizens, and it is difficult to find a starting point for suggestions for reform. Modern police forces are drawn from the societies they serve, and members of the Guyana Police Force are equally exposed to the temptations and negative effects of the drug trade, increasing drug-related violence, the proliferation of illegal weapons, and the ethnic polarization and tensions that tend to escalate during the run-up to national elections. In response to the frequency of deadly attacks from heavily armed criminals, the police have largely gone on the offensive (GHRA 2003). In this climate, it is no surprise that murders remain largely unsolved and prosecutions of police for unlawful killings have been rare, but there has been marked improvement since the new police commissioner took office in 2004 (U.S. Bureau of Democracy 2005), even while he has been under investigation.

Local nongovernmental organizations' and the general public's frustration with the current situation is reflected in a recent joint press release issued by nine organizations,[8] which lamented the disappearance of the rule of law and the attempts by an alleged drug baron (who has been indicted by a U.S. grand jury) to remove the police commissioner from office (Joint Press Release 2006). The organizations lauded the current commissioner's efforts to "re-constitute the GPF [Guyana Police Force] as a professional institution free from political interference, corruption, and capable of effective crime-fighting," to eliminate "rogue elements, such as the 'black clothes' squad . . . and [to place] hundreds of officers and ranks on charges before the courts" (Joint Press Release 2006). The U.S. Bureau of Democracy also noted in its 2005 *Country Report* the commissioner's crime-fighting and anticorruption efforts and his attempt to restore accountability by bringing charges against officers accused of unlawful killings. Apparently, the charting of a new course for the force in recent years may have been the precipitating factor for the developing confrontation between the commissioner and the alleged drug baron.

Apart from the drug trade, economic deprivation and social disorganization of the underclass as well as the social stratification that survived the colonial plantation order may be generating much of the property crime reported in the media, which is usually accompanied by deadly violence against owners of businesses and those perceived to be beneficiaries of the race-based distribution of jobs and economic resources. Ethnic divisions that were created and nurtured during the colonial era have also survived, with disastrous consequences for police-community relations. The almost daily letters to the editor in leading newspapers such as the *Guyana Chronicle* and the *Stabroek News* indicate, for example, that the East Indian population places little confidence in the ability of the African-dominated police to protect them. The East Indian business community has been known to hire and give support to private security groups rather than to the regular police for protection from victimization by criminal elements. Meanwhile, Blacks feel that the East Indian–dominated PPP government is unlawfully excluding them from equal access to employment and the acquisition of economic resources. In this climate, attacks against state agents such as the police may represent a seemingly justifiable protest against what is perceived as an unjust social order, and criminal violence in the course of committing property crime may be seen as a necessary evil in the quest for survival and the redistribution of economic resources.

With the police lies the solution not only to police violence in Guyana, but also to the problems inherent in governing an ethnically polarized society grounded in structural inequality, a system of governance that permits the political and economic exclusion of segments of the population, a self-indulgent and corrupt postcolonial state apparatus, the widespread penetration of the drug trade and organized crime, and a weak judiciary. The commissioner of police and, indeed, the rule of law are currently under siege in Guyana, where it is evident that drug-related criminal elements are taking on political roles and exerting a great deal of political influence. The problem of police violence pales in comparison to the drug-related violence and vigilante justice regularly reported in the media. Recommendations for police reform emphasizing accountability, "partnerships between the community and the police, and respect for human rights," as proposed by the GHRA (2004), as well as for a long overdue program to reduce racial imbalances in the police force are likely to be ineffective in the current climate.

There is urgent need for a political solution to the question of ethnic polarization and the absence of shared governance in Guyana. Political and economic subordination will continue to provide the impetus for the descent into social disorder, law breaking, and resistance to authority. In addition, international assistance is urgently required in order to deal with organized crime and the drug menace, which are primarily responsible for the current breakdown of the rule of law in Guyana. Violence begets violence, and in a society where an alleged drug baron can openly involve himself in a confrontation with the forces of law and order, having every expectation of success, it is difficult to imagine a return to normalcy and the possibility of implementing initiatives to change police culture.

Notes

1. The civilian model adopted under the advice of the Commissioners of the London Metropolitan Police in 1839 was fully transformed into the military model of the Royal Irish Constabulary in 1891, when British troops withdrew from the colony (Jeffries 1952:64). This model was codified by British Guiana Ordinance No. 7 of 1891 and subsequently incorporated into the Police Act of 1957, which currently remains in force, as amended.

2. The Waddington Constitution under which Cheddi Jagan took office in 1953 placed responsibility for defense, the police force, and information in the hands of the chief (colonial) secretary. When that constitution was replaced by a new one in 1961, no changes were made in existing arrangements for operational control of the force, and the colonial governor reserved the PPP government's attempt to transfer operational control of the force to the minister of home affairs by virtue of the Miscellaneous Enactments Bill No. 10 of 1963, so it never became law.

3. Up to the year 2003, the bureau's yearly *Country Report on Human Rights Practices* for Guyana made specific reference to the GHRA as the source of its tallies on the number of persons killed by police. For the years 2004 and 2005, however, there is a discussion of unlawful killings by police, but no numbers are given.

4. The wording used in the U.S. Bureau of Democracy's *Country Report on Human Rights Practices* with reference to its annual reports on Guyana.

5. Indictable crimes in Guyana include offenses for which a penalty of incarceration for a year or more in prison may be imposed, such as murder, manslaughter, rape, robbery, and burglary.

6. Official data are unavailable for this period. As noted in the text, the GHRA no longer releases annual tallies of death caused by police. The most recent *Police Complaints Authority Annual Report 2004* indicates that eleven complaints of unlawful killing were received from the public (PCA 2005), but the actual number of extrajudicial killings, based on media reports, is much higher.

7. CARICOM is the acronym for the Caribbean Community and Common Market, a regional organization constituted by the Treaty of Chaguaramas in 1973 and comprising fifteen Caribbean member states (including Guyana) if Haiti, whose readmission is still pending, is counted.

8. The nine organizations are: Church Women United, Clerical and Commercial Workers Union, Common Ground Guyana, Community Based Rehabilitation Programme —EBD Unit, General Workers Union, Guyana Council of Churches, Guyana Trades Union Congress, Guyana Human Rights Association, and Red Thread Women's Development Organization.

Part 3

Theoretical and Imaginative Spaces

14

Guyana as a Literary and Imaginative Space

Lúcia Sá

Perhaps no region in Amazonia has fueled literary imagination more than "Guayana," the rugged land where the borders of Guyana, Venezuela, and Brazil converge. European travelers and writers of the past, from Walter Ralegh to Arthur Conan Doyle, marveled at the inhospitable environment of high mountains, river rapids, and rain forest, and at the native cultures it sustained. For each one of them, Guayana came to represent lost worlds, present and past, where male colonial fantasy could unleash desires and fears, with astonishing imagination in the case of the Argentine-born W. H. Hudson. But how has Guayana featured in local literatures—that is, in the narratives and songs of the native peoples and in texts by canonical writers from the nation-states imposed on the region?

When Richard Schomburgk visited Guayana in 1842, he mentioned the Arekuna custom of invoking Mount Roraima in song: "For the most part it was the wonders of Roraima, although this extraordinary mountain lay a hundred miles distant, that were glorified. 'Roraima, the red crag wrapped in clouds, the ever-fruitful mother of the streams,' or 'I sing about the red rocks of Roraima on which dark night reigns even by day' were refrains of the songs that we were to hear so often, especially among the Arekuna in the neighborhood of the mountain" (1922 [1848], 2:151). More than half a century later, Theodore Koch-Grünberg transcribed similar songs, each just a single stanza plus refrain, as in the following example:

> Kinatoli poítene-pe kómeme-tana azike loloíme
> haí-a ha-ha-ha haí-a
> (While the japú stays as a servant, come here Roraima
> haí-a ha-ha-ha haí-a). (1979 [1917], 3:145)[1]

The *japú* is a playful, easily domesticated bird prized by native peoples for its black and yellow feathers. The period in which the japú works as a servant indicates, therefore, a time in which one is at home, away from Roraima. The nostalgic invocation of the sacred mountain brings it home, calming down the urge to visit it, to travel again, to set foot on the road once more. Roraima is the place of plenty, the land where animals and fish abound, where trees and crops grow more easily than on the dry savanna. The presence of the domesticated japú at home brings

Roraima's bounty back—a bounty invoked in another lyric poem translated by Koch-Grünberg and the Pemon[2] Mayuluaípu:

> When I go to Roraima I want to eat bananas
> haí-a ha-ha-ha haí-a. (1979 [1917], 3:147)

The vocalic refrain, a kind of lament that is characteristic of all these songs, sets the tone. It expresses desire (I want to eat fruit when I go to Roraima) and the realization that this desire cannot be fulfilled, at least for the moment. Yet going to Roraima is not the only way of experiencing its sacred bounty. In another poem, one's only wish is to dream about it:

> While I sleep come here Roraima
> haí-a ha-ha-ha haí-a.

So imagined, Roraima becomes the paradise that is echoed in the Pemon creation story—"Wazaká," or the Food Tree story, a theme common in Amazonian literature. In the two Pemon versions recorded by Koch-Grünberg, the trickster Makunaíma and his brothers are starving, having only bad fruit to eat. The rodent agouti finds Wazaká, the tree that carries all the good fruit, but he does not tell the brothers, so Makunaíma waits until the rodent has fallen asleep, then checks his teeth to see what he had been eating. In one version, Makunaíma finds maize or corn, and in the other, banana. The agouti then leads the brothers to the tree, and Makunaíma, against his older brother's advice, suggests that they cut it down. The cutting of the tree causes the great flood. Its stump becomes Roraima; the branches fall across the Caroni River, forming the Wazaká-melu waterfall. As Wazaká is falling, it takes with it two other trees, Yulywazaluina-yég and Élu-yég, whose stumps become the mountains Yuluwazaluimá-tepe and Élu-tepe. The branches of these trees also become waterfalls in the Caroni. All of the trees fall across the river, causing the fruit and seeds to grow on the opposite bank—that is, toward the north, beyond Roraima. When Wazaká falls and its branches end up on the other side of Roraima, this place becomes an earthly paradise, a kind of magic garden in contrast with the much poorer savanna. According to Akuli, one of the Pemon narrators, "All of the trees fell on the other side. That's why still today one finds there banana trees, corn, cotton, and many fruits that have not been planted, but which grow on their own in the woods" (Koch-Grünberg 1979 [1917], 2:40). Schomburgk in fact confirmed the abundance of plants in Roraima, calling the region a "botanical El Dorado": "I believed myself transported to some fairy garden, for such a blending of colour, such a multiplicity combined within so small a space, had been a surprise to me until to-day. The border of brushwood that enclosed this botanical El Dorado consisted of the glorious *Thibaudia nutans Klotzsch,* a new and beautiful species" (1922 [1848], 2:209).

Roraima also features prominently in *Watunna,* the stunning cosmogony of the Yekuana, also known as the So'to. There, the tree, called Marahuaka, originally joined earth and sky, like an umbilical cord. Its prototype and counterpart to the east is Roraima (or Dodoima, as the So'to call it), originally a tree grown from a yuca (cassava) splinter. The squirrel Kuchi had planted the yuca after bringing it back from a journey to the sky in search of food. This tree was, for the So'to, the beginning of food as they know it: "Dodoima was the first tree. Now we see it as a very tall mountain. Many wild fruits still grow there. No one plants them. They just grow as reminders" (Civrieux 1980:129)—reminders, that is, of the same botanical paradise celebrated in the Pemon texts. The So'to ancestors took the plants from there and journeyed to Marahuaka along the Pakaraima route (later followed by Koch-Grünberg) to establish their own home at Marahuaka.

In the Carib tradition, the Pemon and So'to Food Tree stories celebrate the bountifulness of nature while recognizing that its resources are limited. Humans have to cut the tree in order to get food, and in doing so they eliminate their own source of nourishment. The solution for this dilemma is planting, which in these Guayana narratives is not a curse, but an important learning process that includes human interaction as well as the relationship between humans and animals. In other words, the felling of the food tree is shown to be a hinge event, marking the transition from a hunter-gatherer society to an agricultural society.[3]

At the same time, the Food Tree narratives highlight the role of humans in shaping the natural environment itself—complicating, in other words, the Hegelian separation of culture from nature.[4] These stories describe the ancestors of the Pemon and the So'to as being responsible for creating the forest as we know it. Further, their actions set landscape into cosmogony and history. Makunaíma's felling of Wazaká in the Pemon creation story defines the topography of the savanna, with its mountains, rocks, and waterfalls. Thereafter, this hero continues to effect a series of changes in this territory, most of them further defining the region geologically. Rocks are an extremely important element in the Pemon culture: they delineate the shape of their territory, creating waterfalls and cliffs that make travel (but also the intrusion of foreigners) more difficult, and they house many spirits. The Precambrian rocks from the Guiana and Brazilian shields, some hundred million years old, are among the oldest geological formations in the planet (Hecht and Cockburn 1989:17). The Pemon know stories that explain the strange shapes embodied in these rocks, and their sense of time is intimately linked to them. Makunaíma left tracks of different animals on the rocks, covered them with wounds from his own body so that people who walked on them would also be wounded, and he transformed people, animals, plants, and artifacts into stone. Such transformations not only explain rocks shaped like animals, humans, plants, and artifacts but are also consistent with the idea that history, in the form of fossils, can be written on stone: stone fish are said to have been left by Makunaíma in several places. But history written on stone exists for the Pemon not only in the form of fossils: in *Tauron Panton* (1964), Cesáreo Armellada's collection of Pemon stories, Makunaíma and his siblings become "the Makunaímas," ancestors who "walked far and wide and painted rocks, and things which now give the Indians much to think about" (57)—a clear reference to what are called *timehri* in Carib, painted or incised rocks. Schomburgk made a similar reference to Makunaíma as creator of timehri glyphs when he came across a rock face with "complete series" of picture writings: "When the Indians first noticed them [the glyphs], they called out in a subdued voice 'Makunaíma, Makunaíma'" (1922 [1848], 2:177).

The Pemon and So'to creation stories are specific to place; that is, they are creations *of* and *in* Roraima. And because these narratives are not static, frozen in time, they also include important events in more recent history. David Guss's (1980) reading of *Watunna,* for instance, highlights moments that tell the So'to history of contact with Europeans and their descendants, as well as the configuration of Guayana as we know it.

The physical and cultural significance of Roraima and its surroundings for the native inhabitants of the region has not gone unnoticed among writers from the countries that share this landscape: Guyana, Venezuela, and Brazil. In *Los pasos perdidos* (1953, The Lost Steps), a novel by Cuban writer Alejo Carpentier, who lived in Venezuela from 1945 to 1956, Guayana represents Latin American culture in its most "authentic" (and to this extent least "Latin") state. The novel's nameless first-person narrator recounts for us in diary form his journey to the Orinoco and Guayana in search of ancient instruments that might help him explain the origins of music. The journey is described as a journey into the past: first, the past of the human race as he encounters ever more "primitive" societies; second, his personal past, marked by memories of his Spanish-speaking mother and a childhood spent in Latin America. The perspective is boldly male, and it could hardly be otherwise as a first-person diary account of a grand adventure lived by a man. The three main female characters in the novel have highly allegorical functions: Ruth, the protagonist's actress wife, represents the coldness and mechanization of the United States and modern urban life in general; Mouche, his mistress, stands for the French and the surrealists, with whom Carpentier himself had been connected and had recently fallen out (the title of the novel is an obvious reference to André Breton's *Les pas perdus*); and Rosario, the woman he falls in love with during the journey, represents both indigenous Amazonia and popular Latin America. As the story of a European traveler who finds a lost world and an ideal woman in the Amazon, *The Lost Steps* apparently emulates European novels such as Arthur Conan Doyle's *The Lost World* (1995 [1912]) and W. H. Hudson's *Green Mansions* (1944 [1904]). What distinguishes it from these earlier models is the ironic disjunction between the first-person narrator and the author himself, which allows the reader to see that neither the cultures nor the "authentic" Woman the protagonist finds in the jungle are as unchanging or timeless as he claims. Rosario, his lover, emerges from this reading as a sexually independent and culturally complex half-Amerindian woman who is irreducible to the simplistic labels the protagonist attempts to project onto her.[5]

Rómulo Gallegos's *Canaima* (1945 [1923]) also deals with the journey of a male protagonist into the jungle. In this case, however, the journey is not so much of exploration as of exploitation. The protagonist, Marcos Vargas, charmed by the stories told to him by a So'to man, goes into the forest in search of riches and ends up swallowed by it. Like Eustasio Rivera's *La vorágine* (1946 [1924], The Vortex), *Canaima* presents the Amazon as a force that attracts young men to the unknown and to destruction. On the one hand, it repeats in local terms the analysis of colonial greed expressed in novels such as Conrad's *Heart of Darkness* (1999 [1899]). On the other hand, it poses a further problem: here, the remote region to be exploited is not a faraway land, but part of one's own nation.

For Timothy Brennan, the novel as a genre gives form to a nation's heterogeneity, combining its different languages and cultures under the same covers, as it were: "It was the novel that historically accompanied the rise of nations by objectifying the 'one, yet many' of national life, and by mimicking the structure of the nation, a clearly bordered jumble of languages and styles" (1990:49). The "heart of darkness" that the Amazon represents in *Canaima* has to be processed as part of the national imaginary. Gallegos conveys this darkness through the Carib term *canaima*, who defined in the novel as "the malign one, the dark divinity of the Waikas and the Makiritares, the frantic god, principle of evil and cause of all ills, disputes the world with Cajuña, the good. Demon with no form of its own and able to assume any appearance, ancient Ahriman reborn in America" (1945 [1923]:252).

Schomburgk called *kanaimà*[6] the "source of all evil" (1922 [1848], 1:288). Koch-Grünberg gave a similar definition but also referred to it as "something unforeseen" and as "hostile neighbor tribes" (1979 [1917], 3:186–187). Ultimately a cause of death, kanaimà is related to revengeful and negative feelings, to people who convey those feelings, and to the malignant power of the shaman. From recent ethnographic work among the Macuxi (or Makushi), Neil Whitehead (2002c) describes kanaimà as violent assassination and mutilation related to shamanic practices. It may also qualify as the struggle for power between different cultural groups. Walter Roth called it "the expression of the law of retaliation" and used it to refer to "the blood-thirsty tribes of Rio Branco" (1915:354, 355), and Henri Coudreau depicted the wild tribes that lived in the mountains as *canaémés* (in Farage 1991:108).

Hence, the term can be used to define the relationship between invaders and invaded. Not only is kanaimà the destruction brought by the invaders, but it is also the self-destructive forces that drive the invaders to act as they do. It carries in itself all the past and present histories of invasions. Along these lines, the So'to define it as an evil passed to them by the Karinya (Caribs, also "Kariña") in the process of negotiating for guns and iron (Civrieux 1980:165–173). In "Visión de América," Alejo Carpentier says that for the Arekuna, kanaimà dwells in the mountain Ayuán and guards native belief, zealously punishing "those who let themselves be convinced by the missionaries" (1990:282).

This complex indigenous concept from Guayana gives coherence to the novel

Canaima, linking the social narrative to the protagonist's psychological quest. It is at the same time a mysterious force that attracts individuals to their own destruction and the exploitation process that enslaves and destroys both Amerindians and mestizos, on the one hand, and their very destroyers, on the other.

The Guyanese writer Wilson Harris also makes use of the concept in the short story "Kanaima" (1971 [1964]). Here, having lost their land, a group of Macuxi are driven to search for a new home. They come to Tumatumari village, where they meet an old Black man who does not like "Indians" and tells them that Kanaima has been looking for them. Too exhausted to go on, they decide to spend the night there. In the middle of the night, an old woman, hypnotized by the roar of the rapids, throws herself off the cliff. The whole tribe then goes in search of her and watches as she tries to climb back up. The narrator comments: "Kanaima alone knows whether she would reach the cliff top" (115).

For both Harris and Gallegos, kanaimà represents the violence against the native populations of the Americas perpetrated by European colonizers, their system, and their immediate descendants—the American nation-states. According to both authors, such violence is intricately linked to the imaginary of the nation itself.

Gallegos's *Canaima* formally resembles the nineteenth-century novel. Its solution to the problems posed by the plot follows the social-realist model: education and fairer working conditions will free the nation from its maladies. Although the protagonist dies at the end of the novel, consumed by kanaimà, his son is sent to be educated in the prosperous farm Tupuquén. The comparison between the degraded village Tumeremo (where rubber and gold are the lure) and the healthy farm environment points to the future that Gallegos (who eventually became Venezuela's president) desired for his nation.

Although many of Wilson Harris's novels also link national identity to the region of Roraima, they do so in ways that are radically different from Gallegos's work, both aesthetically and ideologically. In formal terms, Harris's novels are often seen as extremely difficult, almost impossible to read, to the point that, according to some critics, they cannot be described as novels at all (Sertima 1975: 109). The reasons adduced include the lack of distinction between dream and reality, unclear character definition, and overlapping of different time frames. Harris's first novel, *Palace of the Peacock* (1960), which opens the *Guyana Quartet,* bears all of those traits. N., the narrator, often describes himself in ways that make him indistinguishable from his older brother Donne. Also, the crew of the boat who constantly navigate the river in search of Mariella, Donne's former lover, is identical to a previous crew that died years earlier. The reader cannot know for sure whether the main characters are dead or alive, whether there are two characters who have gone through similar experiences, if there have been two boat crews or just one, and so on. Such uncertainties have led critics to analyze *Palace* as a symbolist novel, as a psychological work that deals with different levels of consciousness, or as a philosophical discussion on life and death. All of these readings are no doubt perfectly acceptable, but in order to understand Harris's novelistic world, we need to look at the geography that engendered it—that is, the region of Roraima. Although not named as such, Roraima is the setting of the novel: the Amazon forest where the crew goes in search of Mariella (in a plot that develops the plot of Hudson's *Green Mansions*) and, more specifically, the high rock walls beside the rapids where the crew of the boat meet their death. The formidable walls correspond to the birthplace of several native cultures of Guayana, celebrated in narratives and songs (as we have seen). When most of the boat crew meet their death in the rapids below, a few try to climb the mountain walls, where they witness nothing other than scenes from Christ's birth.

Parallel to the Christian motif, their ascent of the rock repeats the movement of Arawak creation stories, where humanity is depicted as surfacing from an underworld through a hole, often a water hole.[7] Above all, it resembles the shamanic ascent to the sky (or the journey back from the underworld) in search of knowledge, as it is described, for instance, in the So'to text "Medatia," which accompanies the English editions of *Watunna*. By placing the Christian story of rebirth in the creation space of Amazonian cultures and making it similar to the shamanic journey, Harris forges a culturally mixed creation narrative for his culturally mixed Guyana. The present crew can indeed be the equivalent of other crews of the past, for it represents the colonial adventure that engendered Guyana as a nation. Its members correspond to the different races and social strata that form Guyana. The mestizo Schomburgh evidently evokes (and might indeed be the great-grandson of) the German naturalist Richard Schomburgk, who traveled to Guyana under the British Crown. Donne, N.'s older brother, represents the British Empire in its double role of brutal exploiter of colonial labor and giver of culture (the latter aspect indicated by his name, "Donne," for the English poet who is quoted in one of the epigraphs).[8] Cameron is Black, Vigilante is Amerindian, the da Silva twins are Brazilian, and so on.

Like so many Amazonian creation stories, *Palace of the Peacock* does not tell a complete tale; its plot is repeated and re-created numerous times throughout the novel in the same way that, in native traditions, episodes are repeated within the stories, and creation is reenacted every time a story is told. The death of the crew is, in this sense, a new birth, a new "creation of the world": the legacy of colonial adventure continues to engender the present reality of Guyana. Also, the fact that the boat crew relives experiences that have already been lived by others or even by themselves recalls shamanic stories and experiences of travel through different levels of time.

Palace of the Peacock does not follow the logic of the individualist bourgeois novel: it is instead a creation story that conflates native and Western narratives to forge a national myth. For that reason, its characters cannot be expected to behave as bourgeois individuals: the brothers who at times seem to act in quite opposite ways and at other times appear to be the same person also resemble, to that degree,

Makunaíma and his siblings from the Pemon creation story published by Koch-Grünberg, or many other twins in native creation narratives. In fact, whereas in Koch-Grünberg's version the brothers still have individual names, in a later version published by Cesáreo Armellada they become "the Makunaímas"—brothers who have a major role in giving the world its present shape. If, when reading Harris's novel, we leave aside essentialist notions of the individual, we will find the novel perhaps less illogical than has been claimed. After all, in line with native narrative, human beings (and siblings even more) can appear identical at times and totally different at others; identity can be perceived as a nuanced notion that varies according to time, space, and other circumstances. Moreover, the power struggle between siblings is a major literary motif in the native traditions of Guayana (not least in the Pemon stories I have noted), and in these disputes the roles played by the various siblings are not necessarily fixed.

In addition, the narrator N.'s experiences move frequently from the realm of dream to that of wakefulness so that the reader never knows for sure what really happened. Common enough in twentieth-century experimental literature, this antirealist technique acquires new meanings when seen in the context of Guayana cultural traditions, and these meanings link it, once again, to shamanic experience, which posits the dream world as part of empirical reality. Likewise, the conflation of the place/mission Mariella with the woman Mariella (Donne's lover and motive of the crew's journey through the rapids) gains in significance when read in the context of Guayana native literature, where landscape is alive and an active part of history.

More than thirty years before Wilson Harris's novel was published, the Brazilian Mário de Andrade had already challenged the logic of the realist novel through a hero who is closer to the native American trickster than to bourgeois notions of a constant personality. Not only does his novel *Macunaíma* (1988 [1928]) begin and end in Guayana, but its composition—a collage of texts from different origins—centers on the Makunaíma saga collected by Koch-Grünberg. The quotes from that saga are so many and so close to the original narratives that some contemporaries accused Andrade of plagiarism. The hero in Andrade's novel, like his predecessor Makunaíma, cannot be easily defined by the binary opposition between good and evil. Though acting at times like a Western hero, he is also capable of terrible mischief, incompetence, lust, cowardice, and boredom. As Wilson Harris's novel would do later for Guyana, *Macunaíma* forged a creation story for the Brazilian nation that incorporated its three formative races: the hero is an Amerindian born among a tribe that has unusually dark skin, but he transforms later into a White prince. In other words, he is Indian, Black, and White. His outrageous trickster behavior, however, does not allow the novel to be read as a simple allegory of the nation. Thanks to a thorough involvement with Carib Pemon texts and their trickster heroes, Andrade actually deconstructed what had hitherto been thought heroic and created instead "a hero without a character," a hero and an antihero at the same time. Whereas all the other novels I have mentioned tell the story of a journey into the rain forest, *Macunaíma* moves in the opposite direction, going from jungle to city (São Paulo). The aim of the hero's quest is to invert the process of colonization, so to speak: to transform Brazilian society by incorporating his own tongue into the national dialect and by telling etiological and creation narratives that can help to modify the national myth.

Guayana has played a major, double role in the national literatures of Venezuela, Guyana, and Brazil. On the one hand, this place-concept is the "dark heart" of the nation, the "lost world" that needs to be incorporated into the foundational myth. It is also, however, the source of literary and cultural traditions that allowed Wilson Harris and Mário de Andrade before him to question these very myths, the unidirectionality of time, and the integrity of the bourgeois individual, as their novels show. Rather than a lost world of the past, Guayana may in these terms be read as the cradle of the modern novel in South America.

Notes

1. All translations from non-English texts are mine.

2. "Pemon" is the name by which the Taurepang (called "Taulipang" by Koch-Grünberg), Arekuna, and Kamarakoto call themselves.

3. For further analysis of the Pemon narratives, see Sá 2004.

4. See Brotherston 1992 and Viveiros de Castro 2002 for further discussions of this theme.

5. For further analysis of *The Lost Steps* and its indigenous context, see Brotherston 1993 and Sá 2004.

6. The term *kanaimà* is spelled in many different ways. Here I keep the spelling used by Neil Whitehead in chapter 1 of this volume, except in quotations.

7. The Arawak Tariana, from the Rio Negro region, emerged from a hole in a rock (see Moreira 1994).

8. John Donne is the author of the poem "To his mistress going to bed" (Elegy 19), which compares the exploration of America to a man's exploration of a woman's body. Such a comparison is of course a theme in *Palace of the Peacock*.

15

Inhabiting the Imagined Space
Constructing Waiwai Identity in the Deep South of Guyana

Stephanie W. Alemán

> Here be dragons, and bitter
> cups made of wood; and the hooves
> of horses where they should not
> sound. Yet on the roofs of houses
> walk the carpenters, as once did
> cartographers on the spoil
> of splendid maps. Here is where
> I am, in a great geometry, between
> a raft of ants and the green sight
> of the freedom of a tree, made
> of that same bitter wood.
> —Martin Carter, honored Guyanese poet, "Bitter Wood"

> Dear land of Guyana, of rivers and plains,
> Made rich by the sunshine and lush by the rains,
> Set gemlike and fair between mountains and sea,
> Your children salute you, dear land of the free.
>
> Green land of Guyana, our heroes of yore,
> Both bondsmen and free, laid their bones on your shore;
> This soil so they hallowed, and from them are we,
> All sons of one mother, Guyana the free.
>
> Great land of Guyana, diverse though our strains,
> We are born of their sacrifice, heirs of their pains,
> And ours is the glory their eyes did not see,
> One land of six peoples, united and free.
>
> Dear land of Guyana, to you will we give
> Our homage, our service, each day that we live;
> God guard you, great Mother, and make us to be
> More worthy our heritage—land of the free.
> —Guyanese national anthem

Constructing Waiwai Identity in the Deep South

This chapter addresses the unique configuration of the Waiwai, a group of Carib-speaking Amerindians who historically and currently inhabit the area known differentially as the "forests north of the Amazon," "the Guiana highlands," "the headwaters of the Essequibo River," and, most commonly, "the Deep South of the nation-state of Guyana." Waiwai peoples also inhabit space on the Brazil side of the Acarai Mountains, which form the southern border between Brazil and Guyana (see the chapter by Schuler Zea in this volume). The "Guyanese" Waiwai have inherited and cannot escape an association with the Deep South as it has been both historically and currently imagined by travelers and adventurers, ecotourists and ethnotourists, evangelical missionaries, state officials, the Guyanese populace, poets and artists, and an international array of biological scientists, ethnographers, and development and nongovernmental organization (NGO) personnel. Moreover, the region of the Deep South cannot be disassociated from the Waiwai, who have maintained and assured their presence in the region even to the point of propelling themselves into future imaginings. This chapter explores how the Deep South and the Waiwai together have been integral to so many intertwining discourses, including the ones currently generated by the Waiwai themselves, in order to help us understand not only the processes by which places and cultures are imagined by others but how those who inhabit imagined spaces respond to these processes and perhaps make effective use of them for their own ends.

It is not possible to address the myriad encounters that outsiders of various categories have had with the Waiwai in any detail within the scope of this chapter. Some main categories of persons can be considered, however, including those representing and creating the Guyanese state, missionaries, travel writers and adventurers, biological scientists, and anthropologists. Like the *lianas* (woody vines) that also inhabit this space, these categories intertwine and overlap in often surprising ways. An in-depth analysis of the way in which ethnography has portrayed the Waiwai is vitally important but not within the scope of this chapter. Because other contributors to this volume have outlined some of the dynamics of the Guyanese state in terms of both itself and its relations with Amerindians (see the chapters by Staats, Moreno, Hinds, Mars, and Trotz and Roopnaraine, for example), I make only brief comments on the specific relationship the Waiwai enjoy with the state and its populace as part of a larger matrix within which all are embedded. Lúcia Sá gives some information that applies to the Waiwai in terms of literary imaginings of them, and the other contributions dealing with Amerindians in the Guayana region add to the accretion and layering of discourses that form the body of knowledge regarding the Waiwai.

To begin, the Guyanese nation has a complicated relationship with its Amerindian populations. Walter Rodney points out this fact in his *History of the Guyanese Working People* (1981) by stating that the British Guiana government before independence exploited the labor of Amerindians in certain industries (balata and woodcutting) while simultaneously regulating their involvement in land ownership, economic development, and business ventures, and by legislating it through the creation of the Amerindian Regulations and the Amerindian Act. After independence in 1966 and beyond economics, the new nation of Guyana figured its Amerindian populations as one of the "six peoples" in its national slogan "The Land of Six Peoples" (see the text of its national anthem). The emphasis on the Amerindian as a unique feature of Guyanese nationhood has waxed and waned over time, but two juxtaposed themes continue to emerge.

First, Amerindians represent the deeply rooted history of human occupation of the territorial borders of Guyana and, through place-naming (usually of the interior) and representation in national symbols, form part of the unique fabric of Guyanese life. Therefore, it is argued that they should retain their traditional lifeways as much as possible. Second, it is believed that Amerindians need to be managed and protected until such time as they are able to enter into the modern, national society and become assimilated. Equally strong sentiments and policy decisions coalesce around these two ideas, which are actually diametrically opposed to one another. Should Amerindians be assimilated and homogenized, or should they be kept apart in their traditional cultures and encouraged not to change? As with regard to the other major ethnic populations in Guyana, the East Indian Guyanese and the African Guyanese, Guyana has a continual difficulty in projecting a coherent voice regarding its diverse population. Tacking back and forth between a rhetoric of sameness and a rhetoric of difference, the nation continues to struggle with its role as patriarchal protector of Amerindians. In addition, the nation continually emphasizes its landscape, its geographically unique features and diverse heritage, in relation to Amerindians, further associating them with natural elements (see, again, the national anthem). Other Guyanese are exposed to a national poetic that associates all citizens with a deep and unique connection with the specific geography of Guyana (see Martin Carter's poem at the beginning of the chapter). For these reasons, I focus on the state and its populace and on the landscape of the deep southern region as two loci of the imaginings regarding the Waiwai, but I also continue to emphasize that these categories represent only two of many intertwining discourses concerning them. In addition, these state and landscape categories are ones the Waiwai themselves recognize and interact with in the ongoing project of identity, the formation of which we all are very much involved in through our own processes of acquiring knowledge about the Waiwai.

Those who have encountered the Waiwai in their "cultural space" and have also encountered the Waiwai's landscape can be examined through their role in forming our understanding of the Waiwai themselves. In 1970s Guyana, for example, whereas other Amerindian groups near the coast were enjoying a flurry of interest in their "traditional" cultures, the Waiwai were often overlooked as *actually existing* in the present day and were repeatedly characterized, both in Guyanese rhetoric and in publications, with reference to the work of Niels Fock and Jens Yde of the

1950s (see Fock 1963 and Yde 1965). The Waiwai are still not brought into the present in most Guyanese scholarly literature. Andrew Sanders's works reflect some of the characterizations of Guyanese Amerindians more generally (see *American Indian or West Indian* [1976] and *The Powerless People* [1986]).

In the popular and artistic imagination of the Guyanese, the Waiwai continue to hold a sense of mystery and authenticity. In his memoir *Jungle Cowboy* (1972), Stanley Brock refers to the Waiwai often as he recounts his tale of ranch life on the Rupununi Savannahs, and major Guyanese artists Stanley Greaves and George Simon cite Waiwai symbolism and culture as inspirations to their own work in painting and sculpture, with Simon even having a "Waiwai phase" to his work. The internationally acclaimed Guyanese author Pauline Melville evokes the mystique of the Waiwai in her novel *The Ventriloquist's Tale* (1997) when her two main characters try to flee from society and its constraints by running away to Waiwai country. The contours of a Guyanese representation of Amerindians and of the Waiwai in particular also begin to emerge through a look at the symbolism present in the media and national imagery. In the present day, the Waiwai struggle with these representations in very real ways. For example, the self-representation of a Christian Waiwai is frustrating with respect to a national project that characterizes the Waiwai as "true Amerindians." Tourist literature that promises authentic experiences of Amerindian cultures also do not benefit from what they call "nontraditional" activities (for example, going to church), and those tour operators who have been able to access the Waiwai area often try to script activities to match their clientele's expectations.

The Guyanese population is continually presented with symbols of nationhood that are increasingly complex. In addition, the presence of NGOs (such as Conservation International and the World Bank) and of their funding is beginning to influence government policy in ways that directly affect Amerindians. The Waiwai are no exception in that Conservation International has moved to create a "protected area" covering their entire territory. World Bank funding of grassroots organizations such as the Amerindian People's Association also leads to the impact of outside decision making on the Waiwai community (La Rose and MacKay 1997). Increased interest in Amerindian cultures and in Amerindians' own interpretations of their cultures also leads to the potential commodification of Amerindian identities and the perils it entails (Castile 1996).

In Guyana, there seems to be a less-organized emphasis on recognizing the state's impact on its citizens. As such, even though there does seem to be some element of the "magical state" that Fernando Coronil (1997) outlines for Venezuela, the development of policy and rhetoric concerning Amerindians delineated in their own terms has been comparatively recent in Guyana and noneffectual in terms of their everyday lives in recent times. The situation is more aptly described by Pierre Rivière's thesis in *Absent Minded Imperialism* (1995a), where he discusses the almost disinterested way in which Great Britain pursued its interests in former

British Guiana through the lens of the boundary dispute between the colony and the nation of Brazil that erupted once again in the first half of the nineteenth century. There is also the complex relationship between the missionary presences allowed by Britain and the notion of state and nationhood with respect to Amerindian peoples in Guyana. The obeah-centered regime of Forbes Burnham, with all its connotations of magic and dark spirituality, did not have any discernable impact on the Waiwai in their Deep South territories. Nevertheless, as Peter Kloos reminds us, even as early as 1971 "the Carib village society [was] no primitive isolate" (1971:15). In fact, many or most of the issues presented to the Waiwai in relation to the state have to do with environmental and conservationist concerns, as was and is the case for the Maroni River Caribs. The other issues that affect Waiwai life with the presence of the nation and state center around a market-based economy and national jurisdiction. Just as Kloos described almost forty years ago for Suriname, the issues of elections and political control that seem only to manifest themselves during certain times of the political cycle have some direct, but little penetrating, influence on Waiwai life even in the present day.

In addition, indigenous movements have not gained in strength, numbers, or voice within Guyana, so there are few *indigenous critics* of the state, as in other parts of Amazonia (Warren and Jackson 2002). The muted voices of indigenous peoples in a state of modernity are still to be brought to the forefront of political and social action, and these voices are oftentimes more critical of NGOs and grassroots organizations than they are of the state. The addition of Amerindian voices speaking in the public or global sphere is the next phase in the development of the Guyanese political system, but issues of representation are relatively new as "issues," and the idea of polyphony or even of coming out "against the state" is as yet in its nascent form. Further, what Neil Whitehead argues regarding the Patamuna's "experience of modernity" also applies to the Waiwai experience, though at a lesser level: "Patamuna experience of modernity has largely been in terms of the spread of governmentality, the apparatus of the State by which we are all rendered citizens. However, in spite of being repeatedly surveyed, classified, and converted, the systems of law, education, sanitation and economy that were supposed to bring the Patamuna the fruits of development and progress have failed to materialize" (2006: 169). In the Waiwai's case, there is also no systematic overt violence or "tradition" of violence like a full-fledged assassination "cult" (*kanaimà*), as among the Patamuna (and Macuxi). Although the Waiwai say they are unafraid of the kanaimà and often taunt them to come and "try something" among them because they know magic ways to repel and kill the kanaimà, they are still not engaged in any overt or subverted resistance against the nation or the state and its representations of them.

The state and its populace also provide a bridging discourse that links the Waiwai to the landscape, the landscape to the state, and the state to the larger world. By embedding the Waiwai in the landscape, the discourses that form this aspect of our understanding of the imagined space are again integral to the formation of Waiwai identities. Travel and adventure writers, early scientific explorers, and missionaries also helped to embed the Waiwai in their space as part of textual imaginings, and these imaginings form part of the larger picture of the Waiwai and their range of visitors.

The Waiwai and Their Landscape

> In one mile we passed 130 trees of over 12 inches in diameter belonging to 76 species and this went on mile after mile. And the Waiwai had names for all of them!
> —Nicolas Guppy, *Wai-Wai*

> "Keeping track of where the heck you are is tough in the forest," [Clarke] said. "There are no landmarks, it's hard to see very far, and whatever maps are available are about as reliable as those that say 'Here be dragons.' We climb trees several times a day to get a [global positioning system] reading and re-adjust the compass heading. Normally the best season for plant collection is when the plants are flowering or fruiting. Sometimes it's the only way you can identify them. But during rainy season you'll find different things."
> —H. David Clarke, qtd. in Hillary Mayell, "Biologists Document Rich Plant Life of Guyana"

The landscape within which the Waiwai live affects the formation of a sense of Waiwai identity in two fundamental ways. The first has been discussed previously as part of the way in which the outside world perceives and constructs the Waiwai through an association with the relatively unknown, deep southern forests of Guyana and the historical factors that have kept this area in a comparative state of isolation and essentially undeveloped. This construction includes not only the embellishments of travel and adventure writers, the conversion narratives of missionaries, and the imaginings of the Guyanese state on the coast, but also the legacy of studies relating to the use of environmental resources and the emergence of theories in cultural ecology that form the textual resources available for the construction of an "outside" view of Waiwai society and culture. It emerges as well from the description of the landscape offered by studies that seek to characterize environments.

The second way, more illustrative of a sense of autochthonous Waiwai identity formation as a process, is the use of features of the landscape in the construction of a Waiwai sense of being. As with other topics having to do with the Waiwai, these two fundamental factors interconnect and react with one another in a dynamic and perpetually shifting way to constitute a full sense of Waiwai personhood and a further sense of a collective self. I underscore once again the importance of understanding that Waiwai identity formation does not take place in a sealed cultural vacuum but in fact is influenced in subtle but effective ways by the construction of

"Waiwainess" from all of the outside sources I have named so far. It would be irresponsible to suggest that Waiwai persons are presently unaware of or unaffected by how they are viewed by the outside world. I argue that such unawareness was most probably *never* the case at any point in their social history and that Waiwai are presently quite aware of and in fact actively address and incorporate outside ways of knowing them into their current projection of both an individual and collective self. Balanced with the use of outside perspectives is their own set of ideas about the nature of the world and the movement of persons and substances in it. One of the primary ways to connect a specifically Waiwai theory of nature to their theory of identity is to explore the points at which components of the natural world are employed to construct a sense of "Waiwainess."

The Waiwai people's understanding of the environment in which they live has affected our understanding of their societal makeup and the ways in which they continue to exist. Specifically for the Waiwai, and by association for other Amazonian peoples, the legacy of environmental determinism and early studies in human ecology that focused solely on the adaptive qualities of Amazonian societies deflected attention away from their unique and active reproduction of their society and from one of the key features of Waiwai society in particular—the acceptance and incorporation of a process of continual change and modification into the perpetuation of community. It is important not to fall into the trap of reductionism even in the recounting of deterministic theory, and it thus must be pointed out that one of the main themes of adaptationist arguments is to show how specific cultures manage to integrate aspects of the environment into their belief systems and to engage in a "dynamic interaction" in which they are "neither conqueror [n]or slave, and significantly the native populations recognize this harmony" (Meggers 1971: 146). This sounds close at times to what I want to say about the ways in which Waiwai people use the ambient environment in their construction of personhood and the collective self, but I also want to make clear that I am proposing that the Waiwai people employ aspects of the environment not because they *have to* or are constrained to do so by limiting factors in their environment such as soil quality or protein availability. The emergence of a different theoretical trajectory that has led away from adaptive processes and allowed for considerations of the role of landscape—as a form of symbolic and discursive capital (cf. Bordieu)—in forming indigenous identities has been the much needed answer to the questions of the relationship between people and their environments.

In such works as Christopher Tilley's *A Phenomenology of Landscape* (1994), the discussion of the significance of landscapes is useful to an understanding of how the Waiwai use their surroundings to form their identity. Tilley asserts that space is not neutral and is seen to be so only when it is regarded as a container rather than as a medium for action. Space cannot be divorced from action and is involved in action, so that it does not exist apart from the events and activities within which it is implicated. Space as a social production is always centered in relation to human agency and is amenable to reproduction and change because its constitution takes place as part of the day-to-day praxis or practical activity of individuals and groups.

Tilley goes on to say that space is meaningfully constituted. A humanized space forms both the medium and the outcome of action, both constraining and enabling it. A centered and meaningful place involves a specific set of linkages among physical space of the nonhuman created world, somatic states of the body, the mental space of cognition, and the representation and the space of movement; it also involves encounter and interaction between persons as well as between persons and the human and nonhuman environment. Socially produced space combines the cognitive, the physical, and the emotional into something that may be reproduced but is always open to transformation and change. A social space, rather than being uniform and forever the same, is constituted by different densities of human experience, attachment, and involvement.

This concept of space is relevant to what I have learned among the Waiwai. They perceive the landscape not as a container but as an interactive partner, perpetually changing and always subject to change by human agency, but also changing and moving in a way that influences humans' actions. Their society can be understood in relation to this same idea of motion, change, and reaction. Tilley asserts that a landscape in motion is a necessary component of the description and understanding of any human social group. I have found that marking, moving, controlling, and sometimes succumbing to the ambient environment compose the largest portion of Waiwai activities. Marking, moving, controlling, and sometimes acquiescing to *persons* makes up the other large portion of active life. To describe and understand these two major parts of a Waiwai person's life is to see the contours of what it means to be Waiwai begin to emerge. An outline of human experience that is filled in slowly with events and details is the source from which personhood and identity emerge. When the Waiwai are living out a daily life and at the same time expressing their perception of the world around them through their actions and activities, they are also telling us who they believe themselves to be. They understand identity to be built up through interaction with other sources of vitality. Both other humans and most elements of the environment are such sources. In fact, Waiwai landscapes are brought into being the same way that persons are—through narration and inclusion in discourse, through naming, reference, and interaction. Waiwai landscapes are both trodden and chanted into being.

In the collected volume *The Anthropology of Landscape* (Hirsch and O'Hanlon 1995), Eric Hirsch calls for an unpacking of the landscape concept. He relates the status of landscape in anthropology to that of the body, saying although landscape is "ubiquitous, it remains largely unproblematized" (Hirsch 1995:7). In the same volume, Alfred Gell states that as with landscape, there is no absolute body; the body is a locality, a form of ambience, and a perpetual surround. He explicates the relationship between the body and the landscape in terms of sound: "This landscape is constructed out of the interface between two kinds of experience; distally it is comprised of a codification of ambient sound, that is a soundscape, proximally it comprises the basic unifying armature of the body as a sounding cavity; sensitive to sound and through the autokinetically sensed experience of verbal and mimetic vocalization, productive of sound" (1995:241). Just as with the body, then, the contextual and transformative nature of landscape emerges as a theme in these authors' discussion.

For the Waiwai, the perpetual change in the landscape parallels the perpetual change taking place in humans' bodies. This perception is in part expressed in their spiritual conception of vital energies, which stresses that the physical body is inhabited by a combination of vital forces. A fundamental base of vitality is also present (although unstable) at birth and consists not only of the vital substances contributed by human parents, but also—through mythic understanding—of the vital substances of many other manifestations of being, such as *ekatï*, soul, and in particular *kworokyam*, the soul spirit (from *kworo*, the scarlet macaw). Therefore, although a human person is recognized and constructed as a distinct being, he or she shares and is linked to nonhuman sources of vitality (from the surrounding landscape) from the very beginning of his or her existence in the world. In terms of becoming a "real" Waiwai person, possessing the knowledge of someone who has learned the lessons of Waiwai personhood involves knowing the landscape and its changing nature in intimate ways that non-Waiwai cannot do without proper socialization.

In addition to the recognition of an ever-shifting array of places, naming becomes a central feature of demonstrating Waiwai knowledge. What appears to outsiders as a monotonous wilderness is intimately familiar to a Waiwai person. Not only does knowing the names of places demonstrate knowledge, but evoking them also provides the occasion for narrating stories with regard to such places, as Keith Basso outlines for the western Apache in "Speaking with Names" (1988) and "Stalking with Stories" (1984). Fernando Santos-Granero also highlights the relationship between landscape and knowledge in "Writing History into the Landscape" (1997). There is also a parallel between vision as a powerful motif in landscape interpretation (Cosgrove 1983) and a Waiwai emphasis on good vision or being able to "see" properly as part of the requirements of "proper being" (see Mentore 1993 on properly opening the orifices of the head to receive knowledge). In addition, the root word in the Waiwai phrase for "to be born" and the Waiwai word for "eye" are the same (*ewri*).

In *Landscape and Memory* (1995), Simon Schama also emphasizes the power of social memory in the shaping of identities and the drawing on features of the environment to do so. He asserts that identity is constructed more through the experiencing of others and the environment than through an "autonomous self-consciousness" (10). Schama's treatment of the natural elements of landscape—namely, wood, water, and stone—also allows me to discuss how water holds a great

Constructing Waiwai Identity in the Deep South

deal of symbolic capital for the Waiwai as a natural force and how river rocks can be a powerful source of vital energies for them. What is important here is that the Waiwai have been previously constructed as inhibited and constrained by their environment (Evans and Meggers 1960; Meggers 1971; Steward 1946–59) rather than as engaged in a dynamic interaction with their landscape. The work that has emerged from a rethinking of the relationship between humans and their environments highlights the fact that neither human nor environment is permanently privileged over the other and that any sharp dichotomies between them should be rejected in favor of seeing the two as existing within each other (Croll and Parkin 1992; Ingold 1992). This latter way of thinking about humans and landscapes very much parallels a Waiwai way of looking at the world. That a Waiwai person is formed and continues to exist within a landscape that in turn is formed by him through human agency is one of the foundational ideas of the Waiwai's worldview.

On the other side of this constructed nature of landscape is the view fashioned by the imperial powers and colonial cartography that played into the reception of the Waiwai and the other indigenous peoples of Guyana (the former British Guiana) in the process of mapping the area and claiming its "contents." D. Graham Burnett (2000) alerts us to the constructed nature of "outsiders'" perception of the landscape inhabited by the Waiwai in the activities of the Royal Geographical Society and the work of Robert Schomburgk, who did not have a very positive view of Amerindians as he demarcated the areas of the Deep South in British Guiana (Burnett 2000). Colonial surveying is a subject area that lends itself to interpreting the initial representations of Amerindians and their "emplacement" within landscapes. *Masters of All They Surveyed* is Burnett's contribution to this subject, and his discussion of symbols such as the *Victoria regia* (giant water lily) explains the ways in which Amerindians not only were perceived as elements of natural history (a perception still indicated in their representation at the Smithsonian Institution in Washington, D.C., for example), but were described not by ethnographers and anthropologists but by explorers and geographers. He also describes the process of conducting surveys as "an ambivalent process of progressive erasures" (2000:256), suggesting that those occupying or using landscapes considered "territorial trophies" had to be removed in order to perpetuate an idea of the pristine and to lay open an area for "development."

In his article "It Is Impossible to Make a Step without the Indians" (2002), Burnett addresses this issue head-on as one of complexity and entanglement. He describes the work of explorers and geographers such as William Hilhouse and Robert Schomburgk as "hybrid expeditions—hybrid in the composition of the exploring party itself, as well as hybrid in purpose," and he goes on to assert that these expeditions in turn "shaped European conceptions of the Amerindians of the region, and were in turn shaped by their presence" (4). Of central importance here is the way in which these early experiences shaped what was and still is a complex control of both spaces and identity in which the Waiwai are ultimately enmeshed.

In addition, Richard Drayton's (2000) work highlights some aspects of the European mentalities that associated Amerindians with the flora of their landscapes.

Neil Whitehead (2003a) addresses some of these same issues among the Patamuna with regard to the way in which they characterize and describe certain features of their landscape. In the special case of trees, he notes that a cashew tree can come to represent a fallen, lone warrior; a palm can come to represent the "wild Indians'" refusal of agriculture; and the tree the Patamuna call *kumaka* is the site of a lack of self-control, a threat to the Patamuna model of gender complementarity. In addition, these changing landscapes are in concert with changing persons, and these examples offer evidence of this relationship more generally. In this same discussion, Whitehead offers several key ideas regarding the attempt to understand not only the relationship between indigenous persons and their landscapes, but also the views we have received on these relationships from historical sources. By examining the concept of *historicity,* or the ways that subjective attitudes make the past meaningful, and the act of *historiography,* or how the past is written or discursively narrated, we can, Whitehead tells us, expect multiple historicities and historiographies to emerge. In the special case of the Waiwai, we can expect and do find multiple narrations of both the self and others. In this instance, it is easy to see the mutual, mimetic relations of Amazonians with non-Amazonians, as he also points out. One of the categories for viewing these relations is, of course, landscape. Whitehead tells us that "geographic knowledge means that history is both written into and read from the landscape" (2003a:xiv). In particular, the Waiwai use both what Whitehead refers to as "narratives of emplacement" and narratives that allow for "the unseen world to be made visible" (2003a:75). This use is evident in the narratives of *nuñi kamshikru* (moon-blood place) and of the rock formations with the ekatï (soul substance or vital energies) of past inhabitants in the Essequibo River, but, as with the Patamuna, it is also present in the Waiwai's narrations of the sites of petroglyphs and rock carvings that inevitably evoke the past in the telling of their presence and the interpretation of their often mysterious meanings.

I often think of a large, spiral petroglyph that appears on a rock protruding from the middle of the river near the Waiwai village in Guyana when the water is low enough. This design is reminiscent (mimetic?) of some of the more ancient petroglyphs found in the area, but it has the conspicuous addition of several sets of initials and the year "1989" added to it. It was explained to me that several Waiwai youths made this petroglyph over a period of months, and the *kayaritomo* (village leader) eventually asked them to add the date so that people would not think it was made by the "old ones." I have often thought that this petroglyph, in addition to being somewhat mimetic of past rock carvings, was a way of preserving "sociocultural integrity and continuity," as Whitehead puts it, in the face of this integrity's being "persistently challenged by . . . neocolonial appropriation of lands, resources and intellectual property (2003a:xv). The Guyanese state in this sense is not exactly predatory, but it does engage in the project of becoming a "known feature of the global ethnoscape [that] is central to the political vista of the global economy and the globalized world in general" (Whitehead 2003a:xv). The Waiwai need to concern themselves about this project and do ultimately find compelling and interesting the ways in which the Guyanese nation-state both equates them with and acknowledges them as part of the landscape of the Deep South. History and identity in this case are intertwined in a project that creates narratives of authenticity and presence for both the state and the Waiwai. For the present, the Waiwai in their landscape are a central necessity for the Guyanese state and one it is willing to work to preserve.

Although the history of botanical exploration in the Waiwai area is relatively short, it has come to be extremely important in the story of the Waiwai's relationship with outsiders. To date, little in-depth ethnobotanical work has been done among the Waiwai, although all the botanical expeditions conducted in the area so far have used both Waiwai and Wapishana guides. The exception is the ubiquitous work of Fock and Yde, with Yde providing some very thorough lists of both cultivated and gathered plant species, along with their Waiwai names and supplemental information on their use where available (1965:53–93). Yde used Guppy's (unpublished and now unattainable) report entitled *Plant Exploration in the Sierra Acarai Region* to cross-check some family and species names. Aside from Yde's work, botanical expeditions to the region have provided lists of species names and some information on the dominant families present in the Waiwai's area. The first such expedition was carried out in 1937–38 by A. C. Smith and resulted in two publications (Smith 1939a, 1939b). Following this expedition is one of the typical time gaps in information about the Waiwai and their area; the next botanical work did not occur until Guppy's in the early 1950s, resulting in his reports and book (Guppy 1958). Yde's work is from this same period. A long gap of about thirty years then occurs until the revival of interest in floral composition results in an almost decade-long interaction with the Waiwai and their flora by two international projects. The first, Flora of the Guianas, was a collaborative project between the Dutch at Utrecht University, the British at the Royal Botanic Gardens at Kew, Guyanese scholars at the University of Guyana, and to some extent Americans at the New York Botanical Garden. This project included a collecting trip to the Waiwai area in 1989, and it used their village as a base and drew guides from the village population, usually both Wapishana and Waiwai residents. It marks the beginning of an era of increasing familiarity with biological scientists among the Waiwai, who have used that familiarity to interpret outsiders' meanings and agendas. In 1991, another such international project, the Biodiversity of the Guianas, was undertaken by the Smithsonian Institution. In collaboration with the University of Guyana, this project sent two collectors, Dr. Terry Henkel (1991–93) and Dr. H. David Clark (1995–2000) to the Waiwai region, among other areas, to collect plants and survey the ecological zones present between the southern Rupununi Savannahs and the Sierra

Acarai that forms the border between Guyana and Brazil. The Flora of the Guianas project resulted in publications listing species found in the area (Welle, Jansen-Jacobs, and Lughadha 1989, 1992) but does not relate these species very strongly to Waiwai usages, either practical or symbolic. The same information on a larger scale is present in the Smithsonian project as well. Publications are long in coming from this latter project because they require the positive identification of species by specialists and the preparation of herbarium specimens for several institutions. A number of checklists have come from the project, though (Boggan et al. 1997 and Hollowell et al. 2001 include the Waiwai area). All the collectors over the years, from Guppy to Clark, have mentioned that the Waiwai had names for nearly every herbaceous and tree species they encountered while on expedition. Ironically, B. J. H. ter Welle, N. J. Jansen-Jacobs, and E. M. Nic Lughadha state that Guppy's book was "primarily about the [Waiwai] tribe" and so not very useful biologically (1989:vi). My own assertion is the opposite—that Guppy's 1958 book is mostly about plants, his expedition, and himself, but not much about the Waiwai at all. This is one reason why I have placed it in the travel and adventure genre; his more scholarly botanical work is hard to find, and this book seems to fall short in both botanical and anthropological terms.

Conclusion

All of the Waiwai's "others" (including me) have had a hand in imagining and maintaining the space they currently inhabit. Not to be discounted is the way in which the Waiwai have reacted to and derived agency from these same imaginings. As the Waiwai face the imperative to define themselves for the future, they continue to assert the idea I wish to leave you with in this chapter. A Waiwai conception of the dynamic of human interaction and being emphasizes the role others have in the creation and maintenance of the self. In accordance with their own assertions, by reading this chapter about them, you are now involved in the imagining of them and are entwined in their lives and in the perpetuation of their communities and culture in a way that suggests there is much responsibility in gaining knowledge and allowing the mind to imagine. It is a responsibility that both encourages the Waiwai as it brings others into the project of their continual existence and frightens them with the potential power that comes from beyond their own imaginings.

16

Metaphoric Detours and Improper Translations in the Double Field of Waiwai Anthropology

Evelyn Schuler Zea

Just as there are many and specific *yesamarî* (ways, paths, or detours) interconnecting each household and constituting a so-called *comunidade* Waiwai, there are also many and specific ways and detours to shed light on the so-called Guayana region as an invented space.[1] In this chapter, my aim is to follow Waiwai ways of knowing, with special attention to their understandings of forms of mediation, deviation, and translation between many beings who live close to or far from them, permanently or temporarily, humans and nonhumans. In other words, I let my anthropological approach here be affected by the anthropology of one of the people who live there, who identify themselves and are identified nowadays as "Waiwai." Which ways can enable and convey such affecting? In the attempt to give an answer to this question, I try to revise and expand my metaphoric and conceptual tools as far—that is, as near to Waiwai ones—as I can.

When one reads the ethnographic literature of the Guayana region, it is noticeable that Waiwai ethnogenesis, as happens with the ethnonyms of many other Amerindians, builds a complex exchange between visions *about* this community and visions *of* this community about themselves and about others.[2] I use the name "Waiwai" in the sense that they use this name, knowing that it does not correspond to a single, substantial ethnic unit that exists for itself, but rather to an invention that does and must exist (for intellectual as well as political projects).[3] The statement that there are not many or even any "real" or "true" Waiwai appears repeatedly in the Waiwai literature: for example, William Farabee's reference to only five "real Waiwai" (1924:176), Nicolas Guppy's claim of only two "real Wai-Wais still living" (1958:162), Niels Fock's assertion of only two "true Waiwai" (1963:235), and one Waiwai's explanation that "no one here is *really* Waiwai (*Waiwai ixa*). None of us is Waiwai! The last few original Waiwai (*Waiwainhîrî komo*) were Kîmîya, Porîxa, and Tupuna, but they already died, oh dear.... We just call ourselves 'Waiwai,' but we're not really. That's how it is with us" (Yewîra qtd. in Howard 2001:404).

When one reads Waiwai literature, it is also noticeable that there are many direct and indirect references to the Waiwai's being widespread through large parts of the Guayana region, especially in relation to their trade activities in an expanded regional exchange network. Analyzing this expanded network, Catherine Howard (2001) demonstrates how the Waiwai are renowned in northern Amazonia for their trade specialties of manioc graters, talking parrots, and trained hunting dogs as well as for their expeditions in search of the "unseen people" (*enîhnî komo*) in the surrounding Guayana region. After 1950, when the Waiwai let the Unevangelized Field Mission—and nowadays the Missão Evangélica da Amazônia—establish itself among them, these expeditions continued with the mission's material (for example, boat motors and even sometimes the mission's aircraft) and immaterial (for example, the discourse of evangelical salvation) support.[4]

As groundwork to coming closer to these expeditions and to the differentiations the Waiwai make, I propose here to detach from direct ways of knowing because the object (or subject) to be known is not reachable through them: it does not exist cultivated at one's disposal, but has first to be elaborated and cultivated. In this sense, I propose here three theoretical excursions on notions of *metaphor*, *impropriety*, and *translation* to come closer—not at the conclusion of, but on the journey of these detours—to some Waiwai prospects. In doing so, my interest is neither to apply these theories on Waiwai ways of knowing nor to present them directly as Waiwai theories. As an alternative, I take the position that I can have no immediate access to Waiwai ways of knowing, but that there are many detour possibilities in relating different ways of knowing that let me come closer to them if I succeed.

Before I take these detours, let me describe two field experiences that were fundamental for all thoughts that follow here. The first one took place at the end of 2002 during my second fieldwork, when I accompanied Mikaiasa to interview Makipi, both inhabitants of the Waiwai community of Jatapuzinho. My attention was called to the fact that instead of taking the direct way to Makipi's house, Mikaiasa opted for a way that was considerably longer. When I asked him why he did not take the shorter and more direct way, he answered by drawing with Makipi a map of the different ways that configure the community and beyond (many of which I had not perceived until then). At the same time, they explained to me that I, as a foreign anthropologist, was allowed to take any of the ways, but that among the Waiwai, each person goes his or her own yesamarî, which can be translated as "indirect way" or "detour" and which designates also a certain oblique way of thinking and acting, as I want to discuss in this chapter.

The second experience refers to a certain way of seeing and being seen that called my attention from the beginning of my first fieldwork among the Waiwai in December 2001. In contrast to our (European, non-Waiwai) way of seeing the other frontally, in a direct way, what caught my attention when I arrived at Jatapuzinho (and afterward in other Waiwai communities) was that not a single Waiwai, with the exception of the children, looked at me frontally with this kind of gaze that for us is a first way of recognizing, but rather with an always deviated gaze. As time went by, I realized that this indirectness has nothing to do with mistrust or shame because it persisted without declination. This oblique gaze did not seem to configure something that could be defined in terms of lack (of trust or something similar), but on the contrary indicated something consistent and constitutive of a certain way of seeing and doing.

This form of obliqueness became theoretically more and more challenging as I noted that an increasing number of Waiwai constellations—such as the "unseen people," the "eye-soul," and the "translation rituals of animals," which I discuss in the following pages—seemed also to follow such an awry orientation. Everything seems to indicate that the Waiwai anthropology and their thought images start from the presumption that only indirect and mediated approaches to the things of the world seem to make sense, but not because of ethical or aesthetic reasons and even less because of etiquette or diplomacy, but for the sake of knowledge. A direct and immediate relation, if it still can be called a relation, constitutes in this context a minimal form, a kind of zero level of relatedness and not much more than the instance from which the process of knowledge only starts to develop. A leitmotif among the Waiwai seems to be that there is no knowledge without mediation.

Perhaps ways of hunting can provide a plausible comparison because in hunting, just as in the Waiwai ways of knowing, the attempt is first to surround a fleeing thing/being as widely and broadly as possible and then to close the circle on it patiently. From this perspective, the impulse to apprehend something/someone immediately makes less sense than an overhasty intervention during a hunt. In both cases, the apprehension as well as the comprehension would remain without prey. If we follow this analogy further, the metaphor becomes the linguistic trap that aims to attract and catch new aspects of a thing/being. The trick of metaphor, which is often seen as a risk for the speaker, comes into view as a deliberate and advantageous linguistic strategy to make its respective object/subject appear.[5]

In other words, my attempt here is to find access to Waiwai figures and their cultural procedures through theoretical excursions in the domains of metaphor and translation guided by the notions of detour and impropriety. The methodological option that I assume here thus consists in following the "longer ways" of the Waiwai anthropology, paying attention to the suggestions of their oblique gaze and the meanderings of their yesamarî. The detached and circumspect way of relating that they transmit is reflected in my attempt at capturing indirectly the Waiwai anthropology's indirect forms.

On Yesamarî and Metaphor

First, let me approach the concept of metaphor through references to some of Hans Blumenberg's writings, taking as a starting point his idea of *Umweg*—a concept that can be translated as "detour" and that I suggest as a translation for the Waiwai concept of "yesamarî." Blumenberg (1980 [1960], 1997, 2001) sees the detour not in negative terms as a lack or as a means to be surpassed by an end, but as something culturally constitutive and eminently creative. In opposition to the homogeneity that the institutionalization of the shorter and more direct way promotes, detours enable the openness and receptivity of experience that is a precondition to thinking the diversity of the world and, even more, the plurality of worlds. It is a matter not only of social difference and tolerance, which detours certainly encourage, but in the first instance of the multiplicities of ontologies, which are unfolded also by linguistic detours and which find their shape in metaphor and translation—as exemplary inventions of culture. Like the Waiwai yesamarî, the detours discover the many possible trajectories that lead from one point to the other in the cartographies not only of space but also of culture.

If the detours are multiple, it is because no one of them pretends to overcome another one. In principle, they all are equally inappropriate and disproportional in relation to their end. The impulse of the detour is the training of creativity and, through its means, the affirmations of a singularity. Each yesamarî wants its difference to be recognized; its efficacy consists in being a trace, a singular mark. The detour is not a matter of arriving more rapidly and directly at the aims of the method. The detour's value does not even depend on effectively reaching the presupposed end because it lives from the tension between departing and arriving, beginning and ending. It can persist in this interval, without denying itself, and its art may even lie in this floating form, this never-ending transit.

In the change of perspective that comes with the accentuated effect of decentralization, Blumenberg observes that it is also through the detour that the diversity of the things of the world can gain access to culture and be incorporated. The detour is the counterpart of the *distance* between humans and the world that is given by the inviability of an immediate and exhaustive knowledge, having in view the limitations of the first and the vastness of the second. And yet this distance should not be considered a negative magnitude because it constitutes the condition in which culture grows. If we follow Blumenberg, the relation that saves the distance and constitutes culture is "indirect, circumstantial, provisional, selective and, above all, metaphoric" (2001:415).

In connection to Blumenberg appears the idea of detour as a thought form of metaphor (Konersmann 1999:149). Both metaphor and detour are excessive forms not only because they transpose the uniform channels of communication but also because they present a multiplicity of meanings correlative to the irreducibility of each experience. As the yesamarî Waiwai inscribe their meanderings in the forest, metaphors make detours through the nonconceptual[6] to translate new meanings in the realm of culture.

Seeing the "Unseen People"

This idea may transport us to the famous expeditions the Waiwai organize periodically in search of what they call the "enîhnî komo," the "unseen people" (*enîhnî* indicating "unseen" and *komo* a collective form). These enterprises have no end, and their objects-subjects are continually deferred because the Waiwai indeed think of a new search as soon as they enter in contact with any "unseen people." This is why I agree, in principle, with Catherine Howard when, after a conversation with Yakuta, a famous Waiwai leader, she suggests "that his search was intrinsically interminable" (2001:408). But I do not agree with her conclusion regarding this interminable search, that "at the moment of discovery, the ethereal, hypothetical 'unseen people' *become* humans; conversely, the Waiwai become non-humans, living incarnations of the creator twins, Mawari and Wooxi, or of the missionaries' hero, Jesus Christ. This is why the Waiwai need the 'unseen peoples'" (408, emphasis in the original). Instead, according to her Waiwai interlocutor—"Yakuta told me that he never felt more exhilarated than when he was on the trail of a group" (408)—the truly moving moment in these expeditions seems to happen before and not after the moment of contact; it is in the trace, in the *trail,* in the presentiment rather than in the effectiveness of the encounter with the Other.

By *not* inserting the Waiwai expeditions into a teleological discourse, we can see that it is the process and not the goal that appears with an accentuated meaning—not as a means to a previewed end, but in the form of a persistent detour that figures as reference for the interminable *identité-à-faire* Waiwai. Political goals may be fulfilled in the effective encounter with other groups, but as knowledge enterprises the expeditions continually defer their object-subject in benefice of mediation, where they paradoxically seem to encounter their specific finality. The contours of Waiwai identity achieve a greater level of definition through this process, but only when attention is paid less to the culmination of their enterprises and more to the agility of their images in the transformation of mediation.

The "unseen people" let us see a Waiwai thought image as a way of knowing that is specified through its mediated access to its object or subject by the indirect ways of the detours. In this sense, the "unseen people" can be thought of as an *absolute metaphor*—that is, as a kind of metaphor that is irreducible to and cannot be substituted by a concept (Blumenberg 1980 [1960]:11). As an absolute metaphor, the "unseen people" can be radicalized as an infinite detour and in this way as an image of an unreachable object. In other words, the "unseen people" can be thought of as a metaphor *of* metaphor, conveying the genesis of metaphor rather than a metaphor *about* something or someone. This figure does not stand for something else or build a means of representation, but, as Roy Wagner would say, it stands for itself.[7] In Wagner's formulation, it should not be seen as a conventional symbolization with its property of "standing for" or denoting something other than itself, but as a nonconventional or differentiating symbolization that occurs when "a new referent is introduced simultaneously with the novel symbolization" (1981 [1975]):43).[8]

On Impropriety

As with the revision of detour and metaphor, I propose to look closely at the notion of *impropriety*, which is normally opposed to propriety, especially in its adjective use—that is, "improper" as opposed to "proper." Under the label *impropriety*, many and often-stated reservations against metaphor and translation can be summarized. From a methodic view, it is feared that the detour will miss scientific epistemological aims with its unsuited and excessive means. However, in my view, anthropology works with such means and can hardly do differently because impropriety is anthropology's emblem in the double respect that it turns on the strange through the strange. This is not only a matter of mediation but also a matter of ways of knowing through deviation.[9]

From the perspective of impropriety, the way becomes a detour, or, to be more precise, the way turns out to be a roundabout way—that is, a detour. The premises of its object or subject are taken into account, from which emerges a dense relation that is constitutive of anthropological perspectives. Waiwai anthropological images do not show their objects or subjects as in a smooth mirror but always obliquely, as in a side view, through a visual detour. Many Waiwai figures show that the course of their anthropological knowledge moves through constitutive detours, progressing through strict digression, *metaphorically*, in the same way that its object or subject allows its identity to be seen only through difference, through ambiguous liaison.

Seeing "In the Other's Eye"

Not only the expeditions in search of the "unseen people," but also the Waiwai conception of *yekatî yewru*—translated by Fock, following the missionary's suggestion, as the "eye-soul" (*ewru* indicating "eye" and *ekatî* "soul," but in my opinion better translated as "vitality")—can be seen as visual detours. I would like to pay attention to the way in which the Waiwai explained the eye-soul to Fock in the 1950s as "the small person one always sees in the other's eye" (1963:19). This concept does not designate, as Fock considers in a first instance, "one's own reflected image" or "a general impression of the eye as that which best expresses the soul of a person" (19). Rather, as Fock himself indicates in a second instance, it can better be thought of as related to another Waiwai idea, which he calls the "general idea behind the Waiwai magic: To see oneself is the same as being seen" (122). It is the action of seeing as a form of passion because whoever sees also at the same time suffers the consequences of seeing; or, to say it the other way round, it is the passion of seeing as an intensive kind of action. For this reason, seeing (above all, seeing a supernatural being) is always dangerous because in seeing, one is also seen (and to be seen by a supernatural being means to be affected in multiple ways by it, most commonly by getting sick and most extremely by dying). In other words, in seeing, one encounters counterseeing; that is, assuming a perspective means

Metaphoric Detours and Improper Translations

simultaneously receiving another's perspective because seeing is always a matter of yekatî yewru exchange.[10]

In my conversations with Waiwai regarding yekatî yewru, they told me that "we only have yekatî yewru looking at each other because then there is ekatî, he has ekatî with you, and you have ekatî with him. If you are alone, you have not" (Taytasi translating Totore, from 11 January 2002 in Jatapuzinho). This explanation seems to indicate that yekatî yewru does not exist for itself but exists effectively only through the relation of two persons looking reciprocally, being an action and at the same time a passion.

The missionaries who studied Waiwai ways (including their language) in order to proselytize and induce them to follow the way of God (which the missionaries translated as "Kaan yesamarî") did not miss the importance of ekatî exchange and therefore translated "Holy Spirit" as "Kiriwan Yekatî"—that is, God's "Good Spirit." They preached that everyone must be in constant exchange with Kiriwan Yekatî if one did not want to be punished in purgatory but ascend to heaven.

Yet it is remarkable that, despite allowing many transformations in the past fifty years with the missionaries' presence, the Waiwai continue to describe heaven in a way very similar to how they described it to Fock in the 1950s and to Howard in the 1980s—as a very friendly place full of light where everyone is happy and beautiful:

> The Waiwai believe that after death, their eye-souls are freed from their mortal bodies and ascend to the first heaven, where everybody is dressed in their most beautiful bead and feather finery all the time and engage in perpetual feasting, dancing, and laughter. Each soul obtains a new spouse. No one has to work; nothing ever decays and food and wealth items just appear on their own. . . . The way the Waiwai describe this location is similar to traditional beliefs recorded by Fock (1963:20, 101–103) about the closest of several layers of celestial worlds, the place where the sparkling 'eye-souls' enjoy immortality. Nowadays, they believe that the capture of more souls in the name of Jesus is the surest guarantee that they will be resurrected after death and gain admittance into this domain of eternal effervescence. (Howard 2001:279, 353)[11]

The light that illuminates this beautiful and happy place bridges distances such as those between the different earthly and heavenly cosmic layers, bringing them therefore into communication. The Waiwai associate light with visibility, social thoughts, and actions, and, as Howard describes, its ability to bridge distances and enable communication can also be linked to the importance of the beloved glass beads because they are full of light: "The glint of light reflected off shiny beads is considered pleasing to behold and makes the viewer 'turn towards' the wearer [of beads], creating a bond between them. To capture this quality of shininess, the Waiwai also apply Brazil nut oil to their hair, enhancing it with eagle down (which similarly reflects light) in preparation for public gathering when people catch each other's eyes, even those of God, creating a collectivity of reciprocal gazes" (Howard

2001:272–273). The effect of brilliance through reflected light and its ability to catch other people's eyes enhances the quality of other beloved ornaments as well, especially those (and there are many) that are decorated with brilliant red macaw feathers and, in my opinion, also the currently beloved mirrors and sunglasses.[12]

This notion of light connects to a pervasive Amerindian idea of light as "pure intensity, the intense and intensive 'heart' of reality which establishes extensive distance between beings (i.e., their greater or lesser mutual capacity to become)"; this notion, as Eduardo Viveiros de Castro argues, joins in its turn to the idea of the invisibility of spirits: "the normally invisible is also the abnormally luminous. The intense luminosity of spirits indicates the super-visible character of these beings, which are 'invisible' to the eye for the same reason light is—that is, by being the condition of the visible" (2004:11). Viveiros de Castro also notes that a rather paradoxical picture emerges from the indigenous words we usually translate as "spirits," beings that are beautiful and monstrous, visible and invisible, noniconic and nonvisible. What do we understand by the term *spirits*? Do the Waiwai understand Kiriwan Yekatî the same way the missionaries do? Do both refer to the same conception of light? This subject calls attention to the fundamental question of different ways of thinking what is, can, or should be a translation.

On Translation

Let me begin this fourth theoretical excursion and revaluation—after the ones on impropriety, detour, and metaphor—with a discussion of the essay "The Task of the Translator," in which Walter Benjamin (1996 [1923]) condenses in only a few pages complex questions concerning translation and opens multiple possibilities for thinking about this fundamental subject not only our anthropology, but, as everything seems to indicate, also the Waiwai's. I want to follow here those motives that relate to the figures of detour and impropriety.

Translations create a profound unrest in language, especially in the status of the so-called original that is destabilized and ruined as such. However, it is precisely in this interference and its subsequent disturbing effects that we can see the relevance of translation in its role as agent of living on after—or surviving—the original (cf. Benjamin 1996 [1923]:46). In this sense, translations follow an infinite detour, which does not end because there is no final destination to be perceived as last property.

The detours of translation seem to show the discordance of language with itself. They work under the sign of impropriety because mediation and transformation are immanent to them. As Benjamin notes, translations do not live through an immediate or natural similarity with the original: "No translation would be possible if in its ultimate essence it strove for likeness to the original. For in its afterlife [*Fortleben*]—which could not be called that if it were not a transformation and a renewal of something living—the original undergoes a change" (2004:17). The

Metaphoric Detours and Improper Translations 215

original is not reproduced in the translation, but rather *grows* in it; the original is not substituted but rather *completed* by the translation. In this sense, translations are joining and articulating themselves with the original rather than trying to represent it. Translations thus point rather to the incompleteness than to the self-sufficiency of the original. The impropriety of translations is reinforced by the loss of the original, which does not live anymore as original but only survives when the translation is brought up.

Following Benjamin, the "task of the translator" does not consist in maintaining fidelity to the original or in the immediateness of communication but in elaborating the mediation that permits the survival—the only possible one—of the original. In his lecture about Benjamin's essay, Paul de Man emphasizes decanonization of the original and, through extension, of all absolute instances, specifying the translation precisely for its *distance* from the original. The translation provokes many disjunctions of language, inciting the "errancy of language" (de Man 1985: 44). In the translation's relevance to the original's survival, Jacques Derrida sees the manifestation of an incompleteness that situates the original in the same sequence of imperfection as the translation. The scission between original and translation is therefore only another version of the metaphysical dualism, which can be surpassed only by assuming that the signified does not constitute an instance of transparency but, on the contrary, that the signified shares the dissemination of the signifiers. The migration of the meanings through translation corresponds to nothing less than a process of *transformation* (Derrida 1972:31).

Translation Rituals

Thinking on anthropological translation, Talal Asad (1986) writes in favor of the position that it is not simply a matter of bringing sentences into correspondence in an abstract manner but more a matter of learning the other life form as well. He also argues that the translation of a foreign life form sometimes succeeds better through a theater play, a dance choreography, or a music improvisation than through ethnographic discourse: translation should be not merely a matter of interpretations but of *transformed moments of the original*. This argument may bring us closer to Waiwai anthropology. Let me turn to an example that I consider an especially beloved anthropological praxis among the Waiwai, through which they make remarkable detours in translating different "Others."[13]

The example I am thinking of can be found only marginally in literature on the Waiwai as "animal imitation dances" (Fock 1963:72), "animal imitation games" (Howard 2001:221), or "animal joking (farsa)" (C. Dias 2000:92, 2006:179) in reference to rituals in the course of which some Waiwai actors take on the appearance, language, and behavior of forest animals. These rituals are performed beside other beloved rituals in the context of the Waiwai's annual festivals, which were called Shodewika (Fock 1963) in the 1950s or Shoriwiko (Dowdy 1963) in the 1960s and that nowadays occur on Christmas and Easter, which are called, according to a Waiwai pronunciation of the Christian names, "Kresmus" and "Istu."[14] These festivals maintain several connections with the Shodewika myth (cf. Fock 1963: 56–74) that tells about a Shodewika festival to which a Waiwai couple and other so-called animal people (which in mythic time looked human but during the festival were wearing animal clothes as dance costumes) were invited. On the long way to the festival—which shows itself as one more noteworthy detour—the Waiwai couple composed many songs by imitating the animals they met. These songs became a big success at the feast because everyone wanted to learn and dance to them. After the festival, everyone who returned from it without having married turned into an animal, whereas those who married during the festival remained human and were identified with the Waiwai's neighbors (cf. Fock 1963:56–74). Fock notes the following with regard to the Shodewika festival he saw at the end of 1954:

> The dance festival itself had begun before the Waiwai couple arrived, and the myth thus suggests that the Shodewika festival and dance are a loan from outside, a loan that acquired a Waiwai stamp on account of the fact that the new version employed song texts in Waiwai language. This assumption is supported by the information that the animal imitation dances frequently performed at the Shodewika festivals are regarded by the Waiwai as a loan from the Mouyenna Indians [Mawayana], a neighbouring Arawakan tribe living south-east. (1963:72)

By continuing the performance of these "animal imitation dances," the Waiwai still allude to the mythic account, especially two aspects of it: (1) the human-looking "animal people" were wearing animal clothes as dance costumes during the festival and so were *imitating*—or, to be more precise, *translating*—the animals; (2) the songs are *imitations* or *translations* of different animals' voices as well.

The Waiwai word to designate their performing during these rituals is /yukuknome/, a word that indicates a conjunction of semantic fields of imitation ("amna nukuknomesî," "we [exclusive] are imitating," or, more literally, "we are presenting a sample") and of the visual (/yukuknome-/, /yukuknoke-/, "take a photo, make a drawing")—and is also used by the Waiwai when referring to translation, leading to the important question of how these complex connections can be thought and how they are related.

These animal imitation dances—which I consider "animal translation rituals"—not only still allude to the Shodewika myth but also continue features of the Shodewika festivals, like the one Fock saw in the 1950s. In the busy time of initial contact with non-Waiwai, the Waiwai allowed the establishment of the missionaries among them and some—but not all—of the changes the missionaries proposed (for example, to hold sermons at church during Christmas and Easter and not to prepare manioc beer for the festivals).[15] The Waiwai performed these translation rituals alongside several other dances, games, and rituals during their festivals and, against the missionaries' wishes, often throughout the night.[16]

Metaphoric Detours and Improper Translations 217

In my conversations with the Waiwai regarding these translation rituals—and it is remarkable how much they love to talk about them, doing it a great deal and in an amusing and eloquent way—they always referred simultaneously to a specific animal and to its specific way of speaking and behaving.[17] From among the many examples they gave me and from some of the performances I saw (during their festivals at the end of 2001 and 2002), I choose to describe here the following three examples:

Weñemeñe: a medium-size black animal that likes to eat sugarcane. Every Waiwai performing this animal came to the festival with his body covered with black paint and laden with sugarcane, singing the respective weñemeñe song. They explained to me that when they sing the weñemeñe song, the body becomes light and quick, able to walk crooked and twisted to fight with the *pisko* bird.[18]

Kamara and *poñko:* jaguar and wild pig, two beings of great cosmological relevance, whose translation rituals configure a visible collective plethora involving actors of all ages. In the performance, I saw a big herd of poñko composed of both Waiwai adults and children with their bodies covered with palm leaves. A little poñko was captured by a Waiwai painted like a kamara, jaguar, with a gigantic genital organ that provoked big laughter. The poñko herd pursued the kamara to recuperate the little poñko, but afterward they were in their turn pursued by Waiwai hunters that brought the poñko to the laughing Waiwai women to be prepared as meat to eat.

Yawari: opossum, also of great mythological relevance among the Waiwai, who perform it by night, dancing with few clothes and singing his song or playing his melody with bone flutes. They go from household to household of the *yîmîtîn,* the Waiwai women who are the owners of the beverages during the festivals, and they ask them for beverages, bananas, and mangos and leave dried crocodile or tortoise meat in their houses. When they go away, they steal a chicken or eggs, as the opossums do in their nocturnal wanderings.

These translation rituals point to the correlation between seeing and being seen as one more attempt to deviate from the immediate or frontal or direct gaze. Just as seeing (especially seeing supernatural beings, and all these animals are linked to such beings) is something dangerous and full of risks, in these translation rituals the animals are evoked through redundancy—that is, through a repetition that does not point to identity, as in the case of mere imitation, but to difference. That is what these translation rituals demonstrate through their caricatures and exaggerations and excesses: it is a matter of seeing in between, of using an oblique and lateral gaze for seeing through the nonfamiliar. We might speak of a Waiwai conception of translation of something or someone that cannot be brought or made present but whose surviving can be transmitted as a life through translation.

Interfaces of Translations and Metaphors

"Translation is a form," says Benjamin (1996 [1923]:45), in the sense that translation operates between the languages—that is, not with the referents, but with the arrangement of languages—in the same way as metaphors connect two nets of meaning. Ambivalences constitute the interface of translations and metaphors. It is with such ambivalences that we are allowed to wander from language to language, from word to word. This wandering joins languages' soft places, their vulnerable sides. In this sense, therefore, metaphors and translations can be thought of as work on ambivalences.

Metaphors and translations encounter each other at the moment when the former are withdrawn from arbitrariness and the latter from dependence. It may therefore be expected that the extensive current discussions on metaphor and translation—which, despite mutual motives, move parallel to each other up to this point—will increasingly clarify each other through their resonances. A recurring sign of this convergence is the German word *Übertragung*, which is used for both metaphor and translation and, even more, in the sense of *free* or *poetic* translation, which metaphor seems to approach. By suggesting "transmission" as the translation of *Übertragung*, I try to stress the connection between metaphor and translation, both of which are structured transversally, following an awry way.

Mission and Transmission

To finish here, let me go back to the questions that brought me to the detour on translation and through it to *transmission:* Do the Waiwai understand "Kiriwan Yekatî" the same way the missionaries do? Do both refer to the same conception of light? At a first instance and with the idea in view that both the missionaries and the Waiwai cultivate rich visual traditions, it seems that the light metaphor may provide a bridge of communication between them. Nevertheless, everything indicates that two radically deviating conceptions are at work behind this apparently same use of the light metaphor. The missionaries use it within the bounds of the Holy Message or Representation—that is, as a fixed image in the service of the Lord. The Waiwai, however, seem to cultivate this metaphor for the precise reason that it does not let itself be substituted insofar as it provides both ways of knowing and at the same time the object or subject of knowing.

Through various thought images—such as the enîhnî komo ("unseen people"), the yekatî yewru ("eye-soul"), and the animal translation rituals—the Waiwai seem to be indicating the alternatives of hiding and showing oneself, of seeing and being seen, of seeing as action and as passion. The Waiwai images relate not only to local experiences but transversally also to the working contradictions and ambivalences that mediate between them. The recurrence of these images shows a profound perplexity among the Waiwai and, in response to it, an increasingly sophisticated *transmission*—a metaphoric translation. The missionaries' light metaphors, being in the service of representation, are quickly burned out—and we may be sure that nothing will change as long as the missionaries attribute to light and metaphor a fixed and functional role and exclude their ambivalences as detours of thinking or knowing. Detours are inappropriate to terminal or final destinations and so cannot be understood through them; they define themselves not in function of the straight way, but on behalf of their irreducible diversity.

Acknowledgments

From January 2007 to July 2008, I participated in the postdoctoral program of the Department of Anthropology at the Universidade de São Paulo and am grateful for the research fellowship provided by the Fundação de Amparo à Pesquisa do Estado de São Paulo. I also thank the Research Center "Interweaving Performance Cultures" at the Free University of Berlin for providing a fellowship since August 2008. Last but not least, this chapter could not have been written without the infinite teachings of the Waiwai, especially Makipi, Mikaiasa, Ñawñawa, Panahrui, Powa, Taitasi, Totore, and Yukuma. For Macarwe and Ratarî, in memoriam.

Notes

1. The name "Waiwai" is currently used to designate both a very small subgroup and the actual communities (including different subgroups such as the Mawayana, Katuena, Xerew, Karapayana, Taruma, and Hixkariyana, among others) that speak a Carib language that is also called "Waiwai" and inhabit both sides of the Acarai Mountains on the border region between Brazil and Guyana. Approximately 280 live in Jatapuzinho, 130 in Anaua, 50 in Cobra, 30 in Catual, and 30 in Soma and Samaúma. The numbers are increasing in new villages in the Brazilian state of Roraima, and more than 1,000 live in different villages in the Brazilian state Pará (the largest village still being the Mapuera community). Approximately 270 live in two villages on the Guyana side (see Alemán's chapter) and a few in Suriname, mainly in Tiriyó villages.

2. See the discussion about this kind of relational and context bounded ethnogenesis in Gallois 2000, 2005.

3. Although I concentrated my field research in only one Waiwai community, Jatapuzinho, my aim here is to be writing from a multilocal focus, considering the account of other Waiwai communities from other spaces and other times as well as the accounts of other Amerindians.

4. Considering that the relations the Waiwai established with the missionaries occurred on several levels, I think that instead of simply talking about their "conversion" to Christianity, we should see this ongoing and ever-changing relationship in the context of a complex network of relations with external powers, which are fundamental in the constitution process of their own culture. For the missionaries' version (or conversion), which they present as being made directly through God, see Dowdy 1963, 1995, and Hawkins 1954, 1956. For an anthropological account of the Waiwai and their missionary experience, see Alemán 2005; and for a neighboring Carib example, see Fajardo Pereira 1999.

5. Space can be defined as a domain or, better, a *circumscription* of a metaphor, and its borders as being prescribed by the widest possible detour of a thought image. Again, we

may think of it with the help of orienting analogies to the Waiwai art of hunting because these analogies prescribe the hunting space by an initial detour through which the prey's virtual movements are restricted. To take a space as a metaphor means to shape a virtual space through returning metaphors; put the other way round, it is a matter of reversing or bringing back the metaphors of semantic *fields* as used in linguistics, metaphorically reshaping this time geography.

6. See "Prospect for a Theory of Nonconceptuality" in *Shipwreck with Spectator* (Blumenberg 1997).

7. In *Invention of Culture* (1981 [1975]:43) and then through *Lethal Speech* (1978:25), Wagner expounds this idea of metaphor as "symbols that stand for themselves" (which became the title of his 1986 book).

8. Wagner also calls this mode of symbolization "obviation," which he understands as a process "by which the artificial comes to metaphorize the innate (and the reverse process)" (1978:31).

9. *Improper* is often used as an adjective of *metaphor,* indicating metaphor's provisional and replaceable status and pointing to its subsequent feasible substitution through a literal statement, allegedly without loss of content. The theory of substitution and comparison in classical rhetoric defends this opinion, and the critique of this theory has inaugurated current theories on metaphor. Since the interaction theory of Ivor A. Richards and its display through Max Black, metaphors are rather seen as creative and inventive phenomena. They are not cut out from discourse anymore, but are presented context-bound in the play of their "systems of associated implications" (Black 1983). Metaphors are built out of a multiplicity of linguistic components; they shift from plurality to plurality, which makes it impossible to paraphrase them. Their materials do not remain untouched, but they are shaken and rebuilt, which makes their effects irreducible. Metaphors are also improper in the sense that they belong to nobody; that is, they do not even belong to their supposed creator. As Israel Sheffler formulates this point, "In creating a metaphor, one may surprise oneself" (1997:70).

10. This belief connects to what has been called "Amerindian perspectivism" (Viveiros de Castro 1996) and "Melanesian exchange of perspectives," where "a person's gaze is not returned as such; the man does not see himself but himself, transformed, in another body" (Strathern 1999:255).

11. This "heavenly" place is conceived as a stadium of permanent *tahwore* (joyfulness or elation), where the ethos of *tawake* (congeniality or equanimity) is intensified by the beauty (*cenporem*) of the body adornments (Howard 1991:57).

12. These ornaments "are not so much static objects of aesthetic contemplation (how we tend to view them)," but rather "visual counterparts of processes—of attracting, influencing, acquiring, and assimilating" (Howard 1991:54). See two articles on this fundamental anthropological subject of body adornment among the Waiwai, one written by Howard (1991) and the other by Mentore (1993).

13. These "Others" may live close to or far from the Waiwai, permanently or temporarily, and may be both humans and nonhumans. Whereas Howard (1991, 2001) has focused on the so-called *pawana* ritual, during which the "Other" refers to human visitors, I want to focus on those rituals in which the "Other" refers to what we call "animals."

14. It has to be questioned whether the diverse sectors involved in evangelization effectively substituted their philosophical and cosmological conceptions for native ones. In my view, a logic of transformation and selection seems to make more sense than a logic of substitution, as indicated in the examples I reflect on here.

15. It has to be noted that Waiwai Christmastime and Eastertime coincide with the dry season—that is, with the time during which the festivals were celebrated before the missionaries arrived.

16. Howard describes another proposition by the missionaries that the Waiwai did not accept: "This spirit children [the missionaries] also told them how they reproduced. Although they could copulate like ordinary people, they seemed bizarrely proud of their ability to practice abstinence, even encouraging their spouse to avoid sex despite their mutual desires: They told us, 'The longer we wait, the happier God is. . . .' All of us [Waiwai] just laughed. . . . 'That's certainly not how we practice sex!' we [Waiwai] said. And we still don't. That's a custom we never imitated!' " (Warapuru in Howard 2001:61).

17. Animals such as *amaci* (anteater), *morura* (big armadillo), *kapayo* (small armadillo), *meku* and *poroto* (kinds of monkeys), *pisko* (jacamin bird), *pakria* (little wild pig), *warakaka* (mandi fish), *wayawaya* (otter), *wenu* (bee), *wenayko* (coati), *rere* (bat), *poñko* (big wild pig), *kamara* (jaguar), and *yawari* (opossum).

18. This Waiwai description of song is strongly reminiscent of another Amerindian description: a Yaminahua's explanation to Graham Townsley that the song paths and their "twisted language brings me closer but not too close—with normal words I would crash into things—with twisted ones I circle around them—I can see them clearly" (in Townsley 1993:460).

17

Cultivating a "Culture"
Wajãpi Inventions

Dominique Tilkin Gallois

In November 2003, the United Nations Education, Scientific, and Cultural Organization (UNESCO) announced the results of the second Proclamation of Masterpieces of the Oral and Intangible Heritage of Humanity. One of the twenty-eight selected submissions was "The Oral and Graphic Expressions of the Wajãpi," an indigenous candidate and the first ever to be put forward by Brazil.[1] Thus began one more stage in a long process of reflection among the Wajãpi on the question of their "culture," which this article aims to synthesize. With the support of various public and private institutions, this lengthy process of cultivating a "culture" continues to unfold, and during its course this community—"the Wajãpi"—is emerging with a new profile, both social and political.

My objective here is to illustrate how the production of cultural objects is inseparable from the production of social actors. In the course of recent experiments in cultural "patrimonialization" that have begun to appear among the indigenous communities of Brazil, we have seen both traditional practices configuring new actors and new practices leading to the reappearance of traditional actors—in other words, an intricate network of possibilities that cannot be approached through a simple opposition between the "traditional" and the "new." I aim to illustrate, through the example of the Wajãpi, how cultural regimes are capable of change through a series of transformations and the complexification of the dynamics of cultural transmission.

Plan for Safeguarding Wajãpi Traditional Knowledge in Amapá

Various reasons explain why the Wajãpi chose their *kusiwarã* graphic patterns and the oral wisdom associated with them as the subject of their submission to the UNESCO program. For the younger community leaders, the choice was related to the difficulties they currently face in protecting their graphic art from indiscriminate commercial and public use. Whereas the older members of the community were concerned about affirming the beauty of their corporal paintings, the younger members claimed that in using these works, they were laying themselves bare to prejudiced comments from the *karaikõ*, as they call nonindigenous people. The traditional community leaders also wanted to consolidate their argument that there is little point in "writing" if the young are not capable of "hearing" and in this way learning about their own traditions.

As such, the discussions in preparation for the presentation of their proposal to UNESCO revealed that the choice of their graphic art and the verbal art associated with it was in the interests of both younger and elder Wajãpi. These examples of graphic art are indeed cultural expressions that demonstrate in an exemplary manner the dynamics of the transmission of knowledge in practice among the Wajãpi. Both the graphic patterns and the narratives associated with them are creations marked not only by a particular style—or, rather, a "tradition"—but also by the authorship and innovation of the person making them. This ability to create graphics and narratives in a style marked by constant renovation bears witness to the contemporary nature of Amerindian cultures, which are traditional exactly because they are not constituted only out of things from the past. For the Wajãpi, the challenge is not to eternalize elements of their culture but to secure greater respect for their capacity to incorporate new objects, practices, and reflections into their ways of positioning themselves in the world.

The inclusion of the Wajãpi's forms of cultural expression in UNESCO's Representative List of Masterpieces of Oral and Intangible Heritage may in this way potentially represent an exceptional opportunity to expose—if not to resolve—a series of contradictions in the assistance provided to this and other indigenous groups in the Brazilian Amazon. Although organizations such as UNESCO take care to promote the value of the cultural traditions of native peoples, and Brazilian legislation grants the Amerindians special recognition of their lands and their forms of social and political organization as well as the right to a differentiated education, the implementation of effective measures in these areas continues to be very problematic.

Antecedents: The Construction of an "Indigenous" Identity

In this section, I present a brief history of the long process that led the directors of the Wajãpi Villages Council to submit their proposal to UNESCO. Although UNESCO's acceptance of this proposal would undoubtedly result in the development of new cultural dynamics among the Wajãpi, the initiative behind the Wajãpi candidacy was in itself already the result of certain public policies or, more specifically, of the group's growing involvement in Brazilian indigenist politics.

In dealing with trajectories such as this one in any part of the Americas, it is necessary to consider the specific ways in which each group has developed a particular conception of its own "indianeity" and how, starting from a variety of different perceptions, each group has developed ways of announcing its ethnicity in the context of its relations with national societies. In Brazil, these forms of indianeity are products of the means of appropriation and diverse experiences of each group in relation to the special legal rights granted to Amerindians by the state,[2] for it is in a controlled legal and administrative environment that one learns to be "Indian" or, rather, to occupy the ambiguous space reserved for Amerindians within Brazilian society.[3] It is in this context that Wajãpi adults and young people have been encouraged to produce ideas, projects, translations, neologisms, performances, and objects that conform to what is expected of them: to represent themselves and to explain that they have a "Wajãpi culture."

The appropriation of this condition of being "Indian" was a direct result of a radical transformation in the Wajãpi's pattern of territoriality through the reduction of their territory into a delimited and later demarcated area of land. It was during this movement in the 1980s that the members of a series of dispersed local groups began to refer to themselves as "Wajãpi," principally on occasions that required the affirmation of a social and political unit. These groups had never previously experimented with this unity, and it continues to make little sense in the context of their interpersonal and intercommunity relations. The name "Wajãpi," in fact, is a reference to the language shared by their different subgroups, historically dispersed throughout a vast region along the border of Brazil and French Guiana.[4] For Wajãpi speakers, the use of variants of the same language was never synonymous with any kind of social unity or political consensus but on the contrary enabled the playing out of contradistinctions between subgroups through which they could (as they still can today) enunciate their internal differences and disagreements.

However, as a result of the necessity for dialogue with the karaikõ, formulations began to appear based on relatively homogenous—and necessarily imprecise—factors such as language, collective land (called *jane yvy*), and some valorized elements of *jane reko*, or "our way of being." It was also in this context that the Villages Council, Apina, was created, which aims to bring together "all" the Wajãpi villages in Amapá. These new cultural instruments are played out on the karaikõ's stage, where the Wajãpi do their best to construct a notion of consensus that, in their daily relations, is impossible to sustain precisely due to the value traditionally attributed to difference. In order for the Wajãpi to represent themselves, however, especially in relation to the logic of "projects," it is necessary to suppress divergences. This lesson is, without doubt, one of the most difficult to be learned in the behavior required of those defined by the condition of being "Indian" in Brazil because the idea of unity is totally contradictory for a people who think in terms of the independent trajectories of their local groups and political factions. We can see, however, that whereas during the first stage of the development of a Wajãpi "identity" these communities attempted to obliterate differences, in the current stage they are trying to reelaborate these differences precisely because the younger leaders have come to the understanding that "Wajãpi culture" can be valorized as an instrument for representation that allows the articulation of differences—points of view, big and small variations on names, chants, formulas, practices, and historical experiences.

In this context, notions such as "differentiated culture"—used in indigenist discourse in Brazil—are of real interest to the Wajãpi. For them, worthwhile differences, expressed through the communication that their linguistic identity permits, are not related to a common archive of cultural traits but on the contrary to the possibility of the articulation of internal diversity. It is in this sense that the Wajãpi's specific interpretation of the idea of culture serves to invert the focus of the notion of cultural difference used by conventional actors in the realm of Brazilian indigenist politics. If for the majority of these actors that which is "differentiated" presupposes an undifferentiated ethnic agglomerate, for the Wajãpi valued differences are those that mark distances between their subgroups, emphasizing variations in the archives of their knowledge or affirming autonomy in the political alliances that each subgroup establishes with diverse agencies.

Successive Elaborations on a Wajãpi Notion of "Culture"

During the past two decades, I have been able to accompany the Wajãpi's reflections on questions of culture and politics. In order to document this process of broadened relations, which engages not only the collective that the Wajãpi have been constructing in order to identify themselves in relation to the karaikõ but also new forms of relations among the Wajãpi themselves, I have registered multiple statements on the subject of "culture" made at different stages in this trajectory. The reflections elaborated by ten bilingual teachers with respect to transformations in the relations between generations, between local groups, as well as between the Wajãpi and other Amerindian groups in the same region have been particularly interesting. In these reflections, the teachers have also been concerned to evaluate the alterations that have been brought about in their way of life and the solutions that have been suggested at different moments for the strengthening of "Wajãpi culture." As a starting point, I quote three affirmations:

- "We are ashamed of not knowing how to offer the appropriate replica to the elders, of no longer knowing the right way to speak."
- "We will learn the things of the Whites in school; we have two paths—that of the Wajãpi and that of the Whites."
- "We want to learn to speak our feelings, the way the elders do."

Feeling Ashamed of Being Unable to Dialogue with the Elders

At the beginning of the 1990s, the young people who have today become bilingual teachers and coordinators of Apina were responsible for the production of public "images" of the Wajãpi collective. Assimilating aspects of the special legal rights guaranteed to Amerindians by Brazilian legislation, they understood that cultural difference could be projected to the outside world. Despite the difficulty of promoting unity among the communities, they managed to carry out their role as intermediaries with a certain neutrality, erasing tensions between different local communities and mediating relations within a wider context, where, due to their being literate, they would later become significant actors (for example, in the organization of the Villages Council, the management of a fund for the commercialization of handicrafts, and so on).

In this way, learning to position themselves in relation to other "Indians" and to multiple nationalities, these young people began to use ethnic classifications that had never been used by the older Wajãpi. For the latter, the distinction between Brazilians, the French, and other non-Amerindians held little meaning, just as there was little meaning for them in the difference between the Aparai, the Yanomami, and the Kayapó. These labels are much more restrictive than native categories, which establish subtle counterpoints connected to historical experience and the calculation of social distance.[5] It was perceptible that, when one spoke of other peoples or of pan-indigenous meetings, the difficulties involved in the sharing of reflections between generations increased. It was in this context that the bilingual teachers expressed their embarrassment at not being able to replicate the elders' speech patterns or to sustain a formal dialogue using the refined repertoire of categories of otherness used by their fathers. Neither did they feel capable of using the etiquette appropriate to the reception of visitors, when hosts and guests elaborate their current and respective opinions in relation to the tensions, alliances, and events that affect the network of relations between family groups and when they develop dialogues that "produce" new dissensions or alliances. This inability was in the early 1990s widely criticized by the eldest members of the community, who still today continue to lament the young people's disrespectful attitudes.

It was in this relatively tense environment that expectations of the prestige that might be acquired in the schools began to grow. School was understood to be the place where "knowledge of the karaikõ" could be learned, and many chiefs defended this expectation because of their desire to see their children occupying positions controlled until this point by non-Amerindians, as teachers, health workers, drivers, and so on. For this reason, up until 1998 both the village chiefs and the teachers in the villages refused to allow the use of their mother tongue in the schools. They hoped that this new institution, the school, would offer the possibility of dominating the written word, mathematics, and other subjects in order to access positions and salaries reserved for non-Amerindians.

In this context, a transformed idea of "culture" began to be applied to "Wajãpi craftwork" or, rather, to the adaptation of some items of material culture for sale: miniatures of bows and arrows, ceramics and baskets, necklaces, and so on, the sale of which made possible the acquisition of firearms, ammunition, cloth, cooking pans, and other items they were unable to make themselves. Also defined as being examples "of Wajãpi culture" were the imitations of ritual celebrations presented in the cities at the request of the karaikõ and in return for financial support. All this activity served to strengthen the idea that exhibiting "culture" would bring varied kinds of support. In fact, the Wajãpi were relatively successful in achieving this result, insofar as the logic of most of the funding destined for indigenous peoples requires their visibility. As such, during this phase the idea of cultural valorization in the ambit of the villages made little sense. Tranquillity reigned in relation to the future, alongside a certain disdain for the concerns of anthropologists and educators who sought to problematize the young people's lack of interest in traditional forms of verbal art, corporal painting, and ritual cycles.

Learning to See Yourself from the "White" Point of View

Here it is necessary to exemplify how certain experiences induce or do not induce the construction of new actors through the production of cultural artifacts, be it under the banner of "rescue" or as a form of income generation. Doing so obliges us to evaluate the reflexive process of the exchange of images (between the Amerindians and their public). If Amerindians market themselves to meet the demands of an urban public who are interested in seeing elements of what is identified as "indigenous culture" in Brazil, are these groups therefore subject to a generic indianeity? The situation is not so simple. It has already been recognized that the indigenous groups are not destined to be transformed from "tribal Indians" to "generic Indians."[6]

Since 1998, many Wajãpi, both young and old, have had the opportunity to participate in the production of video documentaries, exhibitions, and books that present aspects of their culture to a diverse public. Through these experiences, one of the most important skills they attained was the ability to select images and the forms of identification for a non-Amerindian public. For the indigenous villages, production of such images raised questions such as "Why write down what I already know?" "Why film these things for my village?" They discovered that mastering these new techniques (drawing up tables, filming, drawing on paper, writing on computers, and so on) was neither the most important nor the most difficult skill. The more difficult tasks were selecting in a "neutral" way among hundreds of drawings and graphic designs and guaranteeing that all the different villages were represented in a display of these designs, especially because the tendency would normally be to select designs from one's own family group. These experiences show that meeting the demand of the Whites' call for "representativeness" of a cultural medium is an extremely complex process. The young directors of Apina continue to face difficulties in selecting pieces of craftwork using the "neutral" criteria of quality, but how can they refuse an object made by their father-in-law, their father, or their grandfather, or say that it is being rejected because it is "badly made"? The production of texts that generalize the idea of a Wajãpi "culture" and gloss over local variations is a politically complex exercise, especially if the local ethic by which no one can speak for another is to be respected and in a context where, as one of the Apina directors suggested, "the collective doesn't exist, only the family."

However, it is recognized that in matters dealing with karaikõ, the negative arguments need to be inverted. Some of such affirmations have been successful—for example, "The Wajãpi aren't poor!" (the title of a chapter in the *Book of Wajãpi Craftwork* [1999]) in response to the conventional discourse with respect to Amerindians' "primitivism" and "poverty." Reacting to prejudice has been an essential step in the process described here. The current interest in these activities stems from seeing the impact that Amerindians had in the city. For example, the ethnographic exhibition set up in the Museum of the Indian in 2002 enabled the Wajãpi who participated to recognize with pride the public's admiration. They began to lose a little of the embarrassment they tend to feel when they are asked about practices such as shamanic cures, forms of marriage between "cousins," and female defense, among many others. They understood that the visitors were interested in the details of these aspects of their culture. That is to say, they recognized that in order to valorize a culture, it is necessary to display it. Yet at the same time the bilingual teachers understood that it was not enough simply to represent themselves to the karaikõ.

Experiments in Cultural Translation

As the bilingual teachers reflected in the education courses they were taking,[7] they became increasingly aware of the complexity of the exercise of cultural translation. They began to discuss openly the problems that arose because of differences in the generations' interpretation of the "Whites'" objects and knowledge. The teachers were troubled by the way in which their understanding of the interethnic situation diverged from the community elders' understanding and practice. The attempt to produce a text in the Wajãpi language dealing with the arrival of the Portuguese to celebrate the five hundredth anniversary of the "discovery" of Brazil was very enlightening in this respect. How were they to translate "Portuguese people," who are not exactly the ancestors of "Brazilians" and as a result are not just karaikõ? How were they to refer to the Amerindians who lived on the coast, such as the Tupinambá? The categories available to the Wajãpi when they want to mark a relationship with a degree of distance go from ally to commercial partner to enemy: *janeanã, panary, apãgwerã, mojutapurukwerã*. However, bearing in mind that we are talking about "Indians" and others from the past, none of these terms is appropriate because the Wajãpi might consider such groups to be their own ancestors, *taimigwerã*. The teachers turned to previous attempts to define such terms,

Cultivating a "Culture" 229

and they spoke with the elders. When the elders found out that the Tupinambá carried out acts of cannibalism, they classified them as *apãgwerã*, former enemies, but the young people preferred the term *janeantakõ*, "allies," for the Tupinambá because they wanted to present evidence that the extinct indigenous populations, like the Wajãpi today, had suffered from the impacts of the karaikõ's occupation of their lands.

As a result of these difficulties, the teachers couldn't reach a conclusion in writing their book about the Portuguese. They preferred to compose texts individually, each in his or her own way, affirming that it would be impossible to decide. For those witnessing these attempts at translation of written texts or explanation of "White knowledge" into the Wajãpi language, it is clear that reaching a consensus will take many years of experimentation. At the same time, it is clear that the writing down of accounts of events connected to colonization by teachers seated at a school desk can only create difficulties in the sense that in this people's interpretative practice, the choice between categories of otherness depends on the context in which each account is presented. In the oral exegesis of an event in relation to past conflicts, fixed categories are not used to identify people or groups because the qualification of these categories depends on the person's point of view, the type of relationships that are being commented upon, and so on. Yet if one of the aims is to write a text for use in schools, it becomes necessary to agree upon a translation for the pupils in *all* the different villages. The experience of choosing terminology to identify groups, types of relationship, and even objects often proves to be a frustrating task for the bilingual teachers. Some give up and continue using Portuguese words instead, even though they regret that the elders, as a result, will not understand them.

Let us consider another example. In 1999, these same teachers had prepared a collection of texts dealing with the demarcation of their land. A year later they went back to these texts to produce school materials and set about reviewing their translations of "White thought." Together, they wanted to choose neologisms that they could use to mediate in meetings with chiefs who spoke only their native language. They became interested in the possibility of being able to incorporate expressions such as *decree, federal, state,* and so on into their own language. It was an arduous task, but they succeeded in creating their own alternatives to differentiate between the various concepts of leadership and forms of representation in the Brazilian state. However, the eldest members of the groups continue to use Wajãpi terms to refer to such activities as well as to government positions, which inhibits their understanding of the actual hierarchies and specifications in each sector. According to the younger group members, if the elders continue to see any authority figure as a *jovijã*—learned elder and village chief—they will never learn to understand the different responsibilities of authorities at the different levels of Brazilian government, municipal, state, and federal. Furthermore, if *jovijã* is also the term used for any person "responsible" for a technical team ("the chief" of a group of nurses, teachers, and so on), there is little space to explain the difference between a government representative and someone in charge of a group of people carrying out a particular job.

This challenge encouraged the teachers to propose translations that would help the elders. At the same time, to try and concretize the usage of the terms, they wrote texts that they piloted in the schools. After two years, they concluded that they would not be able to use the chosen terms to communicate with the elders because the terms were "neither Wajãpi nor karaikõ." More than two years elapsed from the production of the first text to the conclusion of this experiment. It was a productive period during which the teachers acquired the distancing that was vital to their understanding of the cultural transformations that were taking place.

Another example of cultural representation concerned the mathematics used in the demographic census. This subject encouraged debate about the profound changes in the forms of transmitting knowledge among the Wajãpi. It emerged that the people described as *jovijãkõ*, men and women forty-five to seventy-five years old who "knew" or could "explain" traditions, made up only 7 percent of the population. A new issue arose in the debate—"The elders are dying out!"—and the need for an approximation between the generations reappeared, so the younger members of the group could "learn from the elders."

Learning to State Feelings:
The Challenges of a Participatory Inventory

Today, the younger Wajãpi are discovering the "living treasure"[8] embodied by their parents, parents-in-law, and grandparents—thought of as "the elders," the jovijãkõ. It is in this spirit that beginning in 2002 a new stage in their experiments with the representation of their culture started. The research carried out through these experiments aims to construct an inventory of the practices and knowledge transmitted orally. The format of this inventory is still under discussion[9] and brings to light delicate issues with respect to the relationship between the oral and the written. How can forms of expression be developed that by their nature are not destined to serve as ethnic representation or to become heritage?

The purpose of the participatory inventory, which is part of the plan submitted by Apina and selected by UNESCO, is not simply to meet demands for visibility or necessarily to correspond to procedures promoted by public policies in the area of culture, which tend to be particularly concerned with the national dissemination of aspects of Brazilian culture. The discussions of the inventory to be carried out by the Wajãpi deal with one of the principal questions regarding the politics of heritage: Whose heritage and for whom? The young Wajãpi have in the past experimented with a possible answer, encouraging the production of handicrafts, ritual displays, and discourses for consumption by the karaikõ.

At the same time, the older members are more concerned about the continuity

Cultivating a "Culture" 231

of an ethic and aesthetic of "Wajãpi reko," a way of life, rather than about registering it (in writing or through images). In this sense, the elders have continued to follow their own objective, reiterating their interest in transmitting to the younger generations ways of displaying knowledge, points of view, experiences, and trajectories, whether their own or others. It is this challenge that the bilingual teachers accepted when they confirmed that they wanted to learn the traditional forms to express their feelings.

So what will the content of this inventory be? How can forms of expression that are so fluid and ephemeral be registered? What forms of knowledge will be registered? Specialists in the study of mythology and the oral transmission of knowledge have made an important contribution in terms of the risks involved in this kind of process. What happens when oral narratives are transcribed and locked in a text? As Marcel Detienne points out, there is the serious risk that those who spoke the words will not recognize the fixed words used in the written text; in fact, they may well reject the latter. Another challenge lies in the act of transcription and dissemination of narratives, whereby the narratives move from a local context to a wider sphere of visibility (1994:8–9). It is interesting to observe that the Wajãpi teachers reached similar conclusions:

> A lot needs to be recorded because we cannot only have one version; the ways of the elders need to be respected, the versions of the others need to appear too. . . . In my research about *turé* [clarinets], it was not possible to only write; you have to learn to play to be able to respond, to have a dialogue through the turé.
>
> Aikyry

> My father didn't like it when he found out that the younger members were copying down music into a notebook; he said that they would get stuck reading from the notebook, when it should be in your head.
>
> Moropi

> If we teachers only write in books, the students will be dependent on books, they will not be interested in talking with their parents and grandparents; they will say: "I've already got that in my books, so I don't need to ask my father to tell stories."
>
> Seki

A two-way movement is taking place, as illustrated in the experiments described in this article. On the one hand, the movement involves the identification and selection of elements of the body of oral knowledge so that some of them can be transferred into other media for educational use and cultural dissemination. On the other hand, it involves bringing the different generations closer together by valorizing and carrying out local forms of representation that are thought of as "beautiful," "correct," and therefore valuable. This second objective, if achieved, would without a doubt be the most important outcome of this process. Up to now, it has been constituted in an effective but fragile consensus between the bilingual teachers and the traditional chiefs.

The two groups decided together that the school activities would prioritize the "Wajãpi language"—that is, that the teaching of literacy would be carried out in the mother tongue, and not just as a "transition" into Portuguese. Instead of a transition, a comparison would be made between knowledge and points of view, explaining the differences between "Wajãpi thought" and "non-Amerindian thought." The teachers recognize that to carry out this objective, they need to strengthen their ties with the elders, whose help they require to make a comparison between Wajãpi classificatory logics and those learned from the Whites. It is through this process that they will perceive that their mother tongue is capable of describing everything, including "White matters" that they previously thought only non-Amerindian instructors could teach. They can teach Brazilian history in Wajãpi and translate legal concepts, mathematical ideas, and everything else.

This recent stage in the carrying out of translations has effectively contributed to increasing the value of what is called "intangible heritage," whose value can be found in the logic of construction and the organization of cultural items rather than merely in their archiving. In this way, to be able to compare distinct forms of knowledge—distant in time and space—in the school and in the Wajãpi language is without a doubt an extremely important stage in the process of valorization in question. If a program of cultural valorization is not assumed as part of the (political) project, it can remain only in the realm of the memory.

However, depending on the pressure exerted on the indigenous researchers, especially if fixing cultural "products" is demanded of them, the risk will be the production of a collection of pieces of writing, with simplified texts that do not contain the "feelings" that they so want to learn to express. Moving from orality and diffuse forms of transmission to the fixing of these fragments of oral heritage into new media will clearly have new and diverse impacts on the conception of "Wajãpi culture." The dissemination of different versions, the comparison between them, the exchange of family knowledge and traditions will undoubtedly enrich narratives and prevent their pasteurization into generic versions. The biggest problem, however, continues to be the question of how to transpose into these new media the rich contributions that groups with an oral tradition offer to the epistemological debate—or, in the words of Pascal Boyer (1986), the relation between "tradition and truth."

Finally, according to the tradition of the Wajãpi and of the other groups in the southeastern region of Guayana, the majority of cultural elements, such as graphic art, songs, recipes, and so on, neither belong to them nor are creations of a specific group. Because the graphic designs that won UNESCO's recognition are traditional, they do not belong to "the Wajãpi." They were literally captured, or, rather, they are the result of a complex flow of exchange. Furthermore, as has been seen, they are forms of knowledge and practice that logically cannot belong to them or to others, not only because they are ways of bringing people and supernatural entities closer together or of strengthening ties between different Amerindian groups but also because they are generated and expressed within the context of this intense exchange network, testimony to the value of exchange between people and between groups, as well as between humans and nonhumans.

Notes

1. This candidacy was the result of an initiative on the part of the National Indian Foundation's Museum of the Indian and received technical support from the Brazilian Ministry of Culture. In the same year, the Wajãpi's graphic and oral expressions had been registered as Brazilian Cultural Heritage by the National Institute of Historical and Artistic Patrimony under the terms of act number 3551/2000. Both this registration and the candidacy were responses to a specific request by the principal chiefs and indigenous teachers, represented by the Wajãpi Villages Council, Apina, with which the Museum of the Indian has since 2001 maintained a partnership that was established during the preparation of the exhibition Time and Space in Amazônia: The Wajãpi. Apina's partners in the implementation of the Integrated Plan for the Valorization of Traditional Knowledge for the Socioenvironmental Development of the Wajãpi Community of Amapá are the Center for Indigenous Studies at the University of São Paulo, the Institute of Research and Training in Indigenous Education (IEPÉ), and the Department of Education in the Amapá State government. This plan involves the implementation of awareness campaigns aimed at the many agents working directly or indirectly with this community to promote understanding of the value of Wajãpi traditional knowledge. It also involves activities in the villages, such as the training of young people in the registering of aspects of oral knowledge, the continued training of bilingual teachers, and the setting up of a Wajãpi-language school. The plan also promotes the Wajãpi's participation in the control of their lands' natural resources in accordance with their own modes of occupation and management, which need to be valorized by the various agencies offering assistance in the region.

2. Although indigenist politics as configured in Brazil have been concerned mostly with the protection of groups and individuals—and little or not at all with the social, environmental, and economic changes that assistential practices in themselves necessarily provoke—the recent politics of safeguarding are concerned with cultural values, or, rather, with the conditions for their generation. However, because the latter politics arrived later than the former, it encountered indigenous actors already profoundly marked by the tutelage of the Brazilian state, especially with respect to the conditions for the maintenance and reproduction of the specific skills needed for the generation and management of cultural property. In order to verify these transformations, it is important that we evaluate concrete experiences of the generation of cultural property, or the ways in which each group generates values that are able or not able to be appropriated as its own property and as markers of difference.

3. I refer particularly to the ways in which the recognition of cultural diversity and especially of indigenous diversity operate in Brazil, leading to a profusion of contradictory discourses concerning these people's "tradition." Still today, those sectors interested in promoting "cultural rescue" continue to sustain old ideas about "authenticity," "acculturation," and so on. This "sentimental pessimism" (Sahlins 1997) lies at the heart of the "rescue" discourses promoted by these agencies, which are inconsistent

with the clearly integrationist activities that governmental politics continue to develop through the provision of assistance, be it in the area of health or education or economic alternatives.

4. In Brazil, the Wajãpi number around eight hundred people total, distributed among forty-eight villages, all located within Indigenous Land demarcated in 1996. Nearly one thousand Wajãpi live in French Guiana, distributed among several villages on the left bank of the Oyapock River.

5. In a manner similar to the way in which the Greeks defined "mythology": "a way of designating the narratives of others, including those from within, when one wants to mark difference" (Detienne 1994:7). See also Gallois 2007.

6. As Darcy Ribeiro (1970) presumed in his famous analysis of "ethnic transfiguration."

7. The Wajãpi teachers were being trained in education, the training carried out by the nongovernmental organization IEPÉ in partnership with the Amapá State Department of Education.

8. According to Jorge Wertheim, "Living treasures are people who embody to the greatest extent the abilities and techniques necessary for the demonstration of certain aspects of the cultural life of a people and the continuation of their cultural and material heritage" (2003:3).

9. IEPÉ started research training for the bilingual teachers in 2002. It expanded the training in 2005 to include a new group of twenty young people thanks to the collaboration of the Center for Indigenous Studies at the University of São Paulo and the National Institute of Historical and Artistic Patrimony in the Ministry of Culture and to the project "Valorization and Management of Indigenous Cultural Heritage in Amapá and the North of Pará," funded by the Petrobras cultural program.

18

Angles of Vision from the Coast and Hinterland of Guyana

Alissa Trotz and Terry Roopnaraine

For Afro- or Indo-Guyanese "coastlanders," the hinterlands to the south constitute a highly ambivalent space that simultaneously presents the possibility of great wealth and the grave dangers of the truly unknown. The first part of this chapter, written by Alissa Trotz, shows how the spaces and communities of the hinterland, haunting the edges of the coastal imagination and normally an "absent presence" to coastlanders, are rendered visible when they offer redemptive possibilities to the postcolonial Guyanese nation-state. The second part, written by Terry Roopnaraine, turns to a small subsection of the coastal population that has chosen to engage directly and personally with the "bush" and explores how these out-of-place coastlanders make sense of the hinterland.

The first part's argument about making the invisible visible is elaborated through a discussion of the U.S. administration's antitrafficking legislation and subsequent designation of Guyana as a noncompliant country in June 2004. This designation prompted a highly staged local response extensively covered by the local media, which depended for its success on rearticulating narratives of indigenous peoples and women in particular as victims. Drawing on newspaper articles, editorials and letters, documents of the government of Guyana, and interviews with state officials and nongovernmental actors in Guyana, this section explores how "Amerindian women" became central to the debates on trafficking in the service of an indebted postcolonial state apparatus whose actions demonstrated its inscription into broader relations of global capitalism.

Trafficking: Framing the Parameters, Setting the Boundaries

As researchers have noted, trafficking involves the illegal transportation of people across borders for the specific purpose of labor exploitation. Although much of the emphasis tends to be on the crossing of national boundaries, it is the movement of Amerindian women from the interior to the coast that has drawn international attention.

The discourse on trafficking has, at least from the nineteenth century, been highly gendered and sexualized, with international emphasis on rescuing girls and women forced or tricked into prostitution. Recent interventions by the United States reveal the distinct traces of this early approach. In 2000, the U.S. Congress passed the Victims of Trafficking and Violence Protection Act, which requires an annual country report. The 2001 report on this act defines severe trafficking as: "sex trafficking in which a commercial sex act is induced by force, fraud, or coercion, or in which the person induced to perform such act has not attained 18 years of age; or *(b)* the recruitment, harboring, transportation, provision, or obtaining of a person for labor or service, through the use of force, fraud or coercion for the purpose of subjection to involuntary servitude, peonage, debt bondage, or slavery" (U.S. Department of State 2001:2). Countries are ranked in three tiers according to levels of governmental compliance with the minimum standards established by the act for the elimination of trafficking. From 2003 onward, Tier 3 countries— where it is determined that no such efforts have been established—face sanctions, "principally termination of non-humanitarian, non-trade-related assistance. Such countries would also face U.S. opposition to assistance (except for humanitarian, trade-related, and certain development-related assistance) from international financial institutions, specifically the International Monetary Fund and multilateral development banks such as the World Bank. Certain of the sanctions may be waived under certain circumstances, including upon a national interest determination by the President" (U.S. Department of State 2001:8).

Notwithstanding the apparent determination to address the concerns of women and children, the U.S. administration's position is driven more by the logic of a security state and efforts to stem cross-border flows of illegal migrants (Kapur 2003; Kempadoo 2004). The threat of economic sanctions against noncompliant states underscores the report's significance as an important diplomatic instrument to impose conformity with the U.S. foreign-policy agenda, a point Kamala Kempadoo (2004) has made by noting that all the countries that the United States has designated as "rogue" or "terrorist" states fall within the Tier 3 categorization (including Cuba and Venezuela in this region).

The fact that the withholding of aid extends beyond bilateral issues to encompass various international financial institutions holds significant implications for heavily indebted Third World countries such as Guyana, which entered into a structural adjustment arrangement in 1989 that continued with little modification following the return to political democracy in 1992. It is against this backdrop that Guyana's citation in the *Trafficking in Persons (TIPS) Report* and the government's response to it must be assessed.

In 2004, Guyana made its first appearance in the U.S. State Department's *TIPS Report* as "a country of origin, transit, and destination for young women and children trafficked primarily for sexual exploitation" (238). Given Guyana's lack of compliance with the three Ps—prosecution, prevention, protection—for reasons attributed in the report to inadequate resources and a "lack of understanding," the U.S. State Department listed it as a Tier 3 country and gave it sixty days to take steps before it would be reevaluated. In September that year, a White House press release provided details of a Presidential Determination Note authorized by George W. Bush, which upgraded Guyana to a watch list of Tier 2 countries.[1]

What, however, had occasioned the promotion of Guyana to Tier 2? The official local line insisted that various initiatives had been taken "not because we want to satisfy the U.S. State Department. . . . We are doing it because of concern for our people," as Bibi Shadick, the Guyanese human services minister put it (qtd. in *Stabroek News,* 21 June 2004). To be sure, reports had begun to surface in the media as early as April 2004 that the government was establishing a people-trafficking unit and drafting a national strategy (*Stabroek News,* April 23 and 30, 2004). However, a number of interviewees noted that months before the U.S. State Department publicly issued its condemnatory report, a meeting on trafficking had been convened with representatives of the relevant government agencies and the police force where the U.S. findings were discussed. As one interviewee noted, it was highly unlikely that the Guyana government would not have known well in advance of the June publication that the country was going to be named as noncompliant (confidential interviews, July 2005).[2]

In both the external designation as well as the official local responses, Guyana's hinterland communities materialize as sites to be talked about and acted upon in certain ways. The interior appears in the U.S. *TIPS Report* in three configurations, each linked to differently nationalized or racialized groups of women: as a space through which trafficked "foreign" women and children are moved (those coming into the United States from Venezuela and northern Brazil); as an area to which non-Amerindian women from coastal urban centers are taken (closely linked to mining camps); and as a site that generates Amerindian women who are trafficked for prostitution to coastal communities. The latter dominated both the trafficking reports from 2004 to 2006 and the media accounts. This section of the chapter reflects critically on precisely *how* "Amerindian women" in particular were discursively mobilized to become visible in the government's antitrafficking campaign in the second half of 2004.

Several indigenous and other organizations had documented and raised the issue of the sexual exploitation of Amerindian women in the interior and on the coast long before 2004, but to little avail (interview with a Guyana Human Rights Association representative, July 2005; Red Thread Women's Development Programme 1998, 2004; *Stabroek News,* August 2, 2004; see also Colchester, La Rose, and James 2002). Yet between June 2004 (when the *TIPS Report* was made public) and December 2004 (when the Guyana Parliament passed antitrafficking legislation), more than one hundred newspaper articles, editorials, and letters to the press appeared in the three major newspapers—the *Stabroek News,* the *Guyana Chronicle,* and the *Kaieteur News*—giving the impression for the most part that the government was responding to a new phenomenon.

Charged with taking the lead role, the Ministry of Labour, Human Services, and

Social Security (MLHSSS) convened an interagency, interministry steering committee that included the Ministry of Amerindian Affairs and issued a National Plan of Action in April 2004 (Guyana MLHSSS 2004) to combat TIPS in Guyana. Between June and August 2004, Human Services Minister Bibi Shadick and a team visited all ten of the country's administrative regions, covering more than thirty communities and some three thousand people—mostly Amerindian and located in hinterland and riverine areas. The campaign included letters to businesses, meetings with religious and business leaders, development of advertisements, and publication of a TIPS leaflet. Coastal workshops were held, intended to train some three hundred representatives (social workers, police officers, Ministry of Health officials) to recognize and address TIPS. Special workshops were held with community development officers attached to the Ministry of Amerindian Affairs and with police officers stationed in interior communities. Draft legislation on trafficking was presented to Parliament in July 2004, referred to a Select Parliamentary Committee, and passed by the National Assembly less than six months later, on 20 December 2004, to become the Combating of Trafficking in Persons Act (No. 2) of 2005 (Government of Guyana 2005). Under the act, sentences for convicted traffickers range from three years to life as well as the confiscation of assets procured through trafficking. In 2005, a countertrafficking unit was established in the MLHSSS, now recognized as the "focal point for the national programme on TIPS" (Guyana MLHSSS n.d.). Discussions have also begun on assigning a special magistrate to expedite TIPS cases through the judicial system (*Kaieteur News*, 21 June 2006).

In a telling comment by Odeen Ishmael, Guyana's then ambassador to Venezuela, Guyana had fast-tracked plans to avoid a cut in funds from international lending agencies and hoped to be recognized for its efforts in the mid-September evaluation (*Guyana Chronicle*, 1 September 2004). As noted earlier, just a few months after Guyana made the U.S. *TIPS Report* for the first time in 2004, it was moved from a Tier 3 (noncompliant) to a Tier 2 (not fully compliant) watch list. By 2005, the U.S. State Department had again reclassified Guyana, this time securing Guyana's position among Tier 2 countries for the "appreciable progress [shown] over the last year, particularly through its enactment of anti-trafficking legislation, improvement in government coordination and aggressive public awareness campaigns" (U.S. Department of State 2005:117, also qtd. in *Guyana Chronicle*, 6 June 2005). In the 2006 report, Guyana remains at Tier 2, leading Minister Bibi Shadick to complain that the ranking was unfair in light of the significant steps the government had taken (*Kaieteur News* and *Guyana Chronicle*, 21 June 2006).

Amerindians are the only "group" that has shown a consistent population increase in Guyana, a country that in the 1990s was experiencing negative population growth rates, largely due to outward migration.[3] According to the most recent census in 2002, Amerindians constituted 9.2 percent of the population (68,819), up from 6.5 percent in 1991. They reside primarily in the interior (Regions 1, 7, 8, 9) and in Region 2 on the coast, constituting as much as 62 percent, 76 percent, and 89 percent in Regions 1, 8, and 9, respectively. Although the general sex ratio shows an almost equal number of men and women, the ratio is lowest in the interior regions.[4] The smaller numbers of women are possibly indicative of both the movement of Amerindian women to the coast and the inward migration of coastlanders (predominantly men) looking for work in the timber and mining industries that have opened up under structural adjustment.

The interior has become key to national economic growth projections following the implementation of structural adjustment policies: the granting of timber and mining concessions; the promotion of ecotourism; the building of roads connecting Guyana to Brazil; and plans to increase agricultural production (Colchester, La Rose, and James 2002). With its large forest canopies and borders with Venezuela and Brazil, the hinterland has also positioned Guyana as a crucial transshipment location for the international drug trade. Yet whether resources are generated in the hinterland or passing through it, the beneficiaries have not been the peoples who live there and who continue to fare the worst on almost all sociodemographic indicators: almost 80 percent of Amerindians are estimated to be economically below the poverty line; more than 70 percent are engaged in subsistence activities in the agricultural sector; average life expectancy is almost ten years below the national average; few households (less than 13 percent) receive secondary schooling; health services are extremely scarce in the interior in the midst of such diseases as HIV/AIDS, malaria, and tuberculosis, some of which have been introduced or exacerbated by the spurt in the mining industry (World Bank 2004).

These overwhelming structural disparities are accompanied by spatialized representations of Amerindians—which have a long colonial history—as primitive and undeveloped: "successive waves of spiritual and material development have pounded native communities, leading to the continuous ideological construction of indigenous peoples as obstacles to 'progress,'" Neil Whitehead aptly states in the introduction to this volume. Today, 90 percent of the (primarily nonindigenous) population resides on a ribbon of coastal land reclaimed from swamp, and a deep material and imaginative division exists between coast and hinterland. The coast is characterized by a deeply racialized political landscape in which Afro-Guyanese and Indo-Guyanese continually compete over who is more deserving to hold the reins of national power, leaving virtually no room for indigenous peoples, who are seen as living more or less "behind God's back." This marginalization is reflected in the racist term *buck* used casually on the coast to refer to any indigenous person and standing for everything that the modern coastlander is apparently not: traditional, backward, simple, stupid (Mentore 1992).

That these discourses were readily available in 2004 is clear from the Guyanese state's elaboration of its antitrafficking agenda. Official identification of the causes of trafficking has focused overwhelmingly on the problem of individual coastal predators. The machinery of public relations has been geared almost entirely to defining TIPS and training locals to respond to instances of trafficking. Targeting individuals—as both potential predators and civic-minded citizens—dovetails with the U.S. insistence on legal measures via the apprehension, prosecution, and punishment of aggressors. This fit raises the question of the way in which the privileging of technical and legal remedies works to efface more complex analyses of a broad "spectrum of social problems" threatening society (*Stabroek News,* 7 July 2004).

In the opening paragraphs of the Guyanese government's 2004 antitrafficking National Plan of Action, it was recognized that trafficking was associated with migration triggered by "recent developments in mining, logging and related activities in the hinterland locations" (Guyana MLHSSS 2004:3). The report notes that the contributing factors are both supply oriented (poverty, low levels of education and literacy, lack of jobs for women and girls) and demand based (developments in the entertainment industry and the drug trade). Notwithstanding the initial identification of this wider context, the overall strategy focused almost entirely on educating the public, rescuing victims, training personnel, and pursuing perpetrators. By effacing the structural causes of trafficking, the state is thus absolved of any responsibility for the exploitation of Amerindian women's sexual labor in coastal locations.

Consequently, in this narrative the state emerges as the doer par excellence—apprehending, enacting, helping, legislating, organizing, protecting, punishing, reporting, training, visiting, warning—as evidenced by the dizzying array of purposeful measures reported on an almost daily basis in the local newspapers in late 2004. This portrayal sets the stage for the rehearsal of a colonial paternalistic script in which the contemporary state comes to the rescue of trafficked Amerindian women from individual coastal predators. In fact, the production of the state as capable of governing and resolving trafficking is achieved by denying Amerindian peoples any complexity or agency. They exist in official documents and media reports primarily as communities to be spoken on behalf of or as a problem to be solved. The hinterland, for example, is completely flattened in various accounts as a generic place from which victims are recruited for sex work in coastal entertainment spots, notwithstanding the fact that these specific forms of exploitation of Amerindian women and men do not happen uniformly throughout the interior, but rather in those communities that are especially vulnerable because they are closer and more accessible to the coast. Although the National Plan implies the interior in several sections (it talks about remote communities and notes the link among logging, mining, and displacement, and the list of places it identifies for official visits are mainly in the interior), Amerindian communities and peoples are explicitly identified only *once* in this twenty-three-page document: "The [antitrafficking] strategy must also take cognizance of the culture and belief systems of various communities, such as Amerindians" (Guyana MLHSSS 2004:7). At no point are we told exactly what taking Amerindians seriously would entail, how engaging with indigenous notions of personhood might disrupt more familiar racist stereotypes of Amerindian backwardness and helplessness, or how different communities might bring specific histories to bear on the question. Instead, legislative solutions become an easy fix; although important, they should not substitute for a systemic investigation into racism, hinterland poverty, land titles, displacement resulting from timber and mining concessions, and lack of job opportunities (*Stabroek News,* 19 June and 5 August 2005; interview with an Amerindian People's Association representative, July 2005).

Amerindian women emerge in the state's response to trafficking as victims to be rescued and then protected under the provisions of the Trafficking Act, to be put up at shelters until safe return to their communities is possible. The National Plan's description, for instance, of "young people from remote poor communities" conjures images of unsuspecting women being tricked by sophisticated and duplicitous coastal predators. Although the focus is primarily on women, the absence of Amerindian men in both the plan and the U.S. reports implies that Amerindian men are incapable of defending their communities against the illegal migration of women to the coast and subsequent sexual exploitation there.

In this framework, Amerindians also become visible as beneficiaries of the state's tutelage. The majority of TIPS investigative field trips organized in 2004 under the auspices of the MLHSSS occurred in hinterland and riverine areas. The flow of expertise is, however, unidirectional, with state officials and policymakers traveling far distances to educate Amerindians about trafficking. Here, the "problem" materializes as a "lack of information." The ministry's declaration of its intention to collaborate with "other government agencies, NGOs and all stakeholders" (Guyana MLHSSS 2004:7) does not include Amerindians even as junior partners (in fact, the stakeholders involve governmental-social workers, police, health workers, officials from the Geology and Mines Commission, and nongovernmental agencies, overwhelmingly coastal based), but rather relies on the idea of coastal experts bringing knowledge and ultimately salvation to Amerindian communities.

The representation of Amerindian women as requiring rescue was equally pervasive in media reports (Red Thread 2004:19). One letter to a daily newspaper is an example of the place that "the Amerindian" occupies in the general coastal imagination: "Once again the news of the exploitation of Amerindian girls by unscrupulous restaurant owners on the coastland is in the open. This is a blight on the national conscience of Guyanese. . . . I would call on all kind-hearted and peace-loving Guyanese to boycott any restaurant which exploits young girls" (*Stabroek Daily News,* 15 July 2004). Such comments evoke outrage by establishing the difference between the unscrupulous coastlander and his conscientious counterpart, enabling the representation of the coast as a neutral space and its occupants as, for the most part, innocent bystanders. The indignant tone calls forth sympathy and charity from readers, reinforcing a sense of coastlanders as those who must act for and on behalf of (but never with) Amerindian peoples.

Displacing culpability onto individual offenders absolves us from addressing ongoing economic, social, and political inequalities that structure relations between the coast and the interior. Missing from such expressions of concern is any recognition of collective responsibility that would entail an interrogation of historical and contemporary relations that produce Amerindians as subordinate racialized "others." As a result, one Amerindian woman could note of her movement from the North West District to Georgetown to go to school, "Things were different here. I was always called 'Buck Girl' as if it were a curse or a disgrace, as I'm sure many others are called today" (letter to the editor, *Stabroek News*, 25 September 2004). Such a recognition would require the hearing of descriptions of Amerindians as inferior; in response to the Ethnic Relations Commission Hinterland Outreach Programme in region 1, one man stated, "People believe that Amerindians are at the bottom, every other race thinks they are above us and that is how it has always been. I have been told personally that we are nothing and people still say it up to now" (qtd. in *Stabroek News*, 19 June 2005, and *Guyana Chronicle*, 21 June 2005; see also *Stabroek News*, 21 November 2005).

Calling for people to boycott restaurants that exploit young Amerindian women misses the fact that it is also patrons who are the beneficiaries of the so-called buck nights, the racist and misogynist coastal vernacular for bars' practice of offering a night on the town for men that includes being "entertained" by Amerindian women (interviews with representatives of Amerindian People's Association and Amerindian Hostel, July 2005; Red Thread 2004). Moreover, what occurs in the bars is symptomatic of the wider interaction of race, class, and gender that situates Amerindians in the lowest echelons of the occupational hierarchy. Reports that employers threaten to accuse their Amerindian employees of stealing from them if they complain about their working conditions also highlight the confidence among coastlanders that the legal/judicial systems are stacked in their favor. Speaking of the general labor exploitation of Amerindian employees on the coast, one interviewee remarked, "[It] is a cultural advantage. Here at the center we get a lot of calls looking for domestic workers, clothes washer[s], and so. People think Amerindian girls stupid, that there is nobody to represent them, you could do anything to them" (a representative of the Amerindian Hostel, July 2005). Nor can this relationship be reduced to a dynamic that exists only between coastal men and Amerindian women. Non-Amerindian women appear as employers of domestic labor, and some operate as restaurant proprietors. Women were also named as procurers in at least half of the instances of suspected trafficking reported in the media in 2004, their involvement underscoring the significance of gender in the establishment of relationships with Amerindian communities and ensuring the recruitment of women. A general sense, then, that Amerindians "belong" in the interior situates them outside of civilization, thus reinforcing romantic stereotypes of simplicity but also predisposing a culture of abuse toward them because they are not like "us," are less than "us Guyanese." Such widespread sentiments also structure the hierarchical, exploitative, and demeaning experiences Amerindians endure on the coast, encounters that are intended to reinforce the sense that they are out of place there.

*****

This section has explored how Amerindian women became visible as the effect of antitrafficking discourses and media-hyped interventions in Guyana. Immediate local responses to the country's appearance on the U.S. noncompliant list clearly demonstrated the postcolonial state's vulnerability in the international arena. Although Amerindian women appeared to be central to the demonstration of official will to find and protect victims in the national interest, they were in fact the grounds upon which the government could make a claim to take Guyana off the Tier 3 list and ensure that funding from multilateral and bilateral creditors would not be threatened.

Public discussions on trafficking in Guyana have been hypervisible for several years. Yet, notwithstanding this dizzying array of apparently purposeful activity, no successful prosecutions or convictions have been conducted to date; the witness protection program, described as central to successful prosecutions under the Trafficking Act, has not been activated; and there is no independent shelter for women who have been trafficked. For all the resources put into fact-finding missions, creation of specialized antitrafficking units, and educating and sensitizing police, social workers, and the general public, we still do not know how big a "problem" trafficking is, which Amerindian communities are most severely affected, or the numbers of women suspected of being duped or forced to come to the coast.

As this section suggests, however, perhaps we are looking in the wrong place for answers in that these initiatives' intended effect was only to underscore the legitimacy of the state machinery on both a local and an international stage. Insisting on the country's sovereignty in relation to the global antitrafficking campaign and in response to critics deflects attention away from the country's unequal incorporation into the "international family" of nation-states (Alexander 1997; Malkki 1994) and the potentially devastating economic consequences of limited sanctions from the international community if Guyana had remained on the noncompliant list.

In this regard, the interior becomes the solution to the problem, but a solution that has to be managed.[5] The state's redemptive agency is predicated on the feminization of the interior and on the victimhood of indigenous peoples; the idea of the latter as tradition bound, dependent, and therefore requiring outside intervention and rescue becomes the condition of possibility for the modernity of the former, as evidenced in the passage of laws, the geographical concentration of resources on the coast, and the fact that the initiatives go from the coast inland, never the other way around. There is little room to advance the argument that it is precisely such intervention that has historically produced the conditions experienced by peoples in the interior and that leads Amerindians to seek livelihoods elsewhere. Trafficking and Amerindians have now become so synonymous in the public imagination that a more complex reading of patterns of indigenous migration is obscured. What we see here is an example of the hinterland and hinterlanders drifting into sight as the result of externalities (in this case, U.S. foreign policy) in ways that stabilize a set of practices, relations, and identities that reflect coastal preoccupations. In the final analysis, the representation of the Guyanese state as savior of trafficked Amerindian women barely papers over the reality that in fact the main storyline, as usual, was about the salvation of the coast.

Making Miners: Discourse, Praxis, and Transformation in Guyana's Hinterlands

> I sensed, over the years, as a surveyor, that the landscape possessed a resonance. The landscape possessed a life, because the landscape, for me, is like an open book, and the alphabet with which one worked was all around me.
> —Wilson Harris, in Bundy 1999:40[6]

We now turn from the conceptual positioning of the hinterland and hinterlanders in the discourse of Guyana's coastlands to the physical presencing of coastlanders in the hinterland. The coastlanders in question are the itinerant, small-scale miners of gold and diamonds known in Guyana as "porkknockers," and this part of the chapter focuses on their relationship with the landscape and culture of the vast interior lands lying to the south of the coastal belt.[7] Products of a postcolonial coastal culture that is deeply ambivalent about the hinterland and heirs to a trope of extractivism that extends five centuries into the past, porkknockers travel south to attempt to wrest wealth from a disorienting and difficult land. In doing so, they mediate between coast and bush, and merge the chimeras of the past with those of the future.

I (T. R.) carried out the ethnography upon which this section is based in the Pakaraima Mountains of southwestern Guyana principally during 1993–94, with additional field trips in 1997. These mountains constitute the traditional homelands of the Patamona; their southern flanks, which border the North Rupununi Savannahs, are home to the Macuxi.

A Story about a Story about a Story

All around us, the rain beat down through the trees, turning the large holes and trenches in the clearing into treacherous mud baths and dripping through small holes in the weathered tarp. Red Man pulled out a small plastic tube fashioned from a Vicks Nasal Inhaler. He popped off the lid and tipped out a rough diamond. The stone was not very big—perhaps a carat and a half—but it was a beautiful one: a perfect octagon, clean and shining, with no obvious surface flaws. "We were two days out from Chenapau, prospecting a creek which was showing some good indications. One night a man came into our camp, right in the middle of the night, he just walked out of the bush. We still had food in the pot, so we fed him and let him tie up in the camp. His name was Romeo—he was a big strapping guy with big hands and an ugly face. He showed me a diamond and told me he'd got it out of a creek far, far up the Potaro, way behind here. He told me the creek didn't have a name, but you'd know it from the shape of some rocks in the middle, which looked like two tigers. He told me the creek was full of diamonds, but that he'd got fever and had to run and catch landing before he could get them out. I didn't really believe him then, it just sounded like one of those old porkknocker stories." Now Red Man rolled the diamond between his hard fingers and continued, "The next morning, when we got up, Romeo had left the camp already. On the table he'd left a Bible. When I opened the book, I found this diamond inside. I've never sold the diamond, but from then I believed the man's story, and I've always wanted to go up there and take a look, maybe make a few checks. One day I'll go up there and take a look. That was years ago. I never saw Romeo again and I don't know why he left the Bible and the diamond."[8]

Like a piece of thick description that gets thicker with each telling (Geertz 1973:3–30), this is a story about a story about a story. Porkknockers' stories are in many senses mythic, not least in their continual rearticulation and transformation of a set of core themes. These themes would not be unfamiliar to other researchers who have worked among small-scale miners of precious minerals in different contexts.[9] Life in mining camps is experienced through myth and memory expressed as historical narratives about people, diamonds, and places. Red Man's story about Romeo thus plays on certain well-known keys: an itinerant stranger passing through the camp, unannounced and apparently from nowhere; this mysterious stranger telling a strange tale in the night; the traveler then slinking off before dawn, leaving behind some material representation of his tale (here in the form of a diamond). Red Man was reluctant to sell the diamond, not just because it was a reminder of Romeo's story, but because it was a physical piece of both the story and the possibility of a huge strike that it dangled before him: a shining one-and-a-half carat metonym. The story also makes reference to the Bible, anointing it with the moral accents that often accompany these accounts. Romeo's story, as told to Red Man, exhibits a range of tropes we have seen before: a pile of imagined wealth in a little-known part of the forest; the unnamed site marked by stones shaped like jaguars; this mother lode having been just missed because of the encroaching fog of malarial delirium and the panic to get out of the backdam and back to civilization; a single diamond claimed as part of a much larger lode waiting for someone bold enough to go and find it.[10]

This is not simply about discourse (if anything can be *simply* about discourse), but also about practice and the borderlands where discourse and practice meet and infuse each other: in other words, it is about showing that the activities involved in mining for diamonds in Guyana's interior forests are at least in part informed by a cultural logic. In this sense, my position here is both perpendicular and complementary to the theories of the political economy that have so far dominated the analysis of artisanal Amazonian mining—primarily gold mining. Here I am thinking of the excellent studies done by David Cleary and Gordon MacMillan, which go a long way toward sorting out the socioeconomic logic underpinning the mighty gold rushes in Amazonian Brazil during the 1980s and 1990s. Cleary (1990) is particularly strong on the organization of people and labor in the *garimpo* (mining area), whereas MacMillan (1995) closely examines the very important and frequently overlooked articulation of the gold-mining industry with other economic forms and structures in northern Brazil. Neither of these authors, however, directs very much attention toward the relationship between mining as a source of cultural elaboration and mining as a way of making money, and this places certain limits on their analyses. Focusing on the transformation of ritual, Michael Taussig (1980) does seek to recuperate culture in his reanalysis of June Nash's (1979) ethnography of Bolivian miners, but even here the recuperation plays a junior role in what is essentially a Marxist critique of the transition from a moral sociality to an amoral individuality, from reciprocity to greed, from use to exchange, and from subsistence economy to waged proletariat.[11]

Porkknockers' relationship with the hinterland is complex and shaped by the collision of a coastlander ontology with a world of radical difference, both physically and culturally. In this second part of the chapter, the exploration of this relationship maps out along two interpenetrating axes. The first is hermeneutic and contends that in coastlander discourse, the construction of the hinterland and the people who make their home there is defined by a series of contradictions and negative polarities. The second axis explores, through ethnography, processes of self-transformation through the physicality and narration of porkknockers' experience of the hinterland, arguing that *being* in the hinterland is not in fact about survival in an unknown wilderness, but about the gradual acquisition and embodiment of knowledge and physical hardness through processes of enskillment and lived experience: this intellectual and physical transformation makes life in the interior physically and (sometimes) economically viable for persons raised on the comparatively urbanized coastal belt. This part of the chapter ends by examining some aspects of the relationship between praxis and poetics. I argue that porkknocker culture is given shape and form in the resolution, by a transformative rather than a dialectical process, of the oppositions that define coastlander ambivalence toward the hinterland. Thus, poverty becomes wealth, disorientation becomes familiarity, the wild becomes the dominated, and constraint becomes freedom. The porkknockers' discourse forms a backdrop to the day-to-day lived practice of artisanal mining. Is the discursive, then, better regarded as charter or narrative of the physical?

Guyana, squeezed between Amazonia and the Caribbean, a lone Anglophone outpost on a mostly Latinate continent, was a British colony until 1966. The British, succeeding the Dutch colonial rulers in the early nineteenth century, had no real aspirations to open up the Amazonian frontier or to "settle" the hinterland, at least not in any formal or institutionalized sense. With the exception of a handful of hardy individuals who traveled south to start cattle-ranching enterprises in the Rupununi Savannahs, the British preferred to contend with the low-lying coast, combining Dutch techniques of sea defense with the use of an enslaved labor force to reclaim vast tracts of land for sugar plantations (Rodney 1981). This decision would ultimately steer the cultural, political, and economic orientation of Creole Guyanese society northward toward the islands of the British Caribbean and concomitantly away from the harsher continental landscape to the south.[12]

The result of this policy was to create a sharp demographic division between the highly humanized landscape of the coast and (in the coastlander's eyes) the chaotic forests and endless savannas of the interior lands to the south. The coastal belt, as the eighty-kilometer-wide strip of land alongside the Atlantic is called, is where almost all of the Creole population lives. It is the center of the most important national economic activities—sugar and rice cultivation. It is where the capital city and the centers of state power are located. And it is very firmly oriented toward the north: to the islands of the Anglophone Caribbean and beyond that to the diasporic havens of the United States, Canada, and England. Implicit in this northward gaze is a rejection of most of what lies to the south.

What is this land to the south, which after all constitutes more than 90 percent of the country's land area? What does it mean in terms of how coastlanders assign meaning to place? One entry point into such a set of questions is to begin by noting that the Creole Guyanese of Guyana's coastlands express a deep ambivalence about the landscape to the south. On the one hand, these forests and savannas have long dangled the possibility of vast wealth in the form of gold and diamonds. This ur-trope dates to Walter Ralegh's sixteenth- and seventeenth-century quests for the gilded king, El Dorado, and the city he ruled over, Manoa, which Ralegh was convinced lay somewhere between the Amazon and Orinoco rivers. In his work on cartography and exploration in Guyana, the American historian Graham Burnett has referred to this trope as the "Raleghness of Guyana's history" (2000:17). This Raleghness also finds expression in the names that miners post on claim boards, such as "Sir Walter," "Golden City," and the like. The possible wealth, moreover, is of the most democratic kind: there for the taking by anyone stoic or stupid enough to tackle the risks involved in acquiring it. On the other hand, it is a wealth guarded by a landscape of horror: mile after mile of disorienting forest and swamp, populated—so the stories go—by blowpipe-wielding natives and inhabited by dreadful animals, a space teeming with disease and threatening starvation.[13]

Ambivalence about the hinterland regions of Guyana extends to the policy of the state itself, which tends to frame this land as a national larder, a panacea for the country's chronic economic maladies. Thus, the past few administrations have worked hard to attract multinational investors in large-scale logging and mining projects. Yet, at the same time, the state has largely ignored the interests of the approximately seventy thousand indigenous people who live in these forests and savannas, jeopardizing and ignoring time and again Amerindian claims to land rights. There is a strong sense in which the hinterland regions of Guyana are visible to the state only insofar as they offer the possibility of profit, of shoring up claims to wise environmental stewardship, of multiethnic nationhood, and, as Alissa Trotz demonstrates in the first part of this chapter, of cleaving to the interests of powerful neighbors to the north. Following the British lead, the postcolonial Guyanese state has never expressed an interest in the kind of push to open up the frontier that we have seen in other parts of Amazonia, most notably in Brazil during the 1970s. The state has never tried to effect homesteading initiatives of the Brazilian kind, nor have coastlanders made much effort to settle in hinterland locations, although a small number of entrepreneurs have established shops and businesses in mining areas in order to profit from the extractive economy by supplying food, fuel, tools, credit, drink, and prostitutes to miners.

We can see the hinterland—or "bush," as it is more commonly called in Guyana—framed in these different modes by the state and by the coastlander population: as a source of enormous potential wealth and as a place that is variously invisible or dangerous, depending on one's point of view. There exists, however, another perspective on this landscape, concomitant of these two and especially relevant to porkknockers' relationship with the bush. According to this perspective, the interior lands offer the possibility of various kinds of freedom. At one level, drawing on the image of the bush as a place of invisibility, it is freedom both from the surveillance of the domestic household and from the state and its agents. Porkknockers in the hinterland told me again and again that one of the things they liked about being away from the coast was that one could breathe freely: one could smoke a little dope or visit a prostitute without risk of being caught by either the police or one's family.[14] Indeed, one of the central features of the hinterland areas is the relative inapplicability of national laws. Police outposts are few and far between and are chronically underresourced, rendering effective law enforcement difficult or impossible.

At another level, the hinterland offers a different kind of opportunity: freedom from proletarianization. Coastlander porkknockers, most of whom come from poor socioeconomic backgrounds, refer often to this important point. The possibility of mineral wealth, of striking it rich in the forest, incorporates the possibility of breaking away from the drudgery of work at the lower levels of the coastal economic ladder. One of the ideals of being a small-scale miner is to be an independent agent, answerable to no one and free of the shackles of poorly remunerated wage labor on the coast of Guyana. Miners may go weeks on end without a single strike, but they also work with the knowledge and the hope that literally millions of Guyana dollars may lie just inches below the tip of the shovel in a place where no one is obliging them to punch a time card.

The Land, the Mind, and the Body: Learning to Be in the Hinterland

How do porkknockers—products of such a coastlander culture, raised to see the interior lands in such ambivalent terms—come to grips with the art of living (albeit temporarily) and working there? Achieving such a thing depends on resolving the contradictions and oppositions inherent in the coastlander construction of the hinterland; furthermore, such resolution is in turn achieved through processes of intellectual, moral, and physical transformation. This transformation lies at the very core of the ontological shift from proletarian coastlander to porkknocker.

Choosing where to begin digging for diamonds is a complicated and often opaque business. When I first began work with diamond miners, I spent a great deal of time trying to understand how they decided where to begin looking for diamonds in a systematic way. For a long time, their decisions struck me as essentially random; I was unable to see any obvious logic behind choosing one spot over another. Gradually, though, patterns began to emerge. At the surface level, these patterns are based in part on a body of shared general knowledge about where diamonds are found in Guyana. But this alone does not narrow down the search area very much, for huge tracts of land in Guyana are classified as diamondiferous. So, in addition to this very general knowledge about the possible locations of diamonds, miners draw on a constantly unfolding set of narratives about mining and prospecting trips in the past. Narratives such as Red Man's story can form the cartographic basis for prospecting ventures. The point about these stories, then, is that although they embody elements of both myth and history, they also serve as maps and catalysts that point would-be prospectors in the right direction; in other words, they are more than just stories about real or imagined exploits in the past: they are charters for possible action in the future.[15] At night, in mining camps and in the little temporary trade shops that, on mining landings, turn into bars and brothels at sunset, porkknockers constantly tell and retell these stories; as I spent more time in these places, I came to understand that these accounts, traded back and forth, really constitute a kind of forum for the exchange of information, some of it useful and some utterly apocryphal. In exchanging this information, miners gradually and reciprocally fill in the blank spaces in their own internal maps of the landscape. Physical features and landmarks are invested with meaning as places where things happened in the past or as places where things might happen in the future.

Memory also plays an important role in selecting likely places to begin prospecting. In these areas, almost all travel is done on foot. The landscape is therefore experienced slowly and sensuously, as a synaesthestic passage. When passing through the forest, miners will often stop and gaze around, looking for places that might be interesting to prospect in the future, making mental notes of a dry river bed here or a diamond-trapping bend in a shallow creek there. On many occasions when I traveled with a prospecting party, we began prospecting at some point recalled by one of the men as a likely spot he had identified the previous year while en route to somewhere else but in too much of a hurry to stop.

If a prospecting venture is successful—that is, if the assays look promising enough—the work of actually extracting the diamonds can begin. The first stage in this process is staking a claim to the workground. Technically, staking a claim to a workground involves surveying the area, then applying to the Guyana Geology and Mines Commission in Georgetown for a formal claim permit. After this point, as long as the claim owner pays the nominal rent, the claim is exclusively his to work as he wishes. This procedure is, however, rarely followed, not least because it is extremely inconvenient and prohibitively expensive to travel to Georgetown, so in practice the prospectors who have identified a likely workground normally establish their claim by nailing up four signboards to enclose a rectangular piece of land where they intend to mine. A claim sign names the primary owner of the claim and, by tradition, the claim itself. Claim names frequently make reference to historical mining ventures, but the names of girlfriends, wives, and daughters also commonly prefix some optimistic term, as in "Daphne's Luck" or "Mary's Fortune." As noted earlier, references to El Dorado are iconic and popular; the fact that Ralegh's quests were among the most spectacularly unsuccessful prospecting ventures in history is apparently lost on the claimants.

Because such claims have not been registered and gazetted by the state, they have no legal validity. They possess, however, a binding moral validity among other miners. Claim jumping, or working a claim illicitly, is one of the most antisocial offenses among diamond miners. In practice, it is so heavily censured that it rarely happens, existing more as a negative pole of allegorical discourse than as a living action. Miners, depending as they do on a sustaining network of reciprocal relationships, are very reluctant to risk the infamy associated with claim jumping. This raises an important point about diamond fields: although, as argued, the bush is in many ways regarded as a free and lawless place, it is not in fact lacking in ethical codes, but these codes are not necessarily coterminous with state laws. Miners are swift to identify and censure individuals who break these rules, and new porkknockers quickly learn that if they are to be able to function within this particular moral economy, they must learn and abide by its norms. Claim jumping and stealing diamonds, money, goods, or food are regarded as serious offenses; at a minimum, people who perpetrate these kinds of breaches are likely to find themselves ostracized and cut out from the important loops of reciprocity that are so important in the diamond fields.

"You see this scar [a jagged cicatrice running down Douggie's left forearm]? I got that from a cutlass, clearing the bush at our work ground. And look at this one [here he rolled up his trouser leg]: this is where I fell in a pit on top of a mattock. You see these hands [hard and thickly callused]—I am a hard fucking man."

If the mind constitutes a site of intellectual and moral transformation through the absorption of technical skills and ethnical norms, then the body represents a

Angles of Vision from the Coast and Hinterland

site of transformation of a different kind. I refer here to the "hardening" that is an important part of the overall process of self-transformation. Among the many negativities coastlanders assign to the interior forests are the sheer difficulty and danger of such a landscape. Becoming and being a porkknocker depend not only on the acquisition of technical prospecting and mining skills and ethos, but on the ability to live and work in an alien and at times brutally difficult environment. Walking substantial distances through the forest, often "drugging" (carrying) heavily laden *warishi*s (wicker backpacks bought from Patamona and Macuxi communities), and then putting in weeks of backbreaking labor excavating assay trenches and mining pits are tremendously physically demanding. When new porkknockers arrive in the backdam, they are said to be "soft" and "green" because they lack not only knowledge but also physical hardness, resilience, and strength. The process of hardening the body is also set against a moral backdrop that privileges masculinity and self-reliance: complaining about the hardships or, worse, failing to pull one's weight in the camp or on the trail is seen as a sign of weakness. A man must learn to "carry himself" well, "drugging" a full load and participating fully in the work. Conversely, to offer to carry another man's load or to do his work on an excavation is to implicitly and unfavorably judge his strength and masculinity.

As a porkknocker's biography and experience is gradually inscribed upon the surfaces of his body in scars, calluses, and sinewy muscles, so the changes are reflected in the way he situates himself in discourse about the coast and the bush. Where once the bush was the negative pole and the coast represented security and comparative safety, we see a gradual inversion. Porkknockers, now hardened by many forays into the backdam, speak derisively of the "soft," "antiman" (homosexual) life on the coast. The hinterland in turn becomes valorized as a place where a man can—and indeed must—achieve a masculine ideal that is considered to be unattainable on the comfortable coastland.

*****

The main approach of the second half of this chapter has been to present and discuss ethnographic material that points the way to understanding how coastlanders become porkknockers—in other words, how a subpopulation of Guyanese Creole society makes sense of a world that is conceived of as deeply ambivalent. Ambivalence suggests contradiction and opposition, and we may consider this particular ambivalence to be cast in terms of a set of oppositions: poverty/wealth, disorientation/familiarity, wildness/domination, constraint/freedom. I have argued here that becoming a successful porkknocker depends on the coastlander's ability to resolve these oppositions—to transform poverty into wealth and disorientation into familiarity, to dominate the wild and escape constraint. Acquiring this ability in turn requires a process of self-transformation through enskillment, insertion into a new moral economy, and physical tempering. In these various processes of transformation, the discursive achieves a key salience. Almost never empty narrative, porkknocker discourse is in this context a charter and a guide for transformative action.

Redemption, Salvation, Escape, Extraction, Exploitation, and Domination

Like the historical relationship between the Old World and the New, the awkward affinity between Guyana's coast and its polysemic interior can be written in these terms. In this essay of two parts, we have sought to unpack aspects of this relationship by focusing on a pair of complementary perspectives. The first concerns the ways in which the interior and the people who live there are drawn physically and discursively into the coastlands, achieving passing visibility as instruments in the state's crusade to appear both legitimate and obedient under the demanding U.S. gaze. The second perspective reflects on those coastlanders who are drawn physically and discursively into the hinterlands, arguing that such a move ultimately demands engagement with a process of self-transformation and ontological recasting.

Notes

1. See http://www.state.gov/g/tip/rls/tiprpt/2004/.

2. Some of the interviewee names have been kept confidential because these individuals work with or interact with government officials as part of their daily routines; naming them might make them vulnerable.

3. Although this part of the chapter is about the representation of Amerindian women, it is critical to note that diverse sociocultural practices and residential patterns are elided by such a generic application. In Guyana, those whom the state and coastlanders identify as "Amerindians" (the term is also used in different ways by some indigenous peoples, including for purposes of political identification) can more precisely be named Akawaio, Arawak, Arekuna, Carib, Macuxi, Patamona, Waiwai, Wapishana, and Warao, although even these groupings can efface the fact that these peoples have long been part of a larger regional "Guianas" context.

4. The numbers of men relative to every one hundred women are: Region 1 (112); Region 7 (114); Region 8 (132); Region 9 (107).

5. As Terry Roopnaraine notes, one can trace the practice of seeing the hinterland as solution to the earliest days of colonial contact: "at various overlapping moments in history, this [practice] has taken the form of quests for gold, diamonds, wood, medicine, 'the rain forest experience,' 'the Amerindian experience'" (personal correspondence, 15 March 2005).

6. Wilson Harris is intensely preoccupied with the landscape of Guyana's interior, which he experienced intimately as a young man on surveying expeditions. The landscape looms large and oneiric in his magical-realist fiction, which derives much of its richness from the tensions inherent in trying to impose a trigonometric order on a place of bewildering complexity. See Harris 1960, 1971 [1964] and chapter 14 in this volume.

7. As noted, the Guyanese diamond miners referred to in this chapter are known in the vernacular as *porkknockers*. There are several possible etymologies for this name, but the one I think most likely refers to the practice of "knocking" a piece of salted pork on a

pot of rice to impart flavor when there is no meat to add. *Porkknocker* refers particularly to miners of diamonds and gold who practice their trade with little or no mechanized technology, relying chiefly on manual extraction techniques.

8. Direct ethnographic speech was expressed in the Guyanese Creole vernacular, so, for simplicity, I have translated it as much as possible into standard English.

9. See, for example, Candace Slater's fine analysis of the *casos* of Brazilian *garimpeiros* (Slater 1994).

10. The term *backdam* as used here refers to the place of work, the site of mining itself. Conceptually, it is opposed to the "landing," which is an area connected by river, road, or air to larger urban centers. The backdam is typically remote and has no built environment or commerce, but the landing is less remote and may have some dwelling, bureaucratic, and commercial infrastructure.

11. Taussig has been criticized by Michael Sallnow (1989) on the grounds that he has misunderstood history and by Terry Turner (1986) on the grounds that he has misunderstood Marx.

12. The term *Creole* is used here to refer to the 90 percent of the Guyanese population that is for the most part resident on the coastal belt and that traces descent from coerced African and Indian labor forces rather than from any of the indigenous groups in Guyana. It is a term of convenience that in fact obscures much of the ethnic differentiation that is so salient a part of Guyanese life; however, this essay does not depend on disaggregating ethnicities.

13. As George Mentore perceptively notes, "With all the fear and suspicion produced and attached to the unknown and seemingly untameable forest, Guyanese creole society has attributed negativity and inferiority to the Amerindian abode and to the Amerindian person" (1992:1).

14. It is not uncommon for porkknockers who spend a long time in the interior to establish ongoing sexual relations (with a greater or lesser commercial flavor) with Amerindian or Brazilian women living near mining areas. In some cases, such relationships can continue for years, including the possibility of children, and porkknockers will make reference to their "bush family."

15. There are clear parallels between these stories and those of Western Desert Aboriginal people, which serve, among other things, to narrate the land into meaningful human action (Myers 1986).

Bibliography

Absy, M. L.
    1985   Palynology of Amazonia: History of the Forests as Revealed by the Palynological Record. *In* Amazonia. G. T. Prance and T. Lovejoy, eds. New York: Pergamon Press.

Acuña, P. Christovão de
    1891   Colección de libros que tratan de América, raros y curiosos, vol. 2: Nuevo
    [1641] descubrimiento del Gran Rio de las Amazonas. Madrid: Juan Cayetano García.

Albert, Bruce
    1985   Temps du sang, Temps des cendres: Représentation de la maladie, système rituel et espace politique chez les Yanomami du sudest (Amazonie bresilienne). Ph.D. dissertation, Department of Anthropology, University de Paris X Nanterre.

Alemán, Stephanie
    2005   Waiwai Theories of Nature. Ph.D. dissertation, Department of Anthropology, University of Wisconsin–Madison.

Alexander, M. Jacqui
    1997   Erotic Autonomy as a Politics of Decolonization: An Anatomy of Feminist and State Practice in the Bahamas Tourist Economy. *In* Feminist Genealogies, Colonial Legacies, Democratic Futures. M. J. Alexander and C. Mohanty, eds. Pp. 63–100. New York: Routledge.

Alvard, M. S., J. G. Robinson, K. H. Redford, and H. Kaplan
    1997   The Sustainability of Subsistence Hunting in the Neotropics. Conservation Biology 11:977–982.

Amerindian Lands Commission
    1966   Lands Commission Report. Georgetown: Guyanese Government Printing Office.

Amnesty International
    1985–   Amnesty International Report. London: Amnesty International.
    1995

Anderson, C. W.
    1912   Forests of British Guiana, Detail Reports, Series 1: The Forests of the North West District of the Country of Essequibo. Georgetown, British Guiana: Department of Lands and Mines.

Andrade, Mário de
    1988   Macunaíma. Paris: Association Archives de la Littérature latino-améri-
    [1928] caine, des Caraibes et africaine du XXe siècle; Brasilia: CNPQ.

Appun, C. F.
    1893   Roraima. Timehri 8(2) (n.s.):318–348.

Arens, William
    1979   The Man Eating Myth: Anthropology & Anthropophagy. New York: Oxford University Press.

Århem, Kaj.
    1981   Makuna Social Organization: A Study in Descent, Alliance, and the Formation of Corporate Groups in the North-Western Amazon. Uppsala Studies in Cultural Anthropology no. 4. Uppsala, Sweden: Academiae Upsaliensis.

1996   The Cosmic Food Web: Human-Nature Relatedness in the Northwest Amazon. *In* Nature and Society: Anthropological Perspectives. P. Descola and G. Pálsson, eds. Pp. 185–204. London: Routledge.

Armellada, Cesáreo
1964   Tauron Panton: Cuentos y leyendas de los indios Pemon. Caracas, Venezuela: Ediciones del Ministerio de Educación.

Arvelo-Jiménez, Nelly
1971   Political Relations in a Tribal Society: A Study of the Ye'cuana Indians of Venezuela. Cornell Dissertation Series. Ithaca, N.Y.: Cornell University.
1973   The Dynamics of the Ye'cuana (Maquiritare) Political System: Stability and Crisis. International Work Group for Indigenous Affairs (IWGIA) Document no. 12. Copenhagen: IWGIA.

Asad, Talal
1986   The Concept of Cultural Translation in British Social Anthropology. *In* Writing Culture: The Poetics and Politics of Ethnography. J. Clifford and G. Marcus, eds. Pp. 141–164. Berkeley: University of California Press.

Baber, Colin, and Henry B. Jeffrey
1986   Guyana: Politics, Economics, and Society beyond the Burnham Era. London: Frances Pinter.

Barandiaran, Daniel de
1979   Introducción a la cosmovisión de los indios Ye'kuana-Makiritare. Caracas, Venezuela: Universidad Catolica Andres Bello.

Barrington-Brown, C.
1877   Canoe and Camp Life in British Guiana. London: Edward Stanford.

Basso, Ellen, ed.
1977   Carib-Speaking Indians: Culture, Language, and Society. Anthropological Papers of the University of Arizona, no. 28. Tucson: University of Arizona Press.

Basso, Keith
1984   Stalking with Stories: Names, Places, and Moral Narratives among the Western Apache. *In* Text, Play, and Story: The Construction and Reconstruction of Self and Society. E. Bruner, ed. Pp. 77–89. Proceedings of the American Ethological Society.
1988   Speaking with Names. *In* Western Apache Language and Culture: Essays in Linguistic Anthropology. Pp. 34–57. Tucson: University of Arizona Press.

Behling, H.
2002   Impact of Holocene Sea Level Changes in Coastal, Eastern, and Central Amazonia. Amazoniana 17:41–52.

Behling, H., and H. Hooghiemastra
1998   Late Quaternary Paleoecology and Paleoclimatology from Pollen Records of the Savannas of the Llanos Orientales de Colombia. Paleogeography, Paleoclimatology, and Paleoecology 139:251–267.

Belaunde, Luisa Elvira
1992   Gender, Commensality, and Community among the Airo-Pai of Western Amazonia. Ph.D. dissertation, Department of Anthropology, University of London.

Benjamin, Anna
1993   A Preliminary Look at the Free Amerindians and the Dutch Plantation System in Guyana during the 17th and 18th Centuries. Guyana Historical Journal 4–5:21–37.

Benjamin, Walter
- 1996 Die Aufgabe des Übersetzers. *In* Ein Lesebuch, by Walter Benjamin. M.
- [1923] Opitz, ed. Pp. 45–57. Frankfurt: Suhrkamp.
- 2004 The Task of the Translator. *In* The Translation Studies Reader. L. Venuti, ed. Pp. 15–25. London: Routledge.

Berry, P. E., O. Huber, and B. K. Holst
- 1995 Floristic Analysis and Phytogeography. *In* Flora of the Venezuelan Guayana: Introduction, vol. 1. J. A. Steyermark, P. E. Berry, and B. K. Holst, eds. Pp. 161–191. Portland, Ore.: Timber Press.

Biet, Antoine
- 1664 Voyage dans la France équinoxiale en l'Isle de Cayenne. Paris: F. Clouzier.

Bittner, E.
- 1974 Florence Nightingale in Pursuit of Willie Sutton: A Theory of the Police. *In* The Potential for Reform of Criminal Justice. H. Jacob, ed. Pp. 17–44. Beverly Hills, Calif.: Sage.

Black, Max
- 1983 Die Metapher: Mehr über die Metapher. *In* Theorie der Metapher. A. Haverkamp, ed. Pp. 55–79. Darmstadt, Germany: Wissenschaftliche Buchgesellschaft.

Blasco, F., P. Saenger, and E. Janodet
- 1996 Mangroves as Indicators of Coastal Change. Catena 27(3–4):167–178.

Blumenberg, Hans
- 1980 Paradigmen zu einer Metaphorologie. Frankfurt am Main: Suhrkamp.
- [1960]
- 1997 Shipwreck with Spectator. Cambridge, Mass.: MIT Press.
- 2001 Ästhetische und Metaphorologische Schriften. J. Boggan, V. Funk, C. Kelloff, M. Hoff, G. Cremers, and C. Feuillet, eds. Frankfurt am Main: Suhrkamp.

Boggan, J., V. Funk. C. Kelloff, M. Hoff, G. Cremers, and C. Feuillet
- 1997 Checklist of the Plants of the Guianas. 2d ed. Washington, D.C.: Biological Diversity of the Guianas Program, Smithsonian Institution.

Boman, Eric
- 1908 Antiquités de la région Andine de la République Argentine et du D'esert d'Atacama, vol. 1. Paris: Imprimiere Nationale.

Boomert, Arie
- 1980a Hertenrits: An Arauquinoid Complex in North West Suriname. Journal of the Walter Roth Museum of Archaeology and Anthropology 3(2):68–104.
- 1980b The Sipaliwini Archaeological Complex of Suriname: A Summary. Nieuwe West-Indische Gids 54(2):94–107.
- 1983 The Saladoid Occupation of Wonotobo Falls, Western Suriname. *In* Proceedings of the 9th International Congress for the Study of the Pre-Columbian Cultures of the Lesser Antilles. Pp. 97–120. Montreal: International Congress Publications.
- 1987 Gifts of the Amazons: "Green Stone" Pendants and Beads as Items of Ceremonial Exchange in Amazonia and the Carribean. Antropológica 67:33–54.

Boomert, Arie, and Solomon B. Kroonenberg
- 1977 Manufacture and Trade of Stone Artifacts in Prehistoric Surinam. *In* Ex Horreo IPP 1951–1976. B. L. Van Beek, R. W. Brandt, and W. Groenman-van Waateringe, eds. Cingula 4. Pp. 9–46. Amsterdam: n.p.

1987 Gifts of the Amazons: "Green Stone" Pendants and Beads as Items of Ceremonial Exchange in Amazonia and the Carribean. Antropológica 67: 33–54.

Boyer, P.
1986 Tradition et vérité. L'Homme 97–98(1–2):309–329.

Brennan, Timothy
1990 The National Longing for Form. *In* Nation and Narration. H. Bhabha, ed. Pp. 44–70. London: Routledge.

Brett, William H.
1868 The Indian Tribes of Guiana. London: Bell & Daldy.
1880 Legends and Myths of the Aboriginal Indians of British Guiana. London: William Wells Gardner.
1881 Mission Work in the Forests of Guiana. London and New York: Society for Promoting Christian Knowledge and E. & J. B. Young.

Brinkman, R., and L. J. Pons
1968 A Pedo-geomorphological Classification and Map of the Holocene Sediments in the Coastal Plain of the Three Guianas. Soil Survey Papers no. 4. Wageningen, Netherlands: Soil Survey Institute.

Brinton, Daniel
2008 The American Race: A Linguistic Classification and Ethnographic Descrip-
[1891] tion of the Native Tribes of North and South America. New York: N. D. C. Hodges.

British Guiana Commission of Inquiry
1965 Report of the British Guiana Commission of Inquiry: Racial Problems in the Public Service. Geneva: International Commission of Jurists.

British Guiana Forest Department
1935 Forestry in British Guiana. *In* Supplementary Statement Prepared by the Forest Department for Presentation to the Fourth British Empire Forestry Conference (South Africa), no. 8/1935. C.S.O. no. 3421/32. P. 11. Georgetown: British Guiana Legislative Council.

Brock, Stanley E.
1972 Jungle Cowboy. New York: Taplinger.

Broderick, J. J.
1977 Police in a Time of Change. Morristown, N.J.: General Learning Press.

Brotherston, Gordon
1992 Book of the Fourth World: Reading the Native Americas Through Their Literature. Cambridge, U.K.: Cambridge University Press.
1993 Pacaraima as Destination in Carpentier's *Los pasos perdidos*. Indiana Journal of Hispanic Literatures 1(2):161–183.

Brown, K. S.
1977 Centros de evolucao, refugios quarternarios e conservaõ de patrimonios geneticus no regiao neotropical: Padroes de diferenciacaõ em ithomiinae (Lepidoptera: Nymphalidae). Acta Amazonica 7(1):75–137.

Brown, K. S., and A. N. Ab'Saber
1979 Ice-Age Refuges and Evolution in the Neotropics: Correlation of Paleoclimatological, Geomorphological, and Pedological Data with Modern Biological Endemism. Paleoclimas 5:37–48.

Brown, M. K.
1988 Working the Street: Police Discretion and the Dilemmas of Reform. New York: Russell Sage Foundation.

Bundy, A., ed.
  1999 Selected Essays of Wilson Harris: The Unfinished Genesis of the Imagination. London: Routledge.
Burnett, D. Graham
  2000 Masters of All They Surveyed: Exploration, Geography, and a British El Dorado. Chicago: University of Chicago Press.
  2002 "It Is Impossible to Make a Step Without the Indians": Nineteenth-Century Geographical Exploration and the Amerindians of British Guiana. Ethnohistory 49(1):3–4.
Burr, George Lincoln
  1897 Report of the Evidence of the Dutch Archives as to European Occupation and Claims in Western Guiana, vol. 1. Washington, D.C.: U.S. Commission on Boundary Between Venezuela and British Guiana.
Butt Colson, Audrey
  1954 Systems of Belief in Relation to Social Structure and Organization: With Reference to the Carib-Speaking Tribes of the Guianas. Ph.D. dissertation, Department of Philosophy, Oxford University.
  1960 The Birth of a Religion. Journal of the Royal Anthropological Institute 90(1):66–106.
  1973 Intertribal Trade in the Guiana Highlands. Antropológica 34:169.
  1983– The Spatial Component in the Political Structure of the Caribe Speakers of
  84   the Guiana Highlands: Kapon and Pemon. Antropológica 59/62:73–124.
  1985 Routes of Knowledge. Antropológica 63:103–149.
  1998 Fr. Cary-Elwes S.J. and the Alleluia Indians. Georgetown: Amerindian Research Unit, University of Guyana.
Cabalzar, Flora Dias
  1997 Trocas matrimoniais e relações de qualidade entre os Waiãpi do Amap. Master's thesis, Department of Anthropology, Universidade de São Paulo.
Cain, Maureen E.
  1973 Society and the Policeman's Role. London: Routledge and Kegan Paul.
Cancino, Jeffrey Michael, and Roger Enriquez
  2004 A Qualitative Analysis of Officer Peer Retaliation: Preserving Police Culture. Policing: An International Journal of Police Strategies and Management 27(3):320–340.
Capiberibe, Artionka
  2001 Os Palikur e o Cristianismo. Master's thesis, Programa de Pós Graduação em Antropologia Social, Universidade Estadual de Campinas, Brazil.
  2007 O batismo de fuego: Os Palikur e o Cristianismo. São Paulo: Annablume, FAPESP, Nuti.
Carpentier, Alejo
  1985 Los pasos perdidos. R. González Echevarría, ed. Madrid: Cátedra.
  1990 Visión de América. In Obra Completa, 13:281–296. Mexico City: Siglo 21.
Carsten, J., and S. Hugh-Jones, eds.
  1995 About the House: Lévi-Strauss and Beyond. Cambridge, U.K.: Cambridge University Press.
Carter, Martin
  1997 Selected Poems. Georgetown, Guyana: Red Thread Press.
Carvajal, Gaspar de
  1942 Relación del nuevo descubrimiento del famoso Río Grande que descubrió por muy gran ventura el Capitán Francisco de Orellana. Transcripciones

de Fernández de Oviedo y Dn. Toribio Medina y Estudio Crítico de Descubrimiento. Quito: n.p.

Castile, George Pierre
    1996   Indian Identity as a Commodity. American Anthropologist 98(4):743–749.

Certeau, Michel de
    1984   The Practice of Everyday Life. Berkeley: University of California Press.

Chagnon, Napoleon
    1992   Yanomami: The Fierce People. 3rd edition. New York: Holt, Rinehart and
    [1968]   Winston.

Chan, Janet B. L.
    1996   Changing Police Culture. British Journal of Criminology 36(1):109–134.
    1997   Changing Police Culture: Policing in a Multicultural Society. New York: Cambridge University Press.

Chapuis, Jean, and Hervé Rivière
    2003   Wayana eitoponpë: (Une) histoire (orale) des Indiens Wayana, Guyane. Cayenne, French Guiana: Ibis Rouge Éditions.

Charles-Dominique, P., P. Blanc, D. Larpin, M. Ledru, B. Riéra, C. Sarthou, M. Servant, and C. Tardy
    1998   Forest Perturbations and Biodiversity in the Last Ten Thousand Years in French Guiana. Acta Oecologica 19:295–302.

Chevigny, P.
    1995   Edge of the Knife: Police Violence in the Americas. New York: New Press.

Civrieux, Marc de
    1980   Watunna: An Orinoco Creation Cycle. D. Guss, ed. Austin: University of Texas Press.

Clarke, E. C.
    1956   The Regeneration of Worked-out Greenheart (*Ocotea rodiei*) Forest in British Guiana. Empire Forestry Review 35:173–183.

Clastres, Pierre
    1974   La societé contre l'état. Paris: Éditions de Minuit.
    1977   A sociedade contra o estado. Rio de Janeiro: Francisco Alves.

Cleary, David
    1990   The Anatomy of the Amazon Gold Rush. London: MacMillan.

Cohn, Bernard
    1996   Colonialism and Its Forms of Knowledge. Princeton, N.J.: Princeton University Press.

Colchester, M., J. La Rose, and K. James
    1994   The New Sultans: Asian Loggers Move into Guyana's Forests. The Ecologist 24:45–52.
    1997   Guyana, Fragile Frontier: Loggers, Miners, and Forest Peoples. London: Latin American Bureau.
    2002   Mining and Amerindians in Guyana: Exploring Indigenous Perspective on Consultation and Engagement within the Mining Sector in Latin America and the Caribbean. Ottawa: North-South.

Collomb, Gérard
    1997   La question amérindienne en Guyane: Formation d'un espace politique. *In* Anthropologie du politique. M. Abélès and H.P. Jeudy, eds. Pp. 41–66. Paris: Armand Colin.
    2001   Identité et territoire chez les Kali'na: À partir d'un récit du retour des morts. Journal de la Société des Américanistes 86(2):149–168.

Collomb, Gérard, and Félix Tiouka
    2000   Na'na Kali'na: Histoire des Kali'na de Guyane. Cayenne, French Guiana: Ibis Rouge Éditions.
Conrad, Joseph
    1999   Heart of Darkness. Peterborough, Canada: Broadview.
    [1899]
Coronil, Fernando
    1997   The Magical State: Nature, Money, and Modernity in Venezuela. Chicago: University of Chicago Press.
Corrêa, Conceição Gentil
    1965   Estatuetas de cerâmica na cultura Santarém: Classificação e catálogo das coleções do Museu Goeldi. Publicações Avulsas 4. Belém, Brazil: Museu Paraense Emílio Goeldi.
Corsín Jiménez, Alberto
    2003   On Space as a Capacity. Journal of the Royal Anthropological Institute 9(1):137–153.
Cosgrove, Denis E.
    1983   Social Formation and the Symbolic Landscape. Madison: University of Wisconsin Press.
Coudreau, Henri
    1893   Chez nos Indiens: Quatre années dans la Guyane française (1887–1891). Paris: Hachette.
Coudreau, Olga
    1900   Voyage au Cumin. Paris: Hachette.
Crank, J. P.
    1998   Understanding Police Culture. Cincinnati: Anderson.
Craton, Michael
    1996   Continuity Not Change: The Incidence of Unrest among Ex-slaves in the British West Indies. *In* Caribbean Freedom: Economy and Society from Emancipation to the Present. H. Beckles and V. Shepherd, eds. Pp. 420–431. Princeton, N.J.: Marcus Weiner.
Crevaux, Jules
    1883   Voyages dans l'Amérique du Sud, contenant, vol. 1: Voyage dans l'intérieur des Guyanes (1876–1877), exploration du Maroni et du Yary; vol. 2: De Cayenne aux Andes (1878–1879), exploration de l'Oyapock, du Parou, de l'Iça et du Yapura. Paris: Hachette.
Croizat, L.
    1958   Panbiogeography. Caracas, Venezuela: L. Croizat.
Croll, Elisabeth, and David Parkin, eds.
    1992   Bush Base: Forest Farm: Culture Environment and Development. London: Routledge.
Cruxent, José Maria, and Irving Rouse
    1958–59   An Archaeological Chronology of Venezuela. Social Science Monographs no. 6. Washington, D.C.: Pan American Union.
Davis, T. A. W., and P. W. Richards
    1933   The Vegetation of Moraballi Creek, British Guiana: An Ecological Study of a Limited Area of Tropical Rain Forest. Part 1. Journal of Ecology 21:350–384.
    1934   The Vegetation of Moraballi Creek, British Guiana: An Ecological Study of a Limited Area of Tropical Rain Forest. Part 2. Journal of Ecology 22:106–155.

Dawkins, H. Colyear, and Michael S. Philip
  1998   Tropical Moist Forest Silviculture and Management: A History of Success and Failure. Wallingford, Conn.: CAB International.
De Granville, J. J.
  1982   Rain Forest and Xeric Flora Refuges in French Guiana. *In* Biological Diversification in the Tropics. G. T. Prance, ed. Pp. 159–181. New York: Columbia University Press.
De Man, Paul
  1985   Conclusions: Walter Benjamin's "The Task of the Translator." Messenger Lecture, Cornell University, 4 March. *Also in* 50 Years of Yale French Studies: A Commemorative Anthology, Part 2: 1980–1988. C. A. Porter and A. Waters, eds. Pp. 25–46. Yale French Studies no. 69. New Haven, Conn.: Yale University.
De Milde, R.
  1969   Assessment of Hidden Defect of Standing Trees during Inventory Work in Guyana. Proceedings of meeting of IUFRO section 25 working group on mensurational problems of forest inventory in tropical countries, Reinbek, Germany, 1–5 July 1969.
De Milde, R., and D. de Groot
  1970a   Inventory of the Ebini-Itaki Area. Forest Industries Development Survey, Guyana (FIDS). FO:SF/GUY 9. Technical Report no. 9. Georgetown, Guyana: United Nations Development Program, Food and Agricultural Organization.
  1970b   Reconnaissance Survey of the More Accessible Forest Areas, Zone 2. Forest Industries Development Survey, Guyana (FIDS). FO:SF/GUY 9. Technical Report no. 8B. Georgetown, Guyana: United Nations Development Program, Food and Agricultural Organization.
  1970c   Survey of the More Accessible Forest Areas. Forest Industries Development Survey, Guyana (FIDS). FO:SF/GUY 9. Technical Report no. 8. Georgetown, Guyana: United Nations Development Program, Food and Agricultural Organization.
  1971a   Identification of Tree Species on Large Scale Infrared Aerial Photographs of the Coastal Swamp Forests of Guyana. Appendix 12. *In* Inventory of a Selected Area in the Northwest District. Forest Industries Development Survey, Guyana (FIDS). FO:SF/GUY 9. Technical Report no. 10. Rome: Food and Agricultural Organization Forestry Department.
  1971b   Inventory of a Selected Area in the Northwest District. Forest Industries Development Survey, Guyana (FIDS). FO:SF/GUY 9. Technical Report no. 10. Rome: Food and Agricultural Organization Forestry Department.
Derrida, Jacques
  1972   Marges de la philosophie. Paris: Éditions de Minuit.
Descola, P.
  1992   Societies of Nature and the Nature of Society. *In* Conceptualizing Society. A. Kuper, ed. Pp. 107–126. London: Routledge.
Desperes, Leo A.
  1967   Cultural Pluralism and Nationalist Politics in Guyana. Chicago: Rand McNally.
Detienne, Marcel
  1994   Ouverture. *In* Transcrire les mythologies. M. Detienne, coord. Pp. 7–21. Paris: Bibliothèque Albin Michel.

Dias, Carlos M., Jr.
    2000   Próximos e distantes: Estudo de um processo de descentralização e (re)construão de relaões sociais na região sudoeste da Guiana. Master's thesis, Faculdade de Filosofia, Letras e Ciências Humanas, Programa de Pós Graduação em Antropologia Social, Universidade de São Paulo.
    2006   Entrelinhas de uma rede: Entre linhas Waiwai. Ph.D. dissertation, Department of Anthropology, Universidade de São Paulo.

Dowdy, Homer
    1963   Christ's Witchdoctor: From Savage Sorcerer to Jungle Missionary. New York: Harper and Row.
    1995   Christ's Jungle. Gresham, Ore.: Vision House.

Doyle, Sir Arthur Conan
    1995   The Lost World: Being an Account of the Recent Amazing Adventures of
    [1912]   Professor George E. Challenger, Lord John Roxton, Professor Summerlee, and Mr. E. D. Malone of the Daily Gazette. Oxford, U.K.: Oxford University Press.

Drayton, Richard
    2000   Nature's Government. New Haven, Conn.: Yale University Press.

Dreyfus, Simone
    1981   Le peuple de la rivière du milieu: Esquisse pour l'étude de l'espace social palikur. In Orients pour Georges Condominas. Pp. 301–313. Paris: Sudestasie Privat.
    1992   Les réseaux politiques indigènes en Guyane occidentale et leurs transformations aux XVIIe et XVIIIe siècles. L'Homme 122–124:75–98.
    1993   Os empreendimentos coloniais e os espaos políticos na Guiana Ocidental (entre o Orenoco e o Corentino) de 1613 a 1796. In Amazônia: Etnologia e história indígena. São Paulo: Núcleo de História Indigena e do Indigenismo, Universidade de São Paulo, Fundação de Amparo à Pesquisa do Estado de São Paulo.

Drummond, D. S.
    1976   Police Culture. Beverly Hills, Calif.: Sage.

Dumont, Jean Paul
    1978   The Headman and I: Ambiguity and Ambivalence in the Fieldworking Experience. Austin: University of Texas Press.

Ek, R. C.
    1996   Botanical Richness of a Part of the Guyana Shield: The Guianas. In The Guyana Shield: Recent Developments and Alternatives for Sustainable Development. Special issue of Bos Newsletter 15(2):20.

Enmore Enquiry Commission
    1948   Report of the Enmore Enquiry Commission. British Guiana Legislative Council Report no. 10/1948. Georgetown: Guyanese Government Printing Office.

Erikson, Philippe
    1993   Une nebuleuse compacte: Lê marco-ensemble pano. In La remontée de l'Amazone: Anthropologie et histoire des sociétés amazoniennes. Special issue of L'Homme 126–128:45–58.

Evans, Clifford, and Betty J. Meggers
    1960   Archaeological Investigations in British Guiana. Bureau of American Ethnology Bulletin no. 177. Washington, D.C.: Smithsonian Institution.

Fajardo Pereira, Maria Denise

1999 Catolicismo, protestantismo e conversão: O campo de ação missionária entre os Tiriyó. *In* Transformando os Deuses. R. M. Wright, ed. Pp. 245–278. Campinas, Brazil: Editora da Universidade Estadual de Campinas.

Farabee, William Curtis
1918 The Amazon Expedition. Museum Journal, University of Philadelphia 7(4):21–48.
1924 The Central Carib. University of Philadelphia Anthropological Publications of the University Museum no. 10. Philadelphia: University of Philadelphia.

Farage, Nádia
1991 As muralhas dos sertões: Os povos indgenas no Rio Branco e a Colonização. Rio de Janeiro: Paz e Terra and Anpocs.
2003 Rebellious Memories: The Wapishana in the Rupununi Uprising, Guyana, 1969. *In* Histories and Historicities in Amazonia. N. Whitehead, ed. Pp. 107–120. Lincoln: University of Nebraska Press.

Fauque, Elzéar
1839 Lettres édifiantes et curieuses (1729–36). Paris: A. Martin.

Fausto, Carlos
2001 Inimigos fiéis: História, guerra e xamanismo na Amazônia. São Paulo: Edusp.

Fewkes, Jesse
1907 Aborigines of Porto Rico and Neighboring Islands. Washington, D.C.: Smithsonian Institution.

Fock, Niels
1963 Waiwai: Religion and Society of an Amazonian Tribe. Ethnographic Series no. 8. Copenhagen: National Museum of Denmark.

Forte, Janette, and Ian Melville, eds.
1990 The Population of Guyanese Amerindian Settlements in the 1980s. Occasional Publications of the Amerindian Research Unit. Georgetown: University of Guyana.

Friedman, Jonathan
1994 Cultural Identity and Global Process. London: Thousand Books.

Frikel, Protásio
1958 Classificação lingísticoetnológica das tribos indígenas do Pará setentrional e zonas adjacentes. Revista de Antropologia 6:113–189.

Gallegos, Rómulo
1945 Canaima. Buenos Aires: Espasa-Calpe.
[1923]

Gallois, Dominique T.
1986 Migraão, guerra e comércio: Os Waiãpi na Guiana. São Paulo: Faculdade de Filosofia, Letras e Ciéncias Humanas, Universidade de São Paulo.
1988 O movimento na cosmologia Waiãpi: Criacão, expanSão e transformaão do mundo. Ph.D. dissertation, Department of Anthropology, Universidade de São Paulo.
2000 Etnogêneses Waiãpi: Entre diversos e diferentes. Colquio Tempos Índios. Lisbon: Museu Nacional de Etnologia.
2005 (Ed.) Redes de relações nas Guianas. São Paulo: Associação Editorial Humanitas, Fundação de Amparo à Pesquisa do Estado de São Paulo.
2007 Gêneses Wajãpi: Entre diversos e diferentes. Revista de Antropologia 50(1):45–83.

Gallois, Dominique T., et al.
  1999   Caracterização Etnográfica da Região Sudeste das Guianas. *In* Indigenous Societies and Its Boundaries in the Southeastern Region of the Guianas. Fourth Annual Report of the Research Project São Paulo. São Paulo: Núcleo de História Indigena e do Indigenismo, Universidade de São Paulo, Fundação de Amparo à Pesquisa do Estado de São Paulo.

Geertz, Clifford
  1973   The Interpretation of Cultures. New York: Basic Books.

Gell, Alfred
  1995   The Language of the Forest: Landscape and Phonological Iconism in Umeda. *In* The Anthropology of Landscape: Perspectives on Place and Space. E. Hirsch and M. O'Hanlon, eds. Pp. 232–254. London: Oxford University Press.

Gibbs, Allan, and Christopher Barron
  1993   The Geology of the Guyana Shield. Oxford, U.K.: Oxford University Press.

Gibson, Kean
  2003   The Cycle of Racial Oppression in Guyana. Lanham, Md.: University Press of America.

Gillin, J.
  1948   The Tribes of the Guianas and the Left Amazon Tributaries. *In* Handbook of South American Indians, vol. 3. J. H. Steward, ed. Pp. 799–860. Bureau of American Ethnology Bulletin no. 143. Washington, D.C.: Smithsonian Institution.

Glaser, Bruno, and William L. Woods, eds.
  2004   Amazonian Dark Earths: Explorations in Space and Time. Berlin: Springer.

Glissant, Edouard
  1990   Poétique de la relation (Poétique 3). Paris: Gallimard.
  1996   Introduction à une poétique du divers. Paris: Gallimard.
  1997   Traité du tout-monde (Poétique 4). Paris: Gallimard.
  n.d.   Interview d'Edouard Glissant: De la poétique de la relation au tout-monde. Interviewed by Avner Perez. Available at http://le-village.ifrance.com/ATALAIA/glissant.

Goeje, C. H. de
  1924   Guayana and Carib Tribal Names. *In* Proceedings of 21st International Congress of Americanists. Pp. 212–216. The Hague: Society for the International Congress of Americanists.

Góes Neves, Eduardo
  1998   Paths in Dark Waters: Archaeology as Indigenous History in the Upper Rio Negro Basin, Northwest Amazon. Ph.D. dissertation, Department of Anthropology, Indiana University.
  2004   Introduction: The Relevance of Curt Nimuendajú's Archaeological Work. *In* In Pursuit of a Past Amazon: Archaeological Researches in the Brazilian Guyana and in the Amazon Region. C. Nimuendajú and P. Stenborg, eds. Pp. 2–8. Etnologiska Studier 45. Göteborg, Sweden: Världskulturmuseet i Göteborg.

Gomes, Denise Maria
  1999   Reescavando o passado: Um estudio do vasilhame cerâmico da Coleção Tapajônica MAE–USP. Master's thesis, Faculdade de Filosofia, Letras e Ciências Humanas, Universidade de São Paulo.
  2001   Santarém: Symbolism and Power in the Tropical Forest. *In* Unknown Ama-

zon: Culture in Nature in Ancient Brazil. C. McEwan, C. Barreto, and E. Góes Neves, eds. Pp. 134–155. London: British Museum Press.
2002   Cerâmica Arqueológica da Amazônia. São Paulo: Editoria da Universidade de São Paulo.

Gordon, W. A.
1955   The Law of Forestry. Oxford, U.K.: Clarendon Press.

Government of Guyana
2005   Act No. 2 of 2005: Combating of Trafficking in Persons Act. Georgetown, Guayana: Government Printing Office.

Gow, Peter
1991   Of Mixed Blood: Kinship and History in Peruvian Amazonia. Oxford, U.K.: Clarendon Press.
2002   Piro, Apurinã, and Campa: Social Dissimilation and Assimilation as Historical Processes in Southwestern Amazonia. *In* Comparative Arawakan Histories: Rethinking Language Family and Culture Area in Amazonia. J. D. Hill and F. Santos-Granero, eds. Pp. 147–170. Urbana: University of Illinois Press.
2003   "Ex-Cocama": Identidades em transformacão na Amazônia Peruana. Mana 9(1):57–79.

Grayum, G. H.
1971   Logging and Forest Management: Forest Industries Development Survey, Guyana (FIDS). FO:SF/GUY 9. Technical Report no. 12. Georgetown, Guyana: United Nations Development Program, Food and Agricultural Organization.

Green, Lesley Fordred, and David Green
2003   From Chronological to Spatio-temporal Histories: Mapping Heritage in Arukwa, Area Indígena do Uacá, Brasil. History and Anthropology 14(3):283–295.

Greene, J. E.
1974   Race vs. Politics in Guyana. Mona, Jamaica: Institute of Social and Economic Research, University of the West Indies.

Greene-Roesel, Justine
1996   Power, Identity, and Development: The Decline and Rise of Amerindian Agency in Northwest Guyana. Cambridge, U.K.: Cambridge University Press.

Grenand, Françoise, and Pierre Grenand
1987   La côte d'Amapa, de la bouche de l' Amazone à la baie d'Oyapock à travers la tradition orale palikur. Boletím do Museu Paraense Emílio Goeldi (Série Antropologia) 3(1):1–77.

Grenand, Pierre
1981   Agriculture sur brûlis et changements culturels: Le cas des Indiens Wayãpi et Palikur de Guyane. Journal d'Agriculture Traditionnelle et de Botanique Appliquée 28(1):23–31.

Gross-Braun, E. H., P. M. Day, G. H. Robinson, C. C. Applewhite, and R. Brinkman
1966   Soil Mapping. Paris: United Nations Development Program.

Guapindaia, Vera
2001   Encountering the Ancestors: The Maracá Urns. *In* Unknown Amazon: Culture in Nature in Ancient Brazil. C. McEwan, C. Barreto, and E. Góes Neves, eds. Pp. 156–173. London: British Museum Press.

Gumperz, John

1982 Discourse Strategies. New York: Cambridge University Press.
Guppy, Nicolas
    1951 Aerial Photo-interpretation of the Forests of British Guiana. Internal report. Georgetown, British Guiana: Forest Department.
    1952 Aerial Photo-interpretation in British and Dutch Guiana. Internal report. Georgetown, British Guiana: Forest Department.
    1958 Wai-Wai: Through the Forests North of the Amazon. New York: E. P. Dutton.
    1973 A Young Man's Journey. London: John Murray.
Guss, David
    1980 Introduction. *In* Watunna, by M. de Civrieux. D. Guss, ed. Pp. 1–18. Austin: University of Texas Press.
    1986 Keeping It Oral: A Ye'kuana Ethnology. American Ethnologist 13(3):413–429.
    1989 To Weave and Sing: Art, Symbol, and Narrative in the South American Rain Forest. Berkeley: University of California Press.
Guyana Forestry Commission
    2002 GFC Code of Practice for Timber Harvesting. 2d edition. Georgetown: Guyana Forestry Commission.
    2007 Forest Sector Information Report. Year 2006 Review. Georgetown: Guyana Forestry Commission.
Guyana Human Rights Association (GHRA)
    1980– Guyana Human Rights Association Members Annual Report. Georgetown:
    2000 Guyana Human Rights Association.
    2002 Ambivalent about Violence: A Report on Fatal Shootings by the Police in Guyana 1980–2002. Georgetown, Guyana: GHRA.
    2003 Violence: The Most Serious Threat to Human Rights. Press release, 10 December.
    2004 Police Reforms Urgent to Restore Rule of Law. Press release, 26 March.
    2005 Minister Gajraj Should Not Be Re-appointed. Press release, 12 April.
Guyana Ministry of Home Affairs
    2002 Public Consultation on Crime. Georgetown, Guyana: Government Printing Office, 5 September.
Guyana Ministry of Labour, Human Services, and Social Security (MLHSSS)
    2004 National Plan of Action to Combat Trafficking in Persons in Guyana. Georgetown, Guyana: Government Printing Office.
    n.d. Summary of Programme of Activities to Combat Trafficking in Persons in Guyana, 2005. Georgetown, Guyana: Government Printing Office.
Haffer, J.
    1969 Speciation in Amazonian Forest Birds. Science 165:131–137.
    1982 General Aspects of Refuge Theory. *In* Biological Diversification in the Tropics. G. T. Prance, ed. Pp. 42–49. New York: Columbia University Press.
Haman, M., and B. R. Wood
    1928 The Forests of British Guiana. Tropical Woods 15:1–13.
Hammond, D. S., and V. K. Brown
    1991 The Ecological Basis of Recruitment and Maintenance of Timber Tree Species in the Forests of Guyana 3. Interim Group Report DSH3. Ascot, U.K.: Imperial College.
    1993 The Ecological Basis of Recruitment and Maintenance of Timber Tree Species in the Forests of Guyana 5. Interim Group Report DSH5. Ascot, U.K.: Imperial College.

Hannerz, Ulf
1987   The World in Creolization. Africa 57(4):546–559.
Haraksingh, K.
2002   The Guyana Forestry Commission: Code of Best Practice for the Board. Georgetown: Guyana Forestry Commission.
Harris, Wilson
1960   Palace of the Peacock. London: Faber and Faber.
1971   Kanaima. *In* Commonwealth Short Stories. A. Rutherford and D. Hannah,
[1964] eds. Pp. 106–115. London: Edward Arnold.
Havt, Nadja
2001   Representações do Ambiente e Territorialidade entre os Zo'/PA. Ph.D. dissertation, Faculdade de Filosofia, Letras e Ciências Humanas, Programa de Pós Graduação em Antropologia Social, Universidade de São Paulo.
Hawkins, Robert
1954   Bob's Diary: Four Months in the Forests of North Brazil. Dallas: Radio Revival.
1956   The Winning of a Waiwai Witchdoctor: From Fear to Faith. Dallas: Bible Fellowships.
Hecht, Susanna B., and Alexander Cockburn
1989   The Fate of the Forest: Developers, Destroyers, and Defenders of the Amazon. London: Verso.
Heckenberger, Michael J., James B. Petersen, and Eduardo Góes Neves
1999   Village Size and Permanence in Amazonia: Two Archaeological Examples from Brazil. Latin American Antiquity 10(4):353–376.
Henfrey, Colin
1964   Through Indian Eyes. New York: Holt, Rinehart and Winston.
Henley, P.
2001   Inside and Out: Alterity and the Ceremonial Construction of the Person in the Guianas. *In* Beyond the Visible and the Material. L. M. Rival and N. Whitehead, eds. Pp. 197–220. Oxford, U.K.: Oxford University Press.
Herder, Johann
1986   [1772] On the Origin of Language. J. Moran and A. Gode, eds. Chicago: University of Chicago Press.
Hilbert, Peter Paul
1968   Archäologische Undersuchungen am Mitteren Amazonas. Marburger Studien zur Völkerkunde 1. Berlin: Dietrich Reimer.
Hilbert, Peter Paul, and Klaus Hilbert
1979   Archäologische Untersuchungen am Rio Nhamundá, Unterer Amazonas. *In* Beiträge zur Allgemeinen und Vergleichenden Archäologie, vol. 1. Pp. 439–450. Munich: Beck'sche.
Hill, Jane H., and Keith Hill
1986   Speaking Mexicano: The Dynamics of Syncretic Language in Central Mexico. Tucson: University of Arizona Press.
Hill, Jonathan D.
1984   Social Equality and Ritual Hierarchy: The Arawakan Wakuénai of Venezuela. American Ethnologist 11:528–544.
1993   Keepers of the Sacred Chants: The Poetics of Ritual Power in an Amazonian Society. Tucson: University of Arizona Press.
1996a   Ethnogenesis in the Northwest Amazon. *In* History, Power, and Identity:

Ethnogenesis in the Americas 1492–1992. J. Hill, ed. Pp. 142–160. Iowa City: University of Iowa Press.
1996b (Ed.) History, Power, and Identity: Ethnogenesis in the Americas 1492–1992. Iowa City: University of Iowa Press.

Hill, Jonathan D., and Fernando Santos-Granero, eds.
2002 Comparative Arawakan Histories: Rethinking Language Family and Cultural Area in Amazonia. Urbana: University of Illinois Press.

Hill, Jonathan D., and Susan Staats
2002 Redelineando el curso de la historia: Estados Euro-Americanos y las culturas sin pueblos. *In* Colonización, resistencia y mestizaje en las Américas (siglos 16–20). G. Boccara, ed. Pp. 13–26. Quito, Peru: Abya-Yala.

Hinds, David
1998 The Rise of the Authoritarian State in Guyana. Ph.D. dissertation, Department of History, Howard University.

Hintzen, Percy C.
1989 The Costs of Regime Survival: Racial Mobilization, Elite Domination, and Control of the State in Guyana and Trinidad. Cambridge, U.K.: Cambridge University Press.

Hirch, Eric
1995 Introduction: Landscape: Between Space and Place. *In* The Anthropology of Landscape: Perspectives on Place and Space. E. Hirsch and M. O'Hanlon, eds. Pp. 1–30. London: Oxford University Press.

Hirsch, Eric, and Michael O'Hanlon, eds.
1995 The Anthropology of Landscape: Perspectives on Place and Space. London: Oxford University Press.

Hollowell, T., P. Berry, V. Funk, and C. Kelloff
2001 Preliminary Checklist of the Plants of the Guiana Shield Biological Diversity of the Guianas Program, Smithsonian Institution. Unpublished document.

Hoock, J.
1971 Les savanes guyanaises: Kourou. Essai de phytoécologie numérique. Office de la Recherche Scientifique et Technique d'Outre-Mer (ORSTOM) no. 44. Paris: Mém.

Hornborg, Alf
2005 Ethnogenesis, Regional Integration, and Ecology in Prehistoric Amazonia: Toward a System Perspective. Current Anthropology 46(4):589–620.

Hornbostel, Erich M. de
1955–56 La musica de los Makushi, Taulipang y Yekuana. Archivos Venezolanos de Folklore 3(4):137–158.

Horowitz, Donald L.
1985 Ethnic Groups in Conflict. Berkeley: University of California Press.

Howard, Catherine
1991 Fragments of the Heavens: Feathers as Ornaments among the Waiwai. *In* The Gift of Birds: Featherwork of Native South American Peoples. R. E. Reina and K. M. Kensinger, eds. Pp. 50–69. Philadelphia: University Museum, University of Pennsylvania.
2001 Wrought Identities: The Waiwai Expeditions in Search of the "Unseen Tribes" of Northern Amazonia. Ph.D. dissertation, Department of Anthropology, University of Chicago.

Hudson, W. H.
  1944   Green Mansions: A Romance of the Tropical Forest. New York: Random
  [1904] House.

Hurault, Jean
  1968   Les Indies Wayana de la Guyane française: Structure sociale et coutume familiale. Mémoire no. 3. Paris: Office de la Recherche Scientifique et Technique outre Mer (ORSTOM).
  1972   Français et Indiens en Guyane (1604–1972). Paris: UGE 10/18.

Huss, R.
  1971   Logging in Guyana [June–July 1969]. Appendix 1. In Logging and Forest Management. Forest Industries Development Survey, Guyana (FIDS). FO:SF/GUY 9. Technical Report no. 12. Pp. 21–51. Georgetown, Guyana: United Nations Development Program, Food and Agricultural Organization.

Im Thurn, Everard
  1883   Among the Indians of Guiana. London: Kegan, Paul, Trench.
  1934   Thoughts, Talks, and Tramps: A Collection of Papers. London: Oxford University Press.

Ingold, Tim
  1992   Culture and the Perception of the Environment. In Bush Base: Forest Farm. E. Croll and D. Parkin, eds. Pp. 39–56. London: Routledge.
  1995   Building, Dwelling, Living: How Animals and People Make Themselves at Home in the World. In Shifting Contexts: Transformations in Anthropological Knowledge. M. Strathern, ed. Pp. 57–80. London: Routledge.

International Tropical Timber Organization (ITTO)
  2003   Achieving the ITTO Objective 2000 and Sustainable Forest Management in Guyana: Report of the Diagnostic Mission. Document ITTC (34)/8. 34th session of the International Tropical Timber Council, Panama, 12–17 May. Yokohama, Japan: International Tropical Timber Organization.

Isbell, B. J.
  1978   To Defend Ourselves: Ecology and Ritual in an Andean Village. Austin: University of Texas Press.

Jackson, Jean
  1983   The Fish People: Linguistic Exogamy and Tukanoan Identity in Northwestern Amazonia. Cambridge, U.K.: Cambridge University Press.
  1991   Being and Becoming an Indian in the Vaupés. In Nation-State and Indians in Latin America. G. Urban and J. Sherzer, eds. Pp. 131–155. Austin: University of Texas Press.

Jacobs, David, and Jason Carmichael
  2002   Subordination and Violence Against State Control Agents: Testing Political Explanations for Lethal Assaults Against the Police. Social Forces 80(4): 1223–1251.

Jagan, Cheddi
  1997   The West on Trial: My Fight for Guyana's Freedom. St. John's, Antigua: Hansib Caribbean.

Jeffries, Sir Charles
  1952   The Colonial Police. London: Max Parrish.

Jenkins, J. Craig, and Kurt Schock
  1992   Global Structures and Political Processes in the Study of Domestic Political Conflict. Annual Review of Sociology 18:161–185.

Jérémie, S. O., O. Ouraux Nowacke-Breczewski, and S. Vacher
    1993   Archaéologie de sauvetage en Guyane française: Le chantier de Petit-Saut, bilan en juin 1993. Journal de la Société des Américanistes 79:211–224.

Jermier, John M., John W. Slocum Jr., Louis W. Fry, and Jeannie Gaines
    1991   Organizational Subcultures in a Soft Bureaucracy: Resistance behind the Myth and Façade of an Official Culture. Organizational Science 2:170–194.

Joint press release (Church Women United, Clerical and Commercial Workers Union, Common Ground Guyana, Community Based Rehabilitation Programme—EBD Unit, General Workers Union, Guyana Council of Churches, Guyana Trades Union Congress, Guyana Human Rights Association, Red Thread)
    2006   Rule of Law under Threat in Guyana, June 10.

Kappeler, Victor E., Richard D. Studer, and Geoffrey P. Alpert
    1998   Forces of Deviance: Understanding the Dark Side of Policing. 2d edition. Prospect Heights, Ill.: Waveland Press.

Kapur, R.
    2003   The "Other" Side of Globalization: The Legal Regulation of Cross-Border Movements. Canadian Woman Studies 22(3–4):11–23.

Kelly, Robert L.
    1995   The Foraging Spectrum: Diversity in Hunter-Gatherer Lifeways. Washington, D.C.: Smithsonian Institution Press.

Kempadoo, K.
    2004   Victims and Agents: The New Crusade against Trafficking. *In* Global Lockdown: Race, Gender, and the Prison Industrial Complex. J. Sudbury, ed. Pp. 57–66. New York: Routledge.

Kloos, Peter
    1971   The Maroni River Caribs of Surinam. Assen, Netherlands: Van Gorcum.

Koch-Grünberg, Theodore
    1979   Del Roraima al Orinoco. Federica de Ritter, trans. 3 vols. Caracas: Banco
    [1917]   Central de Venezuela.

Koelewijn, C., and P. G. Rivière
    1987   Oral Literature of the Trio Indians of Surinam. Dordrecht: Foris.

Konersmann, Ralf
    1999   Komödien des Geistes: Historische Semantik als Philosophische Bedeutungsgeschichte. Frankfurt am Main: Fischer.

Kulick, Don
    1992   Language Shift and Cultural Reproduction: Socialization, Self, and Syncretism in a Papua New Guinea Village. Cambridge: Cambridge Univ. Press.
    1998   Anger, Gender, Language Shift, and the Politics of Revelation in a Papua New Guinea Village. *In* Language Ideologies: Practice and Theory. B. Schieffelin, K. Woolard, and P. Kroskrity, eds. Pp. 87–102. Oxford, U.K.: Oxford University Press.

Kwayana, Eusi
    1988   More than Survival: A View of the Indo-Guyanese Contribution to Social Change. Unpublished paper.
    1992   Guyana's Race Problems and My Part in Them. The Rodneyite:1–7.

La Rose, Jean, and Fergus MacKay
    1996   Our Land, Our Life, Our Culture: The Indigenous Movement in Guyana. Cultural Survival Quarterly (Winter): 29–34.

Lathrap, Donald W.
    1970   The Upper Amazon. London: Thames and Hudson.

1977 Our Father the Cayman, Our Mother the Gourd: Spinden Revisited, or a Unitary Model for the Emergence of Agriculture in the New World. *In* Origins of Agriculture. C. A. Reed, ed. Pp. 717–751. The Hague: Mouton.

Lehmann, Johannes, Dirse C. Kern, Bruno Glaser, and William I. Woods, eds.
2003 Amazonian Dark Earths: Origins, Properties, Management. Dordrecht, Netherlands: Kluwer Academic.

Lévi-Strauss, Claude
1991 Histoire de Lynx. Paris, Plon.

Lézy, Emmanuel
2000 Guyane, Guyanes: Une géographie sauvage de l'Orénoque à l'Amazone. Paris: Belin.

Lindeman, J. C., and S. A. Mori
1989 The Guianas. *In* Floristic Inventory of Tropical Countries. D. G. Campbell and D. H. Hammond, eds. Pp. 376–390. Bronx: New York Botanical Garden.

Linné, Sigvard
1928 Les recherches archéologiques de Nimuendajú au Brésil. Journal de la Société des Américanistes de Paris (n.s.) 20:71–91.

Linné, Sigvard, and Gösta Montell
1925 Från Brasiliens Indianer i Forntid och Nutid. C. Nimuendajús Arkeologiska och Etnografiska Forskning. Göteborg, Sweden: Göteborgs Museum, Etnografiska Avdelningen.

Lynch, T. F.
1998 The Paleoindian and Archaic Stages in South America: Zones of Continuity and Zones of Segregation. *In* Explorations in American Archaeology: Essays in Honor of Wesley R. Hurt. M. G. Plew, ed. Pp. 89–100. Lanham, Md.: University Press of America.

MacMillan, Gordon
1995 At the End of the Rainbow? Gold, Land, and People in the Brazilian Amazon. Man 25(3):412–433.

Magaña, Edmundo
1993– La palabra, el silencio y la escritura: Notas sobre algunas tribus de las Gua-
94 yanas. Revista Chilena de Antropología 12:99–112.

Malkki, Lisa
1994 Citizens of Humanity: Internationalism and the Imagined Community of Nations. Diaspora 3(1):41–68.

Manning, P. K.
1995 Police Occupational Culture in Anglo-American Societies. *In* The Encyclopedia of Police Science. W. Bailey, ed. Pp. 472–475. New York: Garland.

Mars, Joan R.
2002 Deadly Force, Colonialism, and the Rule of Law: Police Violence in Guyana. Westport, Conn.: Greenwood.

Marshall, Woodville
1996 Notes on Peasant Development in the West Indies since 1838. *In* Caribbean Freedom: Economy and Society from Emancipation to the Present. H. Beckles and V. Shepherd, eds. Pp. 27–42. Princeton, N.J.: Marcus Weiner.

Mayell, Hillary
2001 Biologists Document Rich Plant Life of Guyana to Aid Conservation. National Geographic News, May 8. Available online at http://news.national geographic.com/news/2001/05/0507_guayanaplants.html.

Mazière, Guy, ed.
   1997   L'archéologie en Guyane. Cayenne, French Guiana: APPAAG.
McCallum, Cecilia
   1990   Language, Kinship, and Politics in Amazonia. London: Royal Anthropological Institute of Great Britain and Ireland.
McEwan, Colin, Cristiana Barreto, and Eduardo Góes Neves, eds.
   2001   Unknown Amazon: Culture in Nature in Ancient Brazil. London: British Museum Press.
Meggers, Betty J.
   1971   Amazonia: Man and Nature in a Counterfeit Paradise. Washington, D.C.: Smithsonian Institution Press.
   1982   Archaeological and Ethnographic Evidence Compatible with the Model of Forest Fragmentation. *In* Biological Diversification in the Tropics. G. T. Prance, ed. Pp. 483–496. New York: Columbia University Press.
   1987   The Early History of Man in Amazonia. *In* Biogeography and Quaternary History in Tropical America. T. C. Whitmore and G. T. Prance, eds. Pp. 151–174. Oxford, U.K.: Clarendon Press.
   1994   Archaeological Evidence for the Impact of Mega-Niño Events on Amazonia during the Past Two Millenia. Climatic Change 28:321–338.
   1996   Possible Impact of the Mega-Niño Events on Precolumbian Populations in the Caribbean Area. *In* Ponencias: Primer Seminario de Arqueologia del Caribe. M. Veloz Maggiolo and A. Caba Fuentes, eds. Pp. 156–176. Altos de Chavón, Dominican Republic: Museo Arqueologico Regional Altas de Chavón, Organización de los Estados Americanos.
   2007   Mid-Holocene Climate and Cultural Dynamics in Brazil and the Guianas. *In* Climate Change and Cultural Dynamics: A Global Perspective on Mid-Holocene Transitions. D. G. Anderson, K. A. Maasch, and D. H. Sandweiss, eds. Pp. 117–155. Cambridge, Mass.: Elsevier.
Meggers, B. J., and Clifford Evans
   1957   Archaeological Investigations at the Mouth of the Amazon. Bureau of American Ethnology Bulletin no. 167. Washington, D.C.: Bureau of American Ethnology.
   1961   An Experimental Formulation of Horizon Styles in the Tropical Forest of South America. *In* Essays in Pre-Columbian Art and Archaeology. S. K. Lothrop and others, eds. Pp. 372–388. Cambridge, Mass.: Harvard University Press.
Meggers, B. J., and E. T. Miller
   2003   Hunter-Gatherers in Amazonia during the Pleistocene–Holocene Transition. *In* Under the Canopy: The Archaeology of Tropical Rain Forests. J. Mercado, ed. Pp. 291–316. New Brunswick, N.J.: Rutgers University Press.
Melville, Pauline
   1997   The Ventriloquist's Tale. New York: Bloomsbury.
Menezes, Mary Noel
   1977   British Policy Towards the Amerindians in British Guiana, 1803–1873. Oxford, U.K.: Clarendon Press.
   1988   The Amerindians of Guyana: Original Lords of the Soil. América Indígena 48(2):353–376.
Mentelle, Simon
   1821   Voyage géographique de Simon Mentelle, dans l'intérieur de la Guyane Française, allant de Cayenne, par la rivière de l'Oyapok, au Camopi, aux

Indiens Aramichaux, aux Indiens Émerillons, et redescendant par l'Arawoua et le Maroni, pour regagner Cayenne par la côte d'Iracoubo et de Sinamari, en mars et trois mois suivans, 1767. Feuille de la Guyane Française 122–124:700–703, 724–726.

Mentore, George
    1992   The Buck and the Boviander: Being Amerindian in Multicultural Guyana. Paper presented at the Ninety-first American Anthropology Association Annual Meeting, San Francisco, November.
    1993   Tempering the Social Self: Body Adornment, Vital Substance, and Knowledge among the Waiwai. Archaeology and Anthropology, vol. 9. Georgetown, Guayana: Walter Roth Museum.

Migliazza, E. C.
    1982   Linguistic Prehistory and the Refuge Model in Amazonia. *In* Biological Diversification in the Tropics. G. T. Prance, ed. Pp. 497–519. New York: Columbia University Press.

Milne, Robert Stephen
    1981   Politics in Ethnically Bipolar States. Vancouver: University of British Columbia Press.

Moore, Brian
    1987   Race, Power, and Social Segmentation in Colonial Society: Guyana after Slavery, 1838–1891. Philadelphia: Gordon and Breach Science.

Moran, E.
    1993   Through Amazonian Eyes: The Human Ecology of Amazonian Populations. Iowa City: University of Iowa Press.

Moreira, Ismael Pedrosa, and Ángelo Barra Moreira
    1994   Mitologia Tariana. Manaus: Instituto Brasileiro de Patrimônio Cultural.

Morton, J. A.
    1979   Conceptions of Fertility and Mortality among the Waiwai Indians of Southern Guiana. Master's thesis, Department of Anthropology, Oxford University.

Mueller-Eckhardt, Harold
    1969   Feasibility of Re-activation of the Particleboard Plant in Georgetown, Guyana. Vienna: United Nations Industrial Development Program.

Muir, W. K., Jr.
    1977   Police: Streetcorner Politicians. Chicago: University of Chicago Press.

Munn, Nancy
    1990   Constructing Regional Worlds in Experience: Kula Exchange, Witchcraft, and Gawan Local Events. Man 25:1–17.

Musolino, Alvaro A. Neves
    2006   Migracão, identidade e cidadania na Frontera do Oiapoque e Litoral Suleste da Guiana Francesa. Ph.D. dissertation, Center for Research and Postgraduate Studies on the Americas, University of Brasilia.

Myers, Fred
    1986   Pintupi Country, Pintupi Self: Sentiment, Place, and Politics among Western Desert Aborigines. Washington, D.C.: Smithsonian Institution Press.

Nash, June
    1979   We Eat the Mines and the Mines Eat Us. New York: Columbia University Press.

Nimuendajú, Curt
    1927   Streifzug vom Rio Jary zum Maracá. Petermanns Mitteilungen 73:356–358.

1971 [1926]	Die Palikur Indianer und ihre Nachbarn. Göteborgs Kungliga Vetenskapsoch Vitterhets-Samhälles Handlingar 31(2):1–144. French translation by Claudie Jousse. Typescript.
2000	Cartas do Sertão de Curt Nimuendajú para Carlos Estevão de Oliveira. Lisbon: Museu Nacional de Etnologia, Assíro and Alvim.
2004	In Pursuit of a Past Amazon: Archaeological Researches in the Brazilian Guyana and in the Amazon Region by Curt Nimuendajú. Per Stenborg, ed. Etnologiska Studier 45. Göteborg, Sweden: Världskulturmuseet i Göteborg.

Nordenskiöld, Erland
1930 Ars Americana I: L'archéologie du bassin de l'Amazone. Paris: Les Éditions G. van Oest.

Odum, W. E.
1984 The Relationship Between Protected Coastal Areas and Marine Fisheries Genetic Resources. *In* National Parks, Conservation, and Development: The Role of Protected Areas in Sustaining Society. J. McNeely and K. Miller, eds. Pp. 645–656. Washington, D.C.: Smithsonian Institution Press.

Overing, Joanna
1981 [as Overing Kaplan, Joanna] Amazonian Anthropology. Review article. Journal of Latin American Studies 13:151–165.
1983– Elementary Structures of Reciprocity: A Comparative Note on Guianese,
84   Central Brazilian, and Northwest Amazon Sociopolitical Thought. Antropológica 59/62: 331–348.
1986 Images of Cannibalism, Death, and Domination in a "Non-violent" Society. *In* The Anthropology of Violence. D. Riches, ed. Pp. 86–101. Oxford, U.K.: Blackwell.
1993 Death and the Loss of Civilized Predation among the Piaroa of the Orinoco Basin. L'Homme 126–128:191–211.
2003 In Praise of the Everyday: Trust and the Art of Social Living in an Amazonian Community. Ethnos 68(3):293–316.
2004 The Grotesque Landscape of Mythic "Before Time"; the Folly of Sociality in "Today Time": An Egalitarian Aesthetics of Human Existence. *In* Kultur, Raum, Landschaft: Zur Bedeutung des Raumes in Zeiten der Globalität. E. Mader and E. Halbmayer, eds. Pp. 69–90. Frankfurt am Main: Brandes and Apsel/Südwind.

Overing, Joanna, and Alan Passes
2000a (Eds.) The Anthropology of Love and Anger: The Aesthetics of Conviviality in Native Amazonia. London: Routledge.
2000b Introduction. *In* The Anthropology of Love and Anger: The Aesthetics of Conviviality in Native Amazonia. J. Overing and A. Passes, eds. Pp. 1–30. London: Routledge.

Palmatary, Helen Constance
1939 Tapajó Pottery. Etnologiska Studier 8. Göteborg, Sweden: Göteborgs Etnografiska Museum.
1960 The Archaeology of the Lower Tapajós Valley, Brazil. Transactions of the American Philosophical Society 50(3):19–34.

Palmer, Delbert
1969 An Assessment of the Marketing Potentials of Forest Products of Guyana, South America. Washington, D.C.: USAID.

Paoline, Eugene A., III, Stephanie M. Myers, and Robert E. Worden

2000 Police Culture, Individualism, and Community Policing: Evidence from Two Police Departments. Justice Quarterly 17:575–605.

Passes, Alan

1998 The Hearer, the Hunter, and the Agouti Head: Aspects of Intercommunication and Conviviality among the Pa'ikwené (Palikur) of French Guiana. Ph.D. dissertation, Department of Anthropology, University of St Andrews.

2000 The Value of Working and Speaking Together: A Facet of Pa'ikwené (Palikur) Conviviality. *In* The Anthropology of Love and Anger: The Aesthetics of Conviviality in Native Amazonia. J. Overing and A. Passes, eds. Pp. 97–113. London: Routledge.

2001 Arrête! Laisse! Donne! ("Stop It! Leave It! Give It!"): Equality, Power, and the Comical Imperative in Indigenous French Guyana. Paper presented at the workshop "The Ethnography of Laughter, Joy, Humour, and Play," University of St. Andrews, 18 June.

2002 Both Omphalos and Margin: On How the Pa'ikwené (Palikur) See Themselves to Be at the Center and on the Edge at the Same Time. *In* Comparative Arawakan Histories: Rethinking Language Family and Culture Area in Amazonia. J. D. Hill and F. Santos-Granero, eds. Pp. 171–195. Urbana: University of Illinois Press.

2003 You Are What You Speak, or Are You? Identity, Language, Sociocultural Change, and the Pa'ikwené (Palikur). Estudios Latinoamericanos 23:91–108.

2004a The Gathering of the Clans: The Making of the Palikur Naoné. Ethnohistory 51(2):257–291.

2004b The Place of Politics: Powerful Speech and Women Speakers in Everyday Pa'ikwené (Palikur) Life. Journal of the Royal Anthropological Institute 10(1):1–18.

2006 Not Alone in the Multiverse: Borrowing from Others, Remaining Pa'ikwené (Palikur). Paper presented at the conference "Guiana Ameríndia, história e etnologia," Belém, Brazil, 31 October–2 November.

Forthcoming Loud Women: Creating Community from the Domestic in Amazonia. *In* The Domestic Space Reader. C. Briganti and K. Mezei, eds. Toronto: University of Toronto Press.

Petersen, James B., Eduardo Góes Neves, Robert N. Bartone, and Manuel A. Arroyo-Kalin

2004 An Overview of Amerindian Cultural Chronology in the Central Amazon. Paper presented at the annual meeting of the Society for American Archaeology, Montreal, March.

Pierce, W. Edward

1881 Report of W. E. Pierce to the Bishop of Guiana. The Mission Field (January 1881):16–24.

Plew, Mark G.

1997 Recent Evidence of Paleoindian Occupations in the Lower Amazon: Implications for the Early Prehistory of Guyana. Paper presented at the Twenty-fourth Annual Conference of the Idaho Archaeological Society, Albertson's College, Caldwell, April.

2005 The Archaeology of Guyana. BAR International Series 1400. Oxford, U.K.: Archaeopress.

Plew, M. G., G. Pereira, and G. Simon

2007 Archaeological Survey and Test Excavation of the Kabakaburi Shell Mound,

Northwestern Guyana. Monographs in Archaeology no. 1. Georgetown: University of Guyana.

Police Complaints Authority (PCA)
    2005   Police Complaints Authority Annual Report 2004. Georgetown, Guyana: PCA, 9 June.

Pouguet, Martial
    2002   Chronologie de la Période Céramique de l'archéologie Amazonienne: Réflexions théoriques et méthodologiques. Porto Alegre, Brazil: Pontifícia Universidade Católica do Rio Grande do Sul.

Prance, G. T.
    1973   Phytogeographic Support for the Theory of Pleistocene Forest Refuges in the Amazon Basin, Based on Evidence from Distribution Patterns in Caryocaraceae, Chrysobalanaceae, Dichapetalaceae, and Lecthidaceae. Acata Amazonia 3(3):5–28.
    1982   Forest Refuges: Evidences from Woody Angiosperms. *In* Biological Diversification in the Tropics. G. T. Prance, ed. Pp. 34–75. New York: Columbia University Press.

Price, Richard
    1998   The Convict and the Colonel. Boston: Beacon Press.

Prince, A. J.
    1973   The Rate of Growth of Greenheart (*Ocotea rodiaei*) Schomb. Internal report. Georgetown, Guyana: Forest Department. Published in Commonwealth Forestry Review 52(2)(1973):143–146.

Quinn, Ellen R.
    2004   Excavating "Tapajó" Ceramics at Santarém: Their Age and Archaeological Context. Chicago: University of Illinois Press.

Raffles, Hugh
    1999   "Local Theory": Nature and the Making of an Amazonian Place. Cultural Anthropology 14(3):323–360.
    2002   In Amazonia: A Natural History. Princeton, N.J.: Princeton University Press.

Ralegh, Sir Walter
    1997   The Discoverie of the Large, Rich, and Bewtiful Empyre of Guiana. Tran-
    [1596]   scribed, annotated, and introduced by Neil L. Whitehead. Exploring Travel Series, vol. 1. Manchester: Manchester University Press. American Exploration and Travel Series, vol. 71. Norman: University of Oklahoma Press.

Ramjattan, K.
    2002   Policy and Legal Environment of the Guyana Forestry Commission. A consultancy commissioned by Natural Resources International under the Guyana Forestry Commission Support Project. Georgetown: Guyana Forestry Commission.

Record, S. J., and R. W. Hess
    1943   Timbers of the New World. New Haven, Conn.: Yale University Press.

Red Thread Women's Development Programme
    1998   "Givin' Lil Bit for Lil Bit": Women and Sex Work in Guyana. *In* Sun, Sex, and Gold: Tourism and Sex Work in the Caribbean. K. Kempadoo, ed. Pp. 263–290. Boulder, Colo.: Rowman and Littlefield.
    2004   "You Talking 'Bout Everyday Story": An Exploratory Study on Trafficking in Persons in Guyana. Georgetown, Guyana.

Reiner, R.
    1985   The Politics of the Police. New York: St. Martin's Press.
Ribeiro, Darcy
    1970   Os índios e a civilização: A integração das populações indígenas no Brasil moderno. Rio de Janeiro: Editora Vozes.
Richards, P. W.
    1952   The Tropical Rain Forest, an Ecological Study. Cambridge, U.K.: Cambridge University Press.
The Riots in Georgetown: Details of the Outbreak, Its Cause, and the Measures Taken for Its Suppression
    1905   Reprinted from the *Daily Chronicle*. Georgetown, Guayana: Estate of C. K. Jardine, Decd.
Rival, Laura, and Neil Whitehead, eds.
    2001   Beyond the Visible and the Material: The Amerindianization of Society in the Work of Peter Rivière. London: Oxford University Press.
Rivera, Eustasio
    1946   La vorágine. Bogotá: Ministerio de Educación de Colombia.
    [1924]
Rivière, Peter
    1969   Marriage among the Trio. Oxford, U.K.: Clarendon Press.
    1973   Some Problems in the Comparative Study of Carib Societies. *In* Atti de XL Congresso Internazionle degli Americanisti, vol. 2. Pp. 639–643. Genoa: Tilgher.
    1984   Individual and Society in Guiana: A Comparative Study of Amerindian Social Organization. Cambridge, U.K.: Cambridge University Press.
    1993   The Amerindianization of Descent and Affinity. L'Homme 126–128:507–516.
    1995a   Absent Minded Imperialism: Britain and the Expansion of Empire in Nineteenth-century Brazil. London: Tauris.
    1995b   Houses, Places, and People: Community and Continuity in Guiana. *In* About the House: Lévi-Strauss and Beyond. J. Carsten and S. Hugh-Jones, eds. Pp. 189–205. Cambridge, U.K.: Cambridge University Press.
    1997   Carib Soul Matters—since Fock. Journal of the Anthropological Society of Oxford 28(2):139–148. Originally published in Danish as Caribiski Sjæleanliggender—efter Fock. Tidsskriftet Antropologi 35(6):139–148.
    2001a   O indivíduo e a sociedade na Guiana. São Paulo: Editora da Universidade de São Paulo.
    2001b   A predação, a reciprocidade e o caso das Guianas. Mana 7:31–53.
Rivière, P. G., D. F. Grupioni, D. T. Gallois, G. Barbosa, R. Sztutman, and R. Duarte do Pateo
    2007   A propósito de *Redes de Relações*. Mana 13:251–273.
Rodney, Walter
    1981   A History of the Guyanese Working People, 1881–1905. London: Heinemann.
Rodway, James A.
    1891   A History of British Guiana from the Year 1668 to the Present Time. 3 vols. Georgetown, British Guiana: J. Thompson.
Roejkjaer, A. R.
    1967a   Caribbean Market Survey. Forest Industries Development Survey, Guyana (FIDS). FO:SF/GUY 9. Technical Report no. 1. Georgetown, Guyana: United Nations Development Program, Food and Agricultural Organization.

1967b   Marketing of Forest Products. Forest Industries Development Survey, Guyana (FIDS). FO:SF/GUY 9. Technical Report no. 2. Georgetown, Guyana: United Nations Development Program, Food and Agricultural Organization.

Roeleveld, W.
1969   Pollen Analysis in the Young Coastal Plain of Suriname. Geologie en Mijnbouw 48(2):215–224.

Roosevelt, A. C.
1980   Parmana, Prehistoric Maize, and Manioc Subsistence along the Amazon and Orinoco. New York: Academic Press.
1997   The Demise of the Alaka Initial Ceramic Phase Has Been Greatly Exaggerated: Response to D. Williams. American Antiquity 62(2):353–364.
1998   Paleoindian and Archaic Occupations in the Lower Amazon, Brazil: A Summary and Comparison. In Explorations of American Archaeology: Essays in Honor of Wesley R. Hurt. M. G. Plew, ed. Pp. 1–6. Lanham, Md.: University Press of America.

Roosevelt, A. C., M. Lima da Costa, C. Lopez Machado, M. Michab, N. Mercier, H. Valladas, J. Feathers, W. Barnett, M. Imazio da Silveira, A. Henderson, J. Silva, B. Chernoff, D. S. Reese, J. A. Holman, N. Toth, and K. Schick
1996   Paleoindian Cave Dwellers in the Amazon: The Peopling of the Americas. Science 272:373–384.

Rosengren, Dan
2002   The Collective Self and the Ethno-political Movement: "Rhizomes" and "Taproots" in Amazonia. Identities: Global Studies in Culture and Power 10:221–240.

Rostain, Stéphen
1991   Les champs surélevés amérindiens de la Guyane. La nature et l'homme. Cayenne, French Guiana: Office de la Recherche Scientifique et Technique outre Mer (ORSTOM).
1992   La céramique amérindienne de Guyane française. Bulletin de la Société Suisse des Américanistes 55–56:93–127.
1994a   The French Guiana Coast: A Key-Area in Prehistory Between the Orinoco and Amazon Rivers. In Between St. Eustatius and the Guianas. A. Versteeg, ed. Pp. 53–99. Contributions of the St. Eustatius Historical Foundation no. 3. St. Eustatius, Netherlands Antilles: St. Eustatius Historical Foundation.
1994b   L'occupation Amérindienne ancienne du littoral de Guyane. Paris: L'Institut Français de Recherche Scieintifique pour le Développement en Coopération.

Rostain, Stéphen, and Aad H. Versteeg
2003   The Arauquinoid Tradition in the Guianas. In Late Ceramic Societies in the Eastern Caribbean. A. Delpuech and C. L. Hofman, eds. Pp. 233–250. Paris Monographs in American Archaeology 14. London: Hadrian Books.

Roth, Walter E.
1915   An Inquiry into the Animism and Folk-Lore of the Guiana Indians. 30th Annual Report of the Bureau of American Ethnology, 1908–1909. Washington, D.C.: Smithsonian Institution.
1924   An Inquiry into the Arts, Crafts, and Customs of the Guiana Indians. 38th Annual Report of the Bureau of American Ethnology, 1916–1917. Washington, D.C.: Smithsonian Institution.
1929   Additional Studies of the Arts, Crafts, and Customs of the Guiana Indians,

with Special Reference to Those of Southern Guiana. Bulletin of the Bureau of American Ethnology no. 91. Washington, D.C.: U.S. Government Printing Office.

Rull, V.
 1999 Paleoclimatology and Sea-Level History in Venezuela: New Data, Land-Sea Correlations, and Proposals for Future Studies in the Framework of the IGBP-Pages Project. Interciencia 24(2):92–101.

Rydén, Stig
 2004 Introduction. *In* In Pursuit of a Past Amazon: Archaeological Researches in the Brazilian Guyana and in the Amazon Region: Curt Nimuendajú. P. Stenborg, ed. Pp. 9–11. Etnologiska Studier, vol. 45. Göteborg, Sweden: Världskulturmuseet i Göteborg.

Sá, Lúcia
 2004 Rain Forest Literatures: Amazonian Texts and Latin American Culture. Minneapolis: University of Minnesota Press.

Sáez, Oscar Calavia
 2006 O nome e o tempo dos Yaminawa: Etnologia e história dos Yaminawa do Alto Acre. São Paulo: Editora da Universidade do Estado de São Paulo.

Sahlins, Marshall
 1985 Islands of History. Chicago: University of Chicago Press.
 1997 "Pessimismo sentimental" e a "experiência etnográfica": Porque a cultura não é um "objeto" em via de extinção. Mana 3(1):41–47.

Sallnow, Michael
 1989 Precious Metals in the Andean Moral Economy. *In* Money and the Morality of Exchange. J. Parry and M. Bloch, eds. Pp. 209–231. Cambridge, U.K.: Cambridge University Press.

Sampson, Robert J.
 1987 Urban Black Violence. American Journal of Sociology 93:348–382.

Sanders, Andrew
 1976 American Indian or West Indian: The Case of the Coastal Amerindians of Guyana. Caribbean Studies 16(2):117–144.
 1986 The Powerless People: An Analysis of the Amerindians of the Corentyne River. London: Macmillan Caribbean.

Santos-Granero, Fernando
 1991 The Power of Love: The Moral Use of Knowledge Amongst the Amuesha of Central Peru. London: Athlone.
 1997 Writing History into the Landscape: Space, Myth, and Ritual in Contemporary Amazonia. American Ethnologist 25(2):128–148.
 2002a The Arawakan Matrix: Ethos, Language, and History in Native South America. *In* Comparative Arawakan Histories: Rethinking Language Family and Culture Area in Amazonia. J. D. Hill and F. Santos-Granero, eds. Pp. 25–50. Urbana: University of Illinois Press.
 2002b Boundaries Are Made to Be Crossed: The Magic of the Long-Lasting Amazon/Andes Divide. Global Studies in Culture and Power 9:545–569.

Sarmiento, G.
 1984 The Ecology of Neotropical Savannahs. Cambridge, Mass.: Harvard University Press.

Saussure, Ferdinand de
 1966 Course in General Linguistics. New York: McGraw-Hill.

Scace, Robert C.

1993 An Ecotourism Perspective. *In* Tourism and Sustainable Development: Monitoring, Planning, Managing. J. G. Nelson, R. Butler, and G. Wall, eds. Pp. 59–82. Waterloo, Canada: Heritage Resource Centre Joint Publication, University of Waterloo.

Schaan, Denise
 2001 Into the Labyrinths of Marajoara Pottery: Status and Cultural Identity in Prehistoric Amazonia. *In* Unknown Amazon: Culture in Nature in Ancient Brazil. C. McEwan, C. Barreto, and E. Góes Neves, eds. Pp. 108–133. London: British Museum Press.

Schama, Simon
 1995 Landscape and Memory. New York: Vintage Books.

Schmidt, P. Wilhelm
 1913 Kulturkreise und Kulturschichten in Südamerika. Zeitschrift für Ethnologie 45:1014–1124.

Schomburgk, Richard
 1922 Travels in British Guiana during the Years 1840–1844. 2 vols. Leipzig: J. J.
 [1848] Weber. Translated and edited by Walter E. Roth. Georgetown, Guayana: Daily Chronicle.

Sertima, Ivan van
 1975 The Sleeping Rocks: Wilson Harris's Tumatumari. *In* Enigma of Values. W. Harris, ed. Pp. 105–120. Aarhus, Denmark: Dangaroo.

Shahabuddeen, M.
 1978 Constitutional Developments in Guyana: 1621–1978. Georgetown: Guyana Printers.

Sheffler, Israel
 1997 Symbolic Worlds: Art, Science, Language, Ritual. Cambridge, U.K.: Cambridge University Press.

Sider, Gerald
 1993 Lumbee Indian Histories: Race, Ethnicity, and Indian Identity in the Southern United States. Cambridge, U.K.: Cambridge University Press.

Simões, M. F.
 1981 Colectores-pescadores ceramistas do liettoral do Salgado reconstiuição. *In* Cultura indegina. Pp. 5–12. Belém: Museu Paraense Emilio Goeldi.

Sizer, N.
 1996 Profit Without Plunder: Reaping Revenue from Guyana's Tropical Forests Without Destroying Them. Washington, D.C.: World Resources Institute.

Sizer, N., and R. Rice
 1995 Backs to the Wall in Suriname: Forest Policy in a Country in Crisis. Washington, D.C.: World Resources Institute.

Skolnick, Jerome H.
 1994 Justice Without Trial: Law Enforcement in Democratic Society. 3rd edition. New York: Wiley.

Slater, Candace
 1994 All That Glitters: Contemporary Amazonian Gold Miners' Tales. Comparative Studies in Society and History 36:720–742.

Smith, A. C.
 1939a Botanical Exploration of the Interior of British Guiana. Tropical Woods 57:6–11.
 1939b Plant Collecting in British Guiana. Journal of the New York Botanical Garden 40:10–21, 35–39.

Smith, R. T.
    1962   British Guiana. London: Oxford University Press.

Spinden, Herbert J.
    1922   Ancient Civilizations of Mexico and Central America. American Museum of Natural History Handbook Series no. 3. New York: American Museum Press.

Staats, Susan
    1996   Fighting in a Different Way. *In* History, Power, and Identity: Ethnogenesis in the Americas, 1492–1992. J. D. Hill, ed. Pp. 174–196. Iowa City: Iowa University Press.
    2003   Communicative Ideology in Kapon Religious Discourse. Ph.D. dissertation, Department of Anthropology, Indiana University.

Steege, H. ter, C. Bokdam, M. Boland, J. Dobbelsteen, and I. Verburg
    1994   The Effects of Man Made Gaps on Germination, Early Survival, and Morphology of *Chlorocardium rodiei* in Guyana. Journal of Tropical Ecology 10:245–260.

Stenborg, Per
    2002   Holding Back History: Issues of Resistance and Transformation in a Postcontact Setting, Tucumán, Argentina, c. A.D. 1536–1660. GOTARC, series B; Archaeological Theses no. 21. Göteburg, Sweden: University of Göteburg.

Steward, Julian Haynes
    1946–   Handbook of South American Indians. 7 vols. Bulletin of the Bureau of
    59   American Ethnology no. 143. Washington, D.C.: Smithsonian Institution.

Storrie, Robert
    2003   Equivalence, Personhood, and Relationality: Processes of Relatedness among the Hoti of Venezuelan Guiana. Journal of the Royal Anthropological Institute 9(3):407–428.

Strathern, Marilyn
    1999   Property, Substance, and Effect: Anthropological Essays on Persons and Things. London: Athlone.

Swellengrebel, E. J. G.
    1959   On the Value of Large Scale Aerial Photographs in British Guiana Forestry. Empire Forestry Review 38(1):54–64.
    1960   Aerial Photo-interpretation in the Forest Department. Internal report. Georgetown, British Guiana: Forest Department.
    1961a   Aerial Photo-interpretation: Studies of Several Vegetation Types in the Near Interior. Internal report. Georgetown, British Guiana: Forest Department.
    1961b   Estimation of Greenheart Volume from Small Scale Aerial Photographs. Empire Forestry Review 40(2):162–171.

Tardy, Christophe
    1998   Paléoincendies naturels, feux anthropiques et environnements forestiers de Guyane française du tradiglaciaire à l'holocène récent: Approche chronologique et anthracologique. Thesis, Biologie de Populations et Ecologie, Université Montpellier-2.

Tassinari, Antonella
    1998   Contribuicão à historia e à etnografia do Baixo Oiapoque: A composicão das famílias Karipuna e a estruturação das redes de troca. Ph.D. disserta-

tion, Faculdade de Filosofia, Letras e Ciências Humanas, Programa de Pós Graduação em Antropologia Social, Universidade de São Paulo.

Taussig, Michael
1980   The Devil and Commodity Fetishism in South America. Chapel Hill: University of North Carolina Press.

Taylor, Anne Christine
1985   L'art de la reduction: La guerre et les mécanismes de la différentiation tribale dans la culture jivaro. Journal de la Société des Américanistes 71: 159–173.
1993   Remember to Forget: Identity, Mourning, and Memory among the Jivaro. Man 28:653–678.

Tedlock, Dennis, and Bruce Mannheim, eds.
1995   The Dialogic Emergence of Culture. Urbana: University of Illinois Press.

Terrill, William, Eugene A. Paoline III, and Peter K. Manning
2003   Police Culture and Coercion. Criminology 41(4):1003–1034.

Thomas, Clive Y.
1984   The Rise of the Authoritarian State in the Periphery. New York: Monthly Review Press.

Thomas, David
1972   The Indigenous Trade System of Southeast Estado Bolivar, Venezuela. Antropológica 33:3–37.
1982   Order Without Government: The Society of the Pemon Indians of Venezuela. Urbana: University of Illinois Press.

Tilley, Christopher
1994   A Phenomenology of Landscape: Places, Paths, and Monuments. Oxford, U.K.: Berg.

Tilly, Charles
1978   From Mobilization to Revolution. Reading, Mass.: Addison-Wesley.

Tissot, C., M. R. Djuvansah, and C. Marius
1988   Evolution de la mangrove en Guayanne au cours de l'Holocene. Etude palynologique. Institute français de Pondichérry, Travaux de la Section Scientiphique et Technique 25:125–137.

Toland, Judith, ed.
1993   Ethnicity and the State. New Brunswick, N.J.: Transaction.

Tony, Claude
1843   Voyage dans l'intérieur du continent de la Guyane, chez les Indiens Rou-
[1769] coyens, par Claude Tony, Mulâtre libre d'Approuague. In Essais et notices pour servir à l'histoire ancienne de l'Amérique. H. Ternaux-Compans, ed. Pp. 213–235. Paris: Bertrand.

Toppin-Allahar, C.
1995   A Report on Forestry Law and Policy for the Government of Guyana, Guyana Forestry Commission. Port of Spain, Trinidad: Rapid Environmental Assessments.

Townsley, Graham
1993   Song Paths: The Ways and Means of Yaminahua Shamanic Knowledge. L'Homme 126–128:449–468.

Troup, R. S.
1939   Colonial Forest Administration. Oxford, U.K.: Clarendon Press.

Turner, Terry

1986 Production, Exploitation, and Social Consciousness in the "Peripheral Situation." Social Analysis 19:91–119.

U.S. Bureau of Democracy, Human Rights, and Labor
1993– Guyana: Country Report on Human Rights Practices. Washington, D.C.:
2006 U.S. Government Printing Office.

U.S. Congress
2005 International Narcotics Control Strategy Report 2005. Washington, D.C.: U.S. Government Printing Office.

U.S. Department of State
2001– Victims of Trafficking and Violence Protection Act of 2000: Trafficking in
2006 Persons Report. Washington, D.C.: U.S. Government Printing Office.

Vacher, S., S. Jérémie, and J. Briand
1998 Amérindians du Sinnamary (Guyane): Archéologie en forêt équatoriale. Paris: Editions de la Maison des Sciences de L'Homme.

Van Andel, T.
1967 The Orinoco Delta. Journal of Sedimentary Petrology 37(2):297–310.

Van der Hammen, T.
1963 A Palynological Study of the Quaternary of British Guiana. Leidse Geologishe Mededelingen 29:125–180.
1974 The Pleistocene Changes of Vegetation and Climate in South America. Journal of Biogeography 1:3–36.

Van der Hammen, T., and M. L. Absy
1994 Amazonia during the Last Glacial. Paleogeography, Paleoclimatology, and Paleoecology 109:247–261.

Van der Hout, P.
1999 Reduced Impact Logging in the Tropical Rain Forest of Guyana. Tropenbos-Guyana, series 6. Georgetown, Guyana: Tropenbos Guyana Programme.

Van der Hout, P., and G. Marshall
2004 Training in Reduced Impact Logging in Guyana: The Experience of the Guyana Forestry Training Centre. Food and Agricultural Organization Forest Harvesting Bulletin 14:1–4.

Van Maanen, John
1974 Working the Street: A Developmental View of Police Behavior. In The Potential for Reform of Criminal Justice. H. Jacob, ed. Pp. 153–177. Beverly Hills, Calif.: Sage.

Van Roosmalen, Marc G. M.
1985 Fruits of the Guianan Flora. Utrecht, Netherlands: Institute of Systematic Botany.

Vanzolini, P. E.
1970 Zoologia sistematica geographica e a origem das species. Teses Monografias no. 3. São Paulo: Universidade de São Paulo.

Versteeg, A. H.
1978 A Distinctive Kind of Pottery in Western Suriname. Mededelingen Surinaams Museum 23–24:16–27.
1985 The Prehistory of the Young Coastal Plain of West Suriname. Berichten van de Rilksdienst Oudheidkundig Bodmonderzoek 35:653–750.
1998 Habitation and Environment in the Guianas Between 10,000 and 1,000 B.P. Paper presented at the Seminaire Atelair Peuplements Anciens et Acutels des Forêts Tropicales, 16 October, Laboratoire Ermes, Office de la Recherche Scientifique et Technique Outre Mer (ORSTOM), Orléans, France.

2003 Suriname voor Columbus / Suriname before Columbus. Libri Musei Surinamensis no. 1. Paramaribo, Suriname: Stichting Surinaams Museum.

Versteeg, A. H., and F. C. Bubberman
1992 Suriname before Columbus. Mededelingen Surinaams Museum 49a:1–64.

Vieira, V. S.
1967 Considerations for the improvement in the harvesting of the natural forests in Guyana. Special Subject Report, Commonwealth Forest Officers' Course, 1966–67. Oxford, U.K.: Commonwealth Forestry Institute.
1980 Logging in Guyana and Considerations for Improvements. Georgetown: Guyana National Printers.

Viveiros de Castro, Eduardo
1986 Araweté: Os deuses canibais. Rio de Janeiro: Jorge Zahar.
1993 Alguns aspectos da afinidade no Dravidianato Amazônico. *In* Amazônia: Etnologia e história indígena. E. Viveiros de Castro and M. Carneiro da Cunha, eds. Pp. 149–210. São Paulo: Núcleo de História Indigena e do Indigenismo, Universidade de São Paulo, Fundação de Amparo à Pesquisa do Estado de São Paulo.
1996 Os pronomes cosmológicos e o perspectivismo ameríndio. Mana 2(2):52–78.
1998 Dravidian and Related Kinship Systems. *In* Transformations of Kinship Systems: Dravidian, Iroquois, Australian, and Crow-Omaha. M. Godelier, T. R. Trautmann, and F. E. Tjon Sie Fat, eds. Pp. 31–54. Washington, D.C.: Smithsonian Institution Press.
2002 A inconstância da alma selvagem (e outros ensaios de antropologia). São Paulo: Cosac and Naify Editora.
2004 The Forest of Mirrors: A Few Notes on the Ontology of Amazonian Spirits. Available at http://amazone.wikia.com/wiki/The_Forest_of_Mirrors.

Viveiros de Castro, Eduardo, and Carlos Fausto
1993 La puissance et l'acte: La parenté dans les basses terres d'Amérique du Sud. L'Homme 126–128:141–170.

Wagner, Roy
1978 Lethal Speech: Daribi Myth as Symbolic Obviation. Ithaca, N.Y.: Cornell University Press.
1981 The Invention of Culture. Chicago: University of Chicago Press.
[1975]

Warren, Kay, and Jean Jackson, eds.
2002 Indigenous Movements, Self-Representation, and the State in Latin America. Austin: University of Texas Press.

Wassén, S. Henry
1934 The Frog-Motif among the South American Indians: Ornamental Studies. Anthropos 29(3–4):319–370.

Wavell, Stewart, Audrey Butt, and Nina Epton
1966 Trances. London: Allen and Unwin.

Weber, A. F. R.
1931 Centenary History and Handbook of British Guiana. Georgetown, British Guiana: National Printers.

Welch, Ivan
1966 A Study of the Swamp Forest Types of the Region in Relation to Photo-interpretation: Report on Field Trip to the North West District. Internal report. Georgetown, British Guiana: Forest Department.

1975   A Short History of the Guyana Forest Department 1925–1975. Georgetown, British Guiana: Forest Department.

Welch, I. A., and G. S. Bell
1971   Great Falls Inventory. Internal report. Georgetown, British Guiana: Forest Department.

Welch, I. A., O. R. Sampson, and G. S. Bell
1972   Vegetation Types of Guyana: Photo-interpretation Key. Forestry Bulletin no. 4 (new series). Georgetown, Guyana: Ministry of Mines and Forests.

Welle, B. J. H. ter, N. J. Jansen-Jacobs, and E. M. Nic Lughadha
1989   Botanical Exploration in the Wai-Wai Area of Southern Guyana: 26 August–10 October 1989. Utrecht: Institute of Systematic Botany, with RBG-KEW and UG.
1992   ANNEX: IDENTIFICATIONS for Botanical Exploration in the Wai-Wai Area of Southern Guyana. 26 August–10 October 1989. Utrecht: Herbarium Division of Plant Ecology and Evolutionary Biology, with RBG-KEW and UG.

Wertheim, Jorge.
2003   Interview. Museu ao Vivo, Informativo do Museu do Índio 14(25)(December):3.

Westley, W.
1970   Violence and the Police. Cambridge, Mass.: MIT Press.

White, S. O.
1972   A Perspective on Police Professionalization. Law and Society Review 7 (Fall):61–85.

Whitehead, Neil L.
1988   Lords of the Tiger Spirit: A History of the Caribs in Colonial Venezuela and Guyana 1498–1820. Dordrecht, Netherlands: Foris.
1992 [1989]   Tribes Make States and States Make Tribes: Warfare and the Creation of Colonial Tribes and States in Northeastern South America. In War in the Tribal Zone. B. R. Ferguson and N. L. Whitehead, eds. Pp. 127–50. Santa Fe: School of American Research Press. Originally presented as a paper to the H. F. Guggenheim–sponsored advanced seminar "Expanding States and Indigenous Warfare" at the School of America Research, Santa Fe, New Mexico, March.
1993   Historical Discontinuity and Ethnic Transformation in Native Amazonia and Guayana, 1500–1900. L'Homme 28:285–305.
1994   The Ancient Amerindian Polities of the Lower Orinoco, Amazon and Guayana Coast: A Preliminary Analysis of Their Passage from Antiquity to Extinction. In Amazonian Indians: From Prehistory to the Present. A. C. Roosevelt, ed. Pp. 33–54. Tucson: University of Arizona Press.
1995   The Island Carib as Anthropological Icon. In Wolves from the Sea: Readings in the Archaeology and Anthropology of the Island Carib. N. L. Whitehead, ed. Pp. 9–22. Leiden: KITLV Press.
1996   Amazonian Archaeology: Searching for Paradise? A Review of Recent Literature and Fieldwork. Journal of Archaeological Research 4(3):241–264.
2002a   Arawak Linguistic and Cultural Identity Through Time: Contact, Colonialism, and Creolization. In Comparative Arawakan Histories. F. Santos-Granero and J. Hill, eds. Pp. 51–73. Urbana: University of Illinois Press.
2002b   Dark Shamans: Kanaima and the Poetics of Violent Death. Durham, N.C.: Duke University Press.

2002c   Kanaimà and the Poetics of Violent Death. Durham, N.C.: Duke University Press.

2002d   South America / The Amazon: The Forest of Marvels. *In* The Cambridge Companion to Travel Writing. P. Hulme and T. Youngs, eds. Pp. 122–138. Cambridge, U.K.: Cambridge University Press.

2003a   History and Historicities in Amazonia. Lincoln: University of Nebraska Press.

2003b   The Sign of *Kanaimà*, the Space of Guayana, and the Demonology of Development. Cahiers des Amériques Latines 43:67–85.

2004   (Ed.) Nineteenth Century Travels, Explorations, and Empires: Writings from the Era of Imperial Consolidation, 1835–1910, South America. London: Chatto & Pickering.

2006   The Sign of *Kanaimà:* The Space of Guayana and the Demonology of Development. *In* Terror and Violence: Anthropological Approaches. A. Strathern, P. Stewart, and N. L. Whitehead, eds. Pp. 151–71. London: Pluto Press.

Whitehead, Neil L., and Silvia Vidal
2004   Dark Shamans and the Shamanic State: Sorcery and Witchcraft as Political Process in Guyana and the Venezuelan Amazon. *In* In Darkness and Secrecy: The Anthropology of Assault Sorcery and Witchcraft in Amazonia. N. L. Whitehead and R. Wright, eds. Pp. 51–81. Durham, N.C.: Duke University Press.

Wijmstra, T. A., and T. Van der Hammen
1966   Palynological Data on the History of Tropical Savannahs in Northern South America. Leidse Geologische Mededelingen 38:71–90.

Williams, Brackette F.
1991   Stains on My Name, War in My Veins: Guyana and the Politics of Cultural Struggle. Durham, N.C.: Duke University Press.

Williams, Denis
1985   Ancient Guyana. Georgetown: Guyana Ministry of Culture.
1996   The Mabaruma Phase: Origin Characterization and Chronology. Journal of Archaeology and Anthropology 11:3–53.
2003   Prehistoric Guiana. Kingston, Jamaica: Ian Randle.

Williams, Eric
1964   British Historians and the West Indies. Port-of-Spain, Trinidad: People's National Movement.

Williams, Raymond
1976   Keywords: A Vocabulary of Culture and Society. London: Fontana.

Wilson, J. Q.
1989   Bureaucracy: What Government Agencies Do and Why They Do It. New York: Basic Books.

Wood, B. R.
1926   The Valuation of the Forests of the Bartica-Kaburi Area. Report to the Second Special Session of the Combined Court, British Guiana. Georgetown, British Guiana: Government Printing Office.

Woolard, Kathryn A.
1998   Introduction: Language Ideology as a Field of Study. *In* Language Ideologies: Practice and Theory. B. Schiefflin, K. A. Woolard, and P. V. Kroskrity, eds. Pp. 3–47. New York: Oxford University Press.

Worden, R. E.
    1995   Police Officers' Belief Systems: A Framework for Analysis. American Journal of Police 14:49–81.

World Bank
    2004   Guyana HIV/AIDS Prevention and Control Project: Indigenous People's Development Plan (IPDP). Washington, D.C.: World Bank.

Yde, Jens
    1965   Material Culture of the Waiwai. Ethnographic Series, vol. 10. Copenhagen: National Museum of Denmark.

Young, Allan
    1958   Approaches to Local Self-Government in British Guiana. London: Longmans.

About the Contributors

Stephanie W. Alemán is currently an assistant professor of anthropology and coordinator of the anthropology and ethnobotany programs at the University of Wisconsin–Stevens Point. Her work focuses on the Waiwai, a Carib-speaking group of Amerindians who inhabit the Deep South of Guyana and the forests north of the Amazon in Brazil. Her areas of specialization include shamanism and healing as well as women's lives and gender in Amazonia. In addition, she is actively engaged in ethnobotanical research in this region. Her current work centers on the use of Internet and communicative technology among the Waiwai and issues of globalization and change in Amazonia. She has several publications in progress, among them a consideration of the anthropology of natural disaster in small-scale societies and an exploration of medical pluralism among the Waiwai.

Janette Bulkan is a doctoral candidate at the Yale School of Forestry and Environmental Studies, her dissertation focusing on the slippages between forestry policies and practices in Guyana. She has worked as a social scientist at the Iwokrama International Centre for Rainforest Conservation and Development in Guyana (2000–2003), a senior lecturer at the University of Guyana (1985–2000), and first secretary in the Guyana Ministry of Foreign Affairs (1978–83). She has two decades of work experience with indigenous peoples and local communities in Guyana and was elected the first independent chairperson of the Guyana National Initiative for Forest Certification in 2003. She is also a member of the Governing Council of the Commonwealth Forestry Association. She has published on forest peoples and broader forest issues such as illegal logging in Guyana. She is an editor of the online journal *Kacike* (Journal of Caribbean Amerindian History and Anthropology) and cowrote with Arif Bulkan a chapter on forestry issues and indigenous peoples in *Indigenous Resurgence in the Contemporary Caribbean: Amerindian Survival and Revival*, edited by Maximilian Forte (2006).

Gérard Collomb is a researcher at the Centre national de la recherche scientifique (Laboratoire d'anthropologie des institutions). His present research deals with the political organization and collective identity of the Kali'na Amerindians in French Guiana and Suriname, as well as with the emergence of a national idea in the pluriethnic and pluricultural French Guiana.

Francis Dupuy is lecturer in anthropology at the University of Poitiers. His research themes include economic anthropology and interethnic relations, and he has done fieldwork among rural societies in France. He is the author of *Anthropologie économique* (2001) and several articles.

About the Contributors

Denise Fajardo Grupioni received her Ph.D. in social anthropology from the Universidade de São Paulo in 2005 and is currently a postdoctoral researcher for the university's Núcleo de História Indígena e do Indigenismo. Her main anthropological research fields are the indigenous peoples of the Guianas, especially the Tiriyó and Katxuyana on theBrazilian-Surinamese border.

Dominique Tilkin Gallois is currently a professor in the Universidade de São Paulo's Department of Anthropology and coordinator of the Núcleo de História Indígena e do Indigenismo. Her research includes ethnology focused onAmerindian oral traditions, cosmology, cultural heritage, and local knowledge. She is engaged in advising activities with indigenous communities in Amapá and northern Pará in Brazil, as well as in working with public agencies and nongovernmental organizations on sustainable development projects for indigenous communities.

David Hinds, a political scientist, is currently an assistant professor of Caribbean and African diaspora studies at Arizona State University. His areas of teaching and research include race and ethnicity, Black radicalism, culture as political expression, and Black political thought. He has written extensively on ethnicity and politics in Guyana.

Joan Mars is an attorney-at-law and an associate professor of criminal justice in the Department of Sociology, Anthropology, and Criminal Justice at the University of Michigan at Flint. She has researched and written extensively on police deviance and the abuse of force in Guyana, including her 2002 book *Deadly Force, Colonialism, and the Rule of Law: Police Violence in Guyana*. In 2005, she received a Fulbright Fellowship to lecture and conduct research at the University of the West Indies in Trinidad. She is also a founding director of the Linden Legal Aid Center in Guyana, which provides equal access to justice for residents who would otherwise be unable to afford an attorney.

María del Carmen Moreno is a cultural anthropologist (MA 1996 and Ph.D. 2004 from the University of Wisconsin at Madison). Her dissertation and fieldwork in Guyana's Amazon region focused on the ethnic identity and cultural revival of the Lokono, a small and marginal Amerindian group. She served as an agricultural extension agent for the Peace Corps in West Africa and was also the knowledge management coordinator for the World Council of Credit Unions (WOCCU), for which she collaborated in writing "white papers" on topics as varied as model credit union building in conflict and fragile environments, organizational learning, and knowledge management. She is currently working with another researcher to complete a book on personality differences between twins.

About the Contributors

John Palmer is currently a senior associate with the Forest Management Trust, Gainesville, Florida. For more than four decades, he has worked in many aspects of tropical forestry research and management, with field experience in Africa, Southeast Asia, Central America, and South America in national forest services, universities, the private sector, nongovernmental organizations, the Food and Agricultural Organization, and long-term projects supported by bilateral technical assistance. From 1997 to 2006, he was manager of the United Kingdom's Department for International Development tropical forestry research program, with some thirty concurrent projects in up to seventy countries. He has done several studies of forest systems and their governance in Guyana. During 2006, he and Janette Bulkan prepared jointly a management plan for nontimber forest products in the lower Waini River and the legal wording of a successful claim for Amerindian village lands tenure. They have also published papers on forest governance and corrupt practices such as illegal logging.

Alan Passes was born in 1943 and raised in Switzerland, France, and Great Britain. He began to study anthropology in his late forties at the London School of Economics. Since obtaining his Ph.D. in 1998 from the University of St. Andrews, based on some two years of fieldwork with the Pa'ikwené (Palikur) of French Guiana and northern Brazil, he has worked as an independent scholar-researcher in Amazonian studies. His main areas of interest are sociality, the anthropology of the "everyday," ethnolinguistics, and ethnohistory. He has published articles on the Pa'ikwené in a number of journals, including *Journal of Royal Anthropological Institute, EthnoHistory, Anthropology and Humanism, Estudios Latinoamericanos, Revista de Antropologia,* and *Tipiti.* He contributed to the book *Comparative Arawakan Histories: Rethinking Language Family and Culture Area in Amazonia* (2002), edited by Jonathan Hill and Fernando Santos-Granero. He is coeditor, with Joanna Overing, of *The Anthropology of Love and Anger: The Aesthetics of Conviviality in Native Amazonia* (2000) and is currently preparing a monograph on the Pa'ikwené for publication. As well as working in anthropology, he is also a literary translator, novelist, and screenplay writer, his latest film being *The Piano Tuner of Earthquakes* (2005), directed by the Brothers Quay.

Mark G. Plew is professor of anthropology and chair of the Department of Anthropology at Boise State University, where he also serves as director of the Center for Applied Archaeological Science. His primary research interests are hunters and gatherers and human ecology, and he has conducted numerous projects throughout North and South America, working closely with local Amerindian groups such as the Makushi and the Wapishana in the Rupununi Savannahs and the Iwokrama Rain Forest Reserve in Guyana. During the past eighteen years, he has worked cooperatively with the Amerindian Research Unit of the University of Guyana and the Walter Roth Museum of Anthropology. He has served as an associate editor of the *Journal of*

Archaeology and Anthropology, the scientific journal of the Walter Roth Museum, and as a member of the museum's Scientific Advisory Board. He recently authored "The Archaeology of Iwokrama and the North Rupununi," in *Proceedings of the Academy of Natural Sciences, Philadelphia* (2005), and *The Archaeology of Guyana* (2005). He was also recently named director of the Archaeological Field School Program of the Denis Williams School of Anthropology at the University of Guyana.

Peter Rivière is professor emeritus of social anthropology at the University of Oxford and fellow emeritus of Linacre College, Oxford. He has held posts at London, Harvard, Cambridge, and Oxford universities and retired from Oxford as professor of social anthropology in 2001. His interest in the native societies of Lowland South America began when he joined a botanical and filming expedition to the region in 1957, a journey that took him through the Guayana region and to central Brazil, where he spent some time with the Xavante on the upper Xingu. His first period of intensive fieldwork was among the Trio in 1962–63. His main anthropological publications are *Marriage among the Trio* (1969), *The Forgotten Frontier: Ranchers of North Brazil* (1972), and *Individual and Society in Guiana* (1984), in addition to numerous articles and reviews in a variety of journals. He has more recently become interested in the history of the European exploration of Amazonia. His publications on this topic include *Absented-minded Imperialism* (1995) and a two-volume edition of Sir Robert Schomburgk's reports on his Guayana travels, *The Guiana Travels of Robert Schomburgk 1835–1844*. A subsidiary interest is the history of anthropology, with special reference to the nineteenth and early twentieth centuries.

Terry Roopnaraine studied anthropology at Harvard and Cambridge, receiving his doctorate from Cambridge in 2001. He has held a research fellowship at Jesus College, Cambridge, and lectured in anthropology at the London School of Economics. Major research projects carried out during this period include studies of gold and diamond miners and palm heart extraction in Guyana's Pakaraima Mountains and North West District, respectively. With a regional focus on Amazonia and a specialization in the interior regions of Guyana, his research interests include economic anthropology, extractive industries, processes of social and cultural transformation, and the anthropology of development. Since 2001, he has worked as an independent consultant engaged in ethnographic research for poverty alleviation, social protection, and development programs in Guyana, as well as farther afield in Kosovo, Nicaragua, Turkey, and India.

Stéphen Rostain studied archaeology at the Panthéon-Sorbonne University in Paris. After his initial contacts with New World archaeology in Teotihuacán, Mexico, and on the Maya site of Chaguite, Guatemala, he was employed as an archaeologist in French Guiana in 1985. From 1994 to 1996, he was codirector of the archaeological project Tanki Flip in Aruba. Between 1996 and 2001, he lived in Ecuador, where he was

About the Contributors

codirector of the archaeological project Sangay-Upano and director of the Rio Blanco project. In 2001, he returned to France and a post in the National Center for Scientific Research. He is now in charge of a new project on the archaeology and ecology of the Guianas coast.

Lúcía Sá is professor of Brazilian cultural studies at the University of Manchester. She is the author of *Rainforest Literatures: Amazonian Texts and Latin American Culture* (2004) and *Life in the Megalopolis: Mexico City and São Paulo* (2007).

Evelyn Schuler Zea is currently a fellow in the postdoctoral program of the anthropology department of the University of São Paulo and has been connected to the Núcleo de História Indígena e do Indigenismo since 1996. She received her Ph.D. in 2006 from the Institute for Social Anthropology at the University of Bern. Her fieldwork was carried out in northern Amazonia among Amerindians known as the Waiwai. Her ongoing research concerns conceptions of translation and relation in Amerindian anthropologies, grounded in Waiwai conceptual images and their social dynamics.

Susan K. Staats is an assistant professor in the College of Education and Human Development at the University of Minnesota. Her fieldwork in Kapon communities in 1997-98 focused on communicative ideologies in religious discourse. She currently develops interdisciplinary mathematics curricula and studies informal discourses of mathematical argumentation in university algebra classrooms.

Per Stenborg has long experience of work within Latin American archaeology. His research has addressed issues related to the early stages of contact between Amerindian and European populations. His focus has been on processes of change within the native societies that came into contact with Europeans during the sixteenth and seventeenth centuries and on the question of how such changes may be inferred from historical and archaeological sources and materials. He is also interested in the application of digital methods and analyses in archaeology. He is presently working as project director and senior lecturer in the Department of Historical Studies at the University of Göteberg. He edited the volume *In Pursuit of a Past Amazon: Archaeological Researches in the Brazilian Guyana and in the Amazon Region* (2004), based on the manuscripts and correspondence of Germano-Brazilian investigator Curt Nimuendajú. His research on the Spanish-native period in northwestern Argentina resulted in the publication of *Holding Back History: Issues of Resistance and Transformation in a Postcontact Setting, Tucumán, Argentina c. A.D. 1536-1660* (2002).

Alíssa Trotz is an associate professor in women and gender studies, sociology, and equity studies as well as director of the Caribbean Studies Program at the University of Toronto. She is also a member of Red Thread Women's Development Organization in

Guyana. Her publications include *Gender, Ethnicity, and Place: Women and Identities in Guyana* (with Linda Peake, 1999) and articles on race, gender, historicizing the Caribbean family, and nation and the Caribbean diaspora in such journals as *Small Axe, New West Indian Guide, Social and Economic Studies,* and *Global Networks*. She recently guest-edited, with Aaron Kamugisha, a special issue of *Race and Class* to commemorate the two hundredth anniversary of the abolition of the British slave trade.

Neíl L. Whítehead is professor of anthropology and Latin American and religious studies at the University of Wisconsin at Madison. Author of numerous works on the native peoples of South America, he is an expert on sorcery, violence, and warfare on that continent. He is currently studying the cultural dynamics of sex and violence in Brazil and Ukraine as well as the emergence of posthuman and digital subjectivities.

Index

Abary culture, 37
Açahyzal, 59
Acarai Mountains, 17, 195, 219n1
acculturation, 233
adaptations, 13, 29, 33, 34, 35, 43, 75, 226
adaptive responses, 23, 29, 34, 35
adornos, 39, 40
affinity, 97, 98, 99, 107
Africanist models, 118, 170
Africans, 154, 155, 157–163, 170–173
Afro-Guyanese, 146, 148, 149, 239
agency, 14, 126, 133, 141, 201, 203, 206, 240, 243
agential practice, 135
aggregation (social), 105, 117, 139
agouti, 108, 186
agricultural development, 164, 165; productivity, 3, 239; sector, 160, 164, 239; techniques, 69
agriculture, 13, 34, 36, 38, 39, 42, 52, 73, 75, 82, 164, 204
Akawabi, 32
Akawaio, 252
Akuriyo, 108
Alaka Phase, 32, 33
Albert, Bruce, 97, 107, 124
alliances, 3, 7, 105, 109–112, 113, 118, 119, 120, 137, 169, 170, 225, 226
Aluku, 114, 120, 122n8
Amapá, 13, 17, 36, 44, 45, 48, 50, 52, 53, 54, 55, 56–58, 59–62, 72n1, 72n3, 135, 136, 142, 222, 224, 233n1, 234n9
Amazonia, vii, 7, 13, 18, 28, 37, 97, 136, 139, 141, 143, 185, 188, 198, 208, 233n1, 246, 248
Amazon River, 2, 3, 53, 56, 65–67, 72n4, 75
Amerindian Heritage Month, 151–152
Amerindian People's Association (APA), 153n5, 197, 241, 242
Amokokupai, 125, 129
animators, cultural, 148
animic societies, 98, 99, 100

anthropomorphic motifs, 46, 48, 49, 58, 63, 72
apanjat politics, 163–164
Aparai, 104, 110, 226
Appun, C.F., 128
Apure River, 38
aquatic creatures, 100, 116
Araguari-Amaparí River, 58–59
Araguari River, 44, 58–59
Araguayana, 116
Aramayana, 108
Aramiso, 108
Arauquinoid tradition, 36, 38–44, 47, 51–54
Arawak, vii, 6, 7–8, 12, 14, 18, 58, 67, 95, 98, 101n4, 135, 136, 138, 141, 148, 149, 150, 151, 191, 193n7
Arawera, 124, 125, 127, 130, 131, 132, 133
Araweté, 99
Archaic period, 33
Arekuna, 128, 185, 189, 193n2, 252n3
Arenosols, 75
Areruya, 14, 124–133
Århem, Kaj, 98
Aruã phase, 58, 59, 72n1
Arucauá River, 60–61
Arvelo-Jiménez, Nelly, 96
assistance policies, 104, 105
atomism, 102, 104, 106
authoritarianism, 159, 160, 166
Avecinnia, 25
Awacaipu, 128–130

balata latex, 76
bananas, 116, 186, 217
Barabina, 32, 33
Barbakoeba culture, 39, 41, 42, 44, 47, 48
Barima River, 6, 48
Barrancoid tradition, 36–38, 69
Bartica, 78, 80, 82, 127
basralokus, 76
Benjamin, Walter, 214–215, 218
Bennett, John, 148–150, 153n3

Berbice, 39, 76
Bible, 14, 124, 130, 245
biogeographic data, 23, 29, 33
Bixa orellana, 76
Blacks, 15, 159, 172, 181
Boundary Commissions, 102
Brett, William H., 6, 10, 11, 19n5, 127–128, 130
bride service, 113, 122n2
British Guiana, 1, 10, 11, 19n6, 19n8, 76, 77, 79, 80, 108, 125, 127, 130, 172, 182n1, 195, 203
Brysonima, 25
bulletwood, 76
burials, 32, 39, 47, 51, 59, 72
Burnham, Forbes, 85, 145, 155, 158, 161, 198
Butt Colson, Audrey, 118, 125

Cabalzar, Flora, 108
Calçoene River, 59
Cambisols, 75
Camopi River, 117
cannibalism, 3, 6, 7, 8, 97, 99, 229
Carib, vii, 6–8, 12, 16, 18, 58, 98, 99, 103, 111, 113, 114, 118, 128, 133n2, 136, 152, 187–189, 192, 195, 198, 219n1, 219n4, 252n3
Caribbean oyster (*Crassostrea rhizophorae*), 30
Caripo culture, 45
Carsten, Janet, 95
Carter, Martin, 194, 196
Cary-Elwes, Father, 129
cassava, 14, 128, 130, 131, 149, 187
cassiri, 130, 131, 132
causeways, 42
Cayenne Island, 39–42, 53
cemetery, 47, 60, 61
Central Brazilian Societies, 105
centrifugal forces, 120
Chagnon, Napoleon, 103
Chan, Janet, 168
cheniers, 33
chiefs, 47, 117, 119, 141, 226, 229, 232, 233n1
Chinese, 155, 162
church, 125, 126, 129, 131, 132, 171, 182n8, 197, 216
civilization, 9, 124, 142, 146, 147, 242, 245

clans, 7, 47, 53, 105, 111, 135, 138, 139, 141
class, 19, 155, 156, 158–165, 169–173, 242
Clastres, Pierre, 105, 111
climate, 19, 24, 25; change, 23, 29, 34
coastal areas, 23, 50, 121, 122, 145, 235, 237–248 *passim*, 253
code-switching, 138, 141–143
colonial era, 1–16, 47, 50–53, 56, 84, 105, 113–115, 119, 121, 129, 136, 145–146, 154–165, 168–182, 185, 189, 191, 203, 239, 240, 247, 252n5
communication, 114, 167, 210, 215; sacred, 124
communicative ideology, 124
concentric dualism, 97
consanguinity, 97, 106, 107
continuity, 87, 95, 96, 97, 102, 107, 109, 110, 117, 141, 204, 230
Coppename River, 39, 41
Corantijn River, 37
coresidence, 96, 97, 106, 122n1
corporate groups, 102, 105, 110
cosmological schemata, 97
cosmology, 14, 95, 135
Cottica River, 42
cotton, 116, 129, 186
Coudreau, Henri, 102, 122n7, 189
crabwood tree oil, 76
Creoles, 114, 138, 140, 142, 143, 156
crime, 157, 169, 174, 175, 177, 178–181, 182n5
Crown Lands Ordinance, 76–77
Cubeo, 98
cultural animators, 148
cultural revival, 15, 145, 148–152
Cunani River, 59
Curatella, 25

d'Acuna, Cristóbal, 102
D'Aguiar, Peter, 162
dance, 14, 125, 132, 215–216
Demerara River, 25, 127
demographic recovery, 104
Department of Lands and Mines, 76
depopulation, 72n4, 104, 105
descent, 105, 106, 110–112, 122n1, 179, 253n12
Descola, Philippe, 98–100, 101nn4–5,
Dharmic Maha Sabba, 164

Index

diachronic framework, 67, 108
discourse, vii, 7, 16, 17, 19, 99, 102, 115, 119, 124, 125, 137, 139, 145, 146, 150, 152, 156, 158, 195, 196, 198, 201, 208, 211, 215, 220n9, 225, 228, 230, 233n3, 235, 239, 243, 244–252
Dreyfus, Simone, 103
Dumont, Jean-Paul, 96
Dutch West India Company, 76

earthworks, 42
East Indians, 146, 154, 155, 158–165, 171–173, 179
ekatî, 17, 202, 204, 212–213, 218
elections, 141, 150, 155–156, 159–162, 173, 180, 198
Emerillon, 117, 120
empoldering, 75
Ëna, 136
endemism, 14, 75
endogamy, 98, 102, 106, 109–112
English language, 5, 11, 93, 94, 126, 136, 147, 149, 150, 161, 162, 169, 172, 191, 193n1, 253n8
Enmore riots, 171
environmental change, 13, 23, 28, 29, 34, 35
epa'kano, 117, 118
epugenaks, 125
eremu, 125
esegungang, 125
Espérance 1 and 2, 135–143
Essequibo, 30, 33, 76, 77, 82, 127, 195, 204
ëtakpapïtpë, 117
ethnic conflict, 154–158, 162, 166
ethnicity, 130, 139, 154, 158–163, 223
ethnoarchaeological studies, 50
ethnogenesis, 14, 116, 138, 207, 219n2
ethnographic area, 103
ethnopolitics, 154–166
European Conquest, 50, 53
Evans, Clifford, 32, 58, 59, 60, 61
Evans-Pritchard, E. E., 118
ewang, 127, 131, 132
exchange, 5, 42, 73n5, 85, 97–101, 106, 109, 112, 114, 117, 120, 121, 127–131, 207, 208, 213, 220n10, 227, 232–233, 246, 249
exogamy, 98, 109, 110, 112

Farabee, William Curtis, 102, 208
fatal force, 174
Fausto, Carlos, 119
fighting conch (*Strombus pugilis*), 30
Fluvisols, 75
Fock, Neils, 103, 196, 205, 206, 213, 215, 216
forestry, 13, 74, 75, 77, 79, 80–88
forests, vii, 13, 14, 25, 28, 30, 74–89, 125, 195, 199, 245, 247, 248, 251
Franciscans, 102
Frechal River, 59
French Guiana, 1, 14, 25, 28, 30, 33, 34, 36, 39–53 *passim*, 56, 58, 74, 114–117, 122n4, 135–143, 224, 234n4
Frikel, Protásio, 104
frogs, 39, 42

Galibi-Marwono, 104, 110, 111
Galibi-Oiapoque, 104
Gallois, Dominique, 17, 108, 109, 112n1
Georgetown (Guyana), 16, 78, 149, 150, 171, 174–176, 242, 250
geoscientific data, 23
Glissant, Edouard, 137
gold, vii, 3–5, 76, 77, 190, 244, 246, 247, 252n5, 253n7
Great Falls, 83, 127
greenheart wood, 76, 78, 80, 85, 88
green stone pendants (*muiraquitã*), 39, 42, 59
Guiana mosaic, 94
Guiana Shield, 3, 13, 23, 47, 74, 75, 81, 88, 124
Guianas Project, 102, 104, 107, 109, 110, 111, 112n1
Gumilla, Joseph, 102
Guss, David, 94, 96, 188,
Guyana Human Rights Association (GHRA), 174, 237
Guyfesta, 147–148

Handbook of South American Indians, 6, 12, 18, 103
Harris, Wilson, 190–193, 244, 252n6
Havt, Nadja, 108, 109
headman, 96
heaven, 100, 124, 127, 129–133, 135, 136, 140, 142, 213, 220
Hill, Jonathan, 20n10, 98, 124

hinterland, 17, 18, 74, 75, 86, 115, 236–252
Histosols, 75
Holocene, vii, 13, 23–30, 33, 34
homicide, 174, 175, 176
horses, 124, 194
Hosororo pottery, 32
house, 42, 44, 78, 95–97, 100, 134n2, 151, 194, 208, 217, 239, 248
Hugh-Jones, Stephen, 95
hymns, 124–127, 131

identity, 1, 7, 14, 15, 17, 115, 116, 135–143, 145–153, 154, 190, 192, 195, 199, 201–205, 212, 217, 223–225
Ilha do Carão, 59, 60
Im Thurn, Sir Everard, 10, 11, 20n9, 103, 129
infertile soil, 75
Inini statute, 115
itïpï, 108–111
itupon, 116

Jagan, Cheddi, 88, 145, 155, 161, 165, 172, 182n2
Jagan, Janet, 145, 164
Jari River, 56
Jê, 98
Jesuits, 103, 117
Jivaroan peoples, 99, 101n5

Kabakaburi, 32, 148–153
Kako River, 128
kaleidoscope, 94–95, 101n2
Kali'na culture, 14, 53, 54, 113–123
kanaimá, 6, 10, 18n1, 128, 129, 189, 190, 193n6, 198
Kapon, 118, 125–133
Karipuna, 104, 109, 112n2, 137, 138
Katxuyana, 104
Kaurikreek site, 33, 37, 38
kinship, 105, 107, 113, 121, 122n1, 154
Kloos, Peter, 113, 198
Koch-Grünberg, Theodore, 129, 185, 186, 189, 192
Koriabo culture, 32, 47–48, 53
Kourou River, 42
Kukenaan Valley, 128, 129
Kukui River, 125
Kukuyana, 116, 120, 121, 122n11

Kumarawai, 116, 120, 122nn10–11
Kwatta culture, 41
Kwayana, Eusi, 157–159, 162

La Gruta-Ronquín site, 37
Lake Moreiru, 28
La Rose, Sister, 147–151
Late Allerröd period, 25
Late Aristé culture, 44, 45
Leptosols, 75
letterwood, 76
Lévi-Strauss, Claude, 95, 112
Litani River, 117
logging, 74–89, 125, 240, 247

Mabaruma Phase, 32, 37
Magaña, Edmundo, 124, 126
Magdalene, Sister Rose, 147, 148
Maiongong, 126
Makuna, 98
Makunaíma, 186–192
Makushi (Macuxi), 6, 125, 127, 189
Mana River, 117, 118, 121
mangrove crab (*Ucides cordatus*), 30
mangrove swamps, 24, 25
manioc, 6, 37, 114, 208, 216
Maracá culture, 50, 58, 60, 62, 72
Marajoara phase, 58
Maraso, 108
marine shellfish, 25, 30
Maroni River, 14, 114, 115; Caribs and, 113, 198
Maroons, 114, 120, 122n4, 122n8
Marouini River, 115, 116
marriage alliance, 109, 110
marshramany, 153
Master of Game Animals, 100
Master of the Peccary, 100
Mazagão culture, 44, 50, 51, 53
Mazaruni, 78, 126–133
megafauna, 25
megalithic sites, 45
Meggers, Betty J., 28, 32, 34, 58
Mentore, George, 220, 253
Middle Sinnamary River, 30, 33
millennial preaching, 127
missionaries, 7, 10, 127, 189, 195, 199, 211, 213–221
modernity, 1, 9, 17, 130, 142, 198, 243
Monte Mayé site, 59

Moreiru, Lake, 28
mudflats, 24, 25
Mulattoes, 163, 170, 171
multilocal relations, 102
multiverse, 136
Muritaro, 127, 129
music, 14, 124–130, 149, 188, 215, 231

nationalism, 154, 162, 164, 170
nation-state, 14, 16, 147, 186, 190, 195, 205, 235, 243
Ndjuka, 120
Negro River, 1, 2, 12, 38, 56, 70, 95, 98, 193
Nhamundá River, 13, 56, 63–70
Nimuendajú, Curt Unkel, 13, 55–73
Nordenskiöld, Erland, 55
Northwest Amazon, 18, 98
nuclear family, 44, 105, 113

Okomëyana, 116
Opaguana, 116
Orinoco River, 12, 13, 19, 36, 37, 38, 44, 47, 52, 53, 56, 58, 60, 98, 188, 247
Ouanary Hills, 44, 45, 52
Overing, Joanna, 98, 99, 102–106, 136, 143
Oyapock River, 44, 47, 51, 56, 135, 136, 234n4

Paba kareda, 124, 130
Pa'ikwaki, 137–143
Pa'ikwené, 135–144
Pakaraima Mountains, 3, 28, 187, 244
Paleo-Indians, 29
Palikur, 50–54, 58, 60, 104, 110, 136–143
Panare, 96
paper, 14, 124–133
Pará, 13, 17, 56, 66, 219, 234n9
Paramaribo, 119
Paru River, 114
Pata, 108–110
Patamona (Patamuna), 126, 128, 198, 204, 244, 251, 252
Pemon, 118, 125, 128, 129, 144n5, 186–188, 192, 193nn2–3
Petit Saut, 30, 34
piai, piaichang, 125–133
Pianakoto, 116

Piaroa, 98, 99
Pleistocene, 23
Pleniglacial period, 24
Podzols, 75
police culture, 167, 179, 182
political economy of predation, 97
pollen, 25, 28
Polychrome Tradition, 36, 44, 53, 54, 67, 69, 70
Pomeroon River, 127, 128, 149, 152
postcolonial period, 1, 12, 16, 18, 157, 158, 165, 167–181, 235, 243, 244, 248
prayer, 125, 126, 128
predation, 97–101
pregnant female figurines, 39
primo-occupant, 119–120
Prins Bernhard Polder site, 39, 41
prophets, 124–133

quartz crystal points, 29

race, 15, 111, 153, 155, 160–163, 172, 181, 188, 191, 192, 242
Ralegh, Sir Walter, 1, 3–5, 12, 102, 247, 250
razzias, 120
reciprocity, 17, 99–101, 103, 105, 247, 250
refugia, 28
residential mounds, 38
revival, cultural, 15, 145, 148–152
Rhizophora species, 25
rock shelters, 44–45
Rodney, Walter, 156, 195
Roraima, 124, 129, 133n2, 185–191, 219n1
Roth, Walter, 9–12, 19nn3–4, 19n8, 20n9, 103, 189
Roucouyennes, 116, 122n3

Saladoid tradition, 37
Sanday, Mabel, 150
Santarém material, 55, 63, 67, 70, 73n5
Schomburgk, Richard, 4, 10, 102, 185, 186, 188, 189
Schomburgk, Robert, 1, 10, 203
shaman, 7, 14, 18, 45, 49, 96, 99, 100, 117, 118, 120, 125–129, 141, 189, 191, 192, 228

shellfish gatherers, 36
shell mounds, 32
Shuar, 111
Sinnamary River, 42
Sipaliwini Savanna, 30
slash-and-burn techniques, 36, 37, 41, 52
social climate, 180, 181
Solimões River, 38
souls, 17, 100, 124–127, 131, 133, 203, 204, 209, 212–213, 218
subsistence, 24, 32, 34, 239, 246
Suriname, 1, 11, 14, 25, 30, 33, 34, 35, 37–40, 75, 79, 81, 82, 87, 88, 89, 114, 118–120, 122n4, 124, 198, 219

Tampok River, 117
Tapanahoni River, 114
tareng, 125
Temomairem, 116
Terra Firme, 29
tezo, 59
Thémire culture, 39–44, 48
Tiriyó, 104, 108, 110, 114, 116, 119, 120, 219n1
tobacco, 100, 126
totemic, 98
Trio, 14, 97, 99, 100, 124
Trombetas River, 13, 55, 62–73
Tukanoans, 95, 98, 101n5
tulip mussel (*Modiolus americanus*), 30
Tupi, 6, 17, 63, 67, 97, 100, 117, 228, 229

Uaçá River, 60, 72, 136
Ulemali, 117
Upului, 116, 120, 122n13

uxorilocal, 106, 111, 112, 122n1

Van der Hammen, T., 25
Vaupés, 98
Vidal, Silvia, 129
violence, 7, 8, 16, 156, 167–182, 190, 198, 236
Viveiros de Castro, Eduardo, 97, 111, 214

wai, 124
Waiwai, 9, 11, 16, 17, 82, 96, 100, 104, 110, 194–221
Wajãpi, 17, 104, 107, 110, 117, 222–234
Wakapao, 149, 150
Wakuénai, 14, 124
Wanadi, 124
Wanaina Plain, 32
Wanano, 98
war, 4, 7, 16, 97, 99, 102, 103, 105, 115–122, 136, 154
Wayana, 14, 104, 110, 113–123
Westminster model, 159
Whites, 115, 117, 128, 171, 225, 227, 228, 232
Williams, Denis, 11, 25, 33, 58
Wonotobo site, 37
Woolard, Kathryn, 125

Xingu, 18, 98

Yanomami, 97, 104, 124, 226
Ye'cuana, Yekuana, 14, 94, 96, 101, 186

zebra nerite (*Puperita pupa*), 30
Zo'é, 104, 108, 109, 110